Francophone Africa at fifty

Manchester University Press

Francophone Africa at fifty

Edited by
TONY CHAFER AND ALEXANDER KEESE

Manchester University Press
Manchester and New York

distributed in the United States exclusively
by PALGRAVE MACMILLAN

Published by Manchester University Press
Oxford Road, Manchester M13 9NR, UK
and Room 400, 175 Fifth Avenue, New York, NY 10010, USA
www.manchesteruniversitypress.co.uk

Distributed in the United States exclusively by
Palgrave Macmillan, 175 Fifth Avenue, New York,
NY 10010, USA

Distributed in Canada exclusively by
UBC Press, University of British Columbia, 2029 West Mall,
Vancouver, BC, Canada V6T 1Z2

British Library Cataloguing-in-Publication Data
A catalogue record for this book is available from the British Library

Library of Congress Cataloging-in-Publication Data applied for

ISBN 978 07190 8930 5 hardback

First published 2013

The publisher has no responsibility for the persistence or accuracy of URLs for any external or third-party internet websites referred to in this book, and does not guarantee that any content on such websites is, or will remain, accurate or appropriate.

Typeset by Servis Filmsetting Ltd, Stockport, Cheshire
Printed in Great Britain by
CPI Antony Rowe Ltd, Chippenham, Wiltshire

In memory of Joyce Chafer and Wolfgang Keese

Contents

List of illustrations   ix
Abbreviations   xi
Notes on contributors   xv
Acknowledgements   xix

Introduction   1
Tony Chafer and Alexander Keese

Part I: Zero hour approaches

1   Gaston Defferre's *Loi-Cadre* and its application, 1956/57: last chance
for a French African 'empire-state' or blueprint for decolonisation?   15
Martin Shipway

2   A vocation for independence: Guinean nationalism in the 1950s   30
Mairi MacDonald

3   French officials and the insecurities of change in sub-Saharan Africa:
Dakar, 19 August 1960 revisited   44
Alexander Keese

Part II: Military transitions

4   'Saving French West Africa': the French army, African soldiers and
military propaganda during the 1950s   61
Ruth Ginio

5   The French Army and Malian independence (1956–1961)   75
Vincent Joly

6   Transfer of military power in Mauritania: from Ecouvillon to
    Lamantin (1958–1978)   90
    Camille Evrard

Part III: Continuities and connections

7   Franco-African security relations at fifty: writing violence, security
    and the geopolitical imaginary   107
    Bruno Charbonneau
8   French *coopération* in the field of education (1960–1980): a story of
    disillusionment   120
    Samy Mesli
9   Jacques Foccart: *Eminence grise* for African affairs   135
    Jean-Pierre Bat

Part IV: Anglo-French relations

10 Whitehall, the French Community and the Year of Africa:
    negotiating post-independence diplomacy in West Africa   155
    Mélanie Torrent
11 A transnational decolonisation: Britain, France and the Rhodesian
    problem, 1965–1969   171
    Joanna Warson

Part V: Nationalist trajectories, border issues and conflicted memories

12 The changing boundaries of resistance: the UPC and France in
    Cameroonian history and memory   189
    Thomas Sharp
13 A fragmented and forgotten decolonisation: the end of European
    empires in the Sahara and their legacy   204
    Berny Sèbe
14 Through the prism of the *cinquantenaire*: Côte d'Ivoire between
    refondation and Houphouët's legacy   219
    Kathrin Heitz
15 Chad's political violence at 50: bullets, ballots and bases   233
    David Styan

Bibliography   249
Index   275

Illustrations

Figures

6.1 Operation Ouragan in Mauritania (1958). Map based on
G. Chaffard 'La Mauritanie entre Dakar et Rabat', *Le Monde*, 11–12
mai 1958.   95

9.1 Jacques Foccart and General De Gaulle. Reproduced with
permission from the Archives Nationales de Paris.   141

Tables

8.1 Number of teachers working in Africa from 1960 to 1970   124

8.2 Number of teachers by country in 1965   125

Abbreviations

AAMC	Association des Anciens Militaires de Carrière (Former Career Soldiers' Association)
ACCT	Agence de coopération culturelle et technique (Agency for Cultural and Technical Cooperation)
ADS	Association pour le Développement et la Solidarité
ADSSD	Archives Départementales de la Seine-Saint-Denis
AEF	Afrique Equatoriale Française (French Equatorial Africa)
AL	Armée de libération (Army of Liberation)
ALN	Armée de Libération Nationale
AN	Archives Nationales Françaises
ANM	Archives Nationales du Mali
ANOM	Archives nationales d'outre-mer, Aix-en-Provence
ANS	Archives Nationales Sénégalaises, Dakar
AOF	Afrique Occidentale Française (French West Africa)
AQIM	Al-Qaeda in the Islamic Maghreb
AU	African Union
BAG	Bloc Africain de Guinée
BCD	Bureau du Comité Directeur
BCRA	Bureau Central de Renseignements et d'Action (French intelligence service)
BDP	Bureau de documentation et de presse
BIRD	Banque internationale pour la reconstruction et le développement (International Bank for Reconstruction and Development)
BL	Bodleian Library, Oxford
CADN	Centre des Archives Diplomatiques de Nantes
CAR	Central African Republic

CCFD	Comité Catholique contre la Faim et pour le Développement
CEDOC	Centre de documentation (Gabonese intelligence service)
CEFEO	Corps Expéditionnaire Français en Extrême-Orient (Far East French Expeditionary Corps)
CEPER	Centre d'Edition et de Production pour l'Enseignement et la Recherche
CERI	Centre de recherche en sciences sociales de l'international
CHEAM	Centre des hautes études sur l'Afrique et l'Asie modernes
CHETOM	Centre d'histoire et d'étude des troupes de marine (Centre for the History and Study of Overseas Troops)
CIEES	Centre Interarmées d'essais d'engins spéciaux (Interarmy Special Vehicles Test Centre)
CNPCICI	Commission nationale préparatoire du cinquantenaire de la Côte d'Ivoire
CNRS	Centre National de la Recherche Scientifique
CONFEMEN	Conférence des ministres de l'éducation ayant le français en partage (Conference of Education Ministers Sharing the French Language)
CPDC	Coordination des partis pour la défense de la constitution (Coordination of Political Parties for the Defence of the Constitution)
CPNC	Cameroon People's National Congress
CPS	Comité de Salut Public (Committee of Public Safety)
CR	Comité Révolutionnaire
CRO	Commonwealth Relations Office
DAL	Direction Afrique Levant
DAM	Direction des Affaires Africaines et Malgaches
DDF	Documents Diplomatiques Français
DOM-TOM	Départements et Territories d'Outre-Mer (French overseas departments and territories)
DSG	Démocratie socialiste de Guinée
ECOWAS	Economic Community of West African States
EMA	État-major des Armées
l'EMGDN	Etat-major général de la défense nationale (General Staff of National Defence)
ENFOM	Ecole Nationale de la France d'Outre-Mer (National Academy of Overseas France)
ESDP	European Security and Defence Policy
FAC	Fonds d'Aide à la Coopération
FAN	Forces armées du nord
FANT	Forces armées nationales tchadiennes
FAP	Forces armées populaires

FESAC	Fondation de l'enseignement supérieur pour l'Afrique centrale (Central African Foundation for Higher Education)
FESCI	Fédération estudiantine et scolaire de Côte d'Ivoire
FIDES	Fonds d'investissement pour le développement économique et social (Investment Fund for Economic and Social Development)
FJF	Fonds Jacques Foccart
FLN	Front de Libération Nationale, Algeria
FO	Foreign Office
FPR	Foccart private files
FPU	Foccart's office files
FROLINAT	Front de Libération Nationale du Tchad
GEMDEV	Groupement pour l'étude de la mondialisation et du développement
GEMPA	Groupe d'étude des mondes policiers africains
GP	Garde Présidentielle
GPRA	Gouvernement Provisoire de la République Algérienne
GUNT	Transitional Government of National Unity
ICG	International Crisis Group
IRSEM	Institut de recherches stratégiques de l'Ecole militaire, Paris
J.O.R.F.	*Journal Officiel de la République Française*
LMP	La Majorité Présidentielle
MAE	Ministère des Affaires Etrangères (French Ministry of Foreign Affairs)
MEN	Ministry of Education Archives
Miferma	Mines de Fer de Mauritanie
MNLA	Mouvement National pour la Libération de l'Azawad (National Liberation Front of the Azawad)
MPS	Mouvement Patriotique du Salut
NARA	Archives, College Park, MD
OAU	Organisation of African Unity
OCAM	Office pour la Communauté et les Affaires africaines et malgaches (Office for the Community and for African and Malagasy Affairs)
OCRS	Organisation commune des régions sahariennes (Common Organisation of Saharan Regions, 1957–62)
PCF	Parti Communiste Français
PDCI	Parti Démocratique de la Côte d'Ivoire
PDG	Parti Démocratique de la Guinée
PFA	Parti de la Fédération Africaine
PLR	Postes de liaison et de renseignement (Liaison and information posts)

PPT	Parti Progressiste Tchadien
PRA	Parti du Regroupement Africain
PRC	People's Republic of China
PRO	Public Record Office (now the National Archives), London
RDA	Rassemblement Démocratique Africain
RF	Rhodesian Front
RFI	Radio France Internationale
RHDP	Le Rassemblement des Houphouëtistes pour la Démocratie et la Paix
RPF	Rassemblement du peuple français (Gaullist political party)
RPR	Rassemblement pour la République (Gaullist political party)
SAARF	Special Allied Airborne Reconnaissance Forces
SCNC	Southern Cameroons National Council
SCTIP	Service de coopération technique internationale de police
SDECE	Service de documentation extérieure et de contre-espionnage (External Documentation and Counter-espionage Service)
SHAT	Service Historique de l'Armée de Terre, Vincennes
SHD	Service Historique de la Défense
SMR	Service Militaire de Recherche (Military Research Service)
SNIM	Société Nationale Industrielle et Minière de Mauritanie (National and Industrial Mining Company of Mauritania)
TNA	The National Archives
UAM	Union Africaine et Malgache (African and Malagasy Union)
UDD	Union Démocratique Dahoméenne
UDI	Unilateral Declaration of Independence
UDS[-PFA]	Union Démocratique Sénégalaise – [Parti de la Fédération Africaine]
UDSR	Union Démocratique et Sociale de la Résistance
UGTCI	Union Générale des Travaillaurs de la Côte d'Ivoire
UPC	Union des Populations du Cameroun
UPS	Union progressiste sénégalaise
US-RDA	Union Soudanaise-RDA
UTA	Union des transports aériens
VPP	Vice-Présidence et Présidence du Conseil de Gouvernement du Sénégal
VSN	Volontaires du service national (National Service Volunteers)

Notes on contributors

Jean-Pierre Bat is «archiviste paléographe» and «agrégé d'histoire». His PhD in history (University Paris I Panthéon Sorbonne, 2011), based on his PhD in archive science (Ecole des Chartes, 2006), was about Foccart's policy in former French Equatorial Africa, 1956–69. Since 2011, he has been a curator at the French National Archives for Foccart's files.

Tony Chafer is Professor of Contemporary French Area Studies at the University of Portsmouth and Director of its Centre for European and International Studies Research. He is a French historian and has published widely on Franco-African relations in the late colonial and post-colonial eras. He is the author of *The End of Empire in French West Africa: France's Successful Decolonization?* (Berg, 2002) and has recently completed a research project with Gordon Cumming (Cardiff University) on Anglo-French cooperation in Africa, which has given rise to a series of articles and a book entitled *From Rivalry to Partnership? New Approaches to the Challenges of Africa* (Ashgate, 2011).

Bruno Charbonneau is Associate Professor of Political Science at Laurentian University, Canada and Director of the Observatoire sur les missions de paix et opérations humanitaires, Chaire Raoul-Dandurand, Université du Québec à Montréal. His research examines the international politics of African conflicts and peace interventionism. He wrote *France and the New Imperialism: Security Policy in Sub-Saharan Africa* (Ashgate, 2008), co-edited *Peacebuilding, Memory and Reconciliation* (Routledge, 2012) and *Locating Global Order* (UBC Press, 2010), and has published widely on peace and conflict in Africa, including most recently 'War and Peace in Côte d'Ivoire' in *International Peacekeeping* (2012).

Camille Evrard is a doctoral student of contemporary history of Africa at Cemaf, Université Paris I. She is currently undertaking research for a PhD dissertation on the social history of the colonial troops and the creation of national armed forces in Mauritania between 1930 and 1980, financed by the IRSEM (Institut de recherches stratégiques de l'École militaire) Paris. Camille Evrard is a founding member of GEMPA (Groupe d'étude des mondes policiers africains), and has published in *Afrique Contemporaine*.

Ruth Ginio is senior lecturer in history at Ben Gurion University of the Negev. Her publications include *French Colonialism Unmasked: The Vichy Years in French West Africa* (University of Nebraska Press, 2006), *Violence and Non-Violence in Africa*, co-edited with Pal Ahluwalia and Louise Bethlehem (Routledge, 2007), and *Shadows of War: A History of Silence in the Twentieth Century*, co-edited with Efrat Ben Ze'ev and Jay Winter (Cambridge University Press, 2010).

Kathrin Heitz (MA) was trained in social anthropology and history in Basel (Switzerland), Dakar (Senegal) and Tübingen (Germany). She wrote her MA thesis about decolonisation in Senegal and has conducted field research in Côte d'Ivoire and Cameroon. In her PhD project, she analyses social trust and security in rebel-held western Côte d'Ivoire, which is part of a comparative study at the Institute of Social Anthropology in Basel funded by the Swiss National Science Foundation.

Vincent Joly is professor of contemporary history at the Université Rennes 2 (France). He researches on colonisation and decolonisation in sub-Saharan Africa. His most recent publication is *Guerres d'Afrique. 130 ans de guerres coloniales. L'expérience française*, Rennes, Presses Universitaires de Rennes, 2009.

Alexander Keese edited this book while a visiting scholar at the University of Portsmouth. He currently works as research group director at Humboldt University of Berlin (Germany), funded by ERC Starting Grant n° 240898 under the Framework Programme 7 (FP7) of the European Commission. He is the author of *Living with Ambiguity: Integrating an African Elite in French and Portuguese Africa, 1930–61* (2007) and the editor of *Ethnicity and the Long-term Perspective: the African Experience* (2010).

Mairi S. MacDonald is director of the international relations programme at the University of Toronto. She received her PhD from the University of Toronto in history in 2009. Her thesis was entitled 'The Challenge of Guinean Independence, 1958–1971'. Before returning to the academic world in 2002, Dr MacDonald was a lawyer for a number of years, specialising in communications law and policy in Canada and around the world.

Samy Mesli holds a PhD in History from Université Paris 8 and Université du Québec à Montréal (UQAM). He then did a Postdoctorate at Université de Montréal. His research deals with international relations, and particularly with cooperation in the educational field. He is the author of various scholarly articles and is currently teaching as a part-time lecturer at UQAM.

Berny Sèbe (FRGS, D.Phil Oxon.) is a historian and a Lecturer in Colonial and Postcolonial Studies at the University of Birmingham (UK), with research interests in the cultural history of the British and French empires, the colonial conquest and decolonization of the Sahara and Franco-African relations. He has published many articles and book chapters in the above-mentioned fields. His book 'Heroic imperialists' is in press and he is co-editing a volume on the 'Echoes of Empire' and the legacy of European colonialisms in comparative perspective.

Martin Shipway is senior lecturer in Twentieth-Century French Studies at Birkbeck, University of London. He is the author of *Decolonization and its Impact: A Comparative Approach to the End of the Colonial Empires* (Oxford: Blackwell, 2008), and of *The Road to War: France and Vietnam, 1944–1947* (Providence, RI and Oxford: Berghahn Books, 1996/2003), and has written extensively on comparative decolonisation, on late colonialism in Indochina, Madagascar and Africa, and on topics such as colonial psychology and photography, and post-colonial memory.

Thomas Sharp is an AHRC-funded doctoral candidate at the University of Manchester. He obtained his BA (Hons) in History from the University of Warwick in 2006, and an MA in Cultural History from the University of Manchester in 2008. His present research focuses on the UPC uprising in Cameroon and its historical legacy as a means for Cameroonians to negotiate their relationship with the international environment.

David Styan lectures in the Department of Politics, Birkbeck College, University of London. He has written on French foreign policy in both Africa and the Middle East. He has also published extensively on the economies and politics of the Horn of Africa and the Sahel.

Melanie Torrent is senior lecturer in British history and civilisation at Université Paris Diderot, Paris Sorbonne Cité. She works on the history of the Commonwealth of Nations and Franco-British relations in Africa in the era of decolonisation. She has published several articles in this area and is the author of *Diplomacy and Nation-Building: Franco-British Relations and Cameroon at the End of Empire* (I. B. Tauris, 2012).

Joanna Warson has an MSc from the London School of Economics and Political Science. She is currently working on her PhD thesis at the University of Portsmouth, under the supervision of Professors Martin Evans and Tony Chafer. Her doctoral research examines French policy and perceptions of Anglophone Africa from the 1950s to the 1970s, focusing particularly on the case study of Rhodesia. She has contributed a chapter to a forthcoming collection on *Memory and Commemoration in Contemporary France* (University of Wales Press, 2013).

Acknowledgements

The editors would like to thank the Centre for European and International Studies Research at the University of Portsmouth for supporting an international conference, which was held at the university in September 2010, to mark the fiftieth anniversary of political independence in Francophone sub-Saharan Africa. This volume emerged in large part from that conference. They would also like to thank Clive Chafer and Manus McGrogan for translating the chapters by Mesli and Joly, respectively, into English. In addition, Tony Chafer would like to thank Martin Evans and Natalya Vince for their support, collaboration and encouragement. He also wishes to thank students on the undergraduate programmes and the MA Francophone Africa at the University of Portsmouth for their ideas and contributions to debate on Francophone Africa, which are constantly stimulating. Alexander Keese wishes to thank the European Commission which generously supports his work under Framework Programme 7 (ERC Starting Grant n° 240898).

Introduction

Tony Chafer and Alexander Keese

Since political independence in 1960, French relations with Africa have been the preserve of a small group of specialists working, at least until recently, largely away from the public gaze. If French policy towards sub-Saharan Africa between 1945 and the present day had attracted more interest, beyond the narrow circles of African students and academics in French universities, the small group of very active journalists who write about the 'scandals of the Republic' and the handful of scholars working on French decolonisation and neo-colonialism outside France, then France's record in sub-Saharan Africa would have the potential to be a source of controversy in the same way as the actions of the 'imperialist' United States have been. However, many of these practices and their consequences have remained largely hidden from public scrutiny since the moment of the end of empire. They were not publicly discussed and did not find an echo in French or international public opinion. Moreover, French politicians, at least those of the 1960s, felt flattered when French *grandeur* on the world stage was regarded as being expressed through its importance on the African continent, even after it had lost its empire (Vaïsse 1998). To be sure, there were critics who from an early date attacked French involvement in the internal politics of many African countries, through aid and development policy, military interventions and more secret 'advisory roles'. Scandals such as the involvement of the French oil company Elf in high politics and the overthrow of elected governments, or French behaviour during the Rwanda massacres of 1994, occasionally brought French policy into broader public debate (Clark 2002; Dozon 2003). However, for a country that has been so active on the ground in Africa, both as colonial power and as post-colonial player, public comment and debate have been very limited (Golan 1981).

Among the small groups of critics mentioned above, French policy has of course earned itself a controversial reputation. Indeed, thanks to François-Xavier Verschave, the term 'Françafrique' has been popularised to describe the particular mixture between the public and the private, the connections between African presidents, French officials and their friends from multinational companies, and the deployment of troops and advisers, that characterise Franco-African relations in the post-independence period (Verschave 2000). As much as the public debate on French practices on the African continent remains deficient, the particular features of French involvement in its former colonies and some neighbouring countries are taken for granted by both its supporters and its critics. From this perspective, French manipulation is *everywhere* in the story of France's relations with its former colonies. Some former French administrators have helped to create this image: there are quite a few who obviously like, or liked, to present themselves as 'masterminds' of African policy, who controlled and manipulated the internal affairs of African governments. As sources, accounts coming from these former officials are obviously very complex in their nature. Boasters and cynics among the 'informants' dominate this discussion on the French side, starting with the apparently all-powerful brain of the system, the late Jacques Foccart. Foccart started off as Charles De Gaulle's specialist on overseas – in particular African – affairs in the 1950s, when the latter still was without any formal post. In 1958, at the moment of De Gaulle's return to lead the French Republic, Foccart was appointed to a post behind the scenes, as technical adviser to his mentor. Only in early 1960 was Foccart given a leading role, as Secretary-General of the moribund French Community (or Communauté), and later as Secretary for African and Malagasy Affairs at the Presidency. During this period, he built networks of influence with African leaders and French officials. His extraordinary influence and capacity for intervention in, and manipulation of, African politics have become famous. Foccart did everything to underline his own importance in retrospect, through his own testimony. However, his account and those from other self-declared shadow men and spies are difficult to handle, since attempts to corroborate their information, or to come to conclusions on the basis of other empirical data, have only really begun in earnest over the last fifteen years – and they are not very far advanced.

Thus, scholarly analysis by historians and academics from the neighbouring fields of political science, sociology or anthropology has so far been at best incomplete. 'The longest scandal of the French Republic', as Verschave called it (1998), has not yet been adequately treated in the scholarly literature. There is an impressive amount of archival information that remains unread; there are oral testimonies that are insufficiently interpreted; and the links between 'African' and 'French' perspectives – if we believe that there was a public perception and one or more secret agendas – have not always been found.

The present edited collection represents an attempt to fill this gap. Its contributors are engaged in making accessible new empirical findings concerning a relationship that is an important part of the history of African populations after independence and that is significant both for the process of 'modernisation' of

French politics after 1960 and for Europe's role on the African continent in the past and in the future. It seeks to offer a fresh perspective on developments that started long before 1960, the fallout from which continued to manifest itself long after political independence. At the same time it seeks to challenge three approaches to Franco-African relations from the colonial period to the end of the millennium and beyond that have typified much of the academic work on the subject published to date. We will seek to question two of what we will here describe as the three 'master narratives' that have been used to describe the French role on the African continent and its effects: the narrative of a planned and reasonably successful decolonisation and the narrative of conspiracy and French manipulation. At the same time, we will integrate within our approach the third 'master narrative', which relates to the long-lasting military relations between different African groups and the French.

The 'planned decolonisation' narrative

From the moment when the colonial empire in sub-Saharan Africa waned, there was a sustained attempt at reinterpreting this decolonisation process as something intended and guided by leading French politicians and planners. This perspective came in large part from the top of the government hierarchy itself. It was made possible by the rather unusual situation of a French president regarding himself as the 'man of Africa' (or *homme de l'Afrique*), who wove ideas about the part he played in sub-Saharan Africa during the war into a broader myth regarding his role as 'saviour' of France (De Gaulle 1970). This vision was supported by other personalities belonging to the political establishment in the 1960s, whose career had been linked to the process of decolonisation in sub-Saharan Africa. A particularly impressive example of such trajectories is the career of Pierre Messmer, who occupied the post of Governor of Côte d'Ivoire between 1954 and 1956, when this territory became for a time the model country for a future reformed 'French Union' in sub-Saharan Africa; Messmer acted as High Commissioner in all key territories or groups of territories (Cameroon, French Equatorial Africa, French West Africa), then became War Minister and Prime Minister in governments of the Fifth Republic. Messmer is a prototype for the emergence of a positive discourse on French decolonisation on the African continent: in the academic context his activity as author and first-hand witness gave him unique opportunities in this respect (Messmer 1992, 1998).

In the last two decades, the testimony of French administrators has also become part of this discourse. In a number of edited volumes, many of these officials have insisted on their conscious participation in a planned decolonisation process. One of the main ideas defended here is that, during the 1950s, colonial administrators became aware of the inevitability of a decolonisation of some sort. Many claim they helped in the process. While some administrators admit that at least in the early 1950s they were not sufficiently aware of the process going on around them, most hold that they had the necessary insights (Clauzel 1989, 2003; Gauthereau 1986; Colombani 1991; Ecole nationale de la France d'outre-mer 1998).

The French public has become familiar with this notion of a planned decolonisation mainly because it is embedded in the discourses of aid policy, *coopération* (for a definition of this term, see Chapter 8 by Mesli in this volume), Francophonie and 'French civilisation' or the 'civilising mission' (Cumming 2005). In this context, it is suggested (if not explicitly stated) that French governments added to their main goal – the maintenance of a sphere of political influence – the attempt to guarantee a role for French language and culture on the continent. This idea has been linked to the deployment of a considerable number of French citizens involved in projects of cooperation on the ground and generous financial support for African states (Bossuat 2003). The notion, expressed in the contested Law of 23 February 2005, that the beneficial aspects of French colonisation should be made stronger in secondary education, is intrinsically linked to this narrative and represents, in a way, its culmination (Liauzu and Manceron 2006).

Academics have not fully bought into the 'planned decolonisation' narrative. However, many have taken from this interpretation the more general idea that French colonial politicians were indeed preparing a careful retreat, at the moment when they understood that sub-Saharan Africa could face problems similar to those of Indochina and Algeria that had always been in the spotlight, or when they became aware that maintaining an empire was just too costly (Benoist 1982; Cooper 1996; Bancel 1999). At the same time most historians have appeared to accept that the retreat from empire in sub-Saharan Africa was a poisoned gift.[1]

The 'conspiracy' narrative

French decolonisation has become a favourite theme of a particular type of journalistic investigation. With regard to their role on the African continent, French activities have earned themselves a reputation for being controlled by especially manipulative, successful schemers.[2] The magic name in this context is, again, that of Jacques Foccart (see Chapter 9 by Bat in the present volume), who did his best to make the French public believe that he indeed was a successful 'mastermind' – and autobiographical accounts by other former French agents active in sub-Saharan Africa in the 1960s have contributed to this picture. The 'conspiracy' narrative is sustained by the fact that French governments, on the basis of defence and military assistance agreements, came to the aid of authoritarian leaders in the former French colonies and other African countries: Léon M'Ba in Gabon, 1964, Félix Houphouët-Boigny in Côte d'Ivoire in 1969/70, then Joseph-Désiré Mobutu in Congo-Kinshasa in the 1990s and Idris Déby in Chad as late as 2005 and 2008. The decision by French political leaders to intervene in the Great Lakes region after the Rwanda genocide in 1994, by in effect protecting the Interahamwe militia (who were held responsible for most of the atrocities) and providing them with a safe escape route into neighbouring Zaire, further damaged France's public image in relation to African issues. Semi-private scandals have underscored the particular nature of French involvement on the continent: the notion of 'Françafrique' means a system deliberately created by semi-official French agencies (such as, in the early years of the Fifth Republic, the Office led by Jacques Foccart) and their allies in French industry, a system in which they replaced colonial rule by partnership with particular African leaders and their networks of family and friends, to the obvious detriment of ordinary Africans (Péan 1983; Martin 1995).

This interpretation has then been transposed onto the last decade before decolonisation. The view of France's decolonisation process in sub-Saharan Africa as sinister and manipulative has also been put forward by the more 'radical' African leaders of the period. French colonial planners were accused of deliberately 'balkanising' their former colonies, which had been grouped into federations, in order to weaken them (Morgenthau 1964: 72; Suret-Canale 1970: 193; Suret-Canale 1982: 471; Gallisot 1984: 53). Again, some colonial administrators of this period have been happy to contribute to this version (see for example Sanmarco and Mbajum 2007). In short, the French are suspected of having pushed more 'radical' political leaders into marginal positions and isolating more 'radical' regimes that managed to take over power (such as in Guinea-Conakry) (Schmidt 2007). Other versions of this narrative, which are often to be found in the contemporary African press, see African ministries filled with French specialists, who led the new national governments by the nose as if they were mere *marionnettes* (see for example Deltombe et al. 2011: 389–90).

The 'conspiracy' narrative remains very popular among the more critical commentators, and readers, of French involvement in sub-Saharan Africa (see for example the Dossiers noirs de la politique africaine de la France, of which 23 have been published, 1995–2009; Verschave 1998, 2000; Deltombe et al. 2011). Indeed, conspiracy theories find fertile ground in the literature on Franco-African relations precisely because they have been dominated by secrecy. Moreover, France has in many cases done precisely what the conspiracy theories claim that it does – destabilise or prop up African regimes that are perceived as pro-French in order to further French interests. Moreover, this literature tends to convey very homogeneous views to the reader. Everything seems to fit together quite well in this perspective – nearly all French actions appear to have significance in a context of secrecy and manipulation. However, there have been almost no systematic attempts to look more closely at the different moments when French protagonists appear to have taken over the process – and to measure the degree of French control over these processes. Much work remains to be done in this area.

The 'military bond' narrative

The study of relations between the French army and its former African members is not just a variant of the 'conspiracy' narrative; it has long found an important niche within discussions about France's past on the African continent. The history of African soldiers serving in both World Wars, and in the two major wars against French colonial rule in Indochina and in Algeria, is essential for understanding the social structures of both colonial and post-colonial societies on the African continent. Hundreds of thousands of Africans served under the French flag; apart from the tiny number of African students, academics and, from 1945, politicians who went to France, they are the major group that travelled to the metropole, and which, at the same time, got to know other war theatres (Echenberg 1991; Michel 2003). Immediately before independence, these veterans were, moreover, a group that still had major expectations in terms of political, economic and social compensation for their role. When the 1958 referendum drew near, soldiers continued formulating such demands, not to the new African elites slowly taking over, but to De Gaulle and his right-hand man at the time, Jacques Foccart.[3]

This fact has recently been linked to a far more emotional and polemical theme. While African soldiers had been an essential part of the French armed forces during a number of armed conflicts, the government of the former metropole had, by 1959, denied a part of its responsibility for these groups. In what appears to be a unique legislative act, the French parliament froze the military pensions of all veterans who were not French citizens, thus leading to discriminatory treatment of these veterans as compared to their army colleagues who held a French passport (Onana 2003; *Le Monde* 12 May 2010). Over the last decade, several organisations and African governments have again brought the issue to public attention, referring to France's 'blood debt' towards former soldiers. This process has been full of ambiguities. This is first because many of the post-colonial African governments had deliberately sought not to touch on this question, fearing the close relations that former veterans would then again build up with the French army. Second, the rhetoric has been taken up by associations that are not directly related to veteran issues, namely with regard to French immigration policy. The argument here is that France cannot deny access to individuals whose compatriots saved the country from military threats in an earlier age (Mann 2006: 195–209).

Finally, the question of a common social history of military experiences brings into play the effects of the French military presence after 1960. It is interesting to understand how a parallel transfer of power played itself out in the military sector, most spectacularly in former territories such as Mauritania and Cameroon, where the French army remained on the ground after 1960 to fight against 'insurgents'. The particular interest of these continuities also relates to the fact that many of the *coups d'état* staged against post-colonial governments from the early 1960s were carried out by African military officers who had been educated in the French service. When deciding for or against intervention in a putsch situation, France's African affairs specialists always had to take into account that such leaders had an older, military-related connection with France (Rouvez 1994).

Agents of 'Françafrique': understanding the structures of a new network of relations

The two principal 'master narratives' have a clear tendency to describe processes during the decolonisation period as in some way rationally shaped – although their interpretations go in opposite directions. However, even a short glance at structures of French involvement in sub-Saharan Africa between 1958 and 1960 allows us to cast doubt on this reading. The fact that explicit challenges to these dominant interpretations have rarely been formulated over decades of research shows how dependent this research still is upon the established 'narratives'. Under these circumstances, a revision that leaves more room open to complexities is important.

Who were – beyond a French administration in retreat and African politicians taking over – the early members of the emergent network of French post-colonial policy-making in sub-Saharan Africa in 1958 and the years immediately following? With the return of Charles De Gaulle to political power in May 1958, some of the principal protagonists of 'African issues' were already in place, namely Jacques Foccart and his network of correspondents, informants, collaborators and 'friends'. Their testimonies show, in contrast to the narratives described above, the ambiguities and insecurities of a transition process that only with hindsight can be regarded as straightforward. A brief discussion of the different 'types' of friends and informants involved in African policies at the moment of the transfers of power demonstrates these ambivalences (see also Chapter 9 by Bat in this volume).

One such type is, in the case of Upper Volta, settler representative and territorial assembly member Victoria Tauziède. Deeply concerned by the dangers of a possible 'Communist takeover', she criticised the apathy of the European settlers in the territory who, in the context of a broad Gaullist mobilisation campaign, were to be called on to engage in civic duties. At the same time, Tauziède attempted to safeguard her own career prospects as a high-level official in a future autonomous member state of the French Community (which is what, in 1958/59, she believed Upper Volta would become), hoping that Foccart (and

De Gaulle) would put in a word in her favour with the territorial leaders. By 1960, these attempts had failed.[4] Robert Fournier-Bidoz had similar hopes and was disappointed in a similar way in Côte d'Ivoire.[5]

A second type of network member is those officials and members of technical and educational staff who were deeply frustrated with the evolution of the former French colonies and who express this frustration through (deeply racist) accounts of what they saw as a 'Communist victory'. The Professor of Technical Education in Conakry, Dupuy, is a good example of this group: he accuses the French political establishment of not having understood a minimum of 'African realities' and of having helped Sékou Touré and other 'radicals' to come to power in Guinea-Conakry.[6] The few administrators posted in rural zones, who knew members of the group of new 'African affairs specialists' in Paris, are often equally frustrated informers. This is exemplified by Paul Lavenon, administrator in the 'bush' of Upper Volta, who saw the process from 1958 that led up to independence as xenophobic, anti-white and 'Communist' takeover.[7]

A third group were French officials who in the late 1950s and early 1960s entered the service of African governments – and had a key role in leading the directorates of the national ministries in various countries. These officials have often been characterised as Trojan horses of a power-hungry, neo-colonial French state (Gounin 2009: 24–5; Deltombe et al. 2011). The reality is, once again, more complex: already in 1959, Nigret, technical adviser to Félix Houphouët-Boigny, gave De Gaulle's administration a hard time when it came to negotiating projects that were vital for the economic development of former French West Africa, such as the construction of the Cotonou wharf. Nigret operated both as informant for the French government and as stubborn negotiator on behalf of Côte d'Ivoire interests![8]

However, above all, the early 'African affairs' networks seem to have been a giant bazaar of career perspectives in an insecure world of transition. A handful of examples are sufficient to illustrate this particular situation. In July 1958, Daniel Doustin saw himself as a client of Foccart and De Gaulle, and his nomination as Secretary-General in French Equatorial Africa as the outcome of the latter's wish to 'secure' Congo-Brazzaville with a reliable representative.[9] Doustin's superior, High-Commissioner Yvon Bourges, received requests from Paris to put in some other clients, administrators who had served in middle-level posts in Indochina, and he was not always open to such 'advice'.[10] Jean-Louis Bruhat, *cercle* administrator in Sangha, Congo-Brazzaville, was transferred to become secretary in Laurent Péchoux's cabinet in French Polynesia, after Foccart's intervention had helped to overcome a veto by Houphouët-Boigny, who knew both Péchoux and Bruhat as colonial adversaries in Côte d'Ivoire from the late 1940s.[11] Some, like the High-Commissioner of Congo-Brazzaville, Paul-Charles Dériaud, or his colleague in Dahomey, René Tirant, set all their hopes for further career progression on lobbying in Paris.[12] And even the officials put at the service of African governments, such as Thadée Diffre, director of the cabinet of Ivoirian Prime Minister Auguste Denise, participated in these affairs, accusing French officials in 'their' territory behind the back of the latter and commenting on decisions regarding personnel, including in their own favour![13] Some, like French official in independent Guinea-Conakry Georges Brouin, even threatened to enter the service of an African government if their career wishes were not respected.[14]

Where are the African collaborators in these attempts at network-building? While of course the African services of the French Republic continued to be interested in all kinds of territorial – later national – issues, the participation of Africans within the network is surprisingly limited. Instead of being a well-organised chain of command from Paris to African collaborators in neo-colonial schemes, the French, as the 'zero hour' of independence came and went, appear to have been preoccupied mainly with themselves. Obviously, a small number of African leaders were insiders within the system – this was the case of Félix Houphouët-Boigny without any doubt, followed later by Léopold Sédar Senghor of Senegal, and some others. However, other African leaders struggled behind the scenes to get themselves access to the advantages of French support.[15] Even so, relations between Africans and French by 1960 were far from unambiguous, and far from being sufficiently understood. More than fifty years later, these complex themes require further analysis.

Themes versus narratives: Francophone Africa at fifty

This book will address the many open questions regarding the Franco-African (or Afro-French) experience through five major themes. All of them engage with the two major narratives, while the second part focuses in detail on the more concrete issue of the 'military bond' narrative. The issues analysed start at the end of the Second World War or even earlier, and some are followed through to the end of the first decade of the new millennium, in particular with regard to legacies, continuities and memory. 1960 will be understood in all contributions as a major landmark, but not necessarily as a rupture or turning point.

The first part analyses the late colonial state, and discusses some of the essential politico-administrative decisions taken in the last years of the French colonial empire in sub-Saharan Africa and in the first months after the transfers of power. Do we find indications of manipulated processes and hidden agendas? How should we understand the different dimensions of the nationalist policies of African leaders, such as Sékou Touré, Mamadou Dia and Léopold Sédar Senghor? Martin Shipway in Chapter 1 considers the *loi-cadre*, the Gaston Defferre Law that, in 1956, brought about the creation of territorial institutions with wider responsibilities in the African colonies. Mairi MacDonald focuses in Chapter 2 on Guinea-Conakry, apparently a model country of nationalist activities in the 1950s, whose leader Sékou Touré was the first to demand and receive independence from France in September 1958 – the Guinean trajectory therefore seems to be characterised by a 'vocation for independence'. In Chapter 3, Alexander Keese interprets the behaviour of French officials in August 1960 in one of the first important political crises immediately after the independence of Senegal and French Soudan (today Mali), which led to the break-up of the federation between the two countries.

The 'military bond' narrative and military continuities are addressed in the second part of this book. It describes the efforts of the French command to maintain the loyalty of African veterans and discusses the particular processes of the military transfer of power that ran in parallel to the political processes that led to independence. Ruth Ginio in Chapter 4 investigates the forms of propaganda employed by the French army to motivate African soldiers in French West Africa to continue to identify with the colonial empire in times of change. In Chapter 5, Vincent Joly focuses on a case of military transition, in French Soudan/Mali, in which the new government in Bamako was sceptical, if not hostile, towards French military objectives and the French agents on the ground had to steer a complicated path between the loyalty of Malian veterans and the distrust of the government of Modibo Keïta. Finally, Chapter 6 by Camille Evrard examines how French troops continued to run a colonial war against Mauritanian insurgents after independence, in support of a friendly government.

The third part sheds light on key elements of continuity in relations between Africans and French. Bruno Charbonneau suggests in Chapter 7 that the particular continuities of violence that characterised France's colonial experience in sub-Saharan Africa should be examined more closely. In Chapter 8, Sami Mesly gives a critical account of one of the pillars of the 'successful decolonisation' narrative: the question of educational cooperation. Finally, Jean-Pierre Bat's Chapter 9 interprets the role of the shady 'Mr Africa' of France's post-colonial African activities, Jacques Foccart, and thereby introduces the personal dimension into this long-term perspective.

The relationship between different European experiences of decolonisation is an important, but under-researched, question, beyond a few very basic hypotheses. The fourth section therefore sets the French and the British trajectories in relation to each other. Mélanie Torrent in Chapter 10 gives an account of the British vision of French decisions taken in the 1960s, which enables us to understand the possibilities and limits of the mirror effect between the two colonial experiences. Chapter 11 by Joanna Warson studies the attempt by the French to make a diplomatic and military entry into Southern Rhodesia, a territory that chose 'white independence' in 1965 and became a target region for French activities in the 1960s and 1970s.

Naturally, the French decolonisation experience had very distinct effects in different territorial arenas. The final part of the book thus looks at three case studies of the effects of the memory of processes that took place both during the transfer of power itself and during the establishment of post-colonial relations between African leaders and the former metropole. Cameroon, a territory where a *maquis* organised by the Union des Populations du Cameroun (UPC) dominated the internal situation between 1955 and 1971, is analysed in Chapter 12 by Thomas Sharp, who follows UPC activities into the post-1990 changes and democratisation. The territories located in the Sahara region are discussed by Berny Sèbe, whose Chapter 13 gives an account of their development and the impossibility of any joint political structure in this region. Focusing on the regional centre of Man, Chapter 14 by Kathrin Heitz discusses the celebrations to mark fifty years of independence and the efforts that were made to harness these celebrations for political goals. Finally, in Chapter 15, David Styan then reviews, from the starting point of the (rather muted) celebrations of Chadian independence in 2010, the tradition of violence established from the end of colonial rule.

Fifty years after independence, the legacy of the manifold relations between Africans and French has an important place, not as a result of the continuities of political and socio-economic connections, but also in memories. This book engages with each of these different dimensions.

Notes

1 Only in the recent decade has this vision been challenged, by studies pointing to the very late reaction of the French administration to the gathering pace of events (Chafer 2002b) or to the heterogeneity and lack of vision that characterised opinions on the colonial side (Keese 2007b).

2 This tradition was started very early, with Chaffard (1965), and continues to the present day; see for example the recent book by Deltombe, Domergue and Tatsitsa (2011).

3 See for example Archives Nationales Françaises (AN), Fonds Jacques Foccart (FJF), 'Fonds privé', 164 (AN AG/5(FPR)/164), Foccart, *Note sur les Doléances des Anciens Combattants de l'A.E.F* (without number), n.d.

4 AN, FJF, 'Fonds privé', 207 (AN AG/5(FPR)/207), Victoria Tauzede to Foccart (without number), 10 September 1958.

5 AN, FJF, 'Fonds privé', 197 (AN AG/5(FPR)/197), Fournier-Bidoz to Foccart (without number), 10 October 1958.

6 AN, FJF, 'Fonds privé', 207 (AN AG/5(FPR)/207), Paul Lavenon, Cercle Commander of Dédougou, Upper Volta, to Foccart (without number), 20 August 1958.

7 ANF, FJF, 'Fonds privé', 200 (AN, AG/5(FPR)/200), Dupuy to Nocher of Radio Télévision Française (without number), 1 November 1958.

8 AN, FJF, 'Fonds privé', 138 (AN, AG/5(FPR)/138), Nigret, Technical Adviser of Houphouët-Boigny, Minister of State, *Note relative au Port de Cotonou* (without number), 11 February 1959.

9 AN, FJF, 'Fonds privé', 164 (AN, AG/5(FPR)/164), Doustin, acting Secretary-General of French Equatorial Africa, to Foccart (without number), 23 July 1958.

10 AN, FJF, 'Fonds privé', 164 (AN, AG/5(FPR)/164), Bourges to Foccart (n° 185/H.C.), 7 October 1958.

11 AN, FJF, 'Fonds privé', 164 (AN, AG/5(FPR)/164), Bruhat, Commander of Region of Sangha, to Foccart (without number), 28 November 1958.

12 AN, FJF, 'Fonds privé', 164 (AN, AG/5(FPR)/164), Dériaud, High-Commissioner of Congo-Brazzaville, to Foccart (without number), 16 December 1958; AN, FJF, 'Fonds privé', 138 (AN, AG/5(FPR)/138), Tirant to Foccart (without number), 3 April 1959, p. 1.

13 AN, FJF, 'Fonds privé', 175 (AN, AG/5(FPR)/175), Diffre, Director of Cabinet of Denise, Prime Minister of Côte d'Ivoire, to Foccart (without number), 8 December 1959.

14 AN, FJF, 'Fonds privé', 197 (AN AG/5(FPR)/197), Brouin, member of French Mission in Guinea, to Foccart (without number), 6 October 1958.

15 ANF, Fonds Jacques Foccart, 'Fonds privé', 137 (AN, AG/5(FPR)/137), Emile Zinsou, Minister of General Economy of Dahomey, to Senghor, President of Parliamentary Group of Parti du Regroupement Africain in Paris (without number), 19 July 1958.

Part I
Zero hour approaches

1

Gaston Defferre's *Loi-Cadre* and its application, 1956/57: last chance for a French African 'empire-state' or blueprint for decolonisation?

Martin Shipway

Although 1960 is rightly celebrated as the 'Year of Africa', the series of independence ceremonies across Francophone sub-Saharan Africa and Madagascar which punctuated that climactic year exude the slightly weary air of *faits accomplis* (Shipway 2008b). If we are looking for the turning point at which France's African territories south of the Sahara took the first decisive steps towards their independence, then high on the list of possible moments must be the passing of the Law of 23 June 1956, better known as the *Loi-Cadre* (Framework or Enabling Law) or *Loi Defferre*, bearing the name of Gaston Defferre, Minister of Overseas France in the Socialist-led government presided over by Guy Mollet. Indeed, 1956 has some considerable claim to our attention as a pivotal year in the dissolution of the European colonial empires. It was the year of independence of Sudan and of Morocco (although both were special cases, one an Anglo-Egyptian condominium, the other a French protectorate). It was the planned year of the independence of Ghana, but this had to be put back to March 1957, as the British sought (and failed) to accommodate a federalist challenge to Kwame Nkrumah's otherwise inexorable rise to power. Not least, of course, it was the year of the ill-fated Suez expedition, in which Britain, France and Israel colluded in an abortive attempt to overthrow the nationalist Egyptian government of President Gamal Abdul Nasser.

Not even Suez marked the definitive beginning of the end of empire, however, and arguably the *will* to empire persisted. Certainly, on the British side, though Suez marked a humiliating setback, it did not precipitate a wholesale retreat of British imperial power from the Eastern Mediterranean and Middle East. More generally, historians have increasingly emphasised the reinvigoration of British imperial enterprise in the mid- to late 1950s (Lynn 2005; Darwin 2005). On the French side, the Suez mission arose from the imperatives of the Algerian campaign, which, earlier in the year, had been hugely escalated by a series of decisions taken by the Mollet government. These included the passing of 'special powers', and the despatch of the *contingent*, that is, France's conscript army of *appelés* and reservists (*rappelés*), which ultimately built up French forces to some 450,000 men, in order to defeat the FLN insurgency. As Martin Evans (2011) has argued, moreover, Mollet's 'surge' must be understood alongside his commitment to an eventual Algerian 'peace', prefiguring De Gaulle's so-called Constantine Plan of October 1958, in which a developed and democratic French Algeria would be fully incorporated into the French Republic.

It would be somewhat strange, therefore, if the *intention* behind Defferre's law had been to bring about the rapid end of French rule in the sub-Saharan African territories of a France extending, as his ministerial colleague François Mitterrand would have reminded him, 'from Flanders to the Congo'.[1] And yet the dominant interpretation of the *Loi-Cadre* has been, in various ways, as a 'big step towards decolonisation, if not in so many words' (Cooper 2002: 78). Indeed, one view of Defferre has been, precisely, as a would-be decoloniser, as for example in Edward Mortimer's view, derived in part from the testimony of Defferre's *chef de cabinet*, Fernand Wibaux:

> Defferre was appalled by the bloodshed in Algeria, convinced that it could have been avoided if a more enlightened policy had been applied in time, and determined to avoid a similar catastrophe in Afrique Noire. He may have seen already that independence was the manifest destiny of the African territories. If so, he must also have seen that this destiny could and should be realised without war or even bitterness between France and the Africans, and without real damage to France's real interests (Mortimer 1969: 233, 234n).

Something does not ring true here, in particular the suggestion that a tough-minded politician of Defferre's calibre would articulate, even privately, an idea of Africa's 'manifest destiny' (though he might have done so in the late 1960s). In any case, Defferre, the Mollet government, and more generally the Fourth and early Fifth Republics, have more usually been charged in this matter with either neo-colonial conspiracy or imperial demission. Thus, in keeping with a critique of French 'neo-colonialism' derived from dependency theory, scholars such as Catherine Coquery-Vidrovitch (1988) and Jean Suret-Canale (1998) pointed to the 'influence of the great capitalist entrepreneurs with African interests', although for Alexander Keese these authors 'have never managed to put forward any convincing source material' (Keese 2003: 34). Tony Chafer has placed the *Loi-Cadre* within the wider context of an 'emerging convergence of interests between French governing élites and African political leaders for the transfer of power to Africans'; these shared interests included the 'defeat of the nationalist movement', and the generation of a series of post-colonial collaborating regimes (Chafer 2002b: 206–7). But perhaps the most sophisticated interpretation of the *Loi-Cadre* is that of Frederick Cooper, who sees it bringing to an end a French tradition of assimilationism. According to this view, the French Republic was starting to count the costs of a decade of African welfare policy, which not least saw African workers gaining the entitlement to be considered the equals of their metropolitan counterparts. By shifting budgetary responsibility to individual territories, the *Loi-Cadre* thus transferred welfare costs to the new government councils (Cooper 1996: 407–13, 424–5; Cooper 2005: 227–9). In effect it also pushed decentralisation of the French Union to its limits, and beyond.

This chapter does not diverge from these interpretations of the *Loi-Cadre* as effectively leading to decolonisation in Francophone sub-Saharan Africa. However, the interest of the reforms of 1956/57, it may be argued, is precisely that they faced both ways. Looking back from 1956, the *Loi-Cadre* was clearly the culminating point of a reform process going back to 1946, or even further, to the 1944 Brazzaville conference; this process was designed to rationalise and strengthen the French late colonial state or, following Cooper (2005), 'empire-state'. But at the same time, the passing of the *Loi-Cadre* may also be seen as marking the point at which that process started to unravel south of the Sahara, just as it already had in Indochina and North Africa.

In effect, the *Loi-Cadre* represents the crossover between two opposing but overlapping conceptions of the 'late colonial state', and in particular of 'lateness', which mirror this dual process of consolidation and dissolution. On the one hand, 'late' may be taken to mean 'advanced'. In this sense, the late colonial state emerged from the profound disruption to the colonial empires caused by the Second World War, which led to a 'late colonial shift' in the expectations of both colonisers and colonised (Shipway 2008a: 12–14). According to this view, political and social reforms after 1945 were designed, not simply to appease local or international challenges to colonial rule, much less to head off a decolonisation which could scarcely be imagined in Africa *circa* 1944 or 1946, but rather to transform colonial rule into something sustainable in a longer term. On the other hand, 'late' may be taken straightforwardly in the sense of 'terminal': in this view, officials and politicians in the French Fourth Republic (though the argument may be applied *mutatis mutandis* in the case of the other empires) were simply resisting, for as long as they could, the impending dissolution of the colonial empires. The problem with the first of these conceptions is that, try as we might, we cannot undo the fact that, as Cooper's oft-quoted dictum has it, 'we know the end of the story' (1996: 6). The problem with the second is that it apparently condemns us, as historians of decolonisation, to raking over the 'details of a single, fundamentally unsound policy of preserving colonial-style hegemony over the dependencies' (Lewis 1998: 276).

Can these two conceptions of the late colonial state be reconciled? One possible way of doing so is to focus on the intentions of the policy makers, or more generally to seek to reconstruct the perspective of the French 'official mind', and to ask, in the case of the *Loi-Cadre*, what French politicians and officials really thought they could achieve by the reforms. Were they simply plotting the devolution of onerous budgetary responsibilities to territorial level (as Cooper would have it), the 'balkanisation' of their late colonial domains, or the establishment of France's post-1960 (or post-1958) neo-colonial *'chasse-gardée'*? Such Machiavellian prescience seems unlikely. But conversely, to what extent did they believe in the likelihood of consolidating the French Union sustainably after 1956/57, or in their capacity to restrain the political ambitions of an emerging generation of African politicians? Did they really hope to satisfy Africans with anything less than what Britain was apparently offering (or rather, conceding) to Nkrumah in Ghana, in a process felicitously characterised by *Le Monde* (12–13 November 1956) as 'creative abdication' (*abdication créatrice*)? In what follows, it will rather be suggested that the French 'official mind' was in a sense divided against itself. This is meant not simply in the sense that there were, of course, internal arguments between 'conservative' and 'liberal' officials within the French colonial administration, and differences in outlook (sometimes highly positive and creative ones) between officials and politicians. A distinction has also to be drawn between officials' public recourse to bureaucratic *'langue de bois'* and their own more private opinions (see Shipway 2011: 221). Rather, what is proposed here is a kind of official 'make believe', according to which officials simultaneously believed and disbelieved that far-reaching reforms could be effective; but that they were carried along by the internal logic of their own discourse, and further propelled by the momentum of a new government, a dynamic minister and the increasingly unstoppable force of African political agency.

Constructing the French African 'empire-state'

When Gaston Defferre presented the *Loi-Cadre* to the National Assembly for its first reading, in the debate on 21 March 1956, it was perhaps to be expected that he would quote the key passage from Charles De Gaulle's speech at the opening of the Brazzaville conference twelve years before, on 30 January 1944: 'In French Africa, as in all territories where men live beneath our flag, there would be no progress worthy of the name if men living in their native land did not profit morally and materially from that progress, if they could not improve themselves little by little to a level where they were able to take part in the management of their own affairs'.[2] One reason for this almost obligatory rhetorical gesture was to present the proposed reforms in a light that would meet the approval of potentially hostile Gaullist *députés* in the newly elected chamber (Messmer 1998: 139–40). But aside from this political point-making, the perspective was a not unreasonable one, and though De Gaulle's somewhat paternalist rhetoric at Brazzaville may have resonated strangely in the 1956 chamber, Defferre could look back upon a substantial measure of progress since Brazzaville on which to build his own African reforms. Although that progress had been driven in large measure by the energetic and largely unanticipated engagement in the political process of an emerging African political elite, it was incontestable.

It is easy enough to highlight the insufficiencies, setbacks and *longueurs* of the reform process over the intervening twelve years. The Brazzaville conference itself had been largely a failure, downgraded to a French African conference (rather than the grand imperial conference originally planned), its recommendations watered down by cautious officials, its propaganda message reduced to a faintly absurd 'spirit of Brazzaville' (Shipway 2008a: 127). A ground-breaking recommendation which did emerge from Brazzaville was to include elected colonial *députés* in an eventual Constituent Assembly, but the proposals on this by the 1945 Monnerville Commission were diluted by the Provisional Government, in consultation with senior colonial officials (Shipway 2011: 229–31). The constitution-making process of 1945/46 too was compromised in respect of the French Union. The first constitutional draft was rejected in the April 1946 referendum for reasons that had nothing to do with its strikingly bold provisions on the French Union; however, a backlash over the summer of 1946, triggered by De Gaulle's Bayeux speech on 16 July, led to a more coherent but also more restrictive constitutional framework for the French Union, and to the suspension of provisions for properly representative territorial assemblies in the African territories (ibid.: 242–4).

The Fourth Republic when it came ushered in a period of 'policy sclerosis' in sub-Saharan Africa (Chafer 2002b: 83–4), with a stalled reform agenda further impeded by the working out of France's domestic Cold War, and by a perpetual cycle of political crises and turnover of governments. Even before the inauguration of the new constitution, French forces entered definitively into an unwinnable war with the Viet Minh in Indochina. Three months later, at the end of March 1947, the insurrection in Madagascar further demonstrated the limits of French liberalism; quite apart from the swift brutality with which the insurgency was crushed, the National Assembly lifted the parliamentary immunity of the three Malagasy *députés*, following which they were summarily tried, condemned and incarcerated (and pardoned only by the Mollet government). For a while in 1948/49, it looked very much as if Côte d'Ivoire would be next, and that Félix Houphouët-Boigny's entirely pragmatic relationship with the French Communist Party (PCF) would see him outlawed as a rebel. Meanwhile, in Algeria, a Socialist Governor-General, Marcel-Edmond Naegelen, presided over massive electoral fraud in the 1948 Algerian Assembly elections, neutralising the nationalist opposition, and in effect heading off any possible reformist impact of the 1947 Algerian Statute.

The underlying trend in Africa was nonetheless one in which a distinctive French-African politics was progressively normalised, and the participation of African and other overseas *députés* in French political life was increasingly accepted. Even with a restricted franchise, discriminatory citizens' and non-citizens' electoral colleges, and with each *député* representing two distinct territories, some twenty overseas *députés* in the first Constituent Assembly (1945/46) contributed decisively to the first constitutional text, and passed highly symbolic legislation creating a 'French Union citizenship' and abolishing forced labour; the latter law was a major stepping stone not least for its *rapporteur* in the Assembly, Houphouët-Boigny. In subsequent Assemblies, including the National Assembly, but also the Council of the Republic (upper house) and the consultative Assembly of the French Union, overseas *députés* exerted an influence out of all proportion to their number. This was in part due to the Fourth Republic's shifting pattern of government coalitions, which often relied on the support of small groups to gain or retain office. In the first National Assembly (from late 1946), it was also a function of the formal alignment (*apparentement*) created between the brand-new umbrella party for the African territories, the Rassemblement Démocratique Africain (RDA) and the PCF. When this alignment became a potentially dangerous encumbrance towards the end of the parliament, Houphouët-Boigny was persuaded to re-affiliate the RDA, this time with François Mitterrand's centre-left grouping, the UDSR (Union Démocratique et Sociale de la Résistance); in the 1956 elections, that alliance put Houphouët-Boigny on the winning side. More generally, the electoral cycle, with a franchise progressively widening away from the entitled few to the many, ritually reinforced the practice of an increasingly democratic politics, in what Crawford Young has referred to as a 'golden age' in the associational life of African colonial societies (Young 1994: 237). Officials played their part in this, and increasingly 'played fair' in elections, resisting old habits and the instinct to place 'their' favoured candidates, although intimidation of the oppositional RDA, which was feared and loathed in equal measure, continued right up to the period of the *Loi-Cadre* (Keese 2011). While in the first parliament the emphasis was necessarily on the Parisian pole of influence, the 1951 elections were followed in 1952 by elections to the territorial assemblies, and over the following four years the focus shifted gradually to the prize of territorial control, as exercised most notably by Houphouët-Boigny's hegemonic PDCI (Parti Démocratique de la Côte d'Ivoire). In Guinea-Conakry, also, the influence of Ahmed Sékou Touré's rising star was felt strongly at grassroots level, although it took until the 1956 elections, 'conducted relatively honestly', for his branch of the RDA, the PDG (Parti Démocratique de la Guinée), to break through the barriers of official resistance (Schmidt 2007: 68–96, 105). The *Loi-Cadre* thus did not create the trend to territorialisation, although it did confirm it and make it irreversible.

Guiding principles of the *Loi-Cadre*

Towards the end of the second parliament, several steps taken in the course of 1955 inched the French Union closer to the kind of institutional reforms envisaged in 1956. The first was the introduction of a new Statute for Togo, which as a United Nations Trusteeship Territory fell outside the adjoining Federation of AOF and, given also the inter-territorial and indeed international dimensions of the 'Ewe question', forced the French to work to a more than usually expeditious timetable.[3] The Togo Statute, passed in April 1955, offered a possible model for the reorganisation of territorial assemblies and the introduction of a council of government, although, as it turned out, this was a rather conservative model (Mortimer 1969: 203–4). Secondly, a National Assembly committee chaired by Léopold Senghor, *député* for Senegal and one of the principal authors of the French Union articles in the ill-fated first constitutional draft of April 1946, reported on the possible reform of the existing French Union articles in Title VIII of the constitution (Mortimer 1969: 235); this was not followed up, though Defferre paid Senghor the courtesy of mentioning the proposed reform (even while proposing something radically different) when he presented the *Loi-Cadre* in the National Assembly the following March. Thirdly, the then Minister, Pierre-Henri Teitgen, convened a study group to report on the way forward. Its chairman, Robert Delavignette, described with good reason as 'a spiritual guide to our administrators' (Colombani 1991: 165), was a distinguished former Governor and Director of Political Affairs in the Ministry of Overseas France who had retired from the colonial service to teach at the National Academy of Overseas France (ENFOM), which he had directed during the war years. His report highlighted the contradictions emanating ultimately from the Brazzaville conference, which had failed to reconcile 'the path towards self-government and that of assimilation. It set out to reconcile these tendencies in a vague federation. In fact, it simply juxtaposed them. For too long now we have promised reforms, but failed to implement them' (Ibid.; Chafer 2002b: 164). Finally, Teitgen acted, on advice from ministerial officials led by his Director of Political Affairs Léon Pignon, proposing a law to the National Assembly which would have introduced universal suffrage in the African territories. Before the law could be enacted, however, the National Assembly was dissolved by the prime minister, Edgar Faure, pending general elections (Mortimer 1969: 225).

The *Loi-Cadre* might never have seen the light of day had it not been for the way in which, for once, the institutions of the Fourth Republic were made to work in favour of rapid reform, as the January 1956 elections brought a distinct shift to the Left, ushering in the Socialist-led government of Guy Mollet. Of the key personalities who made the *Loi-Cadre* what it was, two were ministers in the Mollet government, Gaston Defferre at the Ministry of Overseas France, and Félix Houphouët-Boigny, Minister without Portfolio ('*Ministre délégué*') in the prime minister's office; the third was Defferre's senior adviser at the Rue Oudinot, Léon Pignon. Their differing perspectives on the imperatives for reform will be considered in turn. The first, and no doubt most important, was Gaston Defferre, in his mid-forties in 1956 (born 1910) and an experienced political operator, having been Mayor of Marseille at the Liberation (1944/45) and then again from 1953 until his death in 1986, and *député* for Marseille, 1945–58 (and again from 1962 to 1981).[4] It was perhaps the personality of the city boss that impacted more on his office than his ministerial experience, though he had served briefly as under-secretary at the Ministry of Overseas France under Marius Moutet in 1946/47, and had subsequently visited Madagascar on a mission of enquiry into the insurrection, including reporting on allegations of abuse by settlers and officials.[5] He had also been Minister of Merchant Marine in 1950/51, and would already have been Minister of Overseas France under Christian Pineau from February 1955, had not the latter's two-day ministry been voted down in the Assembly (Mortimer 1969: 233). He was the first Socialist to hold the office since Moutet in 1946/47.

The urgency with which Defferre approached the possibility of reform is clear already in a letter he wrote, following a telephone conversation, to the prime minister, Guy Mollet, dated 14 February 1956, less than two weeks after taking office, in which he underlined the 'grave malaise which currently prevails in a number of our overseas territories, especially Cameroon, Madagascar and Chad'. At this stage he was working on the basis of the law drafted by Teitgen the previous December, but which in an enhanced form would introduce universal suffrage and abolish the double college, not only for National Assembly elections (as the 1956 elections had had to be conducted under old rules, with a double college in AEF and Cameroon), but also for territorial assemblies, and hence also for senatorial elections; this reform was indeed incorporated into the eventual *Loi-Cadre*, largely without further discussion. However, although at this point he had not settled upon the formula of the *Loi-Cadre*, or framework law, he was envisaging the introduction of more sweeping institutional reforms, 'within the framework of full powers that the government will be requesting'.[6] Though Defferre never effected this extension of the 'special powers' which were requested and applied in Algeria, the *Loi-Cadre* allowed him precisely to circumvent the 12–18-month delays which he deplored in his letter to Mollet, which meant that any law was 'outdated by the time it was passed, and instead of bringing satisfaction brings only disappointment'. Again, in his eventual '*exposé de motifs*' for the first reading of the *Loi-Cadre*, Defferre underlined how important it was to avoid the long delays which had bedevilled earlier African legislation, notably the four years it had taken to implement the African Labour Code.[7] Conversely, the mechanism of the *Loi-Cadre*, according to which the passing of the law allowed the detail of its provisions to be passed by administrative decree, without further recourse to parliamentary vote, also allowed the possibility of delay: officials at the rue Oudinot were already predicting that, though a preliminary deadline of August 1956 was discussed, the process was likely to drag on well into 1957, as in fact happened.[8]

The second personality who exerted crucial influence on the *Loi-Cadre* was

Félix Houphouët-Boigny, though this influence was exercised, initially at least, largely by default. This was the point at which Houphouët-Boigny's career turned a corner: having transmuted successively from the young champion of African cocoa planters' rights and the abolition of forced labour to party boss and fellow-travelling rebel of the late 1940s, to territorial leader in Côte d'Ivoire still regarded with official suspicion through the early 1950s, he now became a government minister and establishment figure. Defferre sent him a copy of the first draft of the law in late February, on which Houphouët-Boigny commented, somewhat blandly, on 27 February 1956, praising the concept of the *Loi-Cadre*, which had crystallised by this time, and the 'very pragmatic and therefore very realistic presentation'.[9] Defferre seems to have followed Houphouët's advice that he should refrain from mentioning the 'troubles' in Madagascar and Cameroon, but should emphasise only that 'there was still time to act and that the Government can do so without submitting to any pressure'.[10] Houphouët-Boigny's more substantive comments were marginally more pointed, but they largely served to confirm that the proposed legislation was entirely along lines that he could approve, and in particular, that 'it is the attributions of the territorial assemblies that should be extended, and not those of the group [i.e., the Federal] assemblies': as we will see below, this was one of two key battles that was fought around the *Loi-Cadre*, but Houphouët-Boigny was in a sense pushing against an open door in ensuring that the territories, of which Houphouët-Boigny was a major champion, should not give ground to the Federal capitals at Dakar and Brazzaville: Côte d'Ivoire was by far the richest territorial member of the Federation of AOF, and biggest net contributor to its budget. Houphouët-Boigny also placed an interesting emphasis on two elements of the proposed reforms which were of longer-term significance but which largely fell by the wayside: the Africanisation of the civil service, and the development of rural collectivities, to provide representation for the 'peasant masses representing 90% of the population of the Territories'.[11]

The third key figure in the making of the *Loi-Cadre*, Governor-General Léon Pignon, was not a newcomer to the Rue Oudinot by any means, but as Director of Political Affairs since 1954 was in a position to exercise crucial authority in policy-making. His career had been impressive if not exactly glorious since 1943/44, when he was Henri Laurentie's deputy in organising the Brazzaville conference. His instrumental role as political counsellor in Saigon in policy leading up to the outbreak of war in Indochina is well-known (Tønnesson 2009), but even before that, Pignon had been one of the principal authors of the Declaration of 24 March 1945, the abortive blueprint for an eventual late-colonial state in Indochina (Shipway 2008a: 94). As High Commissioner in Indochina (1948–50), he had been responsible for implementing the 'Bao Daï solution' which he had largely invented, and which on a generous interpretation may be seen as a kind of decolonisation of the French regime in Indochina

(Goscha 2011: 32, 107; Shipway 2008b). As Alexander Keese has shown, since taking over at the Rue Oudinot, Pignon had consistently argued in favour of extending the political responsibilities of the African elite (Keese 2003: 41–3). He was backed in this by a small network of like-minded officials whom he had commanded in Indochina, foremost among whom was perhaps Pierre Messmer, who as Governor of Côte d'Ivoire in 1954/55 had formed a constructive relationship with Houphouët-Boigny and who was now Defferre's director of cabinet. In effect, by the time Defferre took office, Pignon had not only drawn up the outlines of what became the *Loi-Cadre* but had also, with his network, fought a number of battles with officials representing, as Keese suggests, the majority opinion within the Ministry and the administration (ibid.). Defferre's appointment was therefore a crucial opportunity for Pignon, who lost no time in recruiting him as a crucial ally in the implementation of the reforms over the following fifteen months or so.

Internal debate surrounding the purpose and direction of the *Loi-Cadre* reforms revolved around three major questions. The first was largely a procedural question, and concerned the legality of the *Loi-Cadre* itself. The upshot of considerable discussion within the Ministry seems to have been the conclusion that, strictly speaking, the proposed mechanisms for introducing reforms through administrative decrees would have required full consultation of both the Assembly of the French Union (whose proposed amendments to the text of the law were largely ignored) and also the existing Territorial Assemblies, which was clearly impracticable, even though not doing so could be 'reconciled only with difficulty with the letter of the Constitution'.[12] This issue appears to have been resolved by the legalistic equivalent of a shrug, and by the general advice that the decrees provided for by the framework of the *Loi-Cadre* were not '*décrets-lois*' (i.e., decrees having legal force) but 'texts having purely administrative value' ('*valeur règlementaire*').[13] In any case, no one appears to have made a serious challenge to the *Loi-Cadre* on the grounds of its unconstitutional nature.

The other two interrelated issues went to the heart of the reforms, and their gradual resolution may be traced through the period of implementation to March 1957: the question of the relative priority to be given to reform at territorial and at federal level; and the composition and powers of the eventual Councils of Government. The first of these questions inevitably revolves around the charge of 'balkanisation' first made by Léopold Senghor in the National Assembly debate on the first reading of the *Loi-Cadre*, in March 1956.[14] Although that accusation prejudged the issue to some degree, it underlines the extent to which the *Loi-Cadre* challenged the prevailing orthodoxy surrounding the Federations of AOF and AEF, an orthodoxy which Senghor himself had followed in his 1955 proposals for reform of Title VIII of the Constitution. As Keese has shown (2003: 44–6), however, this orthodoxy had already been challenged by Pignon and his colleagues in internal debate; while Houphouët-Boigny was a leading exponent of the trend towards territorialisation. Pignon's advice to Defferre in the run-up to the first Assembly debate was entirely pragmatic, namely that, while the reform of the Governments-General and the central administration was one of the 'preoccupations frequently voiced by Parliament and by overseas parliamentarians – M. Senghor', it was nonetheless preferable 'not to undertake reform of the Governments-General before that of the territories had been completed', as this would considerable reduce the options for change, which might include removing the Governments-General altogether (although some form of inter-territorial coordination would still be necessary), or forming territories into new groupings.[15] This apparently open-ended approach to reform did not sit well with orthodox opinion within the administration, and early warning of likely objections to territorialisation came from Paul Chauvet, Governor-General of AEF, who wrote to Defferre in March 1956 to advise against the creation of Councils of Government at the level of the territory, rather than at federal level, as this was likely to lead to the splintering of the Governments-General by reducing them to a 'simple supervisory, coordinating and advisory role'. Chauvet somewhat weakened his case by mentioning his own elaborate plans for reorganising the Union into a series of 'territorial groups' each with its own Council of Government; but he also added some pertinent comment on the role of the Councils.[16]

Chauvet was far from alone in his reservations about the proposed delegation of powers down to the territorial level, and at a Conference of High-Commissioners and Governors over the summer 1956, it was proposed to ditch what was referred to as 'Solution A' in favour of maintaining the status quo, on the basis of which a first set of decrees were prepared. However, when these were passed to Houphouët-Boigny for comment, he responded with a strongly worded ten-page memorandum, and a fourteen-page 'counter-project', effectively reminding the Ministry of the underlying spirit of reform.[17] Although the decision-making following this exchange has not been uncovered, the official Note responding to Houphouët-Boigny's memorandum already suggested that, with some minor reservations, in particular concerning the capacity of a weakened Federation to provide the budgetary resources necessary to balance their budget, his proposals 'seem acceptable'.[18] In effect, following this official 'wobble', the reforms were back on track, and the inexorable trend towards territorialisation continued. Controversy continued in the political sphere, however, as rival tendencies clashed in meetings of the Assembly's Commission of Overseas Territories in early 1957: although the 'balkanising' tendency carried the day (associated on the Commission with the Dahomeyan *député*, Sourou Migan Apithy), it nonetheless made concessions to the 'Senghor' tendency with a greater number of services left in the hand of the Federations.[19]

The second – related, but even more critical – issue concerned the role of the eventual Councils of Government, which were central to the text of the *Loi-Cadre* itself, but the composition and powers of which were left to be sorted out by decree following consultation with African political leaders, notably those sitting on the Commission of Overseas Territories. As already suggested, the proposed model for the Councils was that set up in the 1955 Togolese Statute, which provided for a mixture of 'official' and elected 'unofficial' membership (the British term 'unofficial' being not inappropriate in this context), with the Governor chairing and able to exert executive decision-making power, and indeed the power of veto; this model was championed in explicit detail by Paul Chauvet in his letter to Defferre in March 1956.[20] However, as a model it was rapidly superseded, not least because Togo acquired a new Statute, which ushered in the Autonomous Republic of Togo on 30 August 1956, with a Government led by an African Prime Minister (of half-German parentage), Nicolas Grunitzky, thus bringing to an end Togo's UN Trusteeship status (Mortimer 1969: 241). The eventual structure that was adopted retained the Governor (now a High-Commissioner) as President, with an elected Vice-President and membership drawn from the Territorial Assembly, and no appointed members other than the Governor.[21] In March 1957, Pignon briefed Defferre on the requirements of gubernatorial oversight (*tutelle*) in the face of the elected majority, ruling out the possibility of a veto as being 'inopportune' as it would be a 'copy of the British system, and, for historical reasons, frowned upon (*mal vu*) in France', and so relying on political adeptness on the part of the Governor, backed only by the ultimate constitutional authority of the French Council of State (*Conseil d'Etat*).[22] The sense that the Governors were entering into the new system 'on a wing and a prayer' was even stronger at a Conference of the Governors-General and High Commissioners, chaired by Defferre, that met in Paris on 23/24 April 1957, in the immediate wake of the elections to the Territorial Assemblies.[23] At this point, the die was well and truly cast, and it is fascinating to read the discussions between the pragmatic and still optimistic Defferre, proffering advice from his experience 'as mayor of a big city', and the – presumably – slightly nervous Governors, who would all too soon find themselves presiding over a system in which the rules of the game had been decisively and irreversibly rewritten. More particularly, though the rules governing the role of the Councils of Government had necessarily been couched in terms of procedures and constitutional principles (who is responsible before the Territorial Assembly and on what issues, who sets the Council agenda, what happens when the Governor is absent, in whom are invested the 'powers of the Republic'?), officials were well aware that in practice the success or failure of the new structures would come down to the daily practice of politics.

Conclusion: the *Loi-Cadre* unravels

One conclusion which was not reached at the April 1957 Conference of Governors-General and High Commissioners was any sense that the *Loi-Cadre* reforms were bound to fail, but it is difficult for the historian to conclude otherwise. This was in large measure because of official misreading and miscalculations, whether concerning the presumed unimportance and encumbrance of the African Federations, or the likelihood that the new African leaders would act loyally and 'responsibly' within the new Councils of Government. On the first issue, as Alexander Keese has also argued (2003: 45–6), far from intending to 'balkanise' the African territories in the interests of a presumed neo-colonial future, officials not only downplayed the importance of the Federation in redistributing resources among the territories, but also misjudged its appeal to the African elites, many of whom shared Senghor's well-publicised misgivings. On the second, officials showed a certain nervous awareness of the potential for trouble which turned out to be more than amply justified, as the newly formed Councils of Government rapidly turned against their appointed Presidents. In a broader sense, however, the *Loi-Cadre* serves as an example of a wider problem confronting colonial officials seeking to construct a durable settlement for the late colonial state, which was the tension between, on the one hand, the immense, painstaking effort and detail of the reform process – which, to their credit, the architects of the 1956 reforms had allowed for within the very mechanism of the *Loi-Cadre* – and on the other, the need to recognise and accommodate the dynamism, contingency and sheer untidiness of an unfolding political situation. It is this mismatch between the official imperatives for reform and the undoubted awareness that things could – and would – go seriously wrong that opens a space for what might be termed official 'make-believe', though even this can hardly account for the rapidity with which the reforms unravelled over the course of the following months. In the event, the new structures which had taken more than a year to put in place were shaken to the core barely a year later, by the events of 1958. In bringing to power the 'man of Brazzaville', Charles De Gaulle, first as prime minister and then as President of a new Fifth Republic, the seismic shocks of May 1958, followed by the referendum of September of that year, and not least by Guinée's surprise departure from the newfound French Community, would radically shorten the lifespan of the doomed and ultimately unloved French African 'empire-state'.

Notes

1 From his speech on 1 November 1954; but see also Mitterrand (1953), where the span is given as 'from Lille to Brazzaville'; and Mitterrand (1957).
2 Archives Communales de Marseille, Fonds Gaston Defferre, 100 II 139, Draft of Defferre's speech, n.d.; and see De Gaulle (1970), 394.

3 Togo, a German colony until 1919, was partitioned between Britain and France as League of Nations Mandates (subsequently UN Trusteeship Territories), with the lion's share going to France. The Ewe were divided between French Togo (where some 174,000 lived), British Togoland (137,000) and the Gold Coast (376,000) (Hargreaves 1996: 143; and see Thomas et al. 2008: 252–4). Resolution of the eponymous question therefore involved not only protracted Anglo-French cooperation but also the involvement of the UN Trusteeship Council; in the end, no transfer of territory took place and the Ewe remained divided.

4 After 1981, Defferre returned to ministerial office as Minister of the Interior and Decentralisation, under the presidency of François Mitterrand, and in 1982 turned once again to the device of the *Loi-Cadre* for his decentralisation reforms.

5 See his report and notes, June/July 1947, in Fonds Gaston Defferre, 100 II 338.

6 Fonds Gaston Defferre, 100 II 134, Defferre to Mollet, 14 February 1956.

7 Fonds Gaston Defferre, 100 II 134, draft of 'Exposé de motifs', n.d. (March 1956).

8 Fonds Gaston Defferre, 100 II 134, *Note pour le Ministre, Calendrier*, n.d.

9 Fonds Gaston Defferre, 100 II 134, F. Houphouët-Boigny, Ministre délégué, *Note au sujet du projet de «loi cadre» proposé par Monsieur le Ministre de la France d'Outre-Mer*, 27 February 1956.

10 The 'troubles' in Madagascar were largely unfinished business from the 1947 Insurrection, but are barely mentioned in most accounts, although the 1956 elections led to the creation of Philibert Tsirinana's Parti Social-Démocrate which brought Madagascar to independence in 1960 (Randrianja and Ellis 2009: 278–9; Thomas et al. 2008: 168–9). For Cameroon, the reference is no doubt to the 1955 riots inspired by Ruben Um Nyobé's Union des Populations du Cameroun, a significant stage along the way to sub-Saharan Africa's only armed insurgency against France in this period which started in late 1956 (Joseph 1977; Shipway 2008a: 191–4).

11 Fonds Gaston Defferre, 100 II 134, F. Houphouët-Boigny, Ministre délégué, *Note au sujet du projet de «loi cadre» proposé par Monsieur le Ministre de la France d'Outre-Mer*, 27 February 1956.

12 Fonds Gaston Defferre, 100 II 134, *NOTE sur les modifications apportées par l'Assemblée de l'Union Française au projet de loi no. 895*, n.d. (March 1956).

13 Fonds Gaston Defferre, 100 II 134, *Observations d'ordre général*, n.d. And see Mortimer 1969: 235–6.

14 *J.O.R.F., Débats Parlementaires*, 21 March 1956, 1070.

15 Fonds Gaston Defferre, 100 II 134, *Pignon, NOTE pour Monsieur le Ministre, au sujet du projet de loi no. 895*, 19 March 1956.

16 Fonds Gaston Defferre, 100 II 136, Chauvet to Defferre (n° 643/SPP), March 1956.

17 Fonds Gaston Defferre, 100 II 136, *Note from Houphouët-Boigny to Defferre*, 3 October 1956; Fonds Gaston Defferre, 100 II 136, *Note sur les propositions de M. Houphouët concernant l'organisation des groupes de territoires et les pouvoirs des assemblées*, 4 October 1956.

18 Fonds Gaston Defferre, 100 II 136, *Note sur les propositions de M. Houphouët* …

19 Fonds Gaston Defferre, 100 II 139, *Analyse critique des travaux de la commission*, n.d. (early 1957).

20 Fonds Gaston Defferre, 100 II 136, Chauvet to Defferre (n° 643/SPP), March 1956.

21 Cf. the account of the debate on a Socialist 'counterproject' (n.d., early 1957), in which the case for retaining the Governor alongside an all-elected Council was argued in detail, in Fonds Gaston Defferre, 100 II 139.
22 Fonds Gaston Defferre, 100 II 136, Directorate of Political Affairs, *La tutelle des décisions du Conseil de Gouvernement*, n.d. (March 1957).
23 Full transcript in Fonds Gaston Defferre, 100 II 169.

2

A vocation for independence:
Guinean nationalism in the 1950s

Mairi MacDonald

Within four weeks of its 'no' vote in the referendum of 28 September 1958, newly independent Guinea's president Ahmed Sékou Touré was already hard at work defining independence as the centrepiece of the new country's political culture:

> Independence is a word that is full of nobility; independence is sacred because it must be born in our spirits on the very day that foreign domination takes hold in a country. That is to say that Africa's vocation for independence is not born today, but on the very day when foreign powers extorted from African populations the right to the total exercise of their own sovereignty. (Touré 1958b: 164)[1]

Its decision to opt for immediate independence in 1958 made Guinea an anomaly in French West Africa. With varying degrees of enthusiasm, voters in neighbouring territories in the former Afrique Occidentale Française (AOF) chose, instead, to trust that France's new Fifth Republic would eventually deliver an acceptable path to state sovereignty through the ill-defined mechanism of De Gaulle's proposed new French Community. Historians disagree both about why the dominant Parti Démocratique de la Guinée (PDG) finally decided just two weeks before the referendum to call for its rejection, and about the reasons for De Gaulle's vengeful reaction to Guinea's 'no' (Diallo 2008b: 44–5). What is unarguable is that the PDG did not expect the full force of France's retaliation. De Gaulle ordered the immediate withdrawal of all French administrative personnel and material supports to its erstwhile colony, and conducted a vigorous and wide-ranging diplomatic battle to try to prevent its recognition by France's allies and its membership in the United Nations (MacDonald 2009: 58–76; Lewin 1990: 45–95).

Independence, and France's reaction, thus separated the new country from its neighbours both legally and politically. It also gave Touré the kernel around which he would construct an identity for his new state and, not incidentally, cement his own position as the leader who delivered its freedom from foreign domination. Both popular and scholarly assessments of his legacy tend to acknowledge this accomplishment, even as they excoriate the brutality of his 26-year rule (Kaké 1987; Diawara 1998: 58–76, 96).

The importance of the concept of independence in Guinea's post-colonial history has influenced how the historical literature treats what came before the 'no' vote. Touré's rhetorical conceit that Africa's destiny was set towards a modern concept of state independence from the moment of colonial conquest is an exaggerated version of this tendency to read backwards from the result to trace the antecedents that must have been in place. This literature attributes to canny anti-colonial nationalism the PDG's successful initiative in the summer of 1957 to abolish the institution of *canton* chief throughout the territory. Elizabeth Schmidt, for instance, asserts that the PDG 'was able to capitalise and expand upon preexisting anti-colonial sentiment' in the form of 'rural-based mobilisation against village and *canton* chiefs' (Schmidt 2005: 91). Jacques Rabemananjara goes further to discern prescience in this initiative. He speculates that, had Touré and his party not eliminated the institution and removed the incumbents from power, chiefs would have influenced their followers to vote 'yes' to the referendum and thus defeated the PDG's movement towards independence (Rabemananjara 1958: 11). The reification of independence in this reading ignores the fact that Soudan (now Mali) also abolished canton chieftaincy in 1957, but voters there agreed to join De Gaulle's Community (Mann 2006a: 3). It also ignores the PDG's highly successful electoral track record prior to 1957. More recent work seeks to rebalance our understanding of Guinea's 'no' by crediting Guinea's teachers and students, not the PDG, with the most effective push towards independence. Even this research, however, falls into the trap of assuming that Guinea had a unique inclination based upon the outcome of events, even as it highlights the international and continental connections of the anti-colonial movement in 1950s Africa (Diallo 2008a).

Yet the archival record contradicts these assumptions. There does not seem to have been significantly more talk of independence, sovereignty or even national self-determination in Guinea before 1958 than there was elsewhere in AOF. What talk there is – at least as French colonial officials reported it – portrays independence as an emotional state, rather than a practical, legal and material aspiration. It is the actions, not the words, of the Guinean arm of the Rassemblement Démocratique Africain (RDA) that distinguish this colony. A careful reading of both French and British archival records from this period conveys the impression of a party pushing the boundaries of power, both against the French colonial state that officially exercised sovereignty over the territory, and against British colonial officials in the neighbouring territory of Sierra Leone. The resulting disjunction between anti-colonial speech and the practical exercise of independent authority points to what really was different about

Guinea before the events of September 1958 severed it from its Francophone neighbours.

Anti-colonial speech

The French colonial archives disclose almost no talk of independence in Guinea before 1957, except at the most general level – a level that echoed the 1946 constitution of the Fourth Republic itself, which promised that France 'intended to conduct the peoples in its charge to the freedom to administer themselves and democratically to manage their own affairs' (quoted in Siriex 1957: II). The RDA manifesto, for instance, issued the same year, defined the party's objectives in very similar terms. It would seek 'equal political and social rights, individual and cultural liberties, and democratically elected local assemblies' within 'a freely chosen union between the populations of Africa and the people of France' (quoted in Chafer 2002b: 72–3). Writing in 1955, when he was high commissioner of AOF, Bernard Cornut-Gentille read more into propaganda from the RDA's earliest period. 'Aiming for the liberation of all of black Africa and taking credit for measures of "Liberation" through effective propaganda, it recommended a struggle for emancipation and openly preached war on "imperialism and colonial exploitation"', he argued. Such aggression peaked in the 1949/50 period when the RDA was closely allied with France's Communist Party (the PCF), but by 1950–52, Cornut-Gentille observed, the African party had revised its methods and was collaborating with the colonial administration.[2]

The RDA's local rivals in Guinea were no more forthcoming in expressing anti-colonial ambitions. An Arabic-language tract discovered early in 1955 boasted that the new party called Démocratie socialiste de Guinée (DSG) 'is the guarantee of the total independence of man, woman and child, the enjoyment of their rights, and the safeguard of all their customs, based on equality and brotherhood'. The tract, which French colonial officials believed to have been distributed by Barry Ibrahima (also known as Barry III), went on to define the liberty and independence that it was seeking for Guinea as a matter of ending the territory's 'subjection to foreign power'. Despite French worries, however, this power was not colonial but 'capitalist domination'.[3] The Bloc Africain de Guinée (BAG), like the DSG, was formed in response to the wave of PDG-led post-election violence that began in June 1954. Unlike the DSG, however, the BAG was at pains to distance itself from any hint of communism, reflecting its base of support in the most powerful families of the Fouta Djallon region. The BAG 'affirmed [its] attachment to the Republic One and Indivisible' although it specified that this should not preclude the new party from seeking to enforce the 1946 constitution's promise of eventual self-government. The Republic should also be indivisible, the BAG noted, only to the extent that France treated its black 'sons' as it did its 'own white sons'.[4]

Certainly it is understandable that political parties would be circumspect in expressing anti-colonial sentiment in a colonial territory. Senior leaders within the RDA, in particular, reaped the political benefits in France – as well as the disaffection of more radical elements in AOF – of its 1950 decision to disaffiliate from the PCF and to adopt a new policy of cooperation with the colonial administration (Chafer 2002b: 117–18). But other social circles in Guinea generated few anti-colonial comments that French officials deemed worthy of reporting to Paris. This was not due to lack of attention on the part of the officials, who were, on the contrary, anxious to report every hint of potential resistance. In February 1955, Governor Jean-Paul Parisot reported that available evidence of PDG-led unrest in Conakry and Coyah suggested it was premeditated. He found it most significant that PDG rioters had designated an area within Conakry as 'Dien Bien Phu' and used the term 'Indochina' as a code-name for Coyah.[5]

French officials finally began to report unequivocal demands for independence from Guinean politicians during the election campaign of March 1957. Running for election to the territorial assembly, whose powers had been augmented by the *Loi Gaston-Defferre* (the *loi-cadre*) the previous June, RDA candidates Sory Condé and Lansana Diané were unusually frank in stump speeches they gave in Kankan. 'The *loi-cadre* is intended to put us back to sleep, to set back our independence', said Condé, warning that Guineans would achieve independence 'no matter what the sacrifice'. Diané was more specific. The *loi-cadre* gave the territory no power over the army, police or currency and was, consequently, inadequate. It had been written and enacted in Paris, 'not in the interests of the territories but of France alone'. The RDA, he promised, would not stop until Guinea controlled its army, its finances and its diplomatic relations – not, in fact, until 'Africa is tied to France by nothing more than the links of friendship'. Though he made no explicit mention of Indochina or of Algeria's ongoing liberation struggle, Diané clearly had France's colonial precedents in mind: 'we are determined, for a country has never found its freedom except at the price of human lives, at the cost of position and fortune'.[6]

The leader of Guinea's RDA branch remained circumspect, issuing no explicit calls for independence within direct earshot of French officials until July 1958. Only after Sékou Touré had been made president of French Guinea did he risk expressing disappointment that De Gaulle's draft constitution did not spell out the rights of the territories to 'internal autonomy' or 'self-determination'. In a telegram to Bernard Cornut-Gentille, by now the minister of overseas France, Touré wrote of the elevation of the (African) leaders of AOF's territorial assemblies to their respective presidencies that: 'I consider [it] to be an important step towards the precise definition of the [respective] powers of the Republic and of the African states, whose right to independence must unequivocally be recognised so that their association with France can come about in dignity and with respect for their reciprocal interests'.[7] Touré had chosen both his tone and his audience carefully. Cornut-Gentille had been one of his strongest champions within the French ministry since his term as high commissioner in Dakar from 1951 to 1956, occasioning rumours that his interest in the attractive young Guinean politician was personal, rather than professional (Lewin 2009: 206).

Whatever the source of Cornut-Gentille's sympathy towards Touré, the latter's discretion concerning independence was reflected even in the most incendiary of his speeches: the address to Charles De Gaulle that he delivered in Conakry on 25 August 1958. Here he described the right to independence as an essential component of 'a first and indispensable need' for all Africans: their dignity. There could be no dignity without freedom, he argued, famously adding 'we prefer poverty in freedom to riches in slavery'. Beneath the fiery rhetoric, though, was a streak of pragmatic appreciation for Guinea's ongoing need for French support. Touré listed four areas where the new French community could act effectively on Guinea's behalf – so long as it took those actions on the basis of mutual recognition, and the effective exercise, of the territory's people's right to independence. Those four areas were defence, diplomatic relations, currency and higher education. Guinea would 'voluntarily' cede its sovereign powers over these matters as part of an interdependent entity. Thus, he argued, Guinea's position should not be confused with secession. Instead, Guinea intended to remain tied to the metropole, cooperating with France to 'open up our common wealth' (Touré 1958a: 17–25).

Sékou Touré always maintained that the 'poverty in freedom' speech was the product of a collective effort by a number of the PDG's leaders (Kaba 1989: 105–6). Though he was responsible for its delivery – in a tone that Pierre Messmer called 'offensive' and Lansiné Kaba termed 'hateful' (Messmer 1998: 148–9; Kaba 1989: 114) – its echo of Diané's list of the powers reserved to France by the 'insufficient' *loi-cadre* suggests that its content did, indeed, reflect debate among his colleagues. Elizabeth Schmidt argues that there was a division within the Guinean RDA pitting pro-independence forces, led by trade unions, students and youth, against the more conservative position of Touré. She notes that the leader did not finally concede to these more radical elements within the party until a PDG Congress held on 14 September, the day that Touré finally called for the 'no' vote (Schmidt 2007: 160–2). Touré was not in the forefront of demands for independence, at least until he suddenly obtained it for his new state in October 1958. But the archival record suggests that with the exception of elements like Sory Condé and Lansana Diané, who expressed their disappointment that the 1956 *loi-cadre* did not go further towards complete autonomy, Touré's rhetorical reticence on the subject may not in fact have been a great disappointment to many in his party. Because the fact was that even without calling for independence, Touré's RDA had been able to go further than most other territorial governments towards de facto autonomy, and as early as 1955 enjoyed a freedom of movement that may have made independence not much more than a formality – at least in material, as opposed to emotional, terms.

Anti-colonial behaviour

Though there may have been some circumspection in its rhetoric, the Guinean branch of the RDA was far from shy in practice. Historians eager to dispel the triumphal version of Touré's legend as the champion of Guinean independence have focused on the PDG's orchestration of violence and mayhem to protest against election results that went against the party (Charles 1992). Even Charles's focus on violence as the means by which the PDG took power, however, misses the significance of the party's achievement. Long before formal independence, the French colonial administration had become aware that the PDG was running a local administration in which its own influence was rapidly dwindling.

The earliest indication that French officials recognised what the PDG was becoming dates from August 1954. In June, the administration had held partial elections in Guinea to replace Yacine Diallo as the territory's representative in the French National Assembly following Diallo's death in April. The by-election spurred complaints from both sides. The local RDA complained that the French administration was favouring Barry Diawadou, like Diallo a Fulbe from the Fouta Djallon. Barry, in turn, objected that the administration's attitude 'permitted Sékou Touré to claim that he had official approval'. The president of Barry's election committee, Keïta Ouremba, complained that the RDA was bringing supporters in from Côte d'Ivoire to conduct 'violent' propaganda in favour of Touré, 'absolutely contrary to African customs'. When Barry won the election – despite what even French authorities acknowledged was 'tardy and insufficient' campaigning beyond the Fouta – the local RDA protested. The party complained of irregularities in voter registration in the Faranah subdivision and other majority Fulbe-populated *cercles* in the Fouta. The PDG's Macenta committee proclaimed itself 'astonished' that Sékou Touré, 'the only candidate for whom the people of Guinea had freely voted', had not won, and objected that Barry Diawadou 'in no way represented the Guinean people'.[8] Violent incidents followed at Boké on 14 and 15 July and in Conakry when Barry arrived in the capital on 24 July.

A formal telegram of complaint from Sékou Touré in turn elicited a formal report from the office of Conakry's governor. Noting that 'lies are M. Sékou Touré's favourite dialectic', Secretary-General G. Léglise complained that it was hard to disprove Touré's 'imprecise' allegations. Notwithstanding the difficulties, Léglise denied all assertions that the French administration had improperly pressured RDA members and allies during the election. Touré's complaints were simply part of a campaign to overturn electoral results that were not to his liking. In reality, according to Léglise, Touré 'was a victim of the conservative reaction of customary chiefs towards the theories he propounds', a reaction all the more 'painful because it resulted in his opponent obtaining a crushing majority'. In seeking to discredit Touré and his allegations, Léglise pointed out that his objectives and his actions '[seem] rather far away from the line pursued by M. Houphouet'. The RDA's Ouezzin Coulibaly and 'Guinean parliamentarians who had to intervene in Guinea during the election campaign', said Léglise, 'could recognise that the local RDA is considered to be an opposition party to the Administration'. This accounted for the various forms of PDG organising that French officials had noticed: excessive sales of RDA membership cards, the creation of party sections in rural areas, private meetings in Conakry, even the recruitment of women.[9]

Léglise sought to discredit Touré by accusing him of heading a rogue faction and hinting at treasonous intentions. If he was correct that the PDG aspired to be an opposition party to the administration, though, this also signalled a change – and one that itself made the French authorities somewhat uncomfortable. Since the late 1940s, France had relied on four community organisations, divided along ethnic lines, to control Guinea's population. Even in the run-up to the 1954 by-election, these committees retained a position of some influence. In a letter written late in May 1954, Governor Parisot was blunt: 'First of all', he wrote to Senator Raphaël Saller, 'the ethnic groupings acknowledge that Yacine's successor must be a Fulbe. This is the sentiment of Mamba Sano, Framoi Bérété, Koly Kourouma and Amara Soumah'. The difficulty was that there were two Fulbe candidates: Barry Diawadou and Barry III, who could split the vote among this significant group. In these circumstances, Sékou Touré 'could constitute the outsider'. Indeed, Touré's campaign emphasised that he was the only candidate in 1954 to have risen above Guinea's ethnic rivalries.[10]

By characterising the PDG as an opposition to the administration, Léglise was acknowledging its ambition to operate as a modern political party on a territory-wide scale. It soon became evident to the French that even this was not the limit of the PDG's aspirations. Further outbreaks of politically motivated violence in Guinea in October 1954 and again in January and February 1955 triggered a more thorough investigation of just what might be going wrong for the French administration in this territory. The ministry sent veteran Inspector-General H. Pruvost to conduct an inquiry. Pruvost's initially reassuring reports to Paris soon gave way to a far more alarming view. On 20 February, within days of his arrival, Pruvost described violent incidents in Boffa and Dubréka, up the Atlantic coast from Conakry, as 'manifestations of a pre-insurrectional state', overtly orchestrated by the PDG's 'self-proclaimed administration'. The report itself, sent to Paris in early March, cited with approval the observation that although the party's influence varied across Guinea's regions and ethnic populations, in some places, notably near the capital, 'there is not a single village where an order is carried out, a franc paid of tax, but with the consent of RDA officials. The party, using the existing framework of village society, has put in place an armature parallel to ours, with its village chiefs, its police complete with insignia, even its tribunals ... The most insane *mots d'ordre* circulate through the countryside concerning the invulnerability of anyone carrying a party card, the tax exempt status of RDA members, the legitimacy of refusals to obey any rule that does not emanate from the party'. Pruvost concluded that the incidents were 'signal flares of the success ... obtained by the political action of certain leaders, notably M. Sékou Touré, steeped in Marxist technique'. The ultimate objective of this action, he thought, was the definitive 'eviction of the authority and administration of the French in their current form'.[11] While his finding that the Guinean RDA had the tools to supplant local authority might have echoed much earlier French views of RDA-operated 'parallel administrations' in Côte d'Ivoire and Gabon, Pruvost's strongly worded conclusion left no doubt that in this territory, the PDG intended to rule unopposed – including by the colonial power itself (Keese 2007b: 87–8, 123).

Pruvost's report was never circulated within the colonial ministry or in AOF, in part because its completion coincided with a change of minister. Protesting this silence, Maurice Bayrou, secretary of state for overseas France, noted that the conclusions to be drawn from Pruvost's analysis were alarming and should be acted upon. 'We have seen the birth, within the framework of a political party, of a pseudo-administration, sometimes of a paramilitary character, which has drawn a veil between Guineans and the representatives of [French] authority', he argued. To Bayrou, as to Pruvost, the solution was obvious: take action to 're-establish Guineans' confidence in our Administration'. This would require two initiatives: ensure that the local administration had the means to maintain public order; and buttress the authority of Guinea's 'traditional' chiefs.[12]

Despite Pruvost's findings and Bayrou's pleading, Paris would, or could, do little to counter the PDG's pseudo-administration in Guinea. Arriving to take up his new post as Guinea's governor in October 1955, Charles Bonfils summarised the tenor of the latest outbreaks of violence, especially in the coastal region: 'In Guinea there are no more family quarrels, village disputes, or personal hostilities. Everything is coloured with politics'. In the face of this situation, all Bonfils could do was to assure Governor-General Cornut-Gentille that the fact that administration personnel were being attacked by both sides – the PDG and the BAG – demonstrated that his orders were being carried out with scrupulous 'impartiality'. On reflection a week later, Bonfils decided that the main problem in Guinea was one of class, rather than ethnic, division. Acting on this analysis six months later, he directed his *commandants de cercle* and *chefs de subdivision* to expand and democratise their own activities and councils by including the new collectivities 'that surprise you by behaving like an opposition', including the women of Guinea. These actions were ostensibly to ensure that the 'traditional' chiefs – 'an element of political equilibrium that is indispensible to the life of this country' – regained their popular legitimacy. But implicit in Bonfils's exhortations was an appeal to the members of his own administration to act to shore up their own legitimacy as well.[13]

The next outbreak of violence in Conakry, in early October 1956, demonstrated that neither local administration efforts nor the major reallocation of power and responsibility enabled by the *loi-cadre* would stop the PDG. Bonfils tried to suppress the rioting by issuing a stern warning to Guineans over the radio. Houphouët-Boigny, likely at the instance of the minister, sought to help by calling Touré to Paris. Despite the governor's assurance on 7 October that, the situation having been brought under control, he had no need of supplementary troops, the magnitude of this outburst attracted the attention of the French Union's assembly, which sent a delegation to investigate.[14] The Chiarisini mission concluded that the PDG had been behind this unrest, which resulted in the death of eight locals and the injury of 263 more, listing the means the party had used, including overwhelming the police and administration (Charles 1992: 366–7).

Extending PDG power to British West Africa

For the first time, the October 1956 riots spurred observers to speculate that the PDG had ambitions beyond the French overseas empire. The United Kingdom's Foreign Office (FO) had been watching for evidence of nationalist or independence movements in Francophone West Africa throughout the decade. For most of that time, though, FO officials were content to rely primarily on the assurances and interpretations offered by local French authorities in Dakar to members of the High Commission there and duly relayed to London and Paris. This was particularly true when what they heard accorded with their own easy assumptions about the 'tribal' nature of African society and allegiances. In March 1956, British consul-general G. E. A. Carney responded to a request to provide a 'guess as to the political future of the region' by suggesting 'the leaders of the liberation movement in this territory have most in common with their African counterparts in the British Colonies who have had a similar experience of white domination and now find that it pays to follow a constitutional course to eventual complete freedom with all the advantages that ensue from the support and financial aid of the departing power'. In Carney's view, there was little more to fear from popular agitation or opinion. 'The African's ... strong tribal loyalty' was 'a barrier [in this territory] to his development and presents no foundation on which to build up a national state'.[15]

Reporting on the October riots, the British in Dakar seemed similarly eager to accept at face value the explanations of their French interlocutors in Senegal, filling in the explanation from their own observations and prejudices. Colonial consul David Pearson, assured by director of French security services M. Buisson that a tiny and irrational spark had set off the Conakry riots, opined: 'The coast people are like that, whether it is Freetown, Accra, Lagos or Conakry, – anything can start off a fight, and there is no telling where it will end. Once the original fight was on, political loyalties were invoked, but these were soon forgotten in a general tribal free-for-all. It is only astonishing that there were only seven [*sic*] deaths'.[16]

Despite the attempt to reassure implicit in Pearson's phlegmatic stereotyping, the fact was that by 1956 some of the British were also beginning to exhibit concern about Sékou Touré's intentions – and his growing power to give effect to them, unchecked by nominal French authority. The most acute worries were felt in Sierra Leone, which reacted to the violence in Conakry by expelling a number of 'immigrants' from the British colony back to neighbouring Guinea.[17] This in turn reflected a fear that Touré was trying to establish a local branch of the RDA in Freetown, which he had visited in September 1956. His 'public utterances' on that occasion, according to Sierra Leone's governor Maurice Dorman, 'were nationalistic or rather Pan-African and … advocated mutual help between Africans of British and French territories'. In 1956, British authorities in Sierra Leone interpreted these 'utterances' as 'meaning participation by French Africans in the mineral wealth of this country'. A year later, Dorman worried that renewed signs of RDA involvement in Sierra Leone had more profound implications for both direct and indirect British rule: RDA activities were 'manifesting themselves in anti-chief propaganda and in an attitude of disrespect and defiance of local authority'. The British district commissioner for Bo, Dennis Kirby, summarised the platform of this most dangerous insurgent as: '(i) rabid pan-African nationalism (ii) destruction of all traditional authority (iii) the removal of the hated white man from Africa and (iv) the establishment of a dictatorship of the RDA throughout West Africa. Militant Mohamedanism', he added, 'is also part of the creed'. Both Kirby and Dorman were reacting to a significant increase in 1955 and 1956 in anti-chief agitation, especially in Sierra Leone's northern provinces, which appears to have stemmed largely from internal discontent rather than external agitation (Tangri, 1976, pp. 315–17). Perhaps in recognition of the true origins of their difficulties, neither Dorman in Freetown nor Oldham in Dakar recommended any direct action to counter the RDA in Sierra Leone. Instead, they felt, and London agreed, that any influence that could be brought to bear on Touré would have to be initiated in Paris and exercised through Houphouët-Boigny as head of the RDA. As Oldham put it, 'Chef de Territoire Ramadier in Guinea is in a position vis-à-vis Sékou Touré which prevents him doing little of practical use in this connexion (at least that is our view in this Consulate) and, in fact, so is the High Commissioner (again our view)'.[18]

Oldham's contacts in the French administration in Dakar were clearly the source of the consulate's understanding. The consul met with the French high commission's Franco-British liaison officer, M. Robin, on 19 December 1957. Robin made it clear both that France considered Touré as a dangerous element, and that no one in the French administration seemed able to exercise any authority over him. He 'was sure that Sékou Touré must be well aware of the "RDA" activities in Sierra Leone'. The colonial administration knew how dangerous he was: 'In fact, as [Robin] put it, had any administrator in French Guinea during the last few years read Mr. Kirby's report he would have declared: "But this is all old stuff, we know it all".' The novelty of the British report was its indications that the PDG leader's influence had spread to a neighbouring territory. What was now undeniable, even by the British, was that the PDG had escaped the control of the French administration. As Oldham reported: 'M. Robin went on to remark, with a slight hesitation, that the French are looking discreetly for some means of curbing the influence of M. Sékou Touré' and were looking to Houphouët-Boigny to play a role of which his French colonial masters seemed incapable.[19]

The late colonial state had lost control of Guinea, without its local opposition ever having to declare independence as an explicit goal. Bernard Charles argues that the PDG won by demonstrating to Guinea's masses that the colonial state was incapable of achieving its *raison d'être*, keeping public order. Yet the party's triumph went beyond disproving the capacity of the nominal power of the French. By establishing a parallel administration, the PDG had made the official colonial administration irrelevant to the daily lives of Guineans. If Robin was correct and Touré knew about efforts to organise a branch of his party in Sierra Leone, the PDG may even have begun to conduct its own foreign relations – even as official European rule persisted on both sides of the border.

Conclusion

Martin Shipway characterises the revolutionary project of Algeria's *Front de libération nationale* (FLN) as that of the 'counter-state', meaning that it was 'ready to replace the colonial state, rather than the usual anti-colonial nationalist strategy of the "counter-society", designed to take over an existing state' (Shipway 2008b: 154). Like the FLN, Guinea's PDG was a counter-state, rather than a nationalist project. Its objective was to replace French authority completely within the territory and even, if the fears of the Sierra Leoneans were well founded, to extend its influence beyond Guinea's borders. Moreover, the French were aware of the nature of the PDG's ambition, and of the extent to which it had been realised. The evidence presented here suggests that before Guinea achieved formal state independence, Touré's was not primarily an ideological project. He only started to create an ideology of independence in the last few months of colonial rule.

In fact, what enabled Touré to make independence the centrepiece of Guinea's political culture was France's reaction. All his oratorical skills could not convince De Gaulle that the arrangement he wanted, one that would recognise Guineans' 'first and indispensable need' for dignity by acknowledging their right to independence, was not simply secession. As De Gaulle had hinted in reply to Touré's most famous speech, once its people voted 'no' Guinea was left to face the consequences of independence. And yet those consequences apparently contradicted the promise De Gaulle had made in August 1958 not to place any obstacles in the way of Guinea's chosen path (quoted in Passeron 1962: 459). In addition to withdrawing the 'civil servants and experts sent to Guinea by the French Government under the *Loi-Cadre*' and abruptly ending 'the financial assistance given by the French State for the development of Guinea' (De Gaulle 1964: 28), De Gaulle attempted at every turn to prevent post-referendum Guinea from enjoying any of the privileges of its new status. France's Ministry of Foreign Affairs (MAE) sought to prevent its closest allies from according diplomatic recognition to Guinea. When the United States and United Kingdom went ahead, desperate to begin to counter the influence of their cold war enemies who had been quick to recognise the new state, France extracted promises that they would delay sending diplomatic representation to Conakry. Acting on De Gaulle's instructions and against the advice of its own staff in New York, the French Foreign Ministry tried and failed to delay Guinea's accession to the United Nations. Their first argument was that UN members should question the ability to abide by its Charter of a so-called sovereign state whose colonial power had not formally agreed to decolonise. When the hypocrisy of that argument became apparent, France relied on the notion that by announcing a proposed union with Ghana Sékou Touré had forfeited Guinea's right to independent statehood. Even after Guinea was a full member of the UN, De Gaulle still managed to ensure that France's diplomatic recognition of Guinea would offend the dignity that Touré sought. He refused to extend formal recognition before the Guineans signed technical protocols intended to restore a fraction of the material aid France had provided its former colony – and then signalled diplomatic recognition by way of an informal comment in a personal communication between the presidents (MacDonald 2009: 60–76).

And yet Guinea survived – and so did its well-entrenched PDG administration. There could be no doubt that the PDG and its leader were now at the head of a sovereign state: diplomatic recognition, trade deals and UN membership all spoke to Guinea's independence, and France's stubborn refusal to acknowledge it made the accomplishment all the more symbolically charged. The lesson was not lost on Guinea's erstwhile partners in AOF. Madeira Keïta, who had a long history of working with the PDG in Guinea, told US ambassadorial staff in Paris in August 1959 that 'Guinea had managed satisfactorily thanks to U.S. and other outside aid' – a statement which, though it vastly overstated the importance of American assistance to the new state, successfully conveyed Keïta's real point. Soudan, the territory of which Keïta was minister of the interior, would follow its neighbour into independence. The only question remaining was one of timing.[20]

The significance of Guinea's status as an independent state was also apparent to De Gaulle. Within fifteen months of Guinea's independence, the French president announced that the Federation of Mali and its constituent parts, Soudan and Senegal, could become independent without having to leave the French Community. Announcing on 13 December 1959 that negotiations would take place, De Gaulle qualified the status that would result:

> I prefer to call [it] 'international sovereignty'. This means that a people takes on its own responsibilities in the world, speaks for itself and by itself, and that it is responsible for what it says and for what it does. It is to this rank that Mali and with it, its component states, will accede with the support, the agreement and the assistance of France. (Quoted in Passeron 1962: 469)

The French president had an answer to anyone who, having observed Guinea's experience, might object that international sovereignty was not true independence. Independence, he said, was 'a desire, an attitude, an intention'. But it was an impossible dream: 'the world being what it is, so small, so narrow, so prone to interference, real independence ... truly belongs to nobody' (quoted in Gautron 1980: 26). The exception, as it had been since the mid-1950s, was the PDG's 'counter-state', whose leaders were as determined to celebrate their achievement as the French president was to denigrate it.

Notes

1 Unless otherwise noted, all translations from the French are the author's.
2 Archives nationales d'outre-mer, Aix-en-Provence (hereafter ANOM), Fonds Ministériel (hereafter FM) 1 Affpol/2143/9, memo by Bernard Cornut-Gentille, *Évenements de Guinée*, 14 March 1955.
3 ANOM, FM 1 Affpol/2143/9, Directorate of Political Affairs, Second bureau, *Note*, 1 February 1955.
4 ANOM, FM 1Affpol/2143/7, memo from Cornut-Gentille, Governor-General of French West Africa, to Ministry of Overseas France, Directorate of Political Affairs, *Congrès du Bloc Africain de Guinée (Août 1955)* (n° 2466/AP/2), 23 August 1955.
5 ANOM, FM 1Affpol/2143/9, Telegram from Parisot, Governor of Guinea, to J. J. Juglas, Minister of Overseas France (n° 58–60), 7 February 1955.
6 ANOM, FM 1Affpol/2199/3, report from Section de Coordination, Ministry of Overseas France *Bulletin de renseignements* (n° 862/SC/FOM), 28 March 1957.
7 ANOM, FM 1Affpol/2181/6, telegram from president of Guinea's territorial assembly to Minister of Overseas France, 27 July 1958.
8 ANOM, FM 1Affpol 1/2143/5, report, *A propos de l'élection législative de Guinée*, n.d. (*c.*16 June 1954); telegrams, Barry Diawadou to Robert Buron, Minister of Overseas France and Keïta Ouremba to Buron, 18 June 1954; telegram from Cornut-Gentille, High Commissioner in Dakar, to Buron (n° 257–258), 26 June 1954; memo from

Buron (per J.N. Adenot) to Cornut-Gentille, 23 June 1954; telegram from PDG Comité Macenta to Buron, 7 July 1954.

9 ANOM, FM 1Affpol/2143/5, memo from Parisot, Governor of Guinea, to Cornut-Gentille, *Claims made concerning by-elections in Guinea – vote of 27 June 1954*, 7 August 1954.

10 ANOM, FM 1Affpol/2143/5, letter from Parisot to Saller, 26 May 1954; memo from Parisot to Cornut-Gentille (n° 265/Cab), 21 June 1954.

11 ANOM, FM 1Affpol/2143/9, telegram from Pruvost in Conakry to Juglas, Minister of Overseas France (n° 1), 16 February 1955; telegram from Pruvost as head of mission of inspection in Conakry to Juglas (n° 2), 20 February 1955; ANOM, FM 1Affpol/2144/1, report of H. Pruvost, *Incidents de 1954–1955 en Guinée Française*, March 1955, pp. 39–40, 78–9.

12 ANOM, FM 1Affpol/2144/1, Note, *Mesures de redressement à prendre en première urgence*, attachment to memo from Bayrou, Secretary of State for Overseas France, to Teitgen, Minister of Overseas France, 31 March 1955.

13 ANOM, FM 1Affpol/2143/7, personal letter from Bonfils in Conakry to Cornut-Gentille, High Commissioner in Dakar, 14 October 1955; ANOM, FM 1Affpol/2143/8, memo from Bonfils, Governor of Guinea, to Cornut-Gentille (n° 520/CAB/APA), 22 October 1955; ANOM, FM 1Affpol/2194/5, memo from Bonfils to Commandants de Cercle and Subdivision Chiefs (n° 26/CAB), 14 April 1956.

14 ANOM, FM 1Affpol/2143/8, telegram from Bonfils to Defferre, Minister of Overseas France (n°. 40.121–40.125), 7 October 1956; ANOM, FM 1Affpol/2194/5, secret telegram from Defferre to Bonfils and Cusin, high commissioner in Dakar (n° 20.178–20.179), 17 October 1956.

15 The National Archives, Public Record Office, London (hereafter TNA, PRO), FO 371/119354, letter from Carney, Consul-General in Dakar to Watson, Foreign Office (n° 16200/10/1), 12 March 1956.

16 TNA, PRO, FO 371/119355, enclosure (report from Pearson) to letter from Oldham (Dakar) to Watson (n° C278/10/1/56), 16 October 1956.

17 TNA, PRO, FO 371/119355, telegram from Dorman, Governor of Sierra Leone, to Oldham, Consul in Dakar (n° 364), 19 October 1956.

18 TNA, PRO, FO 371/125642, report from Kirby, District Commissioner in Bo, *The Rassemblement Démocratique Africain (RDA)* (n° 511/57), n.d., enclosure to letter from Dorman to Stewart-Robinson in Dakar, 11 November 1957, enclosed in letter from Oldham in Dakar to Beith in Paris, 14 November 1957.

19 TNA, PRO, FO 371/131409, letter from Oldham to Beith (n° 511/57), 28 December 1957.

20 National Archives at College Park, MD, Records of the Department of State, Record Group 59, Files of the Office of West African Affairs – France, 1944–1960, *Memorandums of Conversation 1959*, 17 August 1959.

3

French officials and the insecurities of change in sub-Saharan Africa: Dakar, 19 August 1960 revisited

*Alexander Keese**

The history of European decolonisation on the African continent is full of intriguing events, many of which are not easily explicable. Particularly in cases in which opinion -makers in a former metropole attempt to sell the process as a 'successful decolonisation', such as is notably the case for the French decolonisation process (Chafer 2001: 178), these attempts tend to provoke opposition. In negative interpretations, decisions taken by agents of the colonial power seem to be full of hidden subtexts. Overtures made to African nationalists appear to be wilfully poisoned gifts; European officials frequently seem to speak in favour of a transfer of power while undermining the whole process at the same time (Chaffard 1965). Many of these interpretations are now reinforced by knowledge from hindsight: the scheming and plotting by the French Secretariat of African and Malagasy Affairs led by Jacques Foccart in the 1960s and early 1970s is the most notable example.[1] From such a perspective, initiatives by Foccart and others appear to be a reprise of manipulations that already played a role during the decolonisation process.[2]

These views often overestimate the capacities of judgment and planning colonial administrators actually had. They also ignore the fact that, in many cases, the information services the administrations relied on reported mainly upon gossip. The quality of reports was often weak, and some of the information they gave was indeed absurd.[3] In the reports, profound analysis of processes was more the exception than the rule.

I have argued elsewhere that many of the French attitudes towards the processes of decolonisation were built upon profound misconceptions. A nearly paranoid fear of Communist subversion eclipsed a considerable part of the analytic capacities of many members of the administration (Keese 2008: 136–8). When the *loi-cadre* was adopted (see Chapter 1 by Shipway in this volume), introducing a first stage of 'semi-autonomy' in sub-Saharan Africa in 1956/57, the idea of leading French officials was that this reform would help to improve the political situation by co-opting a potentially dangerous African elite without giving up effective power. This idea was built on erroneous interpretations, as the French officials rapidly learned. Another fundamental misunderstanding was the 'observation' that most of the African political leaders wished for a strengthening of individual territories instead of federations of territories; which prompted the 'anti-federal' position of successive French administrations.[4] It therefore appears that misunderstandings – often profound ones indeed – are an essential part of the political process leading to decolonisation, and probably not only in the French case (Neuberger 1976: 527).

Acting under extreme insecurity during a decolonisation process that had not been expected to happen was another problem for European and, especially, French administrations. In this chapter, I will approach this experience of insecurity – as being a companion to misunderstanding and irrational fear – in a very specific case: the failure of the most ambitious union project in western Africa on the road to independence, the Mali Federation between the territories of Senegal and French Soudan (Welch 1966: 13–36). This federation was at the same time a particularly important attempt at group decolonisation and intergovernmental cooperation with significance for the whole of the African continent. From the perspective of this chapter, what is interesting is to 'test' the capacities of the agents of the decolonising French state to interfere in the process. In other words, where most historical contributions to date have merely speculated about French strategies and attitudes towards decolonisation in Africa, I will look at a concrete example, contextualising it, however, within the complex transition process between the Constitutional Referendum of 28 September 1958 and the decolonisations of 1960.

The split of the Mali Federation: French response to a challenge in West Africa?

On 1 September 1960, only days after his deportation from Dakar to Bamako, the Soudanese president and former president of the Mali Federation, Modibo Keïta, was again on good form.[5] During a meeting of members and militants of the Union Soudanaise, the ruling party in the independent country now called Mali, he indeed had an easy game. With a clear view to preparing an international campaign against what he presented as France's neo-colonial attitudes, he attacked the French as schemers behind the split of the federation that had linked his country to Senegal and that had so ingloriously been separated as a consequence of the events of the night of 19 August. Exasperated, the French High Representative in Dakar, Claude Hettier de Boislambert, commented on Keïta's attacks in an internal memorandum:

> Again, there are accusations against the High Representative of France, there is talk of his 'systematic refusal' to apply the clauses of the Franco-Malian military

treaty. Mr. Keïta knows that this claim is based on a lie and the false testimony of the ministers who surrounded him in Dakar, who have attempted, with his compliance, to lay upon France the responsibility for his unsuccessful coup attempt. But it is necessary that the legend created by Mr. Keïta remains strong, as it is useful for him to attempt to make a case for blackmail in which France and Senegal appear as co-defendants.[6]

The split of the Mali Federation was in many ways a major event in West Africa and indeed for the whole of sub-Saharan Africa. Serious questions about the dream of federation had already been raised by the refusal in 1959 of the governments of Niger, Dahomey and Upper Volta to join the proposed federation. With the violent end of the union between Senegal and French Soudan, it received a deadly blow. In the regional panorama, it represented the disappointing end of pro-federal agitation, which had started when African politicians had become aware, with the *loi-cadre* of June 1956, that the Ministry of Overseas France was no longer committed to the federal structures that had characterised French colonialism on the African continent (Benoist 1982: 303–6). More broadly, it was a blow to the optimistic perspective that saw Africa's future well-being in the unification of territories (Rothchild 1966: 290).

It was also, for the decolonising metropole, a first event in which the French had to act in a situation of crisis in a now-independent former colony. In Dahomey, in January 1959, French officials had already intervened with troops in a semi-autonomous territory, but the framework of intervention had been very different. During the crisis of the Apithy government in Dahomey, French military envoys Oury and Gros-Désormeaux had played an essential role, giving these events obvious similarities to the split of the Mali Federation (Keese 2007a: 601–2). What made events in the federation different from the French intervention in Dahomey, and more comparable to the series of *coups d'état* in Togo, Congo-Brazzaville, Upper Volta and, again, Dahomey during the 1960s, was the fact that several leading politicians of the Mali Federation had before taken their distance from French representatives in the territory, and from French policy in general. Not only was the Mali Federation, in August 1960, an independent state. Even more important, its elites had been keen to minimise French influence in the internal affairs of the federation during the months preceding the August crisis (which was complicated, given that the same elites depended upon French help and the French presence for budget, military, defence and police support).

Much has already been written about the critical night, in which the Soudanese ministers of the Federation of Mali were put under de facto house arrest with their staff and later expelled to Soudan, as the key event that effectively ended the long-term project to create a federation of territories in West Africa (which had finally been restricted to only two partners). William Foltz published a whole book about the reasons for which the Mali Federation was destined to fail:

from the perspective of a political scientist, he mainly pointed to the different political cultures of the ruling elites.[7] A number of articles and books address the chronology of events, attempting to identify particular reasons for the failure of the federation – these include Joseph-Roger de Benoist, Paule Brasseur, Modou Ndoye, or Sékéné Mody Cissoko (Benoist 1979, Brasseur 1992; Ndoye 1995; Cissoko 2005). Unsurprisingly, the split of the federation and possible French involvement appear in many studies about decolonisation in sub-Saharan Africa, and they are often seen as characteristic of the new, interventionist trend in French policy towards independent African states (Martin 1985: 191; Roche 2001: 237; Ngom and Diouf 2010).

The hypotheses concerning the particular French role during the event are quite diverse, but there remains the lingering notion of a French conspiracy. In this logic, French politicians and officials saw the Mali Federation as too power-ful an entity in the region, an entity that in the future was likely to endanger France's strategic interests. Another argument put forward is that Modibo Keïta had criticised De Gaulle's Algerian and nuclear policy in public and that the French thus wanted to 'free' Dakar from Keïta's dominance in the federation. Finally, one has to ponder the French fear that Guinea-Conakry could ally to or even enter the Mali Federation. Doubtless, from the point of view of several French officials, Sékou Touré, President of Guinea, had challenged the French government by obtaining the immediate independence of his country in 1958 and, during the period between the referendum of September 1958 and summer 1960, Touré was finally classified in Paris as a long-standing Communist enemy of the French (MacDonald 2009: 109). The French intervention in Dahomey in early 1959 had effectively been a response to the 'Communist' mobilisation of the opposition party, the Union Démocratique Dahoméenne, and the trade unions, and had thus been regarded as a necessary intervention to prevent a swing of this territory towards a Guinean path (although, more than anything else, French officials had responded to pressures from the then-Dahomean prime minister, Sourou-Migan Apithy). There was thus a fear that August 1960 in the Mali Federation could have followed a similar logic.

Other interpretations focus on the obviously divergent positions of Soudanese and Senegalese leaderships, which had poisoned the plans of Modibo Keïta and other Soudanese politicians to create a more strongly centralised union. Starting with William Foltz, scholars have claimed that Senegalese politicians feared domination by their Soudanese partners, whose territory was far more populous. For this reason, Senegalese leaders may have been afraid that the federation was going to be highjacked by Keïta's followers. A parallel interpretation, focusing on commercial questions, claims that the Senegalese were worried about Keïta's radical slogans, as these were likely to disturb relations with one of Senegal's most important commercial and economic partners, the former metropole. From this point of view, the Senegalese had for economic reasons sought the first opportunity to get rid of the structures they had so enthusiastically embraced only a few months earlier (Chafer 2002b: 184–5; Migani 2008).

We are now in a better position to draw conclusions regarding the French role during these events. In the Senegalese National Archives, accessibility to files, including those from the 'Federation of Mali' series, is now satisfactory, and the situation regarding access to archives has also changed during the last decade in France. As concerns the latter, we have finally access to the Foccart files in the French National Archives. Jacques Foccart, who was the future Secretary for African and Malagasy Affairs attached to the French presidency and grey eminence behind several future French operations in sub-Saharan Africa, was of course not yet in charge at the moment of the split of the Mali Federation. Decisions regarding the attitude France was to take towards the longer process of erosion and the final rupture of the Federation were made by the French proconsul in Dakar – the High Representative Hettier de Boislambert, by other French officials still active under formal Senegalese orders and, to a lesser extent, by the central services of the French presidency and the office of the Prime Minister. However, Foccart's secretariat created in 1960 assembled important documentation on the affair, which thereafter remained in its offices. Although since 2002 the Foccart files have become more accessible to scholars and been used somewhat more frequently, there is still much work to be done – even taking into account Jean-Pierre Bat's new, ground-breaking interpretation of Foccart's role.[8] Those files treating the split of the Mali Federation and the different processes that led to decolonisation in the different territories are no exception to this rule.

The recently opened documentation allows us new insights into an affair which was rightly taken by the officials of the Secretariat of African and Malagasy Affairs as paradigmatic for political realities in Francophone Africa in the years to come. It helps us decide if the French, in a crisis occurring at a moment of great insecurity because they lacked any routine for dealing with now-independent former colonial territories, can really be seen as strategic schemers. The documentation contained in the Foccart files is instructive because it includes an essential part of the correspondence between the High Representative, the French commanders of the armed forces, the commander of the Gendarmerie of Senegal, Lieutenant-Colonel François Pierre, and the president and the French prime minister. It is – and this is highly important for our purpose – essential to understand that we have no indication that these documents could be inauthentic. They were assembled to prevent exactly what Hettier de Boislambert had described as his particular worry: namely that the French would be *unjustly* accused of being behind the *coup de force* in Dakar. In order to elaborate a strategy to show that Modibo Keïta was a liar, it was essential to be aware of exactly what had really happened. Thus, the conversations between the different key actors in the events can be seen as, at least, relatively accurate with regard to their intentions and decisions.[9]

We nevertheless have to take into account the *possibility* that behind the decisions and reflections documented in confidential dossiers, there is yet another, hidden agenda of action negotiated at the highest level of French politics. It is no secret that President Charles De Gaulle and his African Affairs Adviser, Jacques Foccart, had by 1960 little sympathy for Modibo Keïta and other Soudanese leaders: in 1959/60, the anti-French opinions coming from Bamako were not only regarded as a nuisance, but also as hostile acts. Under these conditions, De Gaulle and Foccart may still have been behind a secret plan to weaken Modibo Keïta's influence in Dakar. Hettier de Boislambert was an official loyal to De Gaulle and he himself hints in his memoirs at such a more obscure scheme (Hettier de Boislambert 1978). We cannot find absolute proof against the existence of this master plan. However, the historian must ask if such 'dark schemers' behind the curtain would have really been able to operate without leaving any traces in the highly confidential French documentation sent between Paris and Dakar. For these reasons, I will attempt, in the following pages, to present at least a plausible scenario.

Acting in a situation of insecurity: French officials and the moment of instability

The critical days before the night of the break-up of the federation are character-ised by an astonishing passivity of the French protagonists. French officials were aware of tensions that existed between the Soudanese and Senegalese political leaders (Migani 2008: 131–2). Even so, French authorities remained convinced for a rather long period that the crisis of the federation was temporary. Although the information services of the French Prime Minister had already in February 1960 commented that Léopold Sédar Senghor was ready to risk a split of the federation and that he had convinced the Senegalese Prime Minister Mamadou Dia of this radical position, it appears that this interpretation was not taken up by the French officials in Dakar.[10] Therefore, the positions adopted by leading Senegalese politicians, which were explained to Hettier de Boislambert during conversations held on the occasion of the Magal, the Murid celebrations in Touba, religious centre of the brotherhood, in the second week of August came as a complete surprise to French officials.

The French High Representative asked for the opinion of Senghor, who was then leader of the Union Démocratique Sénégalaise – Parti de la Fédération Africaine (UDS-PFA), the dominant political party in Senegal and candidate for the presidency of the Mali Federation. The fact that his candidacy was blocked by the negative vote of the Soudanese politicians within the federation was one of the reasons for internal tension. Hettier de Boislambert had nonetheless expected that the elites of both territories would manage to reach a compromise. The French Representative was therefore quite surprised by the attitude of his interlocutor:

Mr Senghor has taken his decision. There will not be any conference between the [federation's member] states. There will not be any session of Congress with a view to electing a President of the Republic. Mali, in its federal form, has ceased to exist.

Mr Senghor, frustrated by the attitude of 'colonisers' shown by the Soudanese leaders and, like President Dia he says, exasperated in particular by Mr. Keïta; to see the President of the Government [Modibo Keïta] completely short-circuit the Government and act only according to his own interest and as a dictator – he, Senghor, took the decision not to be 'fleeced'.[11]

Also, Hettier de Boislambert learned on this occasion that there was already a concrete, if tentative, plan by the leading Senegalese politicians to finish with future Soudanese attempts to obtain the upper hand in Dakar's political structures – although this was still a plan sold as defensive emergency action. Significantly, France's High Representation in Dakar did not take part in the further elaboration of these projects. Apart from some French administrators who were working for the Senegalese government – as was notably, again, the case of the Commander of the Gendarmerie of Senegal, who had to respond to the requests of Mamadou Dia – the French were mainly passive bystanders. According to Hettier de Boislambert, 'precautions have been taken to prevent a *coup de force*. Yesterday evening, I informed you by telegram about the meeting of the officials responsible for Senegal's security services. This meeting was called by Mr Valdiodio N'Diaye, and I have been informed about the outcome'.[12]

Senegal's leaders were, however, worried about possible French reactions. Was it conceivable that the French interpreted legal issues concerning the federation in a different way and that they supported those who defended the integrity of the federal structures? There obviously was no positive information coming from Paris by mid-August 1960, which would have dispelled such worries: no guarantees had been given. In this respect, Senghor was conscious of another useful card to play. Knowing the psychology of French officials from the late colonial period well enough, the Senegalese leader hinted at the alleged pro-Communist sympathies of the Soudanese (a comment that implied, at the same time, that suspicions about the 'leftist' sympathies of some Senegalese leaders, held by French officials, were erroneous). The logic of Senghor's argument was very neat: even from their own perspective: the French were prepared to admit that they had underestimated the influence of 'Communist agents' who had sabotaged the reform process initiated by the *loi-cadre* and that Moscow's henchman Sékou Touré had seriously damaged the French Republic's reputation during the 1958 referendum campaign. Senghor was, thus, well positioned to alert the French to the danger of another 'Communist' victory – this time through the 'colonisation' of Senegal by Modibo Keïta's Soudan: 'I do not accept to see Senegal invaded by Communist forces, nor to see it colonised by Soudan. We would rather be killed than choose retreat. Our decision is irreversible'.[13]

As regards the attitudes of African politicians towards the genesis of the federal project, Senghor's argument was doubtless somewhat adventurous. The old party notables and other party militants from Senegal's UPS had been among the staunchest supporters of the re-creation of federal structures in former French West Africa. Between 1957 and 1959, key officials of the decolonising French colonial apparatus had regarded the initiatives from Dakar as another example of sabotage and of plans for a Communist takeover. On several occasions, French officials had expressed the view that at least the Senegalese Prime Minister Mamadou Dia and the Senegalese Minister of the Interior Valdiodio N'Diaye were Communist fellow travellers and far worse ones than Modibo Keïta who, before early 1959, had, in the view of the French, maintained a fairly low profile. A number of French administrators were convinced that the involvement of Senegalese leaders in setting up the Mali Federation was to create a vehicle to spread their ideas (with Senghor being an eager, if misled supporter).[14]

In mid-August 1960, enough was at stake for Senegalese leaders to obscure their earlier enthusiasm for the creation of a West African federation. Their attempts at courting the French officials had a very concrete reason: leading personalities within the UPS were afraid that Modibo Keïta, in the case of unrest in Dakar, could convince the French High Representative and the army general to intervene with troops at the request of the President of the Mali Federation. Hettier de Boislambert's response to Senghor during conversations one week before the split was strictly legalistic: there were no grounds whatsoever for employing the French army in support of either side in the conflict. Obviously, the French High Representative sympathised with the Senegalese position; he even promised Senghor to guarantee the personal safety of Senegalese Prime Minister Mamadou Dia and of Senghor himself; 'commenting to him, nevertheless, that at this moment the game would definitely be lost for him'.[15] Thus, while there was much sympathy for the Senegalese cause, the French were neither behind any concrete plan to destroy Modibo Keïta's power base nor mentally prepared to intervene in any way. On the contrary, the Secretary-General of the French Community, Raymond Janot, commented that even with Hettier de Boislambert's understanding shown for the Senegalese position, he was in favour of a peaceful settlement of the difficulties and the continued existence of the federation: 'Under the current circumstances it appears to be far preferable that Senegal and Soudan continue to get along with each other, even at the price of some compromises on each side. In fact, if it is good to imagine some of the hypotheses that are opened up by the perspective of the federation splitting up, it would be adventurous to regard the split as inevitable.'[16]

Under these conditions, the initiative during the events of the night of 19 August 1960 was principally left to officials who served under Senegalese orders. This does not, of course, exclude from the outset the possibility that the French representatives in Dakar were aware, at some point, of the rapidly changing situation and attempted to give it a certain direction. To come to a conclusion about this particular question, it is again useful to interpret the available files – something which has not yet been attempted by historians.

Serving la République or serving Senegal? The dilemmas of French officials under African command during the split of the Mali Federation

Observed with hindsight, the course of events on the evening of 19 August 1960 appears to be straightforward. However, this perspective underestimates the complicated effects that the lack of proper armed forces in the independent Federation of Mali and its member states had on political options. If the French army did not intervene, and taking into account that the Presidential Guard under Modibo Keïta's direct orders was still the rump of a potential future force, this would only leave one significant armed unit: the Gendarmerie of Senegal (which was planned to become the Gendarmerie of the Federation of Mali). This Gendarmerie was commanded by a French official, Lieutenant-Colonel Pierre, who usually took his orders from the Prime Minister of Senegal, but could eventually also be called upon under the planned new rules by the President of the Federation of Mali. Pierre's interpretation of the situation was therefore essential for the process and it comes as no surprise that Foccart subsequently kept Pierre's detailed report in his files. This report definitely reads like a movie plot:

8:45pm

Lieutenant-Colonel Pierre has just arrived at his house and prepares to have his evening meal when the telephone rings.

His interlocutor, who does not introduce himself, announces to him 'that the President calls him to the ninth floor of the Federal Building'.

However, on the ninth floor of the Building one finds both the offices of the cabinets of President Modibo Keïta and of President Dia Mamadou.

Lieutenant-Colonel Pierre invites his interlocutor to give his name: it is Colonel Soumaré [Commander of the Soudanese Army and Keïta's right hand man] who repeats to him that the President is waiting for him regarding a very urgent matter.

Lieutenant-Colonel Pierre asks 'which President?' Colonel Soumaré responds 'President Modibo Keïta'. Lieutenant-Colonel Pierre replies that he is on his way.

After some moments of reflection he arrives, nevertheless, at the conclusion that this particular situation does not allow him to obey this unusual order (this is the first time he has been called by President Modibo Keïta) without taking some precautions.'[17]

In the end, Lieutenant-Colonel Pierre does not follow the order and instead informs his direct superior, Mamadou Dia.

This has a determining influence on the subsequent evolution of events: the employment of the Gendarmerie against the president of the federation, the arrest of Soudanese officials and politicians by Gendarmerie forces, and their subsequent expulsion.[18] In an unpredictable situation, the French official under Senegalese orders chose the secure and, at the same time, most familiar option. Lieutenant-Colonel Pierre was clearly loyal to the African politicians he was *used* to working with – namely, Mamadou Dia and the Senegalese Minister of the Interior, Valdiodio N'Diaye. Pierre was sympathetic to their position as much as Hettier de Boislambert was, but there is no reason to regard his action as an illegal decision. On the contrary, in a turbulent decolonising space where some developments were difficult to understand, French officials could find an easy way out of dilemmas by strictly sticking to the rules.[19] In the framework they had become familiar with in the nearly two years since the constitutional referendum, there seemed to be no legal possibility for the president of the Mali Federation to command the Gendarmerie of Senegal. Therefore, its commander believed he was behaving in accordance with a clearly drawn hierarchy when he arrested Soudanese politicians and officials under the orders of the Prime Minister of Senegal.

In comparison to the very formal attitudes the French officials on Senegalese territory maintained, the Senegalese leaders showed themselves very adept at controlling the situation. Mamadou Dia and Valdiodio N'Diaye were quite prepared to mobilise Senegalese officials in the provinces, even in Casamance where UPS leaders feared that sympathies for Sékou Touré and Modibo Keïta could lead to insurrections against the government in Dakar. (There was, in the end, no indication of any such problem.)[20] As for these leaders, their own heroic acts during the incident were the object of pride and they claimed for themselves the principal role in neutralising the Soudanese in the capital. The speech given by Valdiodio N'Diaye, Minister of the Interior, in Fatick in 1962, when he spoke to the inhabitants of one of his electoral strongholds and integrated into this panorama an important Senegalese military officer, is quite representative of the ways in which the Senegalese built their own legends about their role in the events of 19 and 20 August.[21] Thus, Valdiodio N'Diaye described the seizure of Colonel Soumaré as follows:

> There was an impressive silence in the hall. I followed the colonel [who, when he saw that no one from the gendarmerie, the police, or the republican guard accepted his orders, tried to escape] repeating my order to arrest him, but without any more success. At the door of the building I encountered Captain Tamsir Ba, commander of the Republican Guard, whom I requested to follow me in order to arrest Colonel Soumaré. Tamsir Ba did not hesitate for even a second. Very quickly, Colonel Soumaré was surrounded and overpowered by the two of us.[22]

It is obvious that these Senegalese versions of events did not give prominence to any French role. Even so, it is clear that no particular French strategy was identifiable behind the *coup d'état*. On the contrary, French officials, either as representatives of the former metropole or as employees of African governments, were unable to cope with the unpredictability of events in any more autonomous way. They simply relied upon the established rules and routines they had become used to working with over the preceding months.

Conclusion

In the light of the documentation later transferred into the Secretariat of African and Malagasy Affairs, we can draw a number of conclusions with regard to the developments that led to the split of the Mali Federation. These conclusions might not completely overturn previous interpretations formulated by historians and political scientists between the 1960s and the present day. However, it is noticeable that they give a clearer impression of the lines of thought and, particularly, the limitations of French activities in countries of the former French empire during the decolonisation period.

To be sure, French officials were not in a position, in August 1960, to control events surrounding the split of the Mali Federation. While the officials in charge were conscious of the deterioration of relations between Soudanese and Senegalese politicians at the head of the federation, they were not enthusiastic about the possible end of this political entity. On the contrary, Hettier de Boislambert and military commanders like the French general Brébisson had become used to the existence of the federal structures during the less than eighteen months of their existence. In this period of insecurity, in which for the former colonial officials it seemed even unclear which general lines to follow in sub-Saharan Africa, it appeared that the best way forward was to rigorously respect the routines and established norms that had been established in the regional arena since September 1958. Some administrators, such as Fernand Wibaux, High Representative in Bamako, even remained convinced that the Soudanese, in spite of their rhetoric and their potential pro-Communist attitudes, were the more reliable partners in the federation and reliable behaviour was exactly what French officials judged most important in relations with Africans who had become partners.

Any hypothesis of a central French role in overturning the Mali Federation is the result of an overestimation of the capacities of French officials to plan ahead and to manipulate the situation under conditions of insecurity. Such a misinterpretation is very much in line with others to which we have alluded above. French administrators obviously believed they were fighting an uphill battle against Communism – an idea that was central for the whole period between 1945 and 1960 (and even longer), and that could be used by African parties during conflicts to obtain from the French a kind of benevolent neutrality. This, however, was the maximum Senegalese politicians could secure from the French during the split of the Mali Federation. Indeed, French behaviour during the split was analogous to decisions made by colonial administrators and politicians since 1955. In 1956/57 there are clear indications that French officials had been no 'balkanisers' – for the very simple reason that leading French officials had been *convinced* that most African leaders did not want a federation of territories, before being surprised by, first, the anti-balkanisation and, second, the Mali Federation initiative in French West Africa.[23] Likewise, the French had no coherent plan to break up the Mali Federation – they represented a weak and disoriented (former) administration, which felt it had lost control over the political processes in the former African colonies. These officials needed another decade to define France's new role on the African continent and come to terms with decolonisation or seek a compensation for it. On 19 and 20 August 1960, this process was still in its infancy. In this early period after the effective transfer of power, the communications between the key French personalities illustrate a deeply entrenched sentiment of insecurity that eclipsed any capacities for more rational planning.

Notes

* The research on which these findings are based was funded by the European Research Council under the European Union's Seventh Framework Programme (FP7/2007–2013)/ERC Starting Grant Agreement n° 240898.

1 Foccart created his own myth in these respects, see Foccart and Gaillard (1997). There is a handful of more recent studies that try to give a more balanced picture, see Keese (2007a: 604–5) and Bat and Geneste (2010: 93–4).

2 The 'classical case' for this tradition, with relation to Gabon, is made in Péan (1983: 41–69).

3 See Keese (2007b: 129–33). This analysis is, in a way, a counterpart to Luise White's important interpretation on rumour and gossip on the African side of the colonial society, see White (2000).

4 See Keese (2003). The converging interests towards decolonisation have been discussed in Cooper (1994: 1538). The context of the process of decolonization in French West Africa under French rule is explained in Benoist (1982: 435–49).

5 AN, AG/5(FPR)/230, Telegram from Wibaux, French Consul in Bamako, to Janot, Secretary-General of the French Community (without number), 22 August 1960. 'Soudan' was the name of one of the two territories forming the Mali Federation, and its leaders would rename it 'Mali' as a reminder of the failed attempt at creating a larger federation.

6 AN, AG/5(FPR)/230, Telegram from Hettier de Boislambert, French High Representative in Dakar, to Janot (n° 10.245), 1 September 1960, p. 3.

7 See Foltz (1965), who is followed in this idea by Kurtz (1970: 418), Mortimer (1972: 285–6), and Hesseling (1985: 174).

8 See also Bat (2006).

9 AN, AG/5(FPR)/230, General Charles, Commander of the 3rd Brigade,

Overseas Terrestrial Forces, Zone 1, to Wibaux (n° 3/3334), 1 August 1960; AN, AG/5(FPR)/230, *Annexe II: Griefs contre l'Armée formulés au cours de la conférence de presse du 25 Août du Président Modibo Keïta* (without number), without date; AN, AG/5(FPR)/230, *Annexe III: Griefs contre l'Armée formulés au Consul Général de France, le 25 Août 1960 par le Président Modibo Keïta* (without number), without date; AN, AG/5(FPR)/230, *Annexe IIIBis: Griefs contre l'Armée française formulées en diverses circonstances* (without number), without date.

10 MAE, Direction des Affaires Africaines et Malgaches, Mali, 2518, Secretariat-General of the French Community, Directorate of General and Internal Affairs, *Note sur la situation intérieure du Mali et sur les perspectives d'évolution de cette situation* (without number), 13 April 1960, p. 2.

11 AN, AG/5(FPR)/230, Hettier de Boislambert, *Note à l'attention de Monsieur le Premier Ministre* (without number), 16 August 1960, p. 2.

12 Ibid.

13 Ibid.

14 In a later interview, the contents of which are difficult to confirm but that *could* be authentic, Maurice Yaméogo, the Prime Minister of Upper Volta who later took an anti-federalist position and refused to let his country participate in the scheme, held that he had been intimidated in January 1959, during the Constituent Assembly in Dakar, by groups of 'Wolof ogres' and been forced, fearing for his life, to consent to the federal plans. In Yaméogo's words, Modibo Keïta was one of the staunch supporters of the federation, but the Senegalese were still more aggressive. See Guirma (1991: 109–10). The French debate on the 'radicalism' of Senegalese politicians in 1958/59 can be followed in ANOM, FM 1AffPol/2266/6, Sicurani, replacing Lami, French High Commissioner in Senegal, to Foyer, Secretary of State for Relations with French Community Territories (n° 95/C.P.), 28 January 1959, p. 14; ANOM, FM 1AffPol/2266/6, Lami to Foyer (n° 00065/Cab/Ap), 1 April 1959, p. 5; ANOM, FM 1AffPol/2266/6, Lami to Foyer, *Rapport Mensuel: Période du 25 mars au 25 avril 1959* (n° 135), 29 April 1959, p. 12.

15 AN, AG/5(FPR)/230, Hettier de Boislambert, *Note à l'attention de Monsieur le Premier Ministre* (without number), 16 August 1960, p. 3.

16 MAE, Direction des Affaires Africaines et Malgaches, Mali, 2518, Secretariat-General of the French Community, Directorate of General Affairs, *Note sur la situation politique dans la Fédération du Mali* (without number), 18 August 1960, p. 7.

17 AN, AG/5(FPR)/230, Pierre, *Film des Evénements vécus par le Lieutenant-Colonel Pierre Commandant la Gendarmerie du Sénégal* (without number), 22 August 1960, p. 9.

18 ANS, Fédération du Mali, 000203, *Fiche: Ordres Verbaux donnés par le Colonel Soumaré au Capitaine Sanvoisin – Officier Adjoint au Lieutenant-Colonel Commandant le Groupement de Gendarmerie du Sénégal* (without number), without date.

19 This is confirmed by a secret Senegalese report, see ANS, Fédération du Mali, 000203, *Chronologie des Evènements qui ont abouti à la proclamation de l'indépendance de la République du Sénégal* (without number), without date.

20 ANS, 11D1/1110, Telegram from Mamadou Dia to Governors and Cercle Commanders (without number), without date (copied by the Cercle Commander

of Kaffrine, 22 August 1960). On Senegalese fears of 'Soudanese subversion', see ANS, Fédération du Mali, 000215, Senegalese Ministry of National Defence, Second Bureau, *Fiche de Renseignements: Situation au Soudan.* (n° 7/B.2/S.), 17 September 1960.

21 Such 'invention of tradition' was in particular important for Senegalese leaders, such as Lamine Guèye and Valdiodio N'Diaye, who were suspected of having decided for the action against Modibo Keïta and his supporters at the last possible moment; see ANS, Fédération du Mali, 000203, Calvel replacing Kocher, Director of the Bureau of Information and Press, Senegalese Foreign Ministry, *Information diplomatique* (without number), 14 December 1960.

22 MAE, DAM, Sénégal, 3117, Valdiodio N'Diaye, *Discours prononcé à Fatick le 29 Mars 1962 par Me Valdiodio N'Diaye à la Cérémonie d'Inauguration du Monument de l'Indépendance* (without number), without date, p. 4.

23 Another key document that supports this view (and has not yet been brought into the discussion) is ANS, Vice-Présidence et Présidence du Conseil de Gouvernement du Sénégal (VPP), 126, Latyr Kamara, Minister of Public Employment of Senegal, *Audience du 28 Octobre 1957 de M. le Gouverneur Général Pignon, Directeur Général des Affaires Politiques du Ministère de la F.O.M.* (n° 196/MFP/Cab-Conf), 6 December 1957, p. 2.

Part II
Military transitions

4

'Saving French West Africa': the French army, African soldiers and military propaganda during the 1950s[1]

Ruth Ginio

When the French Army, in the years following the Second World War, was sent to defend the Empire in Indochina, Madagascar, and Algeria, African soldiers recruited in French West Africa (*Afrique occidentale française*: AOF) fought side-by-side with French soldiers against the anti-colonial movements in these turbulent parts of the French Empire. Nevertheless, while each of these subjects – the decolonisation of the French Empire and the military service of African colonial soldiers known as the *tirailleurs sénégalais* – has attracted much scholarly interest, the influence of the soldiers' service in France's colonial wars on decolonisation in the territories from which they originated and the role of the French army in this process have been virtually ignored. While studies about decolonisation in Madagascar, Indochina and Algeria attribute significance to the role of the army, due to its active participation in the repression of the anti-colonial movements, studies on AOF ignore the army altogether. Nevertheless, as the special military relations between France and its ex-colonies in AOF seem to show, the investigation of the French Army's role in the decolonisation of the African colonies, or in attempts to prevent it, is vital for understanding the continuity in the pattern of relations between France and its ex-colonies in West Africa.[2]

This chapter aims to examine the ways in which the French military authorities attempted to halt, or at least forestall, the process of decolonisation in AOF by exploiting the service of Africans in the French army as a tool of propaganda. My focus here is on the French army as a crucial colonial actor that did not always share the perspective of the French government or the colonial administration of AOF regarding the form that African-French relations should take during the years of decolonisation and eventually after independence.

This study dovetails with new approaches to French decolonisation. During the past decade the historiography of decolonisation underwent significant transformation. The emphasis in this field has largely shifted from the national story of anti-colonial struggle, which ends 'happily' with independence, to the perception of decolonisation as the culmination of a history of interaction and conflict between colonisers and colonised. Interaction was influenced by external factors, but that was also determined, at least in part, by internal structures (Shipway 2008b: 5). These approaches also emphasise that the colonisers, on the one hand, and the colonised on the other, are not to be seen as homogenous groups sharing the same interests and visions. The case examined here demonstrates that the French army acted in AOF with its own agenda, which was not always identical with that of the colonial administration. African soldiers and veterans also had their own visions regarding the future of African-French relations. As Frederic Cooper maintained, the outcome of decolonisation should not be regarded as the only possible and inevitable one and 'Africans cannot be reduced to stick figures in a drama with two actors, coloniser and colonised, or a story with one plot-line – the struggle for the nation' (Cooper 2002: 38).

Within the topic of French decolonisation, the violent decolonisation process in Algeria has attracted far more scholarly attention than the non-violent process in AOF. Nevertheless, recent studies on decolonisation in AOF, such as Tony Chafer's *The End of the French Empire in West Africa*, demonstrate that in spite of the non-violent character of the process, it was imbued with tensions and contradictions (Chafer 2002b). The inclusion of the army and its special relations with African soldiers and veterans in the story of the decolonisation of AOF is necessary, in my view, to make it complete and to better understand it. As I will show, after a low period in the relations between the army and its African soldiers and veterans which reached rock bottom at the end of the Second World War, the military reforms of the 1950s improved these relations. The army command in AOF believed that it offered a model of cooperation between French and Africans that could serve as an example for the entire federation and offer a valid alternative to independence and to the violent anti-colonial struggles that the army and its African soldiers experienced elsewhere. This, however, was a viewpoint that was not easily accepted by political actors in AOF – African and French alike – and extensive propaganda was needed in order to 'sell' this idea.

As my earlier studies on the African soldiers demonstrated, the relations between the French Army and its African soldiers can serve as a fascinating case study for the evaluation of the complex and often ambivalent relations between France and its West African colonies. On the one hand, the soldiers were colonial subjects, who often came from lesser social backgrounds. On the other hand, they did not remain in their place of birth, but rather, they were on the move as they were called to defend France and its empire in its direst hours. They encountered other colonial populations in Africa and in Asia, and in France they mingled with the French population and some even married French women. They thus interacted with the coloniser in ways that no other Africans have, except perhaps for a small part of the Western-educated elite who studied in France. Also, as I have shown elsewhere, the special military bond that was forged between African soldiers and their French comrades and commanders often served to blur the boundary between colonised and coloniser and created complex identities and aspirations (Ginio 2006, 2010).

The soldiers' presence in various parts of the French colonial empire and in France also offers us an opportunity to examine the decolonisation of AOF in a wider perspective that does not ignore historical events and processes that took place outside its boundaries. French policies, and African demands and struggles, in West Africa were often influenced by decolonisation processes in other parts of the French empire. For example, West African trade unions and students organisations became more radical in their political demands following the outbreak of war in Algeria (Chafer 2002b: 158). African soldiers and the activities of the French army represented an important linkage between these various historical processes.

The outline of this chapter is as follows: I will first discuss the deterioration of the relations between African soldiers and their French commanders during the Second World War and the military's successful attempts to win the hearts of soldiers and veterans during the late 1940s and early 1950s. I will then briefly describe the African participation in the two major colonial conflicts of that time – the Indochina and Algerian Wars. The bulk of this chapter will consider the propaganda that the French Army attempted to disseminate in AOF in order to convince the population of this federation and their political leaders that the relations between the French army and its African soldiers and veterans offered the best solution for the future of the federation.

The Second World War and its aftermath: loss of trust and its regaining

The first battalion of the African military corps, called the *tirailleurs sénégalais*, was established in 1857 and, despite the corps' name, soldiers were drafted from all French territories, not only from Senegal. The *tirailleurs* played a crucial role in conquering French territories in Africa. In 1910, General Charles Mangin promoted the idea of recruiting Africans to take part in the defence of metropolitan France. Most of the African soldiers were recruited to fight in Europe after 1916, when French casualties were becoming heavy and mutiny was on the rise in the ranks. Some 134,000 *tirailleurs* fought in the trenches of the First World War (Echenberg 1991: 7–8; Fogarty 2008: 19).

Although African soldiers had already served on French soil during the First World War, the grim circumstances of France in the second global conflict as well as the timing of the war made the participation of Africans especially problematic for France as a colonial power. Africans fighting in the battles of 1940 witnessed France's defeat and the German occupation of its soil; they spent considerable time in German POW camps and, finally, took part in the liberation of France in the ranks of the Free French forces. Their experiences on and off the battlefields reshaped their views of French colonialism. During their stay in France they interacted with French civilians who mostly treated them much better than the representatives of French colonial rule they had met in their home territories. They were invited into French homes and sometimes forged friendly and even intimate relations with French women. In sharp contrast with these encounters, African soldiers experienced harsh discrimination within the army. African soldiers were excluded from the victory parade in Paris. The military authorities kept postponing the payment of their discharge grants and often accused African prisoners of war of working for their German ex-captors (Echenberg 1991: 87–104). Towards the end of the war, these grievances were expressed in acts of disobedience and mutinies (Scheck 2010: 420–46). Indeed, by the end of the Second World War, relations between African soldiers and the army in which they served were quite hostile. Dissatisfied and angry soldiers revolted in several camps in France. In AOF, the most famous incident was the soldiers' mutiny at Thiaroye in December 1944, which the French command brutally repressed. Even more alarming for the French authorities was a veteran's attempt in Upper Guinea, in 1947, to organise his comrades politically (Mann 2006: 116–19). Within a few years, however, the French army began to implement measures to render military service more attractive for African soldiers. The equalising of African soldiers' pensions to those of their French counterparts in 1950, which was part of a general campaign to win over African veterans, was the first efficient move in this direction. This was followed by augmenting the percentage of volunteers in the army, improving pay and service conditions, offering professional education to soldiers, encouraging African soldiers to become officers, and perhaps the most symbolic change – replacing the term 'tirailleurs sénégalais' with the much more respectful 'soldats africains' (Echenberg 1991: 105; Mann 2006: 124–9, 171–4).

These extensive reforms doubtlessly contributed to the restoration of the soldiers' trust in the French army and attracted more volunteers after the Second World War who wanted to take advantage of the social and economic opportunities the 'new army' offered them. African soldiers and veterans were thus no obstacle to the continuation of French colonial rule.[3] In fact, alienation between them and France resumed only after the independence of the colonies of AOF and the freezing of their pensions (Mann 2006: 140–4).

Since the so-called Indochina amendment of 11 November 1951, African soldiers could no longer be dispatched to territories defined as 'a theatre of active operations' against their will (Echenberg 1991: 108–9). Therefore, all soldiers who took part in the wars in Indochina and Algeria did so voluntarily, although not all African soldiers serving in the French army at the time were volunteers.[4] The creation of new opportunities for Africans within the French army, such as professional training, education and a military career, can explain to a large extent their willingness to take part in France's wars against anti-colonial movements in other parts of the empire.[5]

The army considered its reforms to be most successful, not only in regaining the African soldiers' trust but also in forming a model of relationship between French and Africans based on a common goal and shared glory and sacrifices. Moreover, as we shall see, military authorities in AOF believed that the model they had created could be applicable not only to the soldiers, but also to the territories from which they came. That is not to say that the soldiers' commanders were not concerned about potential problems that the soldiers' service in turbulent areas of the Empire might cause. After all, African soldiers experienced the harsh conditions of two very challenging colonial wars.

The service of African soldiers in Indochina and Algeria

In 1949, with the communist victory in China, the war in Indochina entered a new phase. The Viet Minh, which until then had conducted guerrilla actions against the French, began to receive open support from the new regime in China, and its numbers were growing steadily. The French army suffered increasingly heavy casualties and loss of morale. The French army in Indochina depended heavily on the professional regulars of the colonial army, the Foreign Legion, and North African soldiers (Clayton 1994b: 53–6). Within the colonial army 18,500 African soldiers served in Indochina (Echenberg 1991: 110). The special conditions of the Indochina war – the harsh climate, the unconventional warfare the Viet Minh imposed on the French, and the difficult battle surroundings – took their toll of all of the soldiers fighting on the French side. Africans had their own additional difficulties. Most African soldiers served in small military posts located near villages (Bodin 2000: 58–61). These outposts were fortified by trenches and barbed fences. The Viet Minh, on the other hand, had a much wider space in which it could operate, especially during night time. In interviews conducted by Aïssatou Diagne in 1991, veterans said that they felt constant fear during their service in these posts. The Viet Minh's psychological warfare affected them and when they heard rumours that soldiers in a certain post would be massacred they could not sleep at night and jumped at the slightest noise, which was usually made by rats (Diagne 1991: 69). Ousmane Niang told Diagne that soldiers felt that every peasant they met could turn into a warrior in a second. Even women were potentially dangerous. When he and his comrades captured a woman who was spying on them in Luang Prabang in Laos, she pulled a hand grenade out of her hair and tried to throw it at them (ibid.: 52).

Apart for these harsh conditions, which other soldiers in Indochina had to face as well, African soldiers suffered from discrimination and disrespect from some of their French officers and from parts of the local population. In some cases, their frustration resulted in violence, either expressed in street fights with

Vietnamese civilians, or, in extreme cases, in the murder of their French officers (Ginio 2010: 69–73).

A few months after the 1954 French defeat in Dien Bien Phu, the Algerian *Front de Libération Nationale* (FLN) launched a widespread attack on French targets that set off the 8-year-long Algerian war. African soldiers were called again to defend the empire against its enemies. During the Algerian war, as French reluctance to serve in the continuing bloody conflict grew, the army had to rely increasingly on pro-French Algerians, known as the Harki, and on soldiers from sub-Saharan Africa.

Around 25,000 African soldiers were serving in Algeria by 1956 (Mann 2006: 22). Some arrived directly from Indochina, and their commanders were concerned about the repercussions of this transfer from one battle zone to the other on their morale and motivation.[6] Unlike Indochina, where the soldiers fought in rural areas and where the big cities served as a space of relaxation and refuge from the horrors of war, in Algeria – at least until the beginning of 1958 – the war was fought in urban areas in the streets, cafés, and even inside private homes. After the Algerian resistance was pushed into the rural areas, the fighting continued in mountainous regions and in the margins of the Sahara desert. The French assigned the dirtiest work of the war to African soldiers. Some even took part in torturing FLN prisoners (Zimmerman 2011: 122–3).

Both the Viet Minh and the FLN used extensive propaganda efforts to persuade African soldiers they were fighting an unjust war against their fellow-sufferers. This propaganda occasionally influenced the soldiers, but in a very limited way. The French military authorities were highly concerned about the potential damage this psychological war might cause their recruits and therefore dedicated a great deal of attention to the development of their own propaganda. While in Indochina and Algeria this propaganda was designated for the soldiers, in an attempt to counter that of the Viet Minh and the FLN respectively, when used in AOF its goals and target audiences were much more varied.

Saving the remains of the empire: military propaganda in AOF

At a time when French rule in Indochina and North Africa was gradually being undermined, the military authorities considered AOF as a territory that could still be saved from external influences. Defending AOF necessitated, however, immense propaganda efforts and, as we shall see, it was not easy to convince Africans of the *grandeur* of the French army while in the background the empire which it was meant to protect was slowly disintegrating.

In spite of hesitations over resorting to propaganda in the aftermath of the Second World War, during which both the Nazi regime and the Vichy government in France had turned the term into a negative one, under the Fourth Republic the colonial wars convinced the French government that propaganda was necessary after all. During the Indochina war French officers developed a theory of counter-insurgency warfare termed '*action psychologique*' (psychological operations). Its aim was to use the same sort of strategy that their enemy, the Viet-Minh, had mastered. Between the autumn of 1954 and late 1955, the French army gradually adapted psychological warfare. In March 1955, an agency for psychological operations was established and given the name *Bureau régional d'action psychologique* (Regional Office for Psychological Operations), which later became simply known as the *Bureau psychologique*. Four months later, the psychological operations were implemented in Algeria as well (Pahlavi 2007–8).

While psychological operations were not successful in Indochina, where they were first applied at a rather late stage of the war, in Algeria the military authorities believed it was crucial in winning the Battle of Algiers in 1957. During most of the war, until De Gaulle officially abolished the unit in February 1960, psychological operations were one of the French Army's major weapons against the FLN. It used various means of propaganda in order to raise the morale of French and colonial troops alike, to convince the Algerian population that support of France was their best option, and to demoralise FLN members.[7]

Psychological operations were not limited, however, to these two areas of conflict. As of 1954, the military and colonial authorities in AOF used them extensively. Although this military propaganda was formally aimed at the entire population of AOF, including individuals living in remote and isolated areas, the main target audience was confined to two groups: African veterans, whom the army considered as a vital link to the general population, and the Western-educated elite. The army attempted to reach these audiences in two principal ways: celebrations around holidays and especially on the *Journée des Forces Armées* (Day of the Armed Forces: 8 May) and expeditions into various regions of the federations, called *tournées de brousse*.

Before I go into the specific activities that took place during these propaganda campaigns and their measure of success, as much as this can be estimated, I would like to discuss the army's choice of target audience. The decision to focus on veterans is quite straightforward and does not require a great deal of explaining. As we have seen, from the beginning of the 1950s the army saw veterans as a potential support group and made serious efforts to correct the inequalities that their former treatment involved. Veterans' support was guaranteed by the equalising of their pensions to those of French veterans. In addition, offices for veterans and war victims were established in all the territories of AOF. These offices collected various demands and requests from veterans under their jurisdiction and forwarded them to the colonial authorities. Apart from financial help, the colonial authorities organised pilgrimage trips to Mecca for veterans. The military authorities began to organise such pilgrimage trips for African and North African soldiers and veterans during the 1950s. Ethan Orwin suggests that the initiative for these organised pilgrimages came from North African veterans at the beginning of the decade. The French military authorities believed in the potential of such expeditions as a tool of propaganda. In speeches French officers delivered before pilgrims they focused on the dual obligation of the soldiers to Allah and to France. However, officers were highly concerned regarding the hazards of anti-French propaganda the soldiers might encounter during their trip (Orwin 2008: 272–6).

In a letter from the president of the main veterans' office of AOF to the governor of Senegal, the former expressed the veterans' deep gratitude for the free pilgrimage they received and said that this gesture made them feel that the French army was deeply attached to them.[8]

African veterans were an essential component of every event that the military authorities organised in order to approach the local population in AOF. They helped organise these events and were invited to all of them. Often, as we shall see, they were the only guests who actually appreciated the efforts invested in these celebrations. Veterans were of course part of their societies, and the army's assumption was that treating them well would encourage their friends and relatives to support the army and its endeavours.

The other target group – the Western-educated elite – is more surprising. In his article on the army's policies towards North African soldiers, Orwin demonstrates that the reluctance to recruit intellectuals (or even people who could express themselves in French, for that matter) was still very much evident during the 1950s. The military authorities believed that 'educated North Africans' were dangerous as they were politically conscious, while uneducated soldiers did not look beyond their village or tribe and had no political convictions whatsoever (Orwin 2008: 277–8). Military documents regarding West African soldiers, however, reflect a deep desire on the part of the army to attract more Western-educated Africans. The idea here is that these individuals were most likely to be involved in politics and to be influenced by the anti-colonial struggles in other parts of the French empire. However, in this case, this danger is quoted as the main motivation for recruiting them into the army. In one document it is stated that military service will expose these 'educated Africans' to an African society of tomorrow in which Blacks and Whites are working together for a better future.[9] The military authorities in AOF thus believed that, unlike 'educated North Africans', the young elites of AOF were not a lost cause yet. They could still be won over, if only they realised that the army reflected a perfect alternative to the dissolution of the empire and to African independence – a future of equality and cooperation for the benefit of both France and its African territories. Indeed, the recruitment policy in AOF changed after the Second World War. While before the war, the army systematically preferred 'non-educated' Africans as soldiers, as well as certain ethnic groups that the army considered as 'natural warriors',[10] during the 1950s, preference was given to Western-educated Africans. It is for this reason that the governor of Dahomey specifically asked the military authorities of AOF to focus their activities on the south of the territory where most 'educated Africans' lived, and to avoid acting among ethnic groups in the North, from where many recruits came before the war, so as not to cause disappointment to frustrated Africans who would be now rejected for not being educated enough.[11]

According to military and administrative reports, young 'educated Africans' were a rather difficult target, as most of these Africans did not envisage a military career and were not attracted to the ostensible lure of uniforms and army discipline. These young individuals also followed international news and knew what was happening in the colonial world. They had heard of Dien Bien Phu, they followed the events in Algeria, and were aware of the winds of change and the growing criticism of colonial powers. Thus, this problematic target audience was not easy to deal with, and the military and colonial authorities had to invest efforts in trying to convince these young Africans that the army was their best friend, and that supporting it was the best way to advance their political and social goals.

The military thus designated its propaganda activities mainly for these two groups – the veterans and young 'educated Africans' – while also trying to expand these activities as far as possible within the vast federation of AOF. Both groups were invited to special days of military celebrations, mainly around 11 November and 8 May. Activities on these days included performances, films, games, sport competitions, horse, car and motorcycle races, concerts and parades.[12]

The colonial administration of AOF usually supported these organised military celebrations. However, the following correspondence regarding the army's request to reserve the Dakar stadium for the Army Day of 1955 suggests that this support was not always enthusiastic and that the colonial administration did not give these grand shows of military power the same importance as the military authorities and the veteran associations did.

On 3 February 1955 the high command of the army in AOF distributed the plans for the Army Day celebrations of 8 May later that year. Almost three weeks later, General Garbay,[13] the superior commander of AOF, asked the Governor-General to reserve the Dakar stadium, which had been used the previous year, for these dates.[14] The request was transferred to the municipality of Dakar, which refused it, saying that the football championship of Senegal and the French West Africa Cup games were already scheduled for these dates. The Governor-General offered Garbay several alternatives, such as the local stadium of Fann, on the fringes of Dakar. Garbay's response was furious. He maintained that the alternatives were unsatisfactory as they lacked the right facilities and were far from the centre, and as it was difficult to move equipment to them. The general was outraged by the fact that one of these stadiums was in a triangular shape, thus rendering horse races impossible. Garbay agreed to postpone the celebrations to the second half of June on condition that the army was allowed to use the Dakar stadium. He then added that if his request was not granted, the celebrations would be cancelled. In case this was not enough to convince the Governor-General, Garbay warned him that the cancellation of the celebrations would severely harm the Nation-Army relations and would create an image of mediocrity and lack of professionalism.[15] The general's request was forwarded to Paul Bonifay, the Mayor of Dakar, and the latter agreed. However, he asked to receive the stadium back in the same state that it had before the military celebrations.[16] This remark, and the scheduling of football games during the same week in which the military celebrations were supposed to take place, reflect the civil authorities' lack of enthusiasm for this form of propaganda.

The second type of propaganda efforts, which the administration seems to have supported more willingly, took place in the framework of what the army termed '*tournées de brousse*'.[17] These military tours took place every year from the early 1950s. They lasted around eight months and encompassed even the most remote districts (*cercles*). According to the military authorities of AOF, these tours had several aims. Their main purposes were to reinforce the friendship and trust between the French army and the African population, to establish contact with veterans all over the federation and to manifest the permanence of the French presence. The tours' secondary aims were to collect information about the districts, to train the soldiers, habituate them to village life and to forge team spirit among the military units.[18]

Unlike the celebrations in urban centres, which aimed to attract Western-educated Africans as well as urban veterans, the tours' main targets were rural veterans, who certainly outnumbered the urban ones and Africans living far away from the colonial centres and who therefore did not have access to urban military celebrations. The soldiers who participated in the tours were equipped with film projectors and radio transmitters so as to bring the military's messages to remote regions. In addition photo exhibitions were organised and soldiers handed out presents to people who came to meet them.[19]

A special service note distributed on 9 May 1955 included specific instructions for soldiers participating in these tours regarding the ways in which they should behave towards the local population. Soldiers were reminded that the aim of the tour was to reinforce the friendship between the army and the local population and thus they were warned to avoid any sort of incident. The population, so the document stated, should not feel that the army considered it as hostile. Soldiers were also asked to show special interest in veterans who received decorations for their service and to show respect towards local African functionaries. In return for food, the soldiers were asked not to offer payment to village or canton chiefs as this might upset them. Instead, the officers leading the tours were instructed to give the chief in question a sum of money saying that it was designated for the community, for example to construct a new mosque.[20]

As we can see, the military authorities in AOF invested tremendous efforts and manpower to spread propaganda among the population and improve the image of the army. However, both major target groups – the veterans and the Western-educated African elite – were aware that the army experienced many difficulties, to say the least, in its battles in other parts of the empire. This fact made the propaganda efforts much more complicated. The process of the selection of films to be projected to African audiences reflects well the problematic nature of these military efforts.

Military propaganda and problematic films

One activity common to both celebrations and tours, and to which the military authorities paid special attention, was the projection of films. The French used films extensively as part of their psychological operations in Indochina and Algeria. The *Service cinématographique des armées* (Army Film Service) was responsible for the production of all propaganda films. Not all of those films targeted audiences in the colonies, though. Some were produced for French audiences, and occasionally these films were shown outside France as well. Their aim was to convince viewers to support the continuation of the French presence in Indochina and later in Algeria. Films about Indochina presented the war's purpose as pacification, and attempted to convince their viewers of its necessity. The films on Algeria presented soldiers as maintaining order and as bringing education, health and aid to the Algerians, and their aim was to deny that a war was actually going on. None of the films projected in AOF was produced specifically for West African audiences. The military and colonial authorities had to rely on the supply of films from France, films which were designed for completely different purposes and audiences. This, as we shall see, proved to be quite problematic.

The films that were sent from France to assist the psychological operations were projected in the major territories once every two months in the main towns of all districts and subdivisions, and occasionally in some villages. The audience mostly comprised veterans and schoolchildren, the two groups that were most accessible to the colonial authorities.[21]

Although the administrators who reported on the projection of films attempted to present many of these events as great successes, a careful reading of the documents points to the contrary. In fact, the only cases in which the film screenings could be regarded as a success were documentaries describing familiar battlefields that were shown to veterans. Most of the other films were actually extremely boring for their viewers or worse, harmful to colonial and military interests. As mentioned before, the main problem of most films was that they were not originally designed for audiences in AOF. In 1954, the governor-general complained to the minister of the colonies that the films sent to AOF did not fulfil their aim. As example he gave the film *Nos soldats en Afrique Noire* which was aimed at attracting young French individuals to the army but was of no interest to the African public.[22] When the film *Le grand cirque* – which tells the story of three men who fought with the Free French in the Second World War – was projected in Bamako, only women and young children attended, and, according to the report, they did not find the film interesting at all.[23] Other films were reported as being too technical or over-long.[24]

Films that could not attract the attention of their African audience for more than a few minutes were of course not practically useful as tools of propaganda, but at least they were not harmful. On the other hand, the projection in AOF of documentaries filmed in Indochina before the French defeat in Dien Bien Phu in 1954, was in fact contrary to the propaganda aims. In 1956, the governor of Upper Volta remarked in his report on the psychological operations in his colony that it did not seem worthwhile to project documentaries filmed in Indochina at a time when it still seemed that the problem would be solved in a favourable manner. He added that the film *Les armées de la paix*, for example, was considered a military propaganda film at the time, but achieved the opposite results when the outcome of that war was taken into consideration. In general, the governor recommended not projecting any film that related to a military operation whose outcome was not politically favourable for France.[25] This, of course, did not leave many options.

At first glance, the extensive use of films that were not adapted for showing to African audiences and that occasionally presented an undesirable image of the French Army might seem surprising. However, in spite of their obvious disadvantages, these military films had a vital role in the so-called psychological operations. They symbolised a shared past glory and a future common aim for French and African soldiers. The military authorities saw African veterans – who apparently were the only ones who appreciated those films – as a key element in reaching the hearts of the African population. The military documentaries sought to emphasise this shared destiny and thus to present the entire colonial project in a different light. After all, even shared defeats can evoke the brotherhood of arms, and it was this brotherhood that had to be demonstrated if AOF was to be saved from following the road other French territories were taking during the 1950s.

Conclusion

It is hardly surprising that the French army's role in post-Second World War AOF has been virtually ignored. A non-fighting army rarely attracts attention. It is enough to see what General Garbay, who commanded the repression of the Madagascar 1947 revolt and fought against anti-colonial movements in Tunisia, was forced to do in Senegal. Obviously, sending angry letters to the governor-general in an attempt to reserve the local stadium for the army's celebrations cannot be compared to his previous military operations, although it was definitely less harmful. But, as this chapter has demonstrated, ignoring the army's role in one of the calmest areas of the French empire is a mistake. The army was a major colonial actor in the federation with its own specific agenda, which occasionally paralleled that of the colonial administration but sometimes offered alternatives to it.

The military reforms of the 1950s reshaped the relations between the army and its African soldiers and veterans. They succeeded in creating a loyal group of colonial subjects who enjoyed economic and social benefits and were in fact treated, at least formally, as equal to metropolitan soldiers and veterans. The success of these reforms prompted the army to attempt to win over the general population of AOF. Although it was difficult for the army to convince Africans of its *grandeur* after its failure in Indochina, it could still resort to the discourse of shared destiny and common goals. Unlike in other parts of the French Empire, the army did not even despair of the Western-educated elite of AOF. In fact, it expended much of its propaganda efforts towards this rather suspect group in the hope of persuading it that it offered a tangible and attractive alternative to political independence.

Even when independence was already a *fait accompli*, the demobilisation of African soldiers was gradual and ended only in 1964, four years after the formal end of colonial rule in AOF. Many of the soldiers were demobilised following the demands of their respective new governments and not of their own will (Zimmerman 2011: 133–6). African veterans were in general not interested in independence. It was in fact independence, and the consequent freezing of their pensions, that put an end to the equality they had managed to attain during the 1950s. The military's attempts to reform colonial relations within the army's ranks had a temporary, partial success. Moreover, such reforms were hardly applicable outside the army, as they would have heavily burdened the French government's budget. In any case, these reforms were certainly not enough to prevent the independence of AOF. Nevertheless, as the continuing post-colonial military relations with France's ex-colonies seem to show, formal independence and decolonisation are hardly equivalent terms.

Notes

1 This research was supported by the Israel Science Foundation (grant no. 882/09).
2 On post-colonial military relations between France and its ex-colonies see Granvaud (2009: 31–43).
3 On the success of these reforms in turning African veterans into supporters of French colonial rule see Mann (2006: 133–4).
4 In 1948, 37.6 per cent of recruits (3,008 out of 8,000) were volunteers. See Echenberg (1991: 108).
5 An example of the attractions the army offered to Africans can be found in the military career of Jean-Bedel Bokassa (1921–96). See Titley (2002: 9–10).

6 Service Historique de l'Armée de Terre, Vincennes (SHAT), 1H 2454 d.1, *Fiche de renseignements concernant le personnel africain venue en renforce de l'AOF*, 7 May 1956.

7 For more information on the psychological operations in Algeria during the 1950s see Villatoux (2007: 5–39).

8 Archives Nationales Sénégalaises, Dakar (ANS), 19G16 (17), *Pèlerinages de la Mecque*, 26 August 1954.

9 ANS, 17G 520, *Cabinet Militaire – Programme d'action psychologique*, 1954/55.

10 On recruitment policy before the Second World War and the notion of 'races guerrières' see Lunn (1999: 517–36).

11 ANS, 17G 520, Bonfils, Governor of Dahomey, to Cornut-Gentille, Governor-General of AOF, 27 February 1955.

12 ANS, 5D 213, Commandement supérieur des Forces Armées de la zone de défense AOF-Togo to Cornut-Gentille, *Action de propagande en faveur du recrutement*, 26 January 1954; ANS, 17G 520, *Haute Volta – Rapport sur l'action psychologique en septembre-octobre 1955*, 1956.

13 General Garbay played an active role in the rallying of Chad to the Free French Forces in 1940. After the liberation of France, in which he also played a decisive role, Garbay continued his military career in Madagascar, where he commanded the brutal repression of the 1947 revolt, in Indochina, Tunisia and finally Senegal.

14 ANS, 5D 213, Garbay, Commandant Supérieur de l'Armée en AOF, to Cornut-Gentille, 22 February 1955.

15 ANS, 5D 213, Garbay to Cornut-Gentille, 28 March 1955.

16 ANS. 5D 213, Bonifay, Mayor of Dakar, to Jourdain, Governor of Senegal, 13 April 1955.

17 It is interesting that this is also the term *commandants des cercles* used for their own periodical tours of their territories, which they often neglected to perform.

18 ANS, 11D-1 903, Lami, Governor of Senegal, to Commandants de Cercle, 30 August 1957.

19 ANS, 11D-1 903, Lami to Commandants de Cercle, 30 August 1957.

20 ANS, 11D-1 195, *Note de service – Tournées de brousse*, 9 May 1955.

21 ANS, 17G 520, Bonfils, Governor of Dahomey, to Cornut-Gentille, Governor-General of AOF, 27 February 1955.

22 ANS, 17G 520, Cornut-Gentille to Jacquinot, Minister of Overseas France, *Action psychologique par des filmes*, February 1954.

23 ANS, 17G 520, Geay, Governor of Soudan, to Cornut-Gentille, 29 May 1954.

24 ANS, 17G 520, Cluset, commandant de la deuxième brigade de l'AOF, 22 July 1954.

25 ANS, 17G 520, *Haute Volta – Rapport sur l'action psychologique en septembre–octobre 1955*, 1956.

5

The French Army and Malian independence (1956–1961)

Vincent Joly

On 20 January 1961, in a solemn statement before the official diplomatic corps in Bamako, the President of the Republic of Mali demanded that the remaining French troops based in his country be withdrawn. While expressing a willingness to cooperate with France, Modibo Keïta explained this 'decision of party and government' by stressing the impossibility of stationing 'troops of the former colonial power' alongside those of the 'young State', on the basis both of sovereignty and non-alignment (Keïta n.d.). Whereas strong ties were maintained between the French army and nascent national armies in other former French colonies, the Malian authorities chose to make a clean break. The event held a special significance because of the place of French Soudan and its people in the culture of the French marines. Indeed, this colony had long been seen as theirs by right, where they enjoyed an unparalleled freedom, managing the country for 20 years and displaying an original 'military imperialism' (Kanya-Forstner 1969).

Soudanese soldiers in the French army and the Algerian war

Soudan had long been a 'reservoir of soldiers'. During the Second World War, in the first, intensive recruitment drive between September 1939 and June 1940, 44,000 men were called up. Re-entry to the war in 1943 saw the recruitment of 21,000 soldiers (Joly 2006). Siding with the French proved costly. For example, around 7,000 Soudanese were taken prisoner by the Germans in 1940, of whom 1,500 died in captivity (ibid.). Moreover, there was scant reward for their sacrifice, such that at the end of the Second World War a number of serious incidents occurred in France and Senegal, culminating in the Thiaroye massacre of December 1944. African soldiers demanded recognition of their service. Traditional paternalism proved unreliable as a means of defusing the tensions that came with demobilisation; the old colonial officers had lost 'their men'. One officer stationed in Kati in 1947 lamented: 'Every free former African soldier of the Second World War is imbued with nationalism. They reject the servility of their predecessors and seek only one thing: the speedy departure of the French. Communism seems to have left its mark on them all'.[1]

Although the officer correctly identified the cleavage between two generations of former soldiers, his political analysis could be questioned, influenced as it was then by a hysterical anti-communism (Villatoux 2005: 51ff.). Many simply wanted equal rights (Akpo-Vaché 1996: 21), while others enlisted in the Corps Expéditionnaire Français en Extrême-Orient (CEFEO: Far East French Expeditionary Corps) in Indochina from the end of 1948. Those who went to the Far East were very rough, uneducated recruits: of the 3,000 Soudano-Guinean volunteers in the period 1948–1953, only 2 per cent were literate (Kouassi 1994: 11). However, these men were keenly aware of their rights. They complained of constant bureaucratic red tape and of being denied the most prestigious honours such as the Croix de Guerre. At the end of the Indochina War, the high command became concerned with their 'bad attitude', but this behaviour had no political fallout in the short term (Bodin 2000: 227). Back home, the African soldiers showed few signs of having being influenced by Viet Minh propaganda. Furthermore, it was feared that the mass redundancies in the CEFEO that followed the Geneva peace accords would spell trouble, but nothing came of it.[2] Whatever their generation, these men did not make open anti-colonialist demands, especially as the French government had met their main demand in 1950. On 8 August that year a bill was passed whose articles 9 and 10 enshrined the principle of pension parity between overseas veterans and those of metropolitan France. Colonial authorities proved considerably more generous towards former soldiers than towards civilians, for obvious political reasons: the soldiers represented a potential bulwark against the nationalists. In the Soudanese milieus of San, Mopti and Bandiagara, they were seen by the administration as anti-Rassemblement Démocratique Africain (RDA) (Mann 2006: 173).

The impact of the Algerian War was felt south of the Sahara from 1956. That year, 10,000 Africans were called into this theatre of war. In August, of the 397,000 men under arms, 3.7 per cent were from sub-Saharan Africa (Clayton 1994: 220). Subsequently, Soudanese soldiers would become the targets of Front de Libération Nationale (FLN) propaganda. In 1957, leaflets addressed to 'our African comrades', some written in Arabic, called on them to desert: 'Algeria has won its independence. Run away! Free yourselves from France' (Ageron 1997: 207). The high command also feared the disruptive influence of religion. But there was little cause for concern. As General André Beaufre remarked in the spring of 1956, 'these men have no compunction when it comes to fighting their religious brothers'. Nevertheless, the military authorities kept a watchful eye. A commander in Algeria, General Lorillot, suggested to his counterpart in the Afrique Occidentale Française-Togo area that he use psychology in handling the

African units. In April 1957, Lieutenant Colonel Soumaré was ordered to imple-ment this approach, and the following July, a decision was made to establish a 5th office in Afrique Occidentale Française (AOF) in the near future (Joly 2000).

In the period 1956/57, it was felt both in Dakar and in Paris that the African question could not be separated from events in the Maghreb. According to offi-cials in the High Commission of AOF, contact had already been made between the Moroccan Istiqlal and the Soudanese (Ageron 1992: 232). In April 1956, the governor of French Soudan highlighted the political and strategic importance of the country's northern region: 'This is where Africa meets the Maghreb' he wrote, 'all political, religious and trade union currents circulating in AOF pass through here.'[3] The authorities sporadically denounced the propaganda of the 'al Azhar veterans', union activities and youth groups. The country's secretary-general declared: 'Young people in education are almost all imbued with nationalist, anti-European ideas.'[4] Despite the vote of African deputies in Paris to grant special powers to the government of Guy Mollet, the mood was changing. Delegates to the RDA inter-territorial congress held in Bamako at the end of September 1957 simply called on the French government to negotiate, but the discussions took on a different tone. On hearing of this, the authorities feared that the RDA would change its view of the 'rebellion' in Algeria.[5] In fact, since the summer, the mood in French Soudan had changed. In July, the paper of the Union Soudanaise-RDA (US-RDA), *L'Essor*, stated: 'Wanting to deny your "rebel" opponent the status of legitimate interlocutor is like trying to hide the sun with the palm of your hand' (Ageron 1992: 250, n. 25). War was inch-ing closer; throughout 1957 there were skirmishes in the Sahara. On 23 October 1957, radio in Cairo and Tunis announced the opening of a 'Saharan front' and *El Moudjahid* warned that: 'The battle is now joined in all parts of the nation, from Oran to Tamanrasset, from Ain Sefrat to Djanet and from Colomb Bechar to Edjeleh' (Frémeaux 1997: 93–110).

It is also worth underlining that the desert held a special significance for the army. From the early 1950s, the Interarmy Special Vehicles Test Centre (CIEES) was set up in Colomb Béchar, providing a site for the testing of a wide range of missiles (Varnoteaux 1998: 535–42). The north of French Soudan thereby acquired a strategic importance. At the end of the summer of 1957, work began on a runway for jet aircraft in Tessalit. The little *bordj* in Adrar des Ifoghas was located less than 100 km from the Algerian border, along an axis bearing north to Tidikelt and Reggane and northwest to Hoggar and Tamanrasset. Southwards, the line followed the valley of Tilemsi in the direction of Bourem and the banks of the Niger. For the military, policy towards French Soudan was determined by the Algerian conflict, even though this had to be resituated in the much wider framework of the Cold War. As Commander Hogard, one of the French army's most important theorists of psychological warfare, explained: 'Currently, we can expect the merest revolt in outlying regions of the French

Union to be supported by the party of Revolution and its allies in metropolitan France; not only in the French Union but in foreign territories' (Hogard 1957: 78). In this context, any criticism of the course of action in north Africa was seen as incontrovertible evidence of collusion with Moscow.

The fighting in Timimoun in October 1957 did not go unnoticed in French Soudan. Furthermore, the development of oil exploration in the southern Sahara was potentially at risk because the resulting increase in trade ultimately threatened to 'spread the rebellion to the south'.[6] These fears were openly aired in an article published in May 1958 in the *Revue de Défense Nationale* by Colonel Jean Muller, who denounced the 'degradation' of the situation along Saharan road no. 2, identified as a line of penetration for a possible West African rebellion via the Soudanese towns of Tessalit and Gao (Muller 1958: 754–58).

Soldiers and politics

The return to power of De Gaulle led to concerns south of the Sahara. In Dakar, the army had shown no signs of movement around 13 May. Yet in Soudan there had been tensions between the administration and the local command that stoked the US-RDA's defiance of the French army (Chaffard Vol. 1, 1965: 341). De Gaulle managed to allay these concerns and in Soudan Modibo Keïta called for a 'yes' vote in the September 1958 referendum, although on this occasion the army did intercede with the veterans, both directly and through the support network for General De Gaulle.[7] These men favoured strong links with France and most of them opposed the US-RDA. Significantly, the only veteran in the leadership, Paul Lalifa Keïta, had been removed from the executive in August 1958 (Campmas 1978: 108).

From 1956, Soudanese veterans showed signs of disquiet. Self-rule and the prospect of independence prompted fears that their gains would be clawed back. They viewed the continued presence of the French, in one form or another, as a safeguard and thus they formed a potential reserve of voters likely to oppose the most radical elements in the US-RDA who were tempted by independence (Mann 2006: 134). Moreover, in July 1958 the political landscape changed. At its founding conference, the Parti du Regroupement Africain (PRA) called for immediate independence. Then, in September, Guinea voted 'no' in the referendum on the creation of the Community. French concerns were further heightened when, despite some dissent, Guinean veterans rallied to Sékou Touré in Conakry (Schmidt 2005: 192). Clearly, the ex-servicemen could not tip the balance in favour of France.

Ever since Guinea attained independence, the Conakry regime was depicted as a threat, and the order had been issued to draw a *'cordon sanitaire'* around the country to prevent the contagion of independence from spreading to the rest of West Africa (Chaffard, Vol. 2, 1967: 218, 235). The establishment of the

Ghana-Guinea Union in November 1958 caused French authorities to panic; they even saw it as the product of shady British manoeuvring (*Le Monde*, 24 November 1958). Intelligence was reactivated in July 1958 at the behest of Pierre Messmer, then high commissioner in Dakar. The Military Research Service (SMR) was created, its purpose to work alongside the civil administration. Thus, in early 1959 Major Py of the leading battalion drew up a mixed assessment of the first few months' activity. Having established that collaboration with civilian authorities was in places proving difficult, he decided to do everything possible to keep his organisation's activities secret. The future depended on putting in place a network of agents and informers to infiltrate different groups (political, trade union and youth), 'using the techniques of the Service de Documentation Extérieure et de Contre-Espionnage (SDECE: External Documentation and Counter-espionage Service)'. He recognised that Senegal, Guinea, and Dahomey already had such infrastructure in place but that it was also under way in French Soudan, Niger and Mauritania.[8]

Yet the mood was not one of panic, as neither communist nor Guinean threats were felt to be imminent at the end of 1958. Concerning the latter, General Gardet, commander of the defence zone of AOF-Togo, thought that the Soudanese government had joined the ranks of Sékou Touré's opponents, as shown by its refusal to accept a Guinean ambassador.[9] But it was the situation in Algeria that caused most concern. The military feared that returning demobilised Guinean soldiers would cause unrest among other African soldiers. In the 11th RIC, for example, 176 of the 476 Africans in the regiment collectively refused to obey orders.[10]

These events did not augur well for the future army of the Community as it was feared that the new states would attempt to bring back their soldiers. Fully aware of the threat, France declared on 7 January 1959 the 'united' defence of the Community, to come under a single command. High Commissioners were assigned responsibility for organising the defence of each state, presiding over ad hoc committees that would comprise local army commanders and heads of government (Guéna 1962: 93ff). That same year a central African strategic zone was created, covering all of France's former colonies and with a threefold brief: holding onto a pool of raw materials, controlling the most important lines of inter-African communication and offering an extended strategic area of operation for Western Europe (Chaigneau 1984: 14).

1959: the turning-point

The image of Soudan changed in 1959. During an intelligence conference held in Algiers in November, the situation in the country was analysed in depth by Lieutenant-Colonel Routier. His study revealed that the 'the *enfant terrible* of the Community' was moving towards an authoritarian regime. This deviation had been noticeable since the March 1959 elections, which French intelligence claimed were preceded by the elimination of opposition figures, particularly in Ségou. Moreover, the US-RDA was preparing a referendum on independence.[11] The report's author noted that the accompanying propaganda affected 'the army of the Community in particular', in other words French troops stationed in French Soudan, who were depicted as a 'major impediment' and whose activities were 'closely monitored and systematically disparaged'. Routier believed that the 'secession of Mali' (from the Federation of Mali) (see Keese, Chapter 3 in this volume) was entirely plausible. It would, 'in the medium to long term', imply a challenge to the French army's presence in the country. He concluded: 'This aspect of the issue is surely the most serious and the most urgent.'[12]

The Communist threat was not explicitly mentioned, even when the SDECE anxiously noted US-RDA suggestions of the possibility of a break with France or even the merits of neutrality. The Algerian War was still the main problem: 'The FLN is gaining ground in sub-Saharan Africa.' In truth, the Algerians could not rely on actual material aid but they did receive moral support. From then on, FLN propaganda played on continental solidarity and called for the withdrawal of African troops from Algeria.[13] However, the Soudanese leaders did not so much adopt an anti-war stance as criticise atomic-bomb testing. In August 1959, following a meeting with the Tunisian Minister of Foreign Affairs, Modibo Keïta condemned the tests for the first time. He clumsily explained away this turnaround several days later in a declaration to the Community's executive committee: 'I agreed to the testing of the French atom bomb but I didn't agree to it being in the Sahara.'[14] There was no attack on French policy in Algeria. On the contrary, Modibo Keïta assured General De Gaulle: 'He has our cooperation for the swiftest possible solution to the Algerian crisis.'[15]

Franco-Soudanese relations were shaken. In early August 1959, during a US-RDA conference in Bamako, Keïta stated: 'Nothing can stop Mali's march to independence', while expressing the hope that this could be achieved 'in friendship with France, leading to a multinational federation, in other words a French-style Commonwealth' (Diagouraga 2005: 64). The demand for independence was officially sent to De Gaulle in September. On 13 December, Paris acceded to the request, thereby signing the death warrant of the Community. De Gaulle had no choice; no separate trial of strength could be contemplated while he sought a resolution to the Algerian conflict. The convergence of Malian demands and Algerian self-determination underpinned his drive to transform Franco-Algerian relations.

But the process was not as straightforward as it seemed. At the very heart of the Federation, Senegalese and Soudanese had differing conceptions of independence and the future of relations with France. Paris grew increasingly suspicious of Modibo Keïta and his entourage. French prime minister Michel Debré wrote, in early January 1959, that Keïta was 'A rebel … he quickly took against

General de Gaulle and myself. He's been influenced by Sekou Touré and plans to remove any allegiance to France' (Debré 1988: 319). This hostile attitude resurfaced during the negotiations for independence. Madeira Keïta occasionally stood in for Modibo. Debré's take on him was still less complimentary: 'This roughneck, trained by Communists, wants the talks to fail ... he particularly abhors our continuing military presence' (Debré 1988: 137).

The Soudanese position hardened during 1959. The prospect of independence appears to have driven Modibo Keïta to formulate more aggressive demands. At the same time, the French government's attitude was less neutral than Debré claimed. Indeed, two controversial matters helped explain the tense climate of negotiations, one related to veterans and the other, more importantly, to northern Soudan and its peoples.

The veterans had become a key political issue. Soudanese officials were worried about the veterans' political attitude and their links with France. In 1959, the Soudanese veterans' association spoke out for independence but was challenged by a new group of former career soldiers, the Association des Anciens Militaires de Carrière (AAMC: Former Career Soldiers' Association) which stood for the maintenance of the Community. At one of its meetings in French Soudan, the closing speaker's comments were revelatory: 'France, the motherland' (Mann 2006: 139).

Soudanese leaders could not afford to ignore these men, who could stall the ruling party's political plans. Madeira Keïta was assigned the task of winning them over, as he was the only member of the party leadership to have performed military service. The Soudanese government resolved to fund a paper, *L'Ancien Combattant Soudanais* (The Soudanese Veteran), to compete with Dakar's *La Voix du Combattant* (The Voice of the Veteran), which it judged too 'Senegalese' and close to military circles in metropolitan France. At the same time the government tried to merge the two organisations. This was achieved by March 1960, but the first president, Captain Mamadou Sidibé, was disowned by the veterans due to his overly anti-French stance (Mann 2006: 140). Veterans were never completely won over to the US-RDA, even after the freezing of war veterans' pensions by the French government early in 1960 (Mann, 2006). At a 1959 party congress, Modibo Keïta aired his concerns about them. With reference to the psychological warfare being waged in Algeria by the French Army, he stated: 'This enterprise has worked so well, or appears to have worked so well in Algeria, that some are thinking of introducing it to French Soudan. That's why, during exercises, the veterans have attracted attention. Their grievances are taken into account, their tattered military ribbons have been restored, they are identified with the hoisting of the colours. The people are made to watch films of the Indochina War and the Algerian War, to warn them what to expect if they dare to follow the lead of the politicians in Koulouba' (Campmas 1978: 145). (On this see also Ginio in Chapter 4 of this volume).

The second controversy was much more serious. This involved northern Soudan and was closely linked both to the Algerian War and to nuclear testing in the Sahara. A year after the 'yes' vote in the referendum, Modibo Keïta revealed to a US-RDA conference the reasons why he voted yes. Besides the afore-mentioned need for unity of AOF, he asserted that 'We had not yet achieved the unity of the country. Indeed, some district commanders in the northern regions had created the mystique of Black and White, provoking animosity between nomadic whites and resident Africans, even if only embryonic. In these conditions, had we adopted a potentially oppositional stance towards a well-entrenched colonial presence, well ...! Northern Soudan would unquestionably have been severed from the country' (Campmas 1978: 140). Thus, whether Keïta was targeting certain local officials or the metropolitan government, he accused France of threatening the territorial integrity of the country.

These accusations were nothing new and were certainly not baseless. Indeed, when the OCRS was created in 1956 (see Sèbe in Chapter 13 of this volume), Amadou Ba, Soudanese deputy in the Assembly of the French Union, stated: 'The creation of this organisation will have far-reaching effects on Soudan; sooner or later, the country's two most important regions, Gao and Timbuktu, will be cut off' (Boilley 1993: 234). From October 1957 to May 1958, two petitions were launched by the *cadi* of the Ahel Arawan, Mohammed Mahmoud Ould Cheikh. The second petition became a letter to the French President, refus-ing categorically to be absorbed into any territory dominated by black popula-tions (Boilley 1999: 292). According to the testimony gathered by Pierre Boilley, French officers were behind the signing of the petitions (ibid.: 254). In January 1959 the SDECE reported on the Soudanese tour of the cousin of the Hoggar *amenokal*, Marly Ag Amayas, who was known to be for the establishment of an autonomous state bringing together all the nomadic peoples of the Sahara. He travelled to the Niger Loop, meeting the leader of the Kel Ifora, Attaher Ag Illi.[16]

At the end of 1959, French officers summoned to the city of Gao the Tuareg chiefs of Ménaka, Kidal Bourem and Gao. One of the officers told them that if they did not favour independence as it stood, they should write to Dakar to ask that the French stay until they gained their own independence (Boilley 1999: 295). The chiefs seemed unconvinced, especially as they met the town deputy Songhay Alhaman Al-Ousseini, who explained that the French were trying to turn them against their fellow Soudanese. Even so, they were far from converted to the new republic and the rebellious movement persisted. In May 1960, the SDECE spoke of a 'Tuareg movement' led by Ag Akhamouk, the *amenokal* of Hoggar who was said to have united the tribes of French Soudan and Niger and was laying claim to the areas that represented the 'heritage of the Tuareg nation'. In Soudan he had the support of the Ifora but also of important figures such as a Bunama Kunta, *cadi* and the leader of the Oulliminden.[17] In March 1960, Ag Akhamouk's nephew was in Kidal meeting with Attaher Ag Illi, to whom he promised refuge and protection in the event that the Malian authorities gave him a hard time. This was no empty promise as at the same time the *amenokal* of the Ifora accused the Bamako authorities of inciting slaves to leave the camps.[18]

From December 1958 to November 1959 all French administrators in the northern regions were replaced by Soudanese. Bamako was still convinced that France had not given up on its plans to forge autonomous Saharan regions and was continuing to work on the nomads. Once again, they had good reason to be wary. In January 1960, during independence negotiations, the Etat-Major Général de la Défense Nationale (EMGDN: General Staff of National Defence) identified the positions it wanted to keep in French Soudan: the continuing military presence in the area of Bamako airport-Kati army base, the maintenance and use of the garrison of Tessalit 'where a million francs have already been invested' to arrange for the layover of jet fighters and finally 'to put a down payment on the future occupation of Gao'.[19] At the end of the month, an inter-ministerial meeting was held in Paris to consider the adjustment of the physical border between Soudan and Algeria. All of the participants emphasised the importance of Tessalit in the panorama of the Saharan southwest. In a telegram dispatched from Niamey on 18 January, [Jacques] Soustelle even suggested incorporating Tessalit into the Algerian Sahara or, failing this, negotiating special status for the base with the Malian authorities.[20] That July, Michel Debré wrote, in a letter addressed to the chief of staff: 'It would seem that the only practical, lasting solution lies in the African governments concerned recognising the autonomy of their white Saharan provinces, administered by French officials trained in nomad-oriented policy'.[21]

The possible extension of the Algerian War into the region was an additional worry for the French and furnished another motive in their efforts to maintain influence there. FLN pronouncements on the establishment of a 'southern front' following the fighting of October 1957 had not had the desired effect. Still, Mali was increasingly opening up to FLN propaganda. In May 1959, the commander of the AOF-Togo defence zone, General Gardet, discovered that pro-FLN groups existed among the North African communities of the Niger Loop.[22] The French administrator of the subdivision of Kidal, shortly before his departure in October 1959, noticed this too, but was not unduly concerned; he felt that the Touati, who monopolised trade relations with Algeria, did not interpret the conflict politically as a 'war between the French and the fellagha'.[23]

Modibo Keïta's attitude was changing. In an interview with *France Observateur* on 11 September 1959, he stated that 'the Algerian question has become fundamental to us'. Then in April 1960, in the same weekly, Madeira Keïta let it be known that Mali would not in the future support France's stance on the issue. In Kidal in October 1959, he had already paid tribute to 'our Algerian brothers, who have fought for their freedom for the past five years, and (who) will obtain it'.

On 18 January the negotiations got under way in Paris in a tense atmosphere. The Soudanese Minister for Public Works set the tone: 'Once we have achieved independence in Mali, we will not tolerate any loss of sovereignty' (Benoist 1982: 465). On 4 April the agreement for the transfer of powers was signed. In matters of defence, the creation of a national army was envisaged, but France would retain the right to train its officers and supply its equipment. The French held a very narrow interpretation of the text. The general chief of staff insisted that the new governments take full responsibility for their armies but also emphasised that the armies should fully adopt French methods, and that in every Community state they act as a hub of French influence.[24]

One of the first problems to be addressed was the 3,000 Soudanese still based in Algeria. They were not unduly troubled by the news of negotiations or the statement of independence, since those who wanted to stay in the French army could do so if they could obtain their government's consent. However, in Algeria it was felt that they had to be repatriated, as this was what they wanted: in Laghouat in January 1960, an NCO declared that if independence were granted they would all return home.[25]

On 24 June, negotiations opened in Dakar on the formation of the Malian army. These took place in a friendly atmosphere between de Brébisson and Mamadou Dia. However, in early August they encountered their first obstacle, with the Malians demanding that their army wear different uniforms from that of the French. For de Brébisson this was an unfriendly gesture whose aim 'could not be other than to eradicate any last shred of French influence'.[26] The most difficult moments were yet to come.

The crisis

The Senegalese and Soudanese visions of the new state differed markedly. Modibo Keïta did not try to hide the extent of the disagreement. On 16 August he declared in Dakar: 'It's simply a question of how we see the political and economic future of Mali ... We have to make Mali not for Mali's, but for Africa's sake.' At the same time, Mamadou Dia asserted that: 'Before anything is created ... before we have established Mali, we must first see to Senegal' (*L'Année politique 1960* 1961). The issue of the presidency was crucial. On 18 August, Lamine Guèye backed the candidacy of [Léopold] Senghor, thus destroying Modibo Keïta's hopes. This was announced just as a fractious argument broke out over the nomination of the future Malian army chief of staff. There were two candidates, both colonels in the French army; one was the Senegalese Fall, backed by Dia, while the Soudanese Soumaré was supported by Modibo Keïta. Dia refused to sign Soumaré's nomination form but, ignoring this, Keïta had it published in the *Journal Officiel* of the Federation of Mali on 25 July, thus triggering the crisis.

The events of the night of 19/20 August that engendered the break-up of the Federation are well-known (see Keese, Chapter 3 in this volume). On the other hand, France's role in the affair is still hazy. For the Soudanese, it was obvious: by refusing to intercede at Modibo Keïta's request, the French High Representative in Dakar, Hettier de Boislambert, chose the Senegalese camp. On the morning of 20 August the borders between Senegal and Soudan were closed and within a month the Franco-Malian accords were considered void. The US-RDA executive spelt out in a communiqué in November: 'The Republic of Mali [the government of Modibo Keïta renamed French Soudan 'Mali'] is not beholden to the French Republic through any accord, to say nothing of defence'. The issue of the French troops' presence came up on 14 September at a meeting between Modibo Keïta, French Representative in Bamako Fernand Wibaux, who was more sympathetic to the Soudanese position than some of his colleagues, and de Brébisson. In an atmosphere that de Brébisson considered tense, though courteous, the Malian president requested the evacuation of the Gao, Timbuktu, Sevare, Kayes and Nioro bases.[27] The French accepted this and acted promptly. On 19 September the transfer plans were sent to Paris and six days later only a token military presence remained in Koulikoro. Withdrawal was not confined to the troops; on 17 October it was decided that the funding and upkeep of the Malian army should cease from 1 January 1961.

These initial demands were part of a profound change in relations with France, exposed in spectacular fashion during the special congress of the US-RDA on 22 September 1960, the day that Malian independence was declared. Speakers insisted on the 'immediate departure of the Community army'. Resolutions demanded speeding up the formation of the Malian army and the rapid repatriation of Malians still serving in the French army in Algeria or Cameroon, and condemned nuclear testing in the Sahara (*L'Année politique 1960*). Recognition of the Provisional Government of the Algerian Republic (GPRA) was not yet on the cards, but Modibo Keïta took up the issue, having previously raised it in August. The most spectacular clash occurred in the UN. On 22 September 1960, the General Assembly voted to admit Mali on the same day as Senegal. Mamadou Aw, the head of the Malian delegation, vehemently rejected French patronage, accusing France of 'genocide' and declaring that: 'The Algerian War is in itself enough reason for African states to break with France' (*L'Année politique 1960*). In early December, the Malians voted a motion in support of the FLN. In Jacques Foccart's opinion, this outburst represented a real insult [to France] and was without doubt behind the animosity that De Gaulle continued to display towards Mali until 1967 (Foccart 1997: 177, 335–6).

The French army pulled out quickly. In December, only thirty officers remained, all drawn from the medical corps and working alongside local armed forces. Therefore, the decision on 20 January 1961 to officially demand the departure of the last French troops came as no surprise. Yet it was seen as 'an unfriendly gesture', according to *Le Monde*. The deterioration in Franco-Malian relations had been perceptible for several days, after the Bamako government sent several *notes verbales* to Fernand Wilbaux. On 13 January, the Malian authorities had complained about the landing of a French plane on Kati's emergency runway but also against irregular payments made by the military, and finally, they condemned the arrival of goods from Dakar despite the formal trade ban with Senegal.[28] For Philippe Decraene, the evacuation of French bases would 'prejudice' the security of Algeria's southern border, and the air force would encounter difficulties in its liaison missions throughout West Africa. More worrying still, the Malian decision coincided with the setting up of a Soviet Embassy in Bamako, and with some important arms purchases, notably from Czechoslovakia (*Le Monde* 22/23 January 1961).

The reaction in Paris was mild. In early February, Wibaux submitted an official memo to Modibo Keïta demanding that the evacuation of French bases be linked to a complete redefinition of relations between the two countries.[29] His brief was to explain the memo, telling the Malians that if France was prepared to accede to their demands, 'disengagement should not remain unreciprocated'. Tessalit itself being a simple aerodrome, Paris wanted a guarantee that it would not be used for military purposes. Furthermore, the Malian authorities should help with the evacuation by allowing freedom of transport. And finally, France wished to terminate military cooperation by requesting the return of its doctors.[30]

The Malians felt that this was not the time for a total reappraisal because, for the moment at least, they wished to maintain relations with France. Therefore, it was far from a Guinea-style scenario, even though a Malian currency had become increasingly likely since the US-RDA congress in September.[31] On 12 October, the first units of the Malian army stood in line for Modibo Keïta, but he showed little faith in soldiers still marked with the 'colonial' imprint. In mid-November, his government introduced a series of measures that would fashion the image of the new army. Officers were sent for training to the Soviet Union, the immediate supply line for the bulk of Mali's equipment. Soldiers' pay would be cut by 50 per cent from January 1961 to bring it into line with civil service salaries.[32] While this was an unavoidable necessity, the measure created bad feeling and prompted a return to civilian life among soldiers with several years experience in the French army.

Breaking with the colonial past obliged Malians to show greater solidarity with the FLN. In February, Mali recognised the GPRA. In July, the government authorised the construction of a training camp at In Tedeyni; meanwhile in Gao, ten Algerian agents had taken up residence. Their leader was even received by the governor of the region.[33] However, this '*wilaya* of the sands' did not have significant financial resources and had trouble recruiting locally. According to SDECE intelligence reports from September 1961, the Algerians' brutal behaviour at In Tedenyi and the contemptuous attitude they showed in Kidal and Tessalit alienated the nomad chiefs.[34] The French took the presence of this small group of Armée de Libération Nationale (ALN) fighters seriously, but refused to panic. Furthermore, no French pressure was put on Bamako to remove them.

This behaviour may have seemed strange; however, as far as De Gaulle was concerned, the writing was on the wall. The referendum of 8 January 1961 gave him *carte blanche* to end the war in Algeria, while the attempted military putsch in April gave him added incentive. In this context, Mali was a secondary consideration, but it was preferable to settle accounts as quickly as possible. In a note to Jacques Foccart on 25 May he stated: 'Even though we've entered negotiations with Mali, we have to press ahead with the evacuation of our bases which present us with more problems than benefits' (De Gaulle 1986: 91). In May, André Malraux was dispatched to Bamako. Franco-Algerian negotiations opened on 25 June following his visit and ended with a general accord on technical and cultural cooperation in February 1962. On 22 September, Modibo Keïta formally acknowledged the normalisation of relations between the two countries. Only seventeen days earlier, the French flag had been lowered at the Bamako air base and the military facilities in Kati had been given over to the Malian army (Fané 2008: 385ff).

This policy change was part of the wider reorganisation of defence under way since 1959. In Africa this implied the rapid withdrawal of existing French forces. Thus, between 1960 and 1964, numbers based south of the Sahara dropped from 60,000 to 23,000. In ex-AOF, the AOF-Togo defence zone gave way to the no. 1 strategic overseas zone, with its command post in Dakar. France decided to build an airborne intervention force, which, despite its lack of funding, was intended to complete a wide range of missions, including the maintenance of order. The Cold War seemed a long way off. The Soviet Union may have grabbed the lion's share in the training and supply of the new Malian army but not the monopoly. Bamako also sent trainees to Morocco and Israel. A team of Americans arrived in the country for a brief period to supervise the training of parachutists, and French intelligence also reported the visit of British military experts. In September, when a group of ALN fighters was captured northwest of Béni Ounif, the French confiscated an important stash of weapons, including MG 34 light machine guns which Israel had sold to Mali.[35] Fernand Wibaux was sure that Mali had not turned pro-Communist. He commented on the Franco-Malian accords thus: 'Following the break-up of the Federation of Mali, the Malians were eager to assert their independence, which explains their position of neutrality. This policy should not be read as support for the East but is probably determined by their concern to appear balanced' (Diagouraga 2005: 107).

Conclusion

On 5 September 1961, several decades of military collaboration and shared sacrifice came to a close. This was the outcome of both Mali's desire to attain total sovereignty and ill-prepared French policy. Moreover, defence issues were never central within the Community; it was as though they were to remain the preserve of metropolitan France. As one officer noted in April 1959: 'At the moment the Community can't create a mystique in the way that the Empire, or to a lesser extent the French Union, once did.' The officers had lost their spark, and 'the prospect of becoming mere local trainers of the national army, having once been leaders, has caused deep disappointment'.[36] This state of mind reflected the uncertainty that had gripped the army as a whole and which the changes announced in Algeria in mid-September 1959 would intensify, revealing a fear of the unknown. *La coloniale* (The French colonial army) was forced to give up its former mission as the Empire's *Maître Jacques* ('Jack of all Trades') to take on new, more technical assignments that implied a change in relations with the Africans.

Notes

1 Archives Nationales du Mali (ANM). 1E 2. Kati, 30 October 1947. Renseignements. Activités des anciens militaires libérés, 1939–1945. Secret.

2 Service Historique de la Défense (SHD) 14 H 55. Dakar, 20 October 1955, Haussaire AOF à gouv. territoires. Diffusion restreinte.

3 SHD 14 H 52. Bamako, April 1956. Réponse du gouverneur Geay au rapport de l'inspecteur Sriber sur le problème de la sécurité au Soudan.

4 SHD 14 H 52. Dakar, 12 July 1956, Inspecteur général de la FOM à Min. FOM. Secret.

5 SHD 1596-3. Bulletins de renseignements, 3rd trimester 1957. Attitude du RDA.

6 SHD 10 T 708-1. Bulletin de renseignements, Ministry of Overseas France, 11 January 1958 (origin: haussariat AOF).

7 SHD 1398-4. Rapport du chef de bataillon Maury, officier itinérant du 5ᵉ Bureau de la 10ᵉ RM. Liaison avec la 4ᵉ brigade d'AOF.

8 SHD 14 H 40. Dakar, 6 March 1959, Chef de bataillon Py à tous chefs de poste SMR. Secret.

9 SHD 1 H 1398-1. Dakar, 17 October 1958. Géné. Commandant ZD AOF-Togo. Situation en Guinée. Secret.

10 SHD 1 H 1398-1. Note de service signée Salan et divers TO d'unités stationnées en Oranie. At this point there were between 4,000 and 5,000 Guineans in Algeria.

11 SHD 14 H 85. Conférence de renseignements sur l'Afrique. Alger, 13–19 November 1959, fascicule 1, Situation dans l'ex-AOF. Secret.

12 Ibid.

13 SHD 10 T 524-4. Notice d'information. SDECE, L'Afrique noire et le FLN (mars–juin 1959), 25 June 1959.

14 SHD 10 T 708-1. Revue de la presse soudanaise, August/September 1959.
15 Ibid.
16 SHD 10 T 539-1. Note du SDECE, January 1959. Secret. La tour took place in December 1958.
17 SHD 10 T 539-1. Note du SDECE, Paris, 12 mai 1960. Secret.
18 Ibid.
19 SHD 1 R 205-5. Paris, 6 January 1960. Cadre militaire de la négociation avec le Mali. Note de l'EMGDN. Très secret.
20 SHD 10 T 708-1. Paris, 20 January 1960. Note à l'attention de M. le directeur de cabinet. Réunion au sujet des frontières Sahara-Soudan. Très secret.
21 SHD 10 T 701-1. Paris, 11 July 1960. Premier ministre à chef EMGDN. Secret.
22 SHD 10 T 708-1. Dakar, 23 May 1959, Gardet à adjoint CEMA. Secret.
23 SHD 708-1. Kidal, 10 October 1959. Essai sur la conjoncture politique dans la subdivision de Kidal.
24 SHD 14 H 143-2. Directive. Paris, 22 July Ministre Armées à général commandant ZD OM n° 1.
25 SHD 14 H 127-1. Laghouat, 1 February 1960. Fiche sur l'état d'esprit de la 13e CSPIMA.
26 SHD 14 H 222. Dakar, 4 August 1960, de Brébisson à Ministre Armées.
27 SHD 14 H 222. 14 September 1960, de Brébisson à Ministre Armées. Secret.
28 SHD 14 H 222. Bamako, 13 January 1960, Wibaux à Foyer.
29 *Documents Diplomatiques Français* (*DDF*), *1961*, I. Paris, 9 February 1961, Instructions pour le chargé d'affaires au Mali.
30 Ibid.
31 *DDF 1961*, I. Bamako, 6 March 1961, Wibaux à Foyer.
32 SHD 14 H 222. Bulletin de renseignements du commandant d'armes de Kati, 22 November 1961. Secret.
33 SHD 10 T 701. Dakar, 29 November 1961. Bulletin de renseignements. Très secret.
34 SHD 1 H 1596-3. Renseignements, September 1961. Secret.
35 SHD 1596-3. SSDNA/SM, 3 March 1961. Interception. Très secret.
36 SHD 1 H 2454. 14 April 1959, fiche sur l'état d'esprit de certains cadres en AOF.

6

Transfer of military power in Mauritania: from Ecouvillon to Lamantin (1958–1978)[1]

Camille Evrard

Introduction

'Ecouvillon', 'Ouragan', 'Cornue', 'Lamantin' … all of these are names that recall the same reality: French military operations on Mauritanian soil between 1958 and 1978. These operations were all secret in nature, although for different reasons: low stakes for the metropole, an uncertain legal framework, unmentionable allies or, quite simply, classification as military secrets. Nonetheless, they weave into and are part of the story of the transfer of military power at Mauritanian independence.

During the years under examination here there was, within the depths of the French state, a perpetual movement of reforms and adaptation to those reforms, succeeding one another without any real continuity. When the French state finally established a procedure to end the colonial era under conditions it deemed acceptable (the contractual mode of *coopération*), it used this procedure almost mechanically. Furthermore, it applied the painstakingly agreed reforms in each colony, then each overseas territory and lastly each member state of the French Community.

Also of note is the rather tense atmosphere that characterised international relations in the late 1950s, returning every now and again like an echo behind the perception that the French in Africa, especially the military officers at their respective grades, had of their role. The memory of the Second World War and the emergence of colonial conflicts that forced soldiers to fight under entirely new conditions fostered the development of a very particular military ideology, which reached its climax during the Algerian War.[2] Soldiers fighting in Algeria found themselves immersed in this ideology (this being true of those who fought in Indochina as well) and the fates of their subsequent assignments doubtless played a part in its propagation. After 1961, Saharan and sub-Saharan territory became the space most open to military personnel seeking 'action', which is why the facts I study here are so significant.

On closer examination of the Mauritanian case, we see that to these metropolitan and international problems corresponded territorial realities of another kind, which were nonetheless just as important. These were at once political, cultural and historical contingencies creating an environment on Mauritanian soil in which the transition from a colonial army to a national army was particularly significant. The territory adapted to the stages of the transfer of military power in a practical way, because of the urgent need for a pragmatic transition that was created by the struggle against the Moroccan threat to its integrity, a struggle that was shared by both coloniser and colonised.

In addition to being the year of Moroccan independence, 1956 was also the year in which French overseas territories began developing towards internal autonomy after the adoption of the *loi-cadre* (see Keese 2003, and in this volume Chapter 1 by Shipway). This had great significance for the military, as the formation of territorial governments in 1957 meant that the army was obliged to gradually adapt to a 'local' authority on one hand, and to the central authority of the metropole on the other.

Istiqlal claims over Mauritanian territory led to the deployment of a reinforced military presence in the northern regions, starting in 1957. Operation Ecouvillon, led by French troops in 1958, fought off armed rebels led by Moroccans, but the border area remained under close surveillance for many years. The French army intervened again in early 1961, a few months after the proclamation of Mauritanian independence, when defence agreements had not yet been signed. The Community, theoretically still in place, provided a valid legal framework to this action.

After the total evacuation of French forces from Mauritania in 1966, the French embassy in Nouakchott announced that the French government remained determined to lend assistance to the Mauritanian government if needed, through its armed forces stationed in Dakar or even with units coming directly from France. This scaling down of the French military presence was in line with the overall trend across the African continent at the time. However, the situation in northern Mauritania once again created a specific case: the French army intervened again on a significant scale in 1977/78. Indeed, Spanish decolonisation of the Western Sahara in 1975 and the fight of the Polisario Front against the occupation of a part of this territory by Mauritania forced the latter country to call on the French Air Force, which stopped columns of the Front moving towards Nouakchott.

This brief overview points to the toing and froing between the different aspects that make Mauritania both a representative 'case' of what took place elsewhere in former French Africa, and *sui generis*, that is, specific to Mauritania. In the ensuing military interventions that did not take place within the strict legal framework of defence agreements, one of the characteristics of the process of the transfer of colonial power is evident: the hasty, sometimes improvised and, above all, 'case by case' management of events; which implied, in a way, construction by experimentation.

With its focus on the transfer of military power in Mauritania, the analysis presented here, based on a larger study (Evrard 2008), is at the crossroads of political and institutional history on the one hand and military history on the other. It seeks to build conceptual bridges between a vision of State and 'system' on the one hand, and individuals, former military officers operating in the Sahara, thus giving a more pragmatic – an almost sociological – perspective, on the other. We will focus in particular on three periods of the broader chronology: Operation Ecouvillon, the defence agreements, and Operation Lamantin. This examination of the Mauritanian example allows us to explore the direct consequences of the process of decolonisation in the field. It is a context in which military problems were solved with particular attention to local issues, to technical details in the negotiations and through something that could be called an experimental process. It also makes us aware of poorly analysed key events such as Operation Ecouvillon, which have to be interpreted in their relationship to upcoming independence and to the impact of Moroccan-Mauritanian affairs on the creation of the identity of the emerging state of Mauritania.

The Moroccan threat and its impact on the military evolution of the territory in the late 1950s

Moroccan claims over Mauritanian territory were gradually made public in the spring of 1956 in various speeches given by Allal el Fassi, one of the Istiqlal leaders, although these claims were not officially supported by the Moroccan monarchy at the time (Guillemin 1982: 137). The argument, in addition to its cultural and religious aspects, was certainly also political, since linking Mauritania to Morocco was a way, in the propaganda, of not allowing the establishment of a future 'puppet' state on the payroll of 'French imperialism'.

The military aspect of these claims was somewhat difficult to sort out. When Morocco achieved independence on 3 March 1956, some Army of Liberation (*Armée de libération* or *AL*, that emerged in 1955[3]) combatants refused to pledge allegiance to the Sultan and government and did not join the Royal Armed Forces. More specifically, this 'army' was divided into a Northern Army, whose action was focused on the Ifni and Tarfaya enclaves (still Spanish but located in Moroccan territory) and a Southern Army,[4] which recruited Sahrawis from the Spanish West African territories.[5]

At the same time, military capabilities within French West Africa had, since the end of the Second World War, been rather limited, as they suffered from a permanent lack of strength as well as a complex organisational structure. In response to the Moroccan threats, the Senior Commander-General of the Armed Forces of the French West Africa-Togo Defence Zone (Général commandant supérieur des forces de la zone de défense AOF-Togo, General Gabriel Bourgund) sent a rather vindictive memo to Gaston Defferre, the Minister for Overseas France (via the High-Commissioner of Dakar) in March 1957 in an effort to obtain reinforcements as quickly as possible for the new operational command that he wanted to establish:

> The events of January and February and the threat that is becoming clearer from the borders of Spanish West Africa put Mauritania on the same operational level as Algeria, as one cannot accept the contrast between favoured Mediterranean territories and neglected African territories.

> Now, Algeria has 350,000 men on active service.

> Morocco has a French *presence* of 80,000 men.

> French West Africa, to rise to the challenge in Mauritania and to keep the peace in a country seven and a half times as large as France, has only 20,000 men.

> The imbalance is obvious and is a result of the conversion of French West Africa between 1951 and 1956 into an accelerated training depot and transit centre for African reinforcements heading first to Indochina, then to North Africa ...[6]

Bourgund was supported in his request for additional resources by the Governor of Mauritania (Albert-Louis Mouragues), who emphasised the risk of 'contamination' of the populations, and recommended financing auxiliary units to block the path of the Army of Liberation.[7]

After initial operations in early 1957, made possible by units sent from Dakar (notably the 7th Colonial Parachute Regiment and the 1st Autonomous Motorised Detachment of Thiès), the range of needs was met. But these reinforcements withdrew far too many troops from the Dakar region and none of these units could be permanently kept in Mauritania. In May 1957, Bourgund finally secured major reinforcements, comprised of units from North Africa. By the end of May, Mauritania showed its new face as a 'country in arms'. At the time, the Moroccan government still officially condemned the actions of the Army of Liberation, if one is to believe the diplomatic communications between the Moroccan Minister of Foreign Affairs, Ahmed Balafrej, and the French administration.

Roger Chambard, diplomatic adviser to Gaston Cusin, the High-Commissioner in Dakar, tried to defend the Mauritanian cause in Paris at the beginning of 1958. The Minister of Defence in Felix Gaillard's government, Jacques Chaban-Delmas, helped to calm the fears of the Ministry of Foreign Affairs (Chaffard 1965). Because of international opinion, the Spanish had to be put in a position where they were asking for French military support; but above all, the French Socialists had to be convinced about this collaboration with Franco's regime.[8] In the end, the beginning of the operation had to be postponed at the last minute because of the Sakiet Sidi Youssef affair: on 8 February 1958, the French army bombarded and burned down this Tunisian village near the

Algerian border, as retaliation for an attack by Algerian insurgents; the combatants having then fled to the Tunisian side of the border. The bombings caused many civilian victims. Both flanks of Algeria were thus dangerously exposed.

Bourgund had already been working for some time on the details of the Ouragan military operation, which relied on close coordination with Spanish troops. He planned a two-stage offensive: to destroy the bulk of the Army of Liberation stationed in Seguiet el Hamra and to take back Smara. Then, his plan foresaw the 'cleaning up' of Rio de Oro using a coordinated manoeuvre out of Fort Trinquet (now Bir Moghrein), Fort Gouraud (now Zouerat) and Port Etienne (now Nouadhibou) for the French, and El Aïoun and Villa Cisneros for the Spanish. The French forces' manoeuvre plan was named 'Ecouvillon' and the Spanish operation 'Teide'. On the French side, 5,000 soldiers were available for combat, compared to 9,000 on the Spanish side. Operation Ouragan began on 10 February 1958, lasted 15 days and remained south of parallel 27°40 in order to avoid confrontation with the Moroccan Royal Army (the loyal forces, Forces Armées Royales).

Although the operational status was not commensurate with the means engaged, it was agreed to present this operation as a success: the major part of the AL bands had retreated to the north of the Seguiet el Hamra northern border (parallel 27°40), and the rest were completely disorganised in the region south of the border. The rebels suffered 132 dead, 37 injured and 51 prisoners, while French forces claimed 7 dead and 25 injured. On the other hand, the rallying of several hundred Rgaybats[9] to the camp of the French authorities had significant political consequences for Mauritania's future.

It would be tempting to describe these military events of the late colonial period in Mauritania as 'foundational' vis-à-vis the process of the transfer of military power. There are indeed a considerable number of intelligence reports and military instructions related to this episode in the archives, military as well as political and at all levels – local and central. For example, the Government-General in Dakar received reports on these questions from the Service de Documentation Extérieure et de Contre-Espionnage (SDECE) (External Documentation and Counter-Espionage Service) local office.[10] In the meantime, the SDECE informed Jacques Foccart's office of any political event, especially if it was related to the exploitation of the iron and copper mines[11] – this started as early as 1958, when the Secretariat-General of African and Malagasy Affairs had not yet been created (see Bat, Chapter 9 in this volume) and Foccart was merely technical adviser for African affairs to De Gaulle at Matignon. This leads to the conclusion that the military experience played an important but also peculiar role: it involved the military and psychological defence of a territory by its occupant. Great efforts were deployed – logistically, financially and in terms of human resources – for the territory, and the colonial administration tried to rally the population behind it to face the designated enemy, thus fostering a certain territorial unity.

Figure 6.1 Operation Ouragan in Mauritania (1958).

However, the secrecy of operations meant that French military personnel could not have their battle successes recognised and left them with feelings of great frustration: the dead were not honoured as they could have been in more important and well-known theatres of operations. However, the battles nonetheless contributed to strengthening the bonds between French military officers and some of the Mauritanian combatants, who from that point onwards felt a solidarity created by having fought a common enemy.

One of the most important consequences of the success of the Ecouvillon operation, and also of Moktar Ould Daddah's growing influence – he was then vice-president of the government council – was the meeting in Tinketrat in April 1958. This place, situated north of Fort Gouraud, played host to a huge ceremony during which the Rgaybats solemnly swore allegiance to Ould Daddah: more than 400 tents had been pitched for the occasion.

In the spring of 1959, provisional agreements were drafted that established the legal conditions for the intervention of French armed forces in domestic peacekeeping on Mauritanian territory. Agreements on the transfer of jurisdiction from the French Community to the Mauritanian government were signed by mid-1960, and the Islamic Republic of Mauritania officially came into existence on 28 November 1960. To further understand the process of military transfer, agreements and practical aspects of this crucial period of 'independence' need to be analysed.

The defence and technical military assistance agreements of 19 June 1961 and the creation of the national army

Defence agreements most often included – and the case of Mauritania is no different in this respect – a main text stipulating the duty of mutual aid between both countries to prepare and equip a defence force, and the possibility of Mauritania calling on France to help with its internal and external defence, under conditions established in special agreements.[12] It would seem here that these special agreements never saw the light of day; with the result that one would not be mistaken in thinking that French participation in some actions was defined by the contingencies of the situation rather than by clearly established texts. One of the most striking examples of this is Operation Cornue: the maintenance of military cover along the northern border for several years after Operation Ecouvillon. It was put in place at a time when the defence agreements were not yet signed, and few details of the operation are available to the researcher.[13] The defence agreements that were put into effect contained two appendices: the first on the operation of defence committees and the second on cooperation in the area of raw materials and strategic products. Then came the technical military assistance agreement, which set out the conditions for the collaboration required for the successful establishment of the Mauritanian army. The first annex of this second part of the agreement specified the elements to be transferred to or provided for the new army. The second related to the status of French military personnel on Mauritanian soil (specifically with regard to discipline, justice and facilities). Finally, the third annex clarified the areas of mutual help in matters of defence; in reality it listed all the concessions made by Mauritania to the French army (freedom of circulation, tax exemptions, the right to hire civil workers, etc.).

In addition to these texts two exchanges of letters discussed issues regarding the Port Etienne and Atar bases. They have remained secret; were not published and are not reproducible today, but they can be consulted in the Vincennes archives. Port Etienne is a particularly interesting case as Michel Debré had insisted on the French presence here with Moktar Ould Daddah. The port (present-day Nouadhibou) was the hub for processing what would become the country's two vital resources: mineral ore (iron and copper) and, to a lesser extent, fisheries. The railway built with the help of an International Bank for Reconstruction and Development (Banque internationale pour la reconstruction et le développement: BIRD) loan would link the Koedia-Ijill deposits to the port, where major infrastructures were built. Moreover, the city of Nouakchott was anything but a budding capital at that time, with no real link to the port, which made Port Etienne a unique place for French forces and highly significant for a potential overall military strategy for Africa and the Atlantic. The letter signed at the time of the agreements specified the facilities recognised as being under the control of the French Republic's armed forces in the region:

> The territory, territorial waters, airspace are under the sovereignty of the Islamic Republic of Mauritania; the armed forces of the French Republic enjoy, without any limitations concerning the size of the deployment, the right to provide facilities for storage, protection, supply, instruction, liaison, and transmission, and [unrestricted] movement and circulation in the terrestrial, aerial and maritime space relevant to Mauritanian sovereignty.[14]

François Beslay, who participated in the negotiation of these agreements as military affairs adviser to the Mauritanian president, explained that this was the most difficult point to get the Mauritanian government to accept, as the latter feared the establishment of a French base similar in size to the Dakar or Abidjan bases (personal communication, March 2003). The ensuing defence committee meetings maintained this position, with France insisting that the Islamic Republic of Mauritania provide a long lease for the Lévrier Bay area, on which French military installations were to expand.[15] However, Beslay indicated that, despite the fact that such installations were built at the time, the French military had never occupied them as it had more strategic bases elsewhere.

Things were different in Atar, since Moroccan-Mauritanian tensions had driven the French posture to expand considerably in this regional capital: it contained the command for all northern garrisons and nomadic units covering Adrar and Zemmour, from 1957 onwards. During the months before agreements were signed, the Mauritanian government tried to obscure the French presence: in the view of the government, French troops were too visible in a sensitive area where pro-Moroccan sympathies were very present. Despite this, the government in Nouakchott finally allowed French troops to have air force installations at their disposal, so as to provide an essential supply base for the undercover operations in the north.[16]

In any case, the differentiation between French and Mauritanian armed forces finally took shape with the creation of the Mission of Military Cooperation, and the status of French military personnel was defined in the agreement documents. A Military Assistance Bureau administered and organised the payment of the French military personnel made available to the Islamic Republic of Mauritania. The French government was responsible for their appointment, although it was later often the subject of lengthy negotiations. On the Mauritanian side, the Head of State was in charge of defence but delegated technical developments to the Secretary-General of Defence (Mohamed Ould Cheikh). Assisted by Commandant Paul Mourier (François Beslay's successor since August 1961), Ould Cheikh had to prepare all defence issues for the deliberations of the

Council of Ministers, ensure the establishment and organisation of Mauritanian armed forces and prepare legal texts dealing with defence, conscription and the status of troops. Finally, he took the title of Chief of General Staff and was supposed to sit on the Defence Committees – although Paul Mourier seems to have assumed this task most of the time (personal communication, July 2003).

On 1 July 1961, the Mauritanian army consisted solely of eight active African officers (five cadet officers in Saumur, two in Coëtquidan, one in Fréjus) and one at the Grenoble military college. An entrance examination had just taken place to recruit a new pool of candidates to train as reserve cadet officers (*élèves officiers de réserve*: EOR), but their very poor results meant that no more than one or two candidates could be selected. Therefore, the government planned to fill the vacancies via a radio call to all individuals who held the first part of their baccalaureat diploma. Indeed, it did not want to lose the slots set aside for Mauritanian nationals in French schools under the Plan Raisonnable.[17] The embassy in Saint-Louis even sent a request to the Ministry of Cooperation for an exceptional regime to cover candidates with a low level of training or who were ineligible because of age requirements. Referring to Mauritania's 'pressing need' for specialists, the French embassy in Saint-Louis asked for the indulgence of the selection juries in order to enrol such candidates in the Brest Sea Cadets School (École des mousses) and the Saint-Mandrier School for Apprentices in Mechanics.[18] The lack of military executives, particularly strong in Mauritania, led the Mission of Military Cooperation to open a training school for officers in Atar (Ecole de formation des officiers de l'armée de terre). However, as Jacques Eté confirms, the senior staff of the Mauritanian army remained French for a long time.[19]

The status of Mauritanian military personnel was another challenge for the country's Ministry of Defence. It was expected that the units transferred from the French army would remain under the responsibility of the French Republic until 31 December 1961. By this date, Mauritanian officials at the ministry needed to have prepared the statutes of the Mauritanian army, while explaining to new contingents the temporary continuation on the French payroll.[20] As for military service, an 'empirical regime' had been adopted in agreement with the Mauritanian authorities since 1960. As a result, approximately 1,200 men were enrolled at the start of 1962, without having to make military service mandatory.

On 25 September 1961, a brief from the Directorate of Military Affairs at the Ministry of Foreign Affairs indicated the precise number of personnel for the creation of the Mauritanian Army and the forecasts for the coming year. At the end of 1961, a first group of 467 men was being transferred to the Mauritanian army, but the lack of Mauritanian officers and specialists did not allow for other transfers in that year.[21] Whatever additional troops were needed had to wait until 1962, when military aid amounting to 132 million CFA francs was allocated for the army and another 148 million CFA francs for the gendarmerie.[22] It would not take long for the financial issue to affect the maintenance and functioning of the Mauritanian forces, as the Islamic Republic of Mauritania budget would have had a hard time covering the 800 million CFA francs that specialists had calculated were required to manage the total number of personnel to be transferred. The Mauritanian government asked France to take on (in the budget) until 31 December 1961, the elements transferred, which the French side agreed to do. As for the gendarmerie forces, they were in fact already at the 'permanent and direct' disposal of the Mauritanian government, but no official transfer of units or any associated solemn ceremony was planned.

In 1966, the French vacated Atar, where the last permanent military contingent was stationed. This marks the end of the actual transfer of military power as regards the French personnel on the ground. It was a process, when one looks into it in detail, driven by very down-to-earth and essentially pragmatic considerations, despite the existence of the Plan Raisonnable and the delicate balance of power. During the following ten years, the French military presence was progressively reduced to a very low level.

Of particular note here are the process of trial and error and the negotiations that led ultimately to the difficult birth of the Mauritanian army that was in practice scarcely – if at all – autonomous. The process was slow, costly and above all very dependent on conditions on the northern border, where the Moroccan threat remained real. One of the most striking examples of this was Opération Cornue, which provided military reinforcements and increased surveillance of Seguiet between the end of February and mid-May 1961. It enabled the French military command to organise once again the defence of the north against possible Moroccan action at a time when the Algerian war was in full swing and defence accords had not yet been signed with the new Mauritanian government.[23]

Opération Lamantin and the return of the French army to Mauritania

By way of conclusion to our analysis, the resurgence of French military action that took place on Mauritanian soil in 1977 needs to be underlined. While Franco-Mauritanian relations had cooled considerably following what François Constantin and Christian Coulon called 'the murder of the father' (Constantin and Coulon 1979), France nonetheless launched a relatively significant air operation to come to the rescue of the Mauritanian army, weakened by two years of war against the Polisario Front.[24]

Since December 1975, Mauritanian units had replaced the Spanish army in some of the Western Saharan garrisons, after the Madrid agreements had been signed. These agreements made the Spanish retreat effective, and also confirmed the partition of Western Saharan territory between Morocco and Mauritania

– without providing for any process that might lead to self-determination for the Sahrawi (Caratini 2001 and 2003; Mohsen-Finan 1997). Officially, the French government invoked the security of French engineers working for copper and iron mining companies in Zouerat to intervene.

This intervention took place despite the fact that two years earlier, in February 1973, Mauritania had unilaterally revoked the cooperation agreements with France, as well as the defence agreements. It also created its own currency in June 1973 with the support of the Arab world, to which it had been getting closer for some time – the Mauritanian government was in particular aided in these efforts by Algeria, Kuwait and Libya. In November 1974, it nationalised the most important company active in the country, Miferma.[25] In fact, the cooperation agreements had become legally invalid by that time and had to be renegotiated; the new agreements of 15 February 1973 made no mention of defence.

However, the difficult situation into which Mauritania gradually slid in the ensuing years, related to the war with the Polisario Front in Western Sahara, initiated the renewed presence of military *coopérants*[26] at the Atar military school, starting in 1976. This assistance was expanded in early 1977 when military personnel at all levels of the hierarchy were sent over.[27] The whole of Mauritanian society progressively felt the negative effects of this questionable effort by the government (with French support): its army and the economy were much weaker than the means Morocco had at its disposal to face the same military resistance. When attacks from columns of the Polisario Front turned out to be obviously beyond Mauritania's capacity to contain them – on its own soil, to the south of Zouerat, at the very end of 1977 – the French command launched Operation Lamantin. It consisted of direct airborne attacks, concentrated between December 1977 and May 1978, although the operational staff remained in place until May 1980 (Forget 1992: 88). This was well after the fall of President Ould Daddah, who was deposed by a military coup on 10 July 1978.

One can think that the 'Father of the Nation' had disappointed many of his army executives and more generally his people, in calling in Morocco and France to help (Moroccan troops had also been deployed on Mauritanian territory after the creation of a bilateral High Committee of Defence, in May 1977). Ould Daddah's fate is sadly ironic when one remembers that he had spent a significant part of his political career striving to maintain Morocco at bay and minimising Mauritanian dependence on the French after 1970 (Hodges 1983: 305).

Subsequent to the military coup, Lieutenant Colonel Mustafa Ould Saleck took power, announcing Mauritania's disengagement from the Western Saharan campaign (Dabezies 1978; Ould Saleck 1979). He was among the first generation of Mauritanian officers trained in France in 1961/62, like the majority of senior officers who held key positions in the successive military governments in Nouakchott: no fewer than four coups took place between the fall of Moktar Ould Daddah and the taking of power by Colonel Maaouiya Ould Taya on

12 December 1984.[28] This shows the closeness of the relationship between the French colonial army and the national army of Mauritania, which not only played itself out in the army but had important consequences on Mauritania's political life as well.

Conclusion

In this chapter I have attempted to follow the process of the transfer of military power using a chronological framework, but as an alternative I could have taken as starting point the study of the nature of African national armies. One possible analysis of these armies (Evrard 2008: 147–62) suggests that the Troupes de Marine (colonial troops) model was not imposed as a direct copy, but rather was transmitted by gradual permeation. This was a more abstract form of transfer, linked to French mentality and military tradition. Second, criticism of the model shows the conjunction of two 'handicaps' from the beginning of African national armies: an imbalance that could be called sociological, related to the urgent need for training officers, and a second resulting from an ill-defined conception of the role of the army in a newly independent country.

Finally, the analysis of the colonial military model and the criticism of the transfer process become particularly interesting when confronting the problem of the creation of the Mauritanian nation and the 'relative' aspect of sovereignty thus acquired. Apart from the fact that the French military presence was visibly prolonged for a considerable period of time in Africa after the first phase of technical military cooperation and assistance, that the French government made excessive use of bilateral aid (Lacroix 1965) and that it failed to hide its geostrategic and geopolitical interests (Gaillard 1995: 333–4) behind the alleged altruism of its intentions, it is on the very foundations of its management of overseas cooperation that it can best be attacked. Obviously, because the French sought to develop a specific system solely dedicated to its African partners, French governments were accused of neo-colonialism. In military terms, the uniqueness of the African 'regime' is evident, insofar as the other nations with which France has maintained relationships of military cooperation have been directly managed by the Ministry of Defence (Ministère des armées at the time).

This is by no means comparable to the multiplication of actors and obscure distribution of military responsibilities in the several services to which cooperation with African governments was entrusted in the period following independence. Indeed, at the time when defence agreements were signed, the Parisian organisation was, with regards to the Constitution, quite clear. The Prime Minister held the principal responsibility for military cooperation (thanks to his Etat-Major Général de la Défense Nationale: General Staff of National Defence). The two ministries directly involved attempted to work together on the pragmatic aspects of this cooperation: the Ministry of Defence and the

Secrétariat d'état aux relations avec les Etats membres de la Communauté, which became the Ministry of Cooperation in May 1961. This department was born from Michel Debré's attempts to better coordinate French actions in the former colonies of sub-Saharan Africa. Once independent, however, these countries were also of concern to the diplomatic services at the Ministry of Foreign Affairs. Last but not least, France's allies such as the Mauritanian government also had to deal with the preeminent place of the Presidency in the decision-making process regarding African military affairs (under Jacques Foccart as Secretary-General). In short, the system was strongly criticised because it appeared to be tainted by elements that had already existed in the colonial period (Luckham 1982).

An examination of the transfer of military power at the time of Mauritanian independence that focuses on the French army's military operations and the nature of the process that led to the establishment of the national army reveals both the opacity of the French modus operandi and the disreputable alliances that the French authorities were obliged by the local situation to conclude, but above all it demonstrates the pragmatism that ultimately characterised the transfer of military power. The difficult birth of the Mauritanian national army provides another example of the lack of forward planning and the ad hoc nature of the solutions adopted by the late colonial state. At the same time it shows the importance of personal relationships between military men on the ground, who shared military traditions and a certain way of thinking. Finally, it provides an insight into the direct consequences of the French system in the field and heightens our awareness of hitherto little known events such as Operation Ecouvillon, the significance of which is most appropriately analysed against the background of the coming of independence and the shadow that tensions between Morocco and Mauritania cast over the creation of modern Mauritanian identity.

Notes

1 An earlier version of this chapter was published in French in *Afrique Contemporaine*, n° 235, March 2011, 29–42.
2 Especially with regard to new doctrines (psychological warfare and counter-revolutionary war) (Pernot 2002, Géré 2010).
3 This Army of Liberation recalls the Berber desire to oppose the Makhzen (see Rivet 1999, and Vermeren 2006).
4 Many names have been used to designate this army, but in the French archives one mostly finds the term 'Moroccan Army of Liberation'. Even so, some of the former Saharan military use the local name: *Djich Ettharir*.
5 Especially some Rgaybat, nomadic populations covering the whole region: Moroccan, Spanish and French (Algeria and Mauritania) territories. There were also Teknas from Goulimine and Tentane, and Berbers from the Rif (Caratini 1989; Beslay 1984: 166–7).
6 Archives militaires, SHD, Vincennes, 5H33, Gabriel Bourgund, Senior Commander-

General, to Gaston Cusin, High Commissioner of French West Africa (military office) (n°3/3.178/CONFINS), 4 March 1957.

7 Archives Nationales Sénégalaises, Dakar, Senegal (ANS), GGAOF, 17G/616: Albert-Louis Mouragues, Governor of Mauritania, to Gaston Cusin (n°515/Gvr), 28 December 1956, and (n°517/Gvr), 29 December 1956.

8 Few references can be found on the subject of French/Spanish relations during Franco's regime. See for example Dulphy 2005.

9 See note 5.

10 ANS, GGAOF, 17G/616, *Bulletins de renseignements SDECE pour GGAOF* (sent to Mr Campet), February 1957.

11 Archives Nationales (AN), Fonds privé Foccart, AG5/FPR/246, *Note du SDECE pour la Présidence du Conseil* (n°9467/A), 18 July 1958, and (n°12445/IIA), 31 October 1958. See also Bat, Chapter 9 in this volume.

12 Archives militaires, Vincennes, 14h210/2, *Accords de défense avec la République islamique de Mauritanie.*

13 Archives militaires, 15h82 (d.1), *Opération «Cornue» et situation politico-militaire en Adrar 1961*, conserved in Fréjus at the Chetom (Centre d'Histoire et d'Etudes des Troupes d'Outre-Mer/Centre of History and Studies for Overseas Troops) and in Vincennes (microfilms).

14 Archives militaires, Vincennes, 14H210/2, *Accords de défense avec la République islamique de Mauritanie.*

15 A loan of 2,000,000 French Francs was decided in May 1962 to create this base, as it was indeed considered as strategic from a global defence point of view, Archives diplomatiques du Ministère des Affaires Etrangères (MAE), Direction des Affaires Africaines et Malgaches (DAM), 2698/B; *Comités de défense 1962–1965.*

16 Archives militaires, Vincennes, 14H210/2, *Accords de défense avec la République islamique de Mauritanie.* Any definitive decision was therefore postponed to future Defence Committee meetings, which settled these questions only very slowly. French military installations were progressively dismantled during the years that followed and Atar was the last place to be evacuated in 1966.

17 Plan for the transfer of men and military equipment, agreed in the Technical Military Assistance agreements.

18 AN, Fonds public Foccart, AG/5 (FPU)/3, Pierre Anthonioz, Ambassador and Special Envoy, to Jean Foyer, Minister of Cooperation, 22 September 1961.

19 From 1957 to 1962, he served in *méharistes* units in Mauritania (personal communication to the author, 4 August 2003).

20 In order to put these technical elements of the transfer into perspective, its personal relational aspects remain to be further studied.

21 MAE, DAM 2698/A. Pierre Anthonioz, *Note of the Saint-Louis Embassy: Armée mauritanienne 1961–1969*, 25 September 1961.

22 Archives militaires, SHD, Vincennes, 5H150, *Notice sur la Mauritanie, Archives de campagne 3ème trimestre 1962.*

23 *Archives militaires*, 15h82 (d.1) *Opération «Cornue» et situation politico-militaire en Adrar 1961*, conserved in Fréjus, at the Chetom (Centre of History and Studies for Overseas Troops) and in Vincennes (microfilms).

24 Front populaire de libération de la Seguiet el Hamra et du Rio de Oro (Popular
    Front for liberation of Seguiet and Rio de Oro): a rebel movement fighting for the
    independence of the former Spanish Sahara from Morocco.
25 This company (created by the French during the colonial period) was extracting iron
    from the Koedia of Ijill. It became subsequently the SNIM (National and Industrial
    Mining Company of Mauritania).
26 To be understood as part of the cooperation agreements.
27 On the progressive military reinforcement of Mauritania in the late 1970s, see
    Elsa Assidon's article in *Le Monde diplomatique*, February 1978, and Tony Hodges
    quoting *Le Monde* (Hodges 1987: 305–6).
28 For a detailed chronology of this period – although it gives no further analysis – see
    Mohamed Lemine Ould Meymoun (2011).

Part III

Continuities and connections

Franco-African security relations at fifty: writing violence, security and the geopolitical imaginary

Bruno Charbonneau

Violence was intimately linked to colonisation and colonial violence was, in turn, informed and justified by multiple logics. As a practice, it sought, in various ways, to enforce or impose particular dynamics of inclusion and exclusion. As Martin Thomas (2011: xii) writes, the 'organisational cultures of France's colonial security forces ... often acted as a barrier to reflective engagement with colonial people'. The post-Second World War period saw African political demands for reform, liberty or independence often meeting with force and violence. While the wars of Indochina and Algeria are well known, the massacres of tens of thousands by the colonial armies at Sétif (1945), Haiphong (1946), Casablanca (1947), and Madagascar (1947/48) are frequently forgotten as the context of what has often been represented as the 'successful' decolonisation of Francophone sub-Saharan Africa.

This chapter seeks to understand the continuity of Franco-African security relations since decolonisation. It is argued that the year 1960 did not mark the end of violence, but rewrote it as a different type of violence: one coming out of relations said to be international that affected the limits of tolerable and legitimate violence. Statehood and independence created the conditions for interstate relations and cooperation, thus allegedly putting an end to imperial violence. Despite numerous claims that French militarism and policy of intervention changed after 1960 and have changed since the end of the Cold War, the French state was found in the twenty-first century to intervene militarily, again, in Côte d'Ivoire, Chad, Mali and the Central African Republic (CAR). Despite unquestionable transformations, how can one explain that, fifty years after decolonisation, France continues to intervene militarily in African politics? How can one understand, for example, that the French use of force in Côte d'Ivoire led to a regime change in 2011?

The significance of these questions goes beyond the specific context of France-Africa relations because, as the events of the 2010/11 post-electoral crisis in

Côte d'Ivoire showed, both French and United Nations (UN) peace operations invoke comparisons with colonial and imperial violence (Charbonneau 2012a; Cunliffe 2012). The central concern of this book, to discuss the meaning and effects of decolonisation after fifty years, is therefore not an academic exercise without practical and concrete expressions in current Franco-African relations nor without importance for debates over the purpose and legitimacy of today's international peace operations. In fact, the disarming openness with which imperialism is invoked publicly to justify peace operations (Ignatieff 2003; Marten 2004) suggests the urgent need to analyse colonial violence and its legacy.

This chapter argues that the question of violence – how it is deployed, authorised, and legitimised, its representations, and what we are meant to learn about great acts of violence – is central to providing any sort of interesting answer about French-African security relations at fifty. Violence is here understood as more than an act that destroys, but also as a pedagogical tool that works to control narratives of space and identity and as a politically enabling device that affects agency. Edward Said (1993: xiii) emphasised the significance of such control: 'The power to narrate, or to block other narratives from forming and emerging, is very important to culture and imperialism, and constitutes one of the main connections between them.' In today's 'global peace governance' context (Duffield 2007; Richmond 2011), as Michael Shapiro argued, analysts and policy-makers that are preoccupied with the 'geopolitical strategies of violence' interpret national maps as constituting the unproblematic basis for policy action. Hence, decision-making related to violence is both justified by these 'violent cartographies' and works to inhibit alternatives to the dominant state-centric geopolitical imaginary (Shapiro 1997). Problematising the question of violence is meant to highlight how violence writes a specific geopolitical imaginary of France, Africa, and their place in the world, and how this writing affects the formation and enabling of diverse agencies. Put another way, I locate the legacy of colonial violence in its intellectual predispositions and in its control over stories about violence, security and the geopolitical imaginary. I proceed chronologically to underline the changing yet similar ways in which violence and security have been 'written' and to emphasise two periods of significant transformation, namely decolonisation and the end of the Cold War.

Colonial violence

Discussions over the value or relevance of concepts such as neo-colonialism, new imperialism or similar images that carry an implicit understanding of current France-Africa relations are controversial, but at least they point toward the increasing uncertainties about the significance of decolonisation. Historians have demonstrated that colonisation and decolonisation were not straightforward 'us' and 'them' situations, and that colonial authority worked best when the colonised recognised it or contributed to its implementation (Chafer 2002b; Cooper 2005). While there is little agreement on how to characterise post-1960 France-Africa relations (are they 'international', 'neo-colonial', 'neo-imperial', 'special', or something else?), the legalistic interpretation of decolonisation that establishes African statehood seems to be a dominant one. The year 1960 represents a moment where a strict line is drawn temporally and spatially between imperial and international imaginations, worlds and territories. Temporally, the line establishes a narrative of moral evolution from a time of illegitimate imperial dynamics to a time associated with legitimate relations between legally-equal sovereign states. The line also has spatial effects in that it dismantles the geography of empire to transform it into nation-state spaces. This new spatial grid marks these spaces as 'sovereign', thus as outside the realm of imperial intervention and power. Within this mindset, decolonisation is deployed as an authoritative assertion and political strategy to establish the political stability and coherence of these nation-state categories (like 'France' or any African state). However, as students of Franco-African dynamics know, it often proves difficult to distinguish clearly between France and Africa and French and African agencies. As Gary Wilder argued, the 'French imperial nation-state' should be analysed as a whole and as 'an internally contradictory artefact of colonial modernity that was simultaneously imaginary and real, abstract and concrete, universalizing and particularizing, effective and defective, modern and illiberal, republican and racist, welfarist and mercantilist, Franco-African and Afro-French, national and transnational' (Wilder 2005: 21–2; see also Costantini 2008). These contradictions are in fact the locations of incredibly rich and complex mixes of global, imperial, national and colonial processes, structures and relations. Are we to assume that these contradictions disappeared after 1960?

Notions of citizenship, republicanism, nation, sovereignty, democracy and others were constituted within and across an imperial imaginary and space (Stoler and Cooper 1997). Yet, the strong majority of discussions about current France-Africa relations and French African policy is dominated by state-centric conceptions of political space and identity that obscure the contradictions, ambiguity and contingency in the construction of French and African states and identities. As Michael Shapiro argued in the context of the American colonisation of Hawaii, state-centric analyses is where we observe 'static national culture or set of racial and ethnic maps superimposed on state-administrated territories' (2004: 14). Put another way, the contingent and negotiable nature of state agency and national identity is neglected or ignored by the assumption that the agency of the state comes from the ontological stability of the national identity. The risk is to produce ahistorical accounts of state formation and nation building that obscure 'the pervasive incompleteness of state nationalizing initiatives' (ibid.: 40). Decolonisation did not mark definitely the line between France and Africa because the line needs to be endlessly rewritten, as the crises and debates over the *banlieues*, the Roma and immigration in France suggest (see Tshimanga, Gondola and Bloom 2009).

Within this context of moving and contested identities and relationships, the role of violence seems crucial in establishing the authority of state-centric narratives and thus of a geopolitical imaginary that authorises and re-legitimises the practices of Franco-African security relations and associated political agencies. The French twist to state violence was in linking so intimately French and African states in a common writing of violence and security. Indeed, on the one hand, the violence of the colonial encounter created divergent moral spaces that discriminated between the superior 'French' and the inferior 'African', thus authorising intervention, but it also created, on the other hand, a space of common 'Franco-African' identity. The military conquest of Algiers in 1830 generated what Georges Balandier described as the 'colonial situation'; that is, spaces of coercion and racist ideology where Africans had to work with or against imposed structures, norms and rules (Balandier 1951). Yet, the processes through which these structures, norms, and rules were imposed can hardly be described as a national (French) polity projecting its power beyond its borders, and as clearly grounded in a colonised/coloniser opposition. The day-to-day routines of the French empire involved contingent accommodation and experiences of violence that informed processes of identity formation, both in France and in the colonies. Military and police routines and operations included a diverse mix of experiences: 'patriotism, idealism, the romance of the exotic, challenging hardship, close comradeship (not only with other Frenchmen), but also careerism, personal gain, racial assertion and temptations for the weak in character' (Clayton 1988: 19). Until decolonisation, Africans of various origins participated in wars of conquest, pacification campaigns, and other actions of coercion (Echenberg 2009). These shared experiences validated, for some, the purpose of the empire, inspiring loyalty and identification. The armies of Africa were deployed in almost every French war: la Coloniale served in Algeria, the Crimea, Mexico, Italy, the Dardanelles, the Balkans, the Levant, Tunisia, Morocco, the western Sahara, the wars of 1870–71, 1914–18, 1939–45 and the political repression and wars of decolonisation in Madagascar, Indochina and Algeria. Through these varied and numerous soldiering experiences, a Franco-African militarism and associated identities emerged out of contradictions that challenged the commonly accepted opposing binaries of France/Africa, French/African. This military-imperial system was paternalistic, racist and full of tensions and apparent paradoxes, but one that, 'providing so centralised a role for military units raised in the colonies but officered by Frenchmen and providing for regiments of metropolitan Frenchmen dedicated to imperial roles, offered strength and flexibility in the eras of empire-building and empire-policing' (Clayton 1988: 8). For influential French officers such as Joseph Gallieni (1849–1916) and Louis-Hubert-Gonzalve Lyautey (1854–1934), the fact that African soldiers waged wars of French imperialism was not exploitative, but instead contributed 'to the dignity of indigenous cultural peoples' (Clayton 1988: 4). Even among Algerian and other African soldiers, many believed that the military system was more just than the non-military aspects of the colonial system. In spite of discriminatory and racist experiences, revolts and desertion were rare (Joly 2009: 8). Many African veterans are proud of having served under the French flag (Echenberg 2009).

The significance of this Franco-African military system is in how it wrote violence and the use of force not only in ways that made violence acceptable, but also in ways that performed the authority and legitimacy of the empire, and performed 'French' agency in opposition to 'African' agency. Many African soldiers went on to internalise the militarised and militarising values conveyed through practices of imperial building and policing. Many of them would go on to be the core of African national armies and governments after 1960. As the historian Anthony Clayton (1988: 10) wrote, the 'romance of these regiments in varying measure shared by all ranks and races was an important ingredient in their soldiering; no study of them can set it aside as imperial mythology'. Put another way, shared experiences of violence taught them that the geopolitical imaginary of empire was 'real'.

And yet, the same military experiences were also the roots of protest, challenges and resistance against the empire. Some African veterans attached themselves to the Parti communiste français and participated in the Union intercoloniale and the *La Paria* newspaper of Nguyen Ai Quoc (later known as Ho Chi Minh). Frantz Fanon's experiences during the Second World War subjected him to a colonial racism that changed radically his views of French universalism (on Fanon, see Ahluwalia 2010). Shared experiences of violence and warfare, notably the two world wars, produced contradictions: desire, feelings and discourses about the coherence of the empire and the common destiny of different peoples, but they also marked in blood and destruction and through racist tropes and practices the very difference between 'us' and 'them', between the 'civilised' and the 'barbarians' and 'savages', between a moral space (continental France and Europe) and an exceptional space (the colonies) where the laws and rules of war were allegedly different. While France was facing various political demands for reform or independence after the Second World War, violence was still authorised and legitimised through the narratives of a civilising mission that was gradually transformed into 'development' in the late 1950s (see Meimon 2007), and that promised partnership and cooperation within a revised imperial space.

The use of violence, however, was often the quintessential effect of contra-dictions, where the universal claims and particular practices of empire met. The interplay between the contingent circumstances of empire and the actions of specific individuals produced, on several occasions, massacres and other acts of violence, but it also challenged the very functioning of the empire and transformed colonial perceptions. After 1945, as Martin Thomas (2011: xxvii) writes, 'Rapidly changing cultural expectations in the colonies and in France about permissible interventionism and permissible levels of violence – about what colonial administrations could or should be doing – added to the weight on official minds'. Over the long term, colonial violence exposed the contradictions and limits of the French imperial nation-state and associated identities. The universalising ideals of the civilising mission that sustained the idea of empire could only be undermined by the particular national assumptions associated with the construction of French nationhood and nation-state. The historical construction of French nationhood and European national ideologies, perhaps even before African nationalist movements, both needed and challenged modes of imperial governance. In other words, the 1940s and 1950s were a context of increasing tensions between national and imperial modes of governance, of growing ambiguities and uncertainties over the spatial referents of new national ideologies. The end of the Second World War brought the new United Nations Charter that universalised the nation-state as the legitimate form to organise the political community. In this sense, decolonisation is a moment (albeit a crucial one) of various and sometimes competing initiatives and practices to re-build, re-construe, and re-imagine the political community.

Postcolonial violence (or the era of security)

Jacques Foccart argued that the 'oeuvre' of cooperation was 'the essential condition for the success of the gradual evolution of the colonised nations towards running completely their own affairs by giving them the means to construct a state administration without which nothing can subsist and, consequently, without which their cultural, economic and social development cannot be achieved' (Foccart 1964: n.a.). As such, 'military cooperation' after decolonisation was linked to development and should, in theory, have been conceived as a means to support the sovereignty claims of the new African states, although the maintenance of French influence was in reality also a key factor. Insofar as its aim was to build functional African armies, military cooperation can be said to have failed (Bagayoko-Penone 2003: 164–72). Moreover, the transition process from an imperial model of Franco-African troops and armies to a model of national armies was gradual, sometimes tumultuous, and intimately intertwined with the political process of decolonisation. As Camille Evrard has demonstrated in the case of Mauritania, tensions rose from the necessary collaboration between a political apparatus that was becoming African and a military apparatus and command that remained 'white' for years after decolonisation (Evrard 2008, see also Chapter 6 in this volume). In the end, African political leaders had few options, given their very limited resources. The French military quickly became a dependable source of support to consolidate their regimes.

In common discourse, decolonisation rewrote the imperial model as 'international relations' between legally sovereign member-states of the United Nations, thus writing them as between nominally equal partners. They authorised the permanent existence of French military bases (originally in Senegal, Côte d'Ivoire, Chad, Djibouti, Gabon, Cameroon, and the Central African Republic), the presence of 'pre-positioned' French troops, the presence of French officers in the ranks of the African armies and the option for the French state to intervene militarily almost anywhere (Charbonneau 2008a; Granvaud 2009). During the Cold War era, on top of military interventions to support or topple African regimes, numerous routine interventions must be considered: military exercises, protection of French citizens and ambassadors, shows of force, humanitarian deployments, UN missions and undetermined others. Africa became both an exercise ground for French troops (notably Special Forces) that were without any chance to have such 'prestigious training' elsewhere and a place to show the strength of the French military in circumscribed missions. These aspects of a 'muscled presence' represent the routines, habits and effects of the Franco-African security apparatus (Charbonneau 2008a: 68–72). As Robin Luckham (1982, June) argued, this French militarism has represented a permanent state of intervention that has influenced the composition of social forces, the role of the state, and the distribution of material and political resources of many African states.

The Cold War provided the rationale to authorise these particular practices. The rapid construction of a transatlantic security community around NATO played a key role in transforming Franco-African security relations. After the War of Korea (1950–53), Charles De Gaulle could say: 'Finally, France is the only world power whose army currently fights communists' (in Benot 1994: 33). Within this mindset, African social and political movements could be categorised as pro-Soviet or, later, as pro-Chinese and pro-West, thus informing and influencing the kind of independence, violence and security that were deemed tolerable. President of Côte d'Ivoire Félix Houphouët-Boigny was explicit about his pro-West and anti-communist stance as he worked (often with France) against the rise of communism and 'radical nationalists' in West Africa (Schwab 2004). Furthermore, the war in Indochina suggested that the empire could hardly be held together through force any more, while the Suez crisis of 1956 suggested that the French state could not maintain its world influence and power without the at least tacit support of the US government. In short, the 1950s and 1960s were radically changing the global context of the empire: the UN Charter on the one hand, and the Atlantic Charter on the other, combined to define and redefine the political possibilities of a Franco-African field of action.

For Franco-African security relations, the year 1960 is a crucial moment when a new space is generated where the 'transatlantic community' and the 'France-Africa community' converge. This space makes possible to re-imagine the French empire into the *'pré carré'* (i.e., sphere of exclusive influence). The struggle against communism, while obviously not new in 1960, became increasingly important in the context of the Cold War and thus became the official narrative justifying Franco-African violence in Africa; a discourse that is still often found in academic publications to explain French security policy (see Chaigneau 1984; Chipman 1989; Granvaud 2009; Pascallon 2004; France-Sénat 2006). This Cold War rhetoric whereby France is the defender of Western interests in Francophone Africa largely legitimised the various mechanisms, structures and violent practices of post-1960 French militarism. It transformed France into the *gendarme de l'Afrique*. This *gendarme* is impossible to imagine without the transatlantic geopolitical imagination. Africa is re-written and re-imagined as a space for privileged interventions, not because it is under the authority of the empire, but because it is transformed into a site where the perceived necessities and obligations of Cold War politics authorise and justify the subversive and coercive actions of the French state. Where the 'transatlantic community' met with the Franco-African militarism, the epistemological foundations of the Cold War security imagination had fundamental ontological effects: 'France' became an ontologically stable nation-state completely distinguishable from African states. Decolonisation was implicitly conceived as rupture, but in fact also implied ontological commitments that obscured the continuous effects of violence of French-African relations and agencies. African states became separate state entities that were partaking in the geopolitics of East–West confrontation. African agency (whether leaders or various socio-political movements) was fundamentally affected. To seek or ask for change in paternalist and neo-colonial arrangements resulted in being labelled communist. The space for legitimate African political agency narrowed significantly (for more on the transatlantic link, see Charbonneau 2012b).

This global context is not meant to dismiss the particularities of France-Africa security relations that sometimes had little to do with the actual Cold War, nor to underestimate the evolution of the politics of French intervention between 1960 and the end of the Cold War and the struggles in establishing the French dominant position in Francophone African politics. It is to emphasise the structural conditions of possibility that re-authorised a particular writing and understanding of violence, and how this re-writing of violence participated in the transformation of agency. The judgments and claims that were associated with the perceived necessities of Cold War politics obscured the post-1960 violence of Franco-African security relations, if not erasing it at times (for examples, see Verschave 1998). The right to insurrection, to resistance against oppression and inequalities, and even to determine the foundations of one's society was denied by the legitimacy and authority of the *gendarme*, albeit often with the explicit approval or cooperation of African political elites. The transatlantic security community implied that no one would or could question (or only at great personal risks) the effects of introducing violence and a Franco-African militarism as permanent feature of African politics. Informed by Eurocentric habits of mind with respect to global order and the possibilities and necessities of African politics (see Grovogui 2001), the use of force and the French military become useful or necessary instruments to overcome the so-called limitations of African societies and to protect them from perceived unwarranted (communist) influence.[1] The Cold War and the transatlantic community replaced the colonial rationale that was lost at decolonisation and from which the particular claims of France-Africa security practices could be justified and sustained. The end of the Cold War would also require drastic changes in discourse and practice.

Liberal governance

As decolonisation rewrote France-Africa relations, the end of the Cold War destabilised the narrative of the *gendarme*. It was in 1994 that the end of the Cold War fully caught up with French militarism. The French involvement in the Rwandan genocide (see Charbonneau 2008a: 121–48; Kroslak 2007; Périès and Servenay 2007) called into question the legitimacy of French militarism and initiated a rather significant shift in policy. While some have been quick to pronounce the death of the 'special' relationship (Glaser and Smith 2005) or la Françafrique (Smith 2010), events like the Omar Bongo, Denis Sassou-Nguesso and Jean-Marie Bockel saga (Laurent 2008), the unending French military interventions in Chad and the region (Charbonneau 2010a), and the most recent intervention in Côte d'Ivoire in April 2011 (Charbonneau 2012a) suggest that there might be something 'special' left in France-Africa security relations. How can we explain this continuity? Is there any point talking about decolonisation when examining twenty-first-century French security policy in Africa? Is there any link between this 'security policy' and the history of violence explored in the previous sections? Is there a lingering 'colonial legacy' to these interventions?

Continuity can partly be explained by the military infrastructure. The French state retains strategic military bases in Gabon, Senegal, Djibouti and La Réunion/Mayotte. Interestingly, the website of the État-major des Armées (EMA) now lists French deployments in Côte d'Ivoire, Chad and the CAR as ongoing operations rather than bases or pre-positioned forces (as of this writing in April 2012), despite a long and uninterrupted history of military presence in these countries. In any case, with the gradual development of 'projection forces' during the Cold War that permitted troops to be stationed in France but ready to deploy swiftly in Africa through French African bases, the French government has been able to incrementally close some bases and to diminish the number of permanent troops on African soil. The purpose of military bases has gradually changed towards this logistics support role for projection forces. Despite this restructuring, the number of troops deployed on the African continent has held steady at approximately 10,000 since 1997, including pre-positioned forces and 'non-permanent' forces deployed on diverse operations (Charbonneau 2008a). This infrastructure guarantees that the French state remains an inevitable player in African politics and in all kinds of military or humanitarian interventions on the continent. The 2008 defence and security *Livre blanc* is clear in this regard: 'Africa will be at the forefront of our preventive strategy for the next fifteen years … France wishes to stay on the African continent, but the conditions, the purposes and the organisation of this presence must evolve' (France 2008: 154).

The 'conditions, the purposes and the organisation' that must be changed have emphasised multilateralism, but within a conceptual framework reminiscent of 'civilisational' boundaries. The governing assumptions underpinning the changes introduced to French security policy in Africa continue to produce narratives that discriminate between a world of peace and prosperity (i.e., France, Europe, the West) and a world of conflict, underdevelopment and instability (Africa in particular). In this regard, the 2008 *Livre blanc* is telling, notably if it is read in the context of concrete policy changes towards Europeanisation and NATO, interventions in Côte d'Ivoire and Libya (2011), and resurgent dreams about Eurafrica (see Charbonneau 2012a; 2008b).

The *Livre blanc* is construed as a necessary intellectual *state* exercise to counter the risks and threats facing the 'nation'. Indeed, the French state is presented as protecting and assuring the 'security or protection of the nation', or the 'life [vie] of the nation': 'The objective of the national security strategy is to counter the risks and threats that may affect the life of the nation' (France 2008: 62). The expression 'vie de la nation' conveys the idea that the state protects and serves the interests of a national collective identity and community that are unproblematic. This governing assumption allows to externalise all threats and dangers and to justify responses to said threats and dangers. The *Livre blanc* does it in two ways. First, globalisation is offered as the general context that 'does not create a better or more dangerous world' but an 'international system that is clearly more unstable, less controlled, and thus more alarming, that calls for answers that are both global and very specific' (France 2008: 33). The conveyed assumption is that 'France' does not participate in globalisation or in its alarming or destabilising effects; it only suffers them. France is conceived to be at the centre of a continent that is 'at peace with itself and the rest of the world' (Juppé and Schweitzer 2008: 21; see also France 2008: 310). Second, the 'very specific' is identified as a corridor that goes from West Africa to the Oman Sea. In this corridor, Africa is interpreted as the space that produces illegal immigration, religious fundamentalism, terrorism, illicit traffics and health risks that have direct consequences upon French interests (France 2008: 44–6). In short, Africa, much like the rest of the non-European world, is portrayed as a space from which threats and dangers can come to a Europe conceived as peaceful (this view is widespread; see also Assemblée nationale 2008; France-Sénat 2006; Juppé and Schweitzer 2008).

The recent changes in Franco-African security relations must also be examined through the larger construction of hegemonic institutions and mechanisms for global liberal governance that seek to impose the legitimate limits of violence and peace in Africa.[2] The 'Europeanisation' of French policy has brought hopes for new institutions and modes of governance, policy-making and solidarity, and thus hopes for renewing Franco-African relations. 'Europe', from the French government perspective, offers both material and moral resources. It can participate and share the costs of intervention, just as it can re-legitimise the French presence in Africa (see Charbonneau 2008b). Indeed, in many official documents, the reader is constantly reminded that the bilateral approach to Africa must be sustained and prioritised, but that the multilateral approach is likely to be the most common framework for intervention: the 'multilateral framework guarantees in effect the legitimacy of France's actions on the ground, while sharing the risks of standstill or contagion of crises, notably in the case of military intervention' (Assemblée nationale 2008: 68; see also France 2008: 71–4; France-Sénat 2006: 34, 39). The European Union is conceived as the 'multilateral framework' par excellence because it combines legitimacy, as a multinational and multilateral entity, and efficiently, as an international security actor (Charbonneau 2009).

The enlargement of the EU is argued to have been confirmed and consolidated by NATO's own (France 2008: 23). This transatlantic link is, again, crucial. On the one hand, European cooperation is necessary to face the specific threats and dangers coming from sub-Saharan Africa (ibid.: 44). The increasing numbers of illicit traffics transiting through Africa and the 'issues relating to the supply of strategic raw materials, in any event, call for the careful attention [attention redoublée] of European states' (ibid.: 154). France and the EU, it is argued, must be ready to use force and increase their intervention capacity, but should also contribute to the development of an African regional capacity. On the other hand, the transatlantic link confirms 'Europe' as a space distinguishable and separate from an outside world of threats and dangers. The perceived complementary of the EU and NATO (ibid.: 99–101) works to confirm and consolidate a Eurocentric writing of security that isolates Africa and African security problems from the world. In the numerous debates over humanitarian and military interventions, over peacebuilding activities, and over the 'responsibility to protect' or 'human security', what seems to be constant is in how the West is portrayed as an external saviour, one that has not participated in the genesis of any 'humanitarian crisis' and can be called upon to save the day (Orford 2003). This worldview can be seen in the common discourses and narratives about the existential, cultural, ethnic (and racist) sources of African conflicts (Grovogui 2001), in the dominant representations of North-South relations that authorise interventions (Doty 1996; Slater 2004), and in the inequitable power relations between the North and Africa at the United Nations (Adebajo 2009).

This worldview is not particularly new. It is no surprise that some Ivoirians, for instance, invoked comparisons with colonial violence and imperial dominance when the French and UN military intervened to impose 'peace' in April 2011. For some Francophone African elites this provides a useful means to distract attention from their own shortcomings. However, the most significant lingering effects of colonial violence seem to be in how it narrates conflict, violence and security. In a world of 'opposing civilisations', conflicts become existential, violence is largely irrational and references to African 'tribes' or religious allegiance convey already formed explanations to understanding conflict, and thus an implicit programme of action that a priori authorises violence. In a world of opposing civilisations, Africa is the neglected 'child' that must be protected from itself and from undue outside influence, as then Minister of Foreign Affairs Bernard Kouchner made clear when he called for a 'Western alliance' against the negative influence of China in Africa (AFP 2010). In sum, there are two interrelated tropes that suggest the lingering effects of colonial violence that decolonisation (and the end of the Cold War) transformed, but did not fully disrupt: (1) the 'special' character of France-Africa relations that focuses on bilateral mechanisms; and (2) the 'civilisational' prejudice that locates France strictly inside the 'West' and Africa outside of it and that focuses on multilateral institutions and mechanisms of global governance.

Conclusion

The focus of scholarly analysis has usually been on French or French-African interests, whatever or wherever they may be, in order to explain French security policy in Africa. Such explanations are unsatisfactory to understand long-term dynamics because, while they contain elements of the truth, they cannot encompass the obstinate permanence, longevity and uniqueness of Franco-African security relations. The orthodox analysis is based upon and reproduces an antagonist cartography of individual nation-states, despite the increasing uncertainties in the geopolitical boundaries of states. Violence is then construed within this state-centric and geostrategic cartography, which presumes the need to defend these national borders and boundaries.

In the *Livre blanc*, it is argued that defence and security cooperation 'must be based upon *analyses of common security interests*, participate directly in the rise of peacekeeping African forces and promote the role of the European Union' (France 2008: 155, my emphasis). The first point is undoubtedly the one that is never, or very rarely, challenged, but also the one that, as I have argued here, might be the most significant in understanding the continuities within the transformation of Franco-African security relations. The legacy of colonial violence is in its intellectual predispositions, in the control over stories about violence, security and the geopolitical imaginary. This dominant geopolitical imaginary erases the history of older maps and of violently displaced practices of space and identity. Within a specific geopolitical imaginary, the practices of military interventions and their intellectual representations are woven together in narratives that obscure the violence of France-Africa relations. 'Peace' works as the new rhetorical device for legitimising violence (Charbonneau 2012a).

There has been both continuity *and* change in Franco-African security relations: it could hardly be otherwise. From a research standpoint, it would be necessary to complement the analysis proposed here with a detailed examination of African agency, if only to avoid the impression that the processes of knowledge and narrative production are somehow willed or controlled. There is little doubt that African leaders (notably political and military) cannot be dismissed or forgotten in generating and reproducing the practices of 'French' militarism (thus my use of the 'Franco-African' adjective), just as resisting and opposing practices influenced their development. However, despite the need to consider African agency in our analyses of the daily workings and discourses of Franco-African security relations, there has been very little African capacity to offer alternative interpretation, analysis or intellectual framework to understand and explain the role of violence and militarism in Franco-African relations. This is a key reason why the production of narratives and knowledge about 'analyses of common security interests' is fundamental. Where is this knowledge being produced? To ask the question is halfway towards an answer.

Acknowledgements

I wish to thank Tony Chafer, Alex Keese, Geneviève Parent and the anonymous reviewers for their comments and support in improving this article, and the Social Sciences and Humanities Research Council of Canada for its financial support.

Notes

1 On how such a culture continues to predominate in the French Africa-oriented armies, see Leymarie (2010).
2 By 'global liberal governance', I refer to the conventional wisdom (but draw on its critique) of international humanitarian, development and military intervention policies and practices that seek to police the non-Western worlds (see Duffield 2007).

8

French *coopération* in the field of education (1960–1980): a story of disillusionment

Samy Mesli

'From now on, *coopération*,[1] will be a major French undertaking', announced President Charles De Gaulle in 1964. When the territories that made up France's colonial empire in sub-Saharan Africa (Afrique Equatoriale Française [AEF] and Afrique Occidentale Française [AOF]) gained their independence four years earlier, each of them signed a series of bilateral agreements with the former metropole in order to benefit, in particular, from the technical and financial aid that De Gaulle had promised. This policy of *coopération*, henceforth to be based, in theory at least, on the principle of partnership, developed rapidly and covered many fields of activity, including the economy (with the creation of the Franc zone), defence, health, communications and culture. Its goal was to underpin the economic and social development of these young independent nations, while also maintaining France's presence in and continued domination of its '*pré carré*' (sphere of influence) in Africa (Chafer 2002b).

French colonial history has attracted much scholarly attention in recent years, giving rise to a number of debates around the theme of the 'colonial fracture' ('fracture coloniale') (Blanchard and Bancel 2005). However, it must be noted that the focus of much of this literature has been on the political links between France's and Africa's governing elites in the post-colonial period, often referred to by the term 'Françafrique'; (Gounin 2009; Verschave 1998). In comparison, and considering the significance of the resources devoted to it and the wide range of actions covered, it is surprising that, with a few notable exceptions, little attention has been given to *coopération* in these studies. Albert Bourgi (1979) and Bouhout El Mellouki Riffi (1989) have written books on the subject, a small number of articles analysing French development aid policy have been published (Bossuat 2003, Jacquemot 2011) and the activities of the Ministry of Cooperation have been examined by Cadenat (1983) and Meimon (2005). Apart from the work by Claire Visier (2003), cultural cooperation, which is nevertheless an important component of French foreign policy, as evidenced by the network of Alliances Françaises and cultural centres established around the world, remains little studied.

Alongside culture, education is a central element in French diplomacy; in 1963, there were more than 32,000 French teachers working abroad (Jeanneney 1963: 66). Indeed, from 1960 onwards, the extent of this aid to Africa was considerable, mainly because of the poor state of the education system inherited from the colonial period. As Raymond Pourtier states: 'colonial schools were only accessible to a small minority of young people, just sufficient to meet the needs of the colonial administration for "writers" and other auxiliaries'. In 1960 the new states faced three major problems: to increase school attendance, to Africanise syllabuses [and] to establish the relative priority to be attached to primary, secondary and an almost non-existent higher education sector' (Pourtier 2010: 101). Thus, in order to support the efforts of the governments of the newly-independent states, France made *coopération* in the field of education a priority, as can be seen both from the scale of France's financial contributions and the number of French teachers working there – more than 6,000 by the end of the decade, making education the priority area of *coopération*, although this aspect of Franco-African relations remains largely unrecognised.

This chapter sets out to fill this gap by drawing up a review of educational aid from 1960 to 1980, which is the period of the greatest number of exchanges. The following decade was marked by a decline in such *coopération*, in particular as a result of French budgetary constraints. We will first of all examine the goals and principal areas of activity of French educational aid, before focusing on the record educational *coopération*, drawing particular attention to its failure to adapt to African realities.

The goals of *coopération*

Jacques Basso (1992: 257), lecturer in development law at the University of Nice, has noted that the goals for *coopération* were many and various: 'generosity, sometimes extended to include the idea of "historic reparations", solidarity, self-sacrifice; but also safeguarding one's own economic interests, an undisguised assertion of influence, a quest for power which is the opposite of obliteration, but which by the same token perpetuates a type of domination'.

Grafted on to France's stated desire to continue to exercise influence in its former empire, *coopération* has several objectives. First, it aims to promote the development of the newly independent African states by supporting the emergence and modernisation of central government services, economic and rural development and the training of new elites. In this context, education plays a central role and is seen as a lever for promoting the economic and social development of the young nations. Following the 1961 UN conference in Addis Ababa, which set the objective of universal primary education by the 1980s, the development of education became a political priority.

Beyond these aims, it was the whole range of difficulties confronted by the African states that came to form the primary mission for *coopération*. This serves to highlight a paradox: as the scale of French cooperation became massive after 1960, so the review of France's performance as a former colonial power became at the least questionable. The educational structures inherited from the colonial era were in fact skeletal. Even in Algeria, where French structures were most developed, primary school attendance among the Muslim population barely exceeded 15 per cent in 1954 (Léon 1991: 224). The rates for secondary and higher education were even lower, whereas more than 97 per cent of European children were in school. Besides highlighting the inequality between the local population and those from metropolitan France, these figures show how underdeveloped the educational structures put in place by the French were.

Even if some progress was made after 1958 under the aegis of the Community, the situation in the majority of Francophone sub-Saharan Africa remained dire. Before independence, schooling was provided to barely 4 per cent of the population in Upper Volta. The situation in neighbouring countries was not much better: in 1960, the percentage of those attending primary school in Niger and Mauritania was 6 per cent and in Mali 9 per cent. With certain exceptions, like Madagascar and Côte d'Ivoire, the average school attendance rate in the former French colonies south of the Sahara was around 25 per cent, less than in English-speaking countries. That figure also masks some large disparities between towns and rural areas, and between boys and girls.

There was much to be done, then, for the young African states, which had first to come to terms with a shortage of equipment. In 1963, Robert Tric, inspector from the Ministry of Education, had visited Africa and reported that:

> There is a troubling lack of teaching materials for geography and history. I attended a geography lesson about Russia in Dahomey. A miserable, dusty scrap of a map was the only teaching aid available. Apologies are constantly being made for the lack of globes. The teaching of history is generally not supported by any materials.

> The shortage of textbooks is acute in every country. At the teachers' training college in Katibougou (Mali), the philosophy class has only two textbooks at its disposal. My contact with rural primary schools (in Togo and Dahomey) brought to my attention the acute hardship brought on by the shortage of elementary textbooks in reading and arithmetic. Some states are much worse off than others. There is a huge amount of work to be done.[2]

Equally revealing is the case of Chad. In 1968, the Chadian authorities gave an alarming account of the state of the school system there:

> Our primary schools operate in terrible conditions: the teachers lack the necessary qualifications; there are not enough classrooms and teachers, which results in situ-

ations incompatible with serious education (in some classes in the south, there are between 100 and 200 pupils); nine classes out of ten are conducted inside grass or mat walls, which have to be put up again every year by the students when they return to school; school furniture is almost non-existent; and overall the courses are not fit for purpose, contributing to migration from the countryside and not preparing children to work on the land.[3]

As this report demonstrates, added to the lack of equipment was a shortage of qualified teachers. At the same time as these school systems were facing a rapid increase in the number of pupils, teacher-training institutions, already too few in number, proved themselves incapable of supplying enough qualified teachers, particularly for secondary education. Finally, France's objective was to defend the position of the French language. This cultural link and the use of a common language were priorities for De Gaulle that were shared by African leaders such as Senghor, Diori and Bourguiba. Moreover, the Ministry of Education attached central importance to maintaining French as an official language on the African continent, in the face of the advances made by English because of the presence of Western teachers and the establishment of schools and universities financed by Western states and private partners, notably American foundations and missionary congregations. In bilingual countries, such as Cameroon, France also supported the development of educational institutions to ensure the place and standing of French language and culture. This effort was to be strengthened by the creation of various francophone organisations, including the Conference of Education Ministers Sharing the French Language (Conférence des ministres de l'Education ayant le français en partage: CONFEMEN) in 1960, and the Agency for Cultural and Technical Cooperation (Agence de coopération culturelle et technique: ACCT) ten years later.

The different types of aid

This particularly bleak picture of the educational systems inherited from the colonial period underlines the scale of the task ahead. French aid would consist of two main types. On the one hand, there was financial aid granted to the African states, of which a large part was for the construction of school and university infrastructure; on the other, aid came in the form of a huge number of teaching personnel, with France sending several thousand *coopérants* to African countries every year.

At the start, the financial aid and subsidies given by France were granted through the Aid Fund for *Coopération* (Fonds d'Aide à la Coopération: FAC). This organisation, established in 1959, would devote part of its budget each year to education, in order to support the development of school infrastructure. In 1961, 27 million francs were granted under the aegis of the FAC. These investments increased rapidly in subsequent years as, by 1967, investment in education by the FAC exceeded 44 million francs.

The large scale of this investment facilitated the construction or extension of numerous schools across the continent. Although in its early years this effort was directed towards primary education in order to absorb the rapid increase in the number of children being schooled, the government also gave priority to second-ary education by establishing secondary schools, sixth-form colleges (*lycées*), and further education with the opening of technical and teacher training colleges.

However, higher education was also a priority of the French efforts: between 1959 and 1967, universities absorbed more than 38 per cent of the FAC's budget. During the same period 27 per cent of the budget went to secondary education and around 13 per cent to the primary sector, whereas only 7.4 per cent was invested in technical and professional education. The remainder of the FAC's budget was mainly for the purchase of teaching materials and equipment (Labrousse 1971: 117).

Beyond these financial contributions, French aid was notable for the number of individuals sent to African countries. In fact, no other country has staked as much on this type of intervention: every year, several thousand French teachers were sent abroad in the cause of cultural *coopération*. In 1960, out of 10,000 technical *coopérants* sent to Francophone Africa, only 2,416 were teachers. As Table 8.1 shows, that number had increased to 4,675 by 1964, the first year in which military *coopérants* were included, numbering 255 National Service Volunteers (Volontaires du service national – VSN) that year. The creation of this new category of technical assistants, which had been proposed the year before in the Jeanneney Report, allowed the number of teachers and managers being sent abroad to be reduced by using these young graduates, who would thus perform their military service as civilians (Grossetti 1986).

By the end of the decade, the number of teachers had practically tripled, partly

Table 8.1: Number of teachers working in Africa from 1960 to 1970

Date	Teachers	Number in VSN Programme
1/1/1960	2,416	
1/1/1961	2,794	
1/1/1962	3,233	
1/1/1963	4,040	
1/1/1964	4,675	255
1/1/1965	5,182	698
1/1/1966	5,517	887
1/1/1967	6,121	961
1/1/1968	6,502	1,082
1/1/1969	6,274	906
1/1/1970	6,671	1,119

Source: (Bourgi 1980: 412.)

thanks to the increased number of military volunteers, who made up around 20 per cent of the 1970 total. From then on, the number of volunteers continued to increase at the same rate: by 1974, 7,090 teachers were based in Africa. By the start of the 1980s, the number of individuals posted to black African countries by the French had reached 13,000, of which two-thirds were teachers. So in the field of education, the effort was sustained. However, in the area of technical *coopération*, there were by 1970 fewer than 4,000 expatriate technical assistants, indicating a marked decline in the importance of this sector.

While *coopération* should have been temporary and transitional, the continuation of French aid raised some real issues. Indeed, if the presence of these teachers undeniably contributed to the development of education in the 1960s, by becoming permanent, *coopération* seems in the long term to have applied a brake to the emergence of truly African school systems. The transition from a system of *coopération* based on *training* to one based on *substitution* (of African by French teachers) thus undoubtedly impeded the process of Africanisation of syllabuses and school structures.

Table 8.2 shows the situation in 1965 and illustrates how the amount of aid varied considerably from country to country. Certain states, like Madagascar, Côte d'Ivoire and Senegal, appear privileged in the amount of aid accorded to them, in part because they played host to the largest number of French

Table 8.2: Number of teachers by country in 1965

Country	Civilians	Military	Total
Cameroon	390	74	464
Congo	259	41	300
Côte d'Ivoire	840	165	1,005
Benin	116	26	142
Gabon	153	40	193
Burkina Faso	189	50	239
Madagascar	952	125	1,077
Mali	220	51	271
Mauritania	74	17	91
Niger	141	58	199
Central African Republic	200	40	240
Senegal	862	124	986
Chad	163	79	242
Togo	74	8	82
TOTAL	4,633	898	5,531

Source: MEN-19770641, art. 1, *Activity Report from the Directorate of Cooperation, Ministry of Education, 1965-1966*, pp. 4–5.

expatriates, but also because they had the biggest universities on the continent, where the posts were filled by French teachers.

The majority of overseas teachers were in secondary education, representing 68 per cent of the 4,633 civil servants assigned to Africa. This is explained by the slow rate of Africanisation of secondary school teachers. By contrast, primary school teachers made up barely 10 per cent of the total, the rest of these positions being held by Africans.

The training and management of teachers in such numbers required a commensurate amount of administrative support, involving several stages: advertising the exchange, recruitment, selection, preparing the *coopérants*, posting and onsite management and, finally, reintegration of the teachers into schools on their return to France. Before leaving for Africa, the teachers, national service personnel and administrators took part in a training course, during which they learned about the geography, history, political and administrative structures, ethnography, sociology, economy, religions and art of the country where they were to work. A further course covered the countries' educational structures and programmes, and the ways their teaching methods would need to be adapted.[4]

Another important aspect of *coopération* was the training of African teachers. To this end, training and retraining sessions were organised in the schools, under the direction of French educational inspectors or conducted by specialists from the metropole. African teachers also benefited from training in French educational establishments. In 1961, 259 African teachers were being trained in teacher training and other colleges and in regional educational centres, but also in special schools for maladjusted children, and in school planning and administration.[5] These courses in France, lasting from a few months to one or two years, depending on the course, involved first and foremost teachers in primary, secondary and technical education, but also personnel working in administration, libraries and information services, and specialists in educational research.[6]

Other examples on a larger scale are worth noting. During the school year 1974/75, 100 Tunisian primary school teachers were admitted to teacher training classes throughout France as unregistered students.[7] Similar training was offered to around 50 Moroccan primary school teachers. A more elaborate scheme saw the establishment of twinning arrangements between certain institutions: for example, in 1964 the training college in Grenoble was twinned with the primary school training college in Monastir, which enabled 20 Tunisian students to come to Grenoble for two weeks, while twenty French students undergoing professional training made a corresponding visit to Monastir.[8] Similar exchange programmes were also established between directors of teacher training institutions in France and Morocco.[9]

The example of technical education

Alongside secondary education, the development of technical education also became a priority. With the exception of the Maghreb countries, educational organisations in this field were at an embryonic stage. By means of the FAC, governments financed the construction and equipment of technical schools and colleges, as well as apprenticeship schools and agricultural colleges, based on their French equivalents. Likewise, the education of women was encouraged: for instance, in 1969 the FAC released 1,100,000 francs to build a technical college for women in Bangui,[10] as well as financing the construction of a women's training centre in N'Djamena.

These establishments adopted the syllabuses and qualifications in place at that time in France and were staffed with French *coopérants* to carry out the instruction. During the 1965/66 academic year, there were 1,033 teachers in the technical sector, or 22 per cent of the total number of expatriate teachers in Africa and Madagascar.[11]

Before 1960, professional education was neglected, but in the decade that followed, it experienced significant growth. In Senegal, for instance, the school population more than tripled between 1960 and 1972, rising from 2,867 to 9,273 pupils (Bourgi 1979: 258). Yet despite this rapid increase, the technical sectors appeared to meet with a certain disaffection among both students and parents, suffering, as they did in France, from a negative image. In 1964, a high-ranking civil servant from the technical education division of the Ministry of Éducation, André Garcia, who had visited Chad, deplored this situation, emphasising what was at stake in the development of technical education:

> The relatively low regard in which technical education is held is a serious issue. A developed country like France must redress its past shortcomings in this regard. It would be most unfortunate if a country like Chad also adopted the snobbish attitude towards a 'universal culture' conceived at the start of the nineteenth century for the children of the upper middle class. It is by developing the art of being skilled rather than well-spoken that this country will improve its standard of living.[12]

Based directly on the French system, the technical education provided to Africa rapidly demonstrated how poorly it was suited to local conditions. In 1965, a French observer, recently returned from an inspection tour of technical colleges, stated that 'at this stage, the training of the workforce must be sure to respond to the country's needs … It is our responsibility to ensure this, since such technical education as there is has been introduced by ourselves', he continued, before drawing a discouraging picture:

> We have put the emphasis on technical education for industry, while in truth that industry does not yet exist. We are training scores of metalworkers, lathe operators, cutters and electricians for work every year, while the number of lathes and milling

machines is minute, and electricity is only to be found in these countries' major cities, with the exception of Algeria and Morocco ... All technical education is being provided by French personnel, and it is possible that at the end of the day these teachers will find themselves blamed for the unsuitability of this education.[13]

As he saw it, technical education, more than any other, should develop at its own pace and be programmed around job prospects linked to economic and social development. 'Its chief mission is to train those who will improve the quality of life in these countries. Failure would have major repercussions', he concluded, adding that 'every time the recipient of a diploma, trained by the French, fails to find a job, it will be the purpose of French education that will be questioned'.[14] If this account serves to highlight the special role of technical and professional education, which seemed to crystallise the expectations and stakes for development aid, it serves equally to illustrate the failure of *coopération* to connect with the needs of the African states.

Coopération in the field of higher education

In the final analysis, university education appears to have been one of the main beneficiaries of *coopération*. After the founding of the first Institutes of Advanced Studies in Antananarivo, Dakar and Abidjan, France encouraged the opening of new university campuses, as in Cameroon in 1962. Since the number of students remained small, the authorities opted to set up regional universities. In 1961 a convention was signed by Congo-Brazzaville, the Central African Republic, Gabon and Chad setting up the Central African Foundation for Higher Education (Fondation de l'enseignement supérieur pour l'Afrique centrale: FESAC).[15] Following the same model, a university was established by the states of Benin and Togo.

These new universities enjoyed considerable support from the FAC. Research shows that every year this organisation devoted almost 10 per cent of its entire budget to the construction and resourcing of African and Malagasy universities. These funds served to finance new infrastructure, including teaching facilities, libraries, halls of residence and sports centres, as well as university hospitals.

However, French assistance went well beyond the financing of new infrastructure, and the whole functioning of African higher education proved to be broadly dependent on *coopération*. By virtue of the bilateral agreements they signed, France took responsibility for paying lecturers' salaries as well as contributing to the costs of equipment and running costs of the universities. Madagascar's situation is telling: in 1963, the French government contributed up to 98.7 per cent of the budget to run Madagascar's university, amounting to 5,549,659 francs. After this, French funding decreased rapidly as the Malagasy authorities' contribution increased, reaching 1,851,000 francs in 1967, or 30 per cent of the total budget.[16]

In the case of the University of Dakar, France was still covering 80 per cent of its budget (20 million CFA francs) in 1968, while for its part the Senegalese government was paying 5 million CFA francs. The following year, after the student strikes in Dakar and the riots of June 1968, President Senghor demanded greater control over the university, with the result that the proportion covered by Senegal rose to 30 per cent of the total budget (Mesli 2009: 116).

So France took responsibility for the majority of the running costs of the universities, but most important, it maintained its presence through its teaching personnel, by means of its *coopérants*. In 1967, the University of Dakar only had 65 African lecturers out of a total of 289 teaching staff. Taking into account improvements in the situation with regard to assistant lecturers, the Africanisation of teaching staff proved to be particularly slow. This situation caused not a little discontent on the part of the African authorities. In 1966, the Ivoirian Minister of Education, Amon Tanoh, wrote a letter to the Director of Higher Education at the Ministry of National Education in Paris to highlight the case of young Ivoirian graduates who wanted to find jobs at the University of Abidjan. He pointed to the situation of a young doctor of law, who was unable to find a job there 'because a French assistant lecturer, who has yet to complete his thesis … is already in the job which should be his', and stated that:

> The concern to Africanise, under the best possible conditions, teaching posts at the university makes it vital to find a solution to this problem by freeing up certain jobs for the benefit of those Ivoirians who have the required qualifications. Thus it is important to begin studying right away the conditions under which French personnel might be progressively relieved of their posts, while giving them assurances about the possibility of their promotion in France.[17]

In parallel with the development of universities in Africa, scholarships were offered to African students wishing to pursue their university studies in mainland France. This programme was expanded from the end of the Second World War, and by 1960 there were some 5,500 African students in France (Dewitte 2004: 204). Several hundred of these lived at the French Overseas Students' Residence (Maison de la France d'Outre-mer), opened in 1951 in the heart of the International University Centre (Cité internationale universitaire) in Paris, which in 1973 became the Lucien Paye Hall (Résidence Lucien Paye). During the 1970s the number of African students in France increased significantly, and the Ministry of Education listed some 7,700 foreign students from sub-Saharan Africa in French universities, in addition to 15,800 students from the countries of the Maghreb.[18]

To encourage students, African governments and the FAC granted scholarships: from 1965 the latter disbursed around 870 of these each year to African nationals studying in France; but it also offered grants to students in Africa for them to attend the various universities on that continent. The number of these scholarships grew substantially between 1965 and 1968, from 1,600 to 2,250,[19] and continued to rise during the 1970s.

The efforts made during these two decades contributed to the development and spread of higher education in Africa, giving rise to a substantial increase in the number of students. However, it must also be noted that, as with technical education, the structure of university courses and degrees remained a carbon copy of the model used in France, mostly to ensure that African qualifications were accepted as valid within the French system. In 1968 the crises in the universities of Dakar and Abidjan, and four years later in Madagascar, marked the first questioning of French *coopération*, in which two of the protesters' foremost demands were the adaptation of programmes to local realities and the Africanisation of posts in further and higher education.

The disappointments of *coopération* in education

In 1989 Jacques Adda and Marie-Claude Smouts (1989: 50), in their book *La France face au Sud*, drew up an unflattering review of French *coopération*:

> The French programmes that form the basis for education in these countries are poorly adapted to the needs of their recipients – when they are not simply regarded as outmoded in France itself. In particular, technical education has been neglected, just as it has been in France. As André Postel-Vinay has correctly noted, the type of abstract, literary and legal knowledge dispensed by France in Africa contributes to urban unemployment, flight from the countryside and emigration. By failing to take into account employment needs or job openings, it creates candidates for the civil service – the sole supplier of low productivity jobs in economies on their way to disintegration – instead of training local farmers in more productive techniques. Besides being a factor in perpetuating cultural dependence, this also results in an enormous squandering of resources.

To what, then, can we attribute this failure? To begin with, the amount of financial and human resources devoted to *coopération* is beyond question. By means of the FAC, France supported the construction of numerous schools, and financed the development of universities in French-speaking Africa. The thousands of *coopérants* sent abroad each year undeniably contributed to the expansion of local education systems. Through its policy of cultural *coopération*, France played a significant role in developing school structures in Africa, and thus contributed to the progress made in expanding school attendance, even if the needs of these educational systems remained great.

The problem lies elsewhere, and has more to do with the *coopérants*, whose numbers carried on growing, at least until the beginning of the 1980s. The criticisms that came out of Africa in the 1970s and the resulting renegotiation of the agreements on *coopération* did not lead to a slowing of the growth in the number of postings. The African countries did not seriously challenge this, and the archival records show that France did not even manage to fulfil all its partners' demands, a sign that their support for the *coopérants* remained undiminished. Some states, like Côte d'Ivoire and Senegal, encouraged the flow of French or other foreign teachers, either through the mechanism of international *coopération* or by having them sign local contracts.

Their needs were so acute that African governments were forced to demand the continuation of *coopération*. But the French failure to train sufficient African teachers – despite the fact that it would have been cheaper than the posting abroad of large numbers of teachers from metropolitan France – represented one of the most serious shortcomings of *coopération*.

A corollary to this question of schoolteacher training was the issue of the Africanisation of the school systems, heightened by the fact that the provision of aid by France had become permanent: on the one hand was the educational programmes' failure to adapt to local realities; on the other, the failure to create school structures that responded to the needs of the African states. In both respects there was obvious failure.

First and foremost, Africanisation was concerned with the content of what was taught and learned, which in most cases remained modelled on French programmes. Maurice Flory noted that in this respect, the presence of *coopérants* may have put a brake on the 'vague desire for reform', as their influence seems to have been fundamentally conservative: 'Firstly, this was true with regard to the realities of the countries in question, which were largely ignored while the benchmark remained … the French model; further, this was also true because the *coopérants* presumably found it impossible to effect the kind of specific, national changes needed to introduce an alternative model' (Flory 1976: 17).

Some steps, however, were taken under the aegis of CONFEMEN, which, from 1966 on, backed the writing and publication of African textbooks in history, geography and natural science; but then the problem became one of 'training sufficient numbers of teachers capable of delivering an entirely new curriculum' (Bourgi 1979: 265).

However, the problem went well beyond course content: it was its failure to adapt to local conditions that called the entire educational system into question. As we have seen in both technical education and university degree programmes, the failure was palpable.

We can see then that despite repeated warnings, *coopération* continued to develop along the same lines, without really adjusting to the socio-economic conditions in the host countries. One possible reason for this could be the lack of reliable statistical tools at the authorities' disposal. At a CONFEMEN meeting in 1968, the governments decided to create a planning and statistics department, noting that 'statistical errors were undermining programming plans', as had been the case in 1961 at the time of the Addis Ababa Conference.[20]

But the problem was more crucially a lack of planning and control by the states. In 1976, Jean Touscoz (1976: 31) observed that France had not sought to match its *coopération* strategies to African countries 'by any systematic or coherent evaluative process'. Besides the absence of control mechanisms, he highlighted the ineffectiveness of the joint bilateral commissions, whose meetings were either very general and superficial or, at the other extreme, addressed very detailed and limited issues 'such as the wording of new proposals, or recording delays or overspending in the carrying out of projects. The infrequency and duration of their meetings, as well as the way they were prepared for, militated against their being considered in any way as mechanisms for evaluation', he determined.

Conclusion

Launched in 1960, *coopération* aimed to forge new links between France and its former African colonies. Affecting a wide range of areas of activity, but especially education, the financial and human commitment made by France was massive, exceeding by far what had been done in previous decades under colonial administration. But French educational *coopération* presents a mixed picture. On the one hand, it served to develop African educational structures, thereby contributing to improvements in school attendance on the continent; on the other, its activities contained many grey areas, foremost among which was its failure to adapt the training it provided to local conditions, technical education being a particularly telling example.

Since the beginning of the 1980s, *coopération* has been subject to increasingly strong criticism, as the deficiencies of the education systems in francophone countries have become evident, notably in comparison with the Anglophone countries, which have been more successful in terms of both rates of attendance and results. In quantitative terms, it is necessary first of all to underline that the number of schools and educational establishments was too small and unable to cope with the increase in population. But the problems were also qualitative in nature, with the quality of education suffering, notably as a result of inadequate teacher training, the large number of pupils repeating years and the cost of the system, which was much higher, relatively, than in other parts of the world.

In many respects, these difficulties are linked to the nature of *coopération*, which is modelled directly on the French education system. According to Brigitte Nouaille-Degorce writing in 1980, *coopération*, which was introduced at the moment when the colonies were claiming their independence, was 'developed little by little, in response to circumstances rather than following any pre-ordained or rigid plan' (1980: 75). Thus, the way *coopération* was implemented never really reflected local needs, lacking any real planning on the part of France and its African partners. In the opinion of Albert Bourgi, responsibility for this failure 'falls primarily on the African states, which were solely in charge of education policy. But we must also recognise that many factors weighed heavily in the choices they made: the role and place of the French language; the fact that, at the time of independence, the French education model was the only one that existed' (Bourgi 1979: 237–8). On the other hand, what could one expect from France, guided by experience of its own educational model, and its *coopérants*, imbued with the teaching methods practised on the mainland?

While it may be difficult to assign responsibility for this failure, it should be noted that, despite the considerable amounts invested in *coopération*, no truly African model emerged after independence to guide and direct the development of educational structures. As such, the example of French *coopération* in the field of education illustrates once again the difficulties confronting international aid programmes implemented by external actors, whether they be states or international organisations.

Notes

1 *Coopération* in this context means more than simply 'working together toward a common end.' Following independence, a range of bilateral accords were signed with the new governments of almost all the former French colonies in sub-Saharan Africa, covering economic, political, military, technical and cultural cooperation. *Coopération* also referred to the new Ministry of Cooperation, which was established in 1961 to replace the Ministry of Overseas France (former Colonial Ministry) in carrying out the job of managing French aid missions in France's former colonies in sub-Saharan Africa; but perhaps *coopération*'s greatest novelty was that it involved a systematic transfer of expertise via technical aid experts and teachers living in the assisted countries.

2 Ministry of Education Archives (MEN) 19770641, art. 10, Report by Inspector Tric, 8 March 1963.

3 MEN-19770508, art. 120, 'Contribution de la République du Tchad', Document du gouvernement du Tchad pour la CONFEMEN, Libreville, 1968, p. 2.

4 MEN-19770641, art. 1, *Rapport d'activité de la Direction de la Coopération, Ministère de l'Éducation nationale, 1965–1966*, p. 8.

5 MEN-19770508, art. 1, *Rapport d'activité de la Direction de la Coopération, Ministère de l'Éducation nationale, 1962*, pp. 126–8.

6 MEN-19770508, art. 120, *Programme des stages 1963–1964 pour la formation des personnels africains et malgaches de l'enseignement*, 1964.

7 MEN-19780681, art. 18, Document of the International Affairs Directorate of the Ministry of Education, 1975.

8 MEN-19770641, art. 10, *Appariement entre l'Ecole Normale d'Instituteurs de Grenoble et l'Ecole Normale d'Instituteurs de Monastir: Lettre de l'Inspection académique de l'Isère au Directeur de la Coopération avec la Communauté et l'étranger*, 24 December 1963.

9 MEN-19780681, art. 17, *Document de la Direction de la Coopération internationale du ministère de l'Education nationale*, 1972.

10 MEN-19770641, art. 3, Comité directeur du FAC, *Construction d'un collège technique féminin à Bangui*, session of 15 April 1969, p. 5.

11 MEN-19770641, art. 1, *Rapport d'activité de la Direction de la Coopération*, 1966.
12 MEN-19770641, art. 9, *Note sur le développement de l'enseignement au Tchad: Rapport de mission d'André Garcia, Professeur à l'Institut national d'administration scolaire de Paris*, 20 January 1964.
13 MEN-19771257, art. 33, *Note du service de l'Inspection générale du ministère de l'Education nationale: Nécessité en Afrique d'adapter l'enseignement technique à l'économie de chaque pays*, n.d.
14 Ibid.
15 MEN-19770510, art. 8, *Procès-verbal du Conseil d'administration de la Fondation de l'enseignement supérieur en Afrique centrale, tenue à Libreville*, 1–2 March 1966.
16 MEN-19770510, art. 9, *Rapport du Rectorat de Madagascar, Présentation des masses budgétaires de l'enseignement supérieur pour l'exercice 1967: Participation des Républiques français et malgache au budget de fonctionnement des établissements universitaires*, p. 12.
17 MEN-19770510, art. 6, Amon Tanoh to Directeur des enseignements supérieurs au ministère de l'Education nationale, 10 June 1966.
18 MEN-19820128, art. 2, *Note du ministère de l'Éducation nationale: Etudiants étrangers 1972–1973*, n.d.
19 MEN-19770641, art. 1, *Document du Secrétariat d'Etat aux universités*, n.d.
20 MEN-19770508, art. 120, *Document de la CONFEMEN*, 1968.

9

Jacques Foccart, *Eminence grise* for African affairs

Jean-Pierre Bat

A whiff of scandal and secret definitely attaches to Franco-African relations – rightly or wrongly searching for the roots of political deficiencies in Africa today in the nature of the decolonisation process. As early as 1960, Jacques Foccart emerged as the main architect of the political construct that Jean-Pierre Dozon (2003) described as '*L'Etat français contemporain et son double, l'Etat franco-africain*' (The contemporary French State and its *doppelganger*, the Franco-African state).

Due to his fourteen years of handling French interests in Africa, Foccart's shadow still hovers over research on decolonisation and the post-colonial period in Francophone Africa. When he was alive, Foccart was a source of the mythology that surrounded him, among his detractors as well as his supporters. His many nicknames – such as '*L'éminence grise du Général*', '*la bacille*', '*la Foque*', '*le Fantômas*', '*le Raspoutine*', or '*le Père Joseph du régime*'[1] – all vouch for the dark and persistent legend that surrounded this character, and there are as many attempts to uncover the famously secret personality of Charles De Gaulle's most influential adviser (Bat 2012).

By that time, Foccart's name sounded all the more unsettling since he was said to control African policy on the one hand, and France's special services on the other – from the SAC (*Service d'action civique*) to SDECE intelligence Services (*Service de documentation extérieure et de contre-espionnage*). Foccart was identified as '*la grande barbouze*' [head of secret services] in Charles De Gaulle's France (Audigier 2003). Choosing Africa as his main field of action, Foccart so vigorously imprinted his methods on France's decolonisation process that, fifty years on, they continue to cast a shadow over France's relations with its former '*pré carré*' [sphere of influence] in Francophone Africa.

Foccart: the dark legend

In the public mind, Foccart's politics still find an echo in the term '*la Françafrique*'. Used for the first time by Ivoirian President Félix Houphouët-Boigny, this term was supposed to describe the community of views and interests shared by France and its colonies. By the 1980s and 1990s, it had become synonymous with scandal, after French interference in African affairs and neo-colonialism had been exposed (Péan 1983). This neo-colonialism, both economic and political, showed itself through the practices of oil companies such as Elf and then Total, and through the support given to African presidents who had remained 'friends of France'.

François-Xavier Verschave, a fierce detractor of French policy in Africa, ended his work *La Françafrique, le plus long scandale de la République* with a haunting question: 'Is a 'defoccartisation' possible?'(Verschave 1998: 333–8). This statement suggests that Foccart was the all-powerful architect of French relations with its former colonies. In this respect, Foccart cannot but remind us of Cardinal Mazarin, King Louis XIV's most influential and unpopular minister during the Fronde (1648–52). The archives of Foccart's Bureau de documentation et de presse (BDP) show the complex figure of Foccart in the media.[2] Underneath each political operation, people seek traces of the chief adviser's secret influence and manipulations. As the Fifth Republic began, a great number of satirical papers more and more often portrayed him as the head of some 'shadow cabinet'. Among left-wing newspapers, *Le Canard enchaîné* stands as Foccart's most effective and consistent detractor. Two representative moments are worth remembering, though they cannot wholly reflect the vast array and the diversity of articles dedicated to the presidential special adviser on Africa. The first was in 1965, after the kidnapping of Medhi Ben Barka, main opponent of Moroccan king Hassan II, on 29 October at the Brasserie Lipp in Paris. His body has never been found, but it appears that Colonel Oufkir, director of the Moroccan secret service, was responsible for his kidnapping and assassination – thanks to the complicity of the French, including the criminals Georges Boucheseiche and Antoine Lopez, French and Moroccan secret services informers.[3] As the presidential special adviser for security affairs, Foccart was immediately suspected of being part of the plot. The cartoonist Roland Moisan immortalised dignitaries of the Gaullist system (the Prefect of Police and the Minister of the Interior) by sketching them as innocent angels at a time when rumour had it that they were involved in Mehdi Ben Barka's disappearance. At Foccart's feet lies a perfume bottle, as a subtle hint at the French saying '*Foccart est au parfum*' (Foccart is in the know), which was subsequently used by Lopez to clear himself.[4] If anything happened in France, it could not but reach Foccart's ears – to the great satisfaction of the African presidents who were friends of France.[5] In 1969, the Foccart scandal broke. As Alain Poher was made interim President, Foccart was suspended from office. From all sides (not only left and extreme left parties, who considered him as representing the darkest part of the Gaullist system they had been fighting since 1958, but also former OAS members who considered Foccart their main enemy, since he had during the Algerian crisis been responsible for police and intelligence services at the Elysée palace), accusations were made against Foccart that came to focus on a Louis XV console said to conceal a wire-tapping set.[6] These few elements are indicative of the nefariousness of the picture that was sketched in the public mind: all the components of scandal – power, secrets, money, police activities – are brought together.

In this context, Africa – the *'domaine réservé'* (preserve) of the President – appears as a film negative for the fairly disreputable methods used by Foccart behind the scenes (Péan 1990). Endeavouring to outline the boundaries of Foccart's power and influence over African affairs comes down to tracing the thread of a life built on Gaullist militancy.

The Gaullist baron and the RPF in Africa (1940–1958)

Foccart's actual political career began with the French Resistance: under the name of Binot, he enlisted in the Bureau Central de Renseignements et d'Action (BCRA) in occupied France and became head of the M area network (Maine-Anjou). From the 1940s, Foccart underwent three main formative influences. Made an officer at the Liberation, Foccart was trained within the Special Allied Airborne Reconnaissance Forces (SAARF). After 1945, he spent many years in Cercottes, completing his reserve training within the '11e choc' special forces unit, where he bonded with his reservists. He used to meet in Cercottes special officers such as Captains Bob Maloubier, Raymond Muelle, Raymond Bichelot, Marcel Chaumien, alias 'Mr Armand', and also Colonel Jacques Morlanne, the head of the SDECE special forces – Service 29 which became Service VIII after 1958 – to whom he provided information from Africa (personal communications, Bob Maloubier, 29 January, 19 June 2008; Raymond Muelle, 29 February, 3 June 2008). Foccart kept the connection to Morlanne's successor, Colonel Robert Roussillat.[7] In the 1960s, Foccart, who had taken the position of presidential adviser, used these SDECE officers: Marcel Chaumien headed Service VII (SDECE unconventional intelligence service) in Africa (personal communication, Marcel Chaumien's daughter, 9 January 2012); Raymond Bichelot was nominated chief of station in Abidjan (1963–68) where he was up to the 1980s security adviser to President Houphouët-Boigny; and Bob Maloubier, who left the SDECE in 1956, was recalled to establish the presidential security service in Gabon in 1964. Foccart was so close to SDECE Special Forces that, in 1959, he kept a watchful eye on the covert network in Guinea created by Service VIII from Dakar – the story ended with Prime Minister Mamadou Dia's protest after Sékou Touré revealed the 'French Guinean plot' in April 1960.[8] After 1959, Foccart persuaded SDECE General Director Paul Grossin that an African department should be created. Foccart established a direct connection to the SDECE's Africa Director, Maurice Robert, in the 1960s. After 1969, his links to the secret services got weaker. But from the 1940s to the 1960s, the world of intelligence had been structuring Foccart's social and political behaviour. An autodidact, Foccart learnt most of his skills from his action in the Resistance: patriotism, direct action and secret practices had left a deep mark on him. These experiences led him to give his political and personal commitment to General De Gaulle.

In order to remain financially independent, Foccart set up an import-export company, which he entrusted to the care of a very close friend, Robert Rigaud. The income drawn from this company enabled him fully to commit himself to his political battles, which began as early as January 1946 with De Gaulle leaving power just as the Fourth Republic was in the process of adopting a constitution. In December 1946, De Gaulle informed a handful of faithful followers – including Foccart – that he wished to create his own political force. No sooner was the Rassemblement du peuple française (RPF) officially launched in April 1947 than Foccart established himself as one of its mainstays. After his service in the Resistance revealed Foccart's political skills, his activism in the RPF in opposition led to his emergence as De Gaulle's 'Mr Africa'. Invited to the RPF headquarters in 5, rue de Solférino, Foccart came to take a first interest in Africa as he was offered the opportunity to succeed Pierre Lefranc and Pierre Anthonioz as the head of the French overseas departments and territories (DOM-TOM) commission (Turpin 2002). His work mainly focused on the DOM-TOM and Africa. Foccart initiated the publication of *Lettre à l'Union française*, a news bulletin that was to play a major part in spreading his reputation. In March 1950, he was appointed counsellor to the Assembly of the French Union by the RPF parliamentary group. As the new Gaullist representative for Africa he started travelling throughout the continent, endeavouring to build up links with African political figures. Here lies a key characteristic of Foccart's personality: he was, above all things, a networker. The political stakes involved in Foccart's mission were all the more important since the overseas RPF was distinguished by its conservative views, often expressed in a colonial advocacy of European interests in Africa, especially in the 1950s.

Foccart moulded his pragmatic approach to problems by learning how to manoeuvre skilfully among the different Gaullist currents and charting a course that was likely to solve African colonial issues while providing France with some advantages and seeking to avoid another Indochina war. In 1952, he gradually brought about a personal rapprochement with Félix Houphouët-Boigny – their partnership soon became the keystone on which Foccart built his African politics. Even though Félix Houphouët-Boigny was dealing with the French government after he broke with the Communist Party in 1950 and got closer to François Mitterrand's Union démocratique et socialiste de la Résistance (UDSR), he was still considered as the main enemy of the French colonial lobby that organised within the RPF. Comparing Foccart's correspondence as RPF counsellor (kept by the Fondation Charles De Gaulle) and as President De Gaulle's adviser (kept by the Archives nationales) in the 1950s, significant changes can be noticed:[9] while two important landowners in Côte d'Ivoire, Georges Héritier in Abidjan and Robert Fournier-Bidoz in Bouaké, appeared to be the most influential RPF representatives, Foccart ultimately relied on Félix Houphouët-Boigny's team (Alain Belkiri or Governor Guy Nairay). If the declining influence of the landowners' lobby was perceptible in Foccart's letters after 1958, this decline appeared to be the result of a five-year policy: since 1953 and De Gaulle's trip to Africa, Foccart had decided to establish links with Félix Houphouët-Boigny and his African party organisation, the Rassemblement Démocratique Africain (RDA). Throughout the 1950s, Foccart was well aware that he would have to make a choice, but he was also conscious that it was not necessary as long as De Gaulle was not president. Here lies the explanation of Foccart's tactics: to get the widest possible alliance in favour of De Gaulle's return in a crisis situation, in order to make him the undisputed 'providential man'.

Many characteristic features began then to stand out in Foccart's personality, most particularly his appetite for intelligence service issues. Through RPF supporters, he soon wove around himself a web of colonial administrators (such as Governor Roland Pré, former administrator in Cameroon, who faced the beginning of the UPC rebellion – see Sharp, Chapter 12 in this volume), old friends settled in Africa (such as Jacques Mansion, one of the first BCRA officers established in Brazzaville) and even police and military men well-versed in the security services. Through Captain Maurice Robert and Inspector Césari, he built up links with the Dakar SDECE and the Abidjan Security Service (Laurent 2011: 137–55).[10] More generally, Foccart developed a network of well-informed persons, such as Lebanese merchant Mahmoud Bourgi in Dakar, even if he remained very discreet about this particular ally.[11]

His journey through the wilderness started after his 1953 electoral defeat. However, despite De Gaulle distancing himself from his political party, the RPF did not die out. Foccart's main task was to maintain it alive politically, as he was catapulted into the position of last secretary-general of the party to, in his own words, 'save the day' (Foccart and Gaillard 1995: 107). Still a loyal soldier, Foccart intended to solve the last remaining RPF issues and to maintain the institutional and informal links between the numerous 'comrades'. He was willing to link the various social and political forces favourable to De Gaulle, as he was confident that sooner or later De Gaulle would once more assume power. It was not until December 1958, when the RPF was officially dissolved, that Foccart left the party.

Not surprisingly, Foccart was directly involved in the 13 May 1958 events. He went underground during the entire month of May, just as he had in the

Resistance period. Connected to special forces officers, he operated as an invisible but permanent interface between De Gaulle, officially retired, and activist movements from Algiers. With De Gaulle's last loyal soldiers (Michel Debré, Olivier Guichard, Pierre Lefranc, Christian de La Malène and René Ribière) he planned the political agenda necessary for De Gaulle to assume power again: psychological actions directed at French politicians and public opinion, the creation of a link with the Committee of Public Safety (CPS) – in particular by sending Léon Delbecque to Algiers after 12 May 1958, and meetings with the emissaries from Algiers – in particular Major Vitasse and Captain Lamouliatte.[12] Their roadmap was clear, as they wanted to let the pressure rise until De Gaulle appeared as the last resort. However, the 'Resurrection' operation was the Rubicon that they would not overtly cross. Once again, Foccart demonstrated his taste for political operations and his loyalty to De Gaulle. When the latter became the last president of the Council of Ministers of the Fourth Republic, the former was installed as chief adviser to De Gaulle.

Creating the 'Africa cell' at the Élysée palace: the Secrétariat général des affaires africaines et malgaches 1958–1974

Foccart's first mission was to elicit a positive response to the 28 September 1958 constitutional referendum as he organised De Gaulle's tour through France's African colonies of Madagascar, French Equatorial Africa (AEF) and French West Africa (AOF). Even though he succeeded in his undertaking, this feat should not obscure the fact that he also participated in redrawing the map of decolonised French Africa. Indeed, Foccart supported Houphouët-Boigny's conception of a federal French-speaking West African against Dia's and Senghor's idea of a French-speaking West Africa confederation. The federal solution was based on direct, bilateral links between Paris and each capital, links that 'Mr Africa' intended to embody as De Gaulle gave him all the necessary powers to assume this role, whereas the confederation would have kept the federation of French West Africa together as a unit and links with France would then have been channelled through the federation. This choice reflected the fact that Foccart had chosen to rely on Félix Houphouët-Boigny's conception and his RDA network, which included the majority of the governments of the French West African colonial territories at the moment of independence. The federal solution also, of course, had the benefit of weakening African territories and thus facilitating the maintenance of French control.

As technical adviser, Foccart was responsible for Africa, the DOM-TOM (French overseas territories), De Gaulle's relationships with his supporters and with the secret services. In order to fulfil his role, he used to meet daily with the Head of State in the evenings. These one-to-one meetings were to Foccart a genuine holy communion. Even though their content was kept secret, from

Figure 9.1 Jacques Foccart and General De Gaulle.
Reproduced with permission from the Archives Nationales de Paris.

1965 onwards Foccart kept track of these conversations as he religiously took notes at all these meetings, which were later published under the title *Journal de l'Elysée* (Foccart 1997, 1998, 1999, 2000 and 2001). His proximity turned him into De Gaulle's voice as he became the tool that put his policies into action. Thus, Foccart would provide the tactics for the execution of De Gaulle's strategy. In other words, while Foccart was doing the dirty work, De Gaulle would not be compromised. In case of a failed operation, this would enable De Gaulle to accuse his advisers. Of course, there was no plan at the outset to create Foccart's position in this way (the myth of the 'mystery man' propagated by Pierre Péan): rather, he had been gradually slipping into this role before 1958. Between 1954 and 1958, when he was looking after the RPF without De Gaulle, he proved his loyalty but also his competence. In 1958, De Gaulle knew how reliable Foccart was, being his only collaborator who never made a political career. He was able to mobilise Gaullist support (even pro-French Algeria supporters) without personally compromising De Gaulle. In the 1960s, Foccart presented himself implicitly as De Gaulle's Pythia – indeed it was here that his political strength and legitimacy after De Gaulle's death lay, as he could always say 'President De Gaulle told me ...' or 'President De Gaulle thought ...'.[13]

In March 1960, the Office of the Community (the new name for France's colonial empire) at the Elysée palace became Foccart's responsibility. He replaced Raymond Janot as Secretary-General of the Community, which had been conceived as a means of transition from one historical era to another. For De Gaulle, this was the best way of keeping control over the decolonisation of France's sub-Saharan African colonies, and the creation of autonomous republics in 1958 was supposed to facilitate this. However, when the republics achieved independence in 1960, the Community no longer had any *raison d'être*. By choosing his presidential adviser for Africa as its Secretary-General, De Gaulle sought to re-affirm the personal link between Paris and France's 'African friends', who became in turn fathers of the newly-created African republics that were imagined as little sister states of the French Republic. In March 1961, the Office of the Communauté was renamed the Office pour la Communauté et les Affaires africaines et malgaches (Office for the Community and for African and Malagasy Affairs). This was not only a new name but it shows also the extent to which the Fifth Republic based its international policy on African politics to project its power at an international level (Turpin 2009, 2010).

It is easy to understand how Foccart's decisions became more important than the more traditional French protocol and diplomacy. One example of this pattern of politics is the fact that *coopération* (see Mesli, Chapter 8 in this volume) was never under the control of the Foreign Affairs Ministry, but in Foccart's hands. In 1964, Foccart established his authority in an institutional way as he started to call tripartite meetings between his office, the Ministry of Cooperation and the Ministry of Foreign Affairs. (If needed, other ministerial advisers would be invited to join the meetings.) This enabled a better understanding of African affairs as the meetings were led by Foccart.

His relationship with French diplomacy in Africa illustrates his method: he looks for a direct connection to loyal ambassadors, regardless of whether they are professional diplomats or not. His personal and informal correspondence with Jacques Raphaël-Leygues, French ambassador in Abidjan from 1963 to 1979, or Maurice Delauney, French ambassador in Libreville from 1965 to 1972 and 1975 to 1979, illustrates his way of managing African affairs. Following requests from Félix Houphouët-Boigny and Albert-Bernard Bongo, the French ambassador was considered much more as a presidential adviser than a representative of a foreign country.[14] From 1960, Foccart discreetly intervened in the nomination of ambassadors: Roger Barberot, former high officer in the French Army and well-known supporter of De Gaulle, was sent to Bangui where he dealt with every special file under David Dacko's presidency.[15] With Foccart's agreement, from 1960 to 1965 Roger Barberot directly managed Central African security issues with President David Dacko, Captain Jean Portafax – SDECE representative – and Superintendent Robert Allongue – SCTIP representative.[16] Maurice Ligot, Foccart's first principal private secretary at the Office of the Community, admitted that, after the formal interview between the presidential adviser and the ambassador, Jacques Foccart and Robert Barberot used to spend time talking about secret issues, involving security and matters of high politics, without any witness being present (personal communication, Maurice Ligot, 24 October 2007).

A 'Foccart method'?

Within fourteen years, the adviser came to stamp his own imprint onto Franco-African relations. However this ought not to be considered as a real system, but rather as a modus operandi, since Foccart always remained suspicious of any strict method or indeed of actions motivated by ideological considerations. The fact that his method seemed out of phase with classical protocol did not mean Foccart ignored its codes, but the highly political logic behind his handling of African Affairs, in close connection with the presidency, marginalised the Ministry of Foreign Affairs.

After French decolonisation in sub-Saharan Africa, defence of the '*pré carré*' and support for African heads of state who were friendly towards France soon emerged as an absolute priority. Foccart devised a real *Pax Gallica* (Bat 2011) on the continent – and woe betide those who dared to try to disturb it! Hence, the 15 August 1963 overthrow of Fulbert Youlou's regime in Congo-Brazzaville, after three days of street riots known as 'Les Trois Glorieuses', resonated like a thunderbolt in Paris as well as in the capital cities of Francophone Africa – and most strongly in Abidjan. France had to prevent any other coup from taking place in its '*pré carré*'. The 1964 Gabon *coup d'état* led Foccart to show his determination. After sending paratroopers to re-establish President Léon M'Ba in office, he appointed a number of special advisers to Libreville in order to restore state power in Gabon.[17] The concern he showed towards this country was confirmed in the following years when he appointed Maurice Delauney – a former colonial officer who had remained close to Foccart – as ambassador to Gabon. However, his most important victory lay in Albert Bongo's nomination as Léon M'Ba's official successor.[18] Indeed, France defined a clearer tactic for military intervention after the 1963 Brazzaville trauma, which had revealed dysfunctions in the system – France had to intervene within one or two days if French vital interests or the lives of presidents who were allies of France were in danger. Foccart did not hesitate to take personal responsibility for such decisions without officially involving De Gaulle, although of course in so doing he risked being accused of pursuing a neo-colonial policy by public opinion (Keese 2007a).

More generally, 'Mr Africa' set about strengthening links within the '*pré carré*' by means of the French military presence and threats. Maurice Robert offered an original solution to this problem: give every president a special connection to the SDECE through the PLR system (Postes de liaison et de renseignement: Liaison and information posts), the official part of SDECE activity in Africa. Between 1969 and 1972, in order to combat the FROLINAT rebellion and defend a territory he considered as a key military region facing Libya, Foccart decided to deploy the French army to Chad to save Tombalbaye. He took this decision despite difficult relations between Paris and N'Djamena. In this operation, known as the 'Limousin' operation, France for the first time acted as a policeman in Chad and would do so again several times through a whole series of military interventions – among which 'Tacaud' (1978–80), 'Manta' (1983–86) and 'Epervier' (1986–ongoing) remain the most well known over the last four decades.[19]

The specific relations between France and its former African colonies turned out to be less guaranteed by shared institutions than by Foccart's personal involvement. The adviser had been building personal connections with African presidents, creating a kind of political private club that was intended to be one of the main cornerstones of the *Pax Gallica*. This 'Foccart method' made possible the creation of the presidential '*domaine réservé*' for African policy. Hence, Franco-African relations were enacted at the crossroads between public and private spheres. Foccart used to receive African presidents at home, in the Villa Charlotte in Luzarches (Val d'Oise), or to make direct phone calls to them, ignoring in this respect the normal diplomatic channels and etiquette. At the centre of this 'Foccart matrix' was the direct link to the Elysée palace, indicating the special importance France attached to African security.

Jean-Bedel Bokassa appears as the most eloquent illustration of the way Foccart dealt with Africa. France managed to gain control over Bokassa,[20] despite his known personal excesses since the 'St Sylvestre coup' in the early hours of January 1966, which brought him to power in the Central African Republic (Laurent 2011: 199–219).[21] After Foccart's departure in 1974, following the election of Giscard d'Estaing as president, Paris-Bangui relations continued between the two 'cousins', Jean-Bedel Bokassa and Valéry Giscard d'Estaing, until their breakdown in 1979 with the 'Barracuda' operation on 20 September. Two years after he had let Marechal Bokassa become 'Emperor Bokassa I' during a ceremony inspired by Napoleon's coronation, Giscard d'Estaing decided on a tactical intervention to overthrow Bokassa – who had established commercial links with Libya, France's enemy in Africa during the Chad crisis. While this was supposed to be a 'Central African coup', French involvement was immediately revealed (Bat 2012: 378–86). As a consequence, relations between the French president and his counterpart from the Central African Republic were transformed into a media issue throughout the 'diamonds scandal' (this related to a gift of Bokassa to Giscard d'Estaing when the latter was Minister of Finance). It became a tale of Franco-African partnership in the 1970s, developing from political friendship to personal betrayal, and constituted a major political scandal during the French presidential election campaign in 1981. This excessive episode appears as the complete opposite of Foccart's style under the presidencies of de Gaulle and Pompidou (Foccart and Gaillard 1997: 510; Faes and Smith 2000).[22]

Willing to establish and maintain the closest connections with African presidents who were friends of France, Foccart discreetly sent a number of special agents to Africa, initiating a *missi dominici* pattern that would become the most efficient and visible part of his method. These special advisers, usually unofficial, incarnated a physical and permanent link between African presidents and the Elysée, in order to harmonise political decisions. While they offer an integrated-circuit network of communication between the Elysée palace and France's African allies, they simply cut the Ministry of Foreign Affairs out of African affairs.

Among these *missi dominici*, Jean Mauricheau-Beaupré was one of the better known characters (Bat and Geneste 2010). After his first experience as Fulbert Youlou's special adviser in Brazzaville (1960–63), he was sent to Abidjan to be active on Houphouët-Boigny's side, where he stayed until his death in 1996. A former member of the Resistance, a Gaullist supporter in the 1950s and friend of Debré's, who was involved in producing the periodical *Le Courrier de la colère*, he spent some time in Paris as a member of the Office of the Community (1958–61) before going to Congo-Brazzaville. After 1961, officially working under a Cooperation contract in Africa, he kept in touch with Foccart's Office – where he retained his influence through the 1960s. Indeed, he introduced himself as Foccart's messenger when in the field. Mauricheau-Beaupré was obviously given much room for manoeuvre. Managing 'black operations', he considered himself as the kingpin of Gaullist ambitions in Africa.[23] However, this did not prevent him from being involved in major failures, as in Brazzaville on 15 August 1963, when Fulbert Youlou was overthrown despite Mauricheau-Beaupré's negotiations. For nearly 18 months, he was then involved in planning Youlou's escape. When the time came, he allowed public rumour to refer to him as the 'man who saved Youlou from the Congolese Revolution'; although the fact is that Youlou escaped by himself during the night of 25 March 1965.[24] Mauricheau-Beaupré promoted a sort of modern secret diplomacy, known in France since the eighteenth century and Louis XV's reign as '*le secret du roi*'. In 1960, in the former Belgian Congo, he supported Moïse Tshombé's Katanga secessionist movement (1960–63) and later organised Tshombé's comeback as Prime Minister in Léopoldville (1964–65), thus being the first to open this country to the club of former French colonies and bringing it into the '*pré carré*'. Mauricheau-Beaupré and his team were used as an unofficial 'French voice' in Léopoldville: he was to support Tshombé's position against Lumumbist rebels, on the one hand, and the pro-American 'Binza group', on the other. After Tshombé's arrest in Algeria in 1967, Foccart abandoned Mauricheau's political line and started to deal directly with Mobutu, who became an efficient French ally in Central Africa up to 1997. During the Congo crisis (1960–65), Mauricheau was the one who took the decision to recruit French mercenary Bob Denard, thus endowing French policy in Africa with a useful but shameful master trump (Lunel 1991 and Denard 1998). In these obscure activities, Denard could be used whenever SDECE special forces could not be involved. Finally, he also supported the struggle for Biafran independence (1967–70), led by Colonel Odumegwu Ojukwu (Durand 2007: 472), in order to weaken the influence of the 'Nigerian elephant' in West Africa, so close to Côte d'Ivoire. France never took any official position with regard to the Katangan or the Biafran secessions. Using the *missi dominici* and their action, Paris instead intended to rely on its 'sister republics' (a term used by the French revolutionaries to designate their ideological allies) to maintain a French order – the *Pax Gallica* – in Africa. In this respect, Mauricheau embodied the unofficial side of Foccart's tactical conceptions, defining some kind of 'official illegality' within a new political space (Bat 2012: 270–334). Mauricheau's secret correspondence to his deputy, Philippe Lettéron, clearly points to his political conceptions: Houphouët-Boigny's code name is 'Big Brother', while Charles De Gaulle's is – obviously – 'Big Father'.[25]

The '*éminence grise*' and 'Gaullist talisman'[26] (1974–1997)

When Valéry Giscard d'Estaing won the 1974 presidential elections, times seemed to change. With his programme '*le changement dans la continuité*' ('change with continuity'), he disbanded Foccart's office, and the Gaullist adviser was dismissed by the new administration.[27] But in reality, this was far from being the end of an era; after 1974, Foccart's pattern of relations with African powers was adopted by the new political team at the Elysée palace. Although the important Africa Office at the Elysée was definitively closed, the functions of adviser for African Affairs remained intact, under the President's personal control. René Journiac, a former deputy of Foccart's, was chosen by President Giscard d'Estaing to be his special adviser for Africa.[28] The 'Africa cell' appeared to be the main political legacy of Foccart's 'matrix'.

Though Foccart had left the Elysée, he remained connected to his influential African friends, whom he tried to rally to his new political battle: the revival of Gaullism with Jacques Chirac and his party, the Rassemblement pour la République (RPR). A fierce opponent of the Socialists in 1981, he considered the legislative victory in 1986 as the first step on the road to a Gaullist comeback: Jacques Chirac was appointed prime minister, inaugurating a period of 'cohabitation' between a left-wing president and a right-wing prime minister. Foccart became his special adviser for African Affairs at the Matignon palace during these two years. Chirac's failure to win the 1988 presidential elections forced him to rethink his strategy for a Gaullist revival.

From the Paris Town Council, where Chirac had been building his strong-hold, Foccart created his African think tank for the RPR under the obscure name of 'Association for Development and Solidarity' (ADS). It became known very quickly as the 'Martignac cell', in reference to its location. Ably assisted by Fernand Wibaux, former ambassador to Chad during the 'Limousin' opera-tion (1969–72), and by Pierre Voïta, former French officer, Foccart worked to convince France's African partners to support Chirac's presidential election cam-paign in 1995. Thus, operating behind official French policy in Africa between 1974 and 1988, and indeed up to 1995, 'Mr Africa' aimed at exploiting institu-tional deficiencies in order to define policy. His 'Martignac cell', connected to key African personalities, sought to exploit the lack of institutional structures in order to prepare Chirac's African policy after 1995.[29]

On 7 May 1995, Foccart prepared his comeback to the Elysée palace that he had left twenty years earlier. However, it was impossible for him to be his old self again as the leader of a special office for African Affairs, as he had been in the 1960s. Political and administrative customs had changed over these three decades: technicians and technocrats replaced the old guard of the Gaullist Resistance; most positions in ministerial cabinets were now filled by graduates of the Ecole Nationale d'Administration; and finally, diplomats won a clear-cut victory over the Ministry of Cooperation, which had been jealously maintained by Jacques Foccart beyond the sphere of influence of the Ministry of Foreign Affairs since the 1960s. Thus, considering Foccart's personality, Jacques Chirac reached a compromise for his 'Africa cell'.[30] Michel Dupuch, former ambassador to Côte d'Ivoire (1979–93) was appointed head of the official Africa cell, located at 2, rue de l'Elysée, while at 14, rue de l'Elysée, sharing the building with the presidential military cabinet, Foccart, assisted by Fernand Wibaux, was set up as an unofficial adviser and Chirac's personal representative to African presidents.[31]

Despite suffering from illness, the 'Old Man' embodied more than ever the personalised relationships between Paris and its former colonies. On 20 November 1995, the everlasting 'Mr Africa' was awarded by Jacques Chirac the rank of Grand Officer of the Legion of Honour. But, without setting aside the specificity of French connections with the African continent, debates were taking place in the 1990s around the role of the 'Africa cell', in an effort to bring about some kind of 'defoccartisation' – in institutions as well as in minds – and thus create a new legitimacy for French policy.

Conclusion

On 19 May 1997, Jacques Foccart died at home in Paris. His duties were transferred to Fernand Wibaux up to the end of the President's first term of office in
2002. Then the unofficial cell closed. This provides us with an additional clue as
to how Foccart built himself political and institutional influence (since becoming
a leading figure in the first Gaullist party, the RPF). His legacy shows its effects
so much in the practices of post-colonial relations between France and its former
colonies that it seems to shape behaviours even after his death. The unofficial
rules are kept tacit, based on the *Pax Gallica*, never written down, but known
and followed by everyone involved.

Jacques Foccart remains a controversial and polemical figure, fifty years
after the independence of France's sub-Saharan African colonies. He is a major
reference point for those who deal with fantasy, myth and conspiracy in public
opinion. We can conclude that he left his imprint – in the political field, but also
in historiography and public memories – and that this is finally stronger in the
collective mind than in the republican institutions. The enduring '*Françafrique*'
springs from this imprint. The publication of his interviews with Philippe Gaillard
between 1992 and 1997 (*Foccart parle*) and of his personal diary written between
1965 and 1974 (*Journal de l'Elysée*) have become the main sources on Foccart
after his death and have further fuelled this view of him as the 'mystery man', as
much for what they do not say as what they do. In fact, Foccart had been thinking
about how he would be remembered very much earlier: on 12 November 1980,
after one year of discussions following the colloquium held in October 1979 in
Bordeaux on De Gaulle's Africa policy, he decided to give his personal files to
the Archives nationales (creating the FPR files – 'Foccart private files'). At the
same time, between 1977 and 1984, under the new archival practices instituted
under the Giscard d'Estaing presidency, the Elysée (in particular René Journiac)
gave papers from the Office of the French Community to the Archives nationales
(thus creating the FPU files – 'Foccart's Office files'). Here lie the most important
sources on Foccart's African activities, and certainly the most important collection
of files written by De Gaulle's advisers. These files do finally destroy one myth –
that of a 'mystery man' who never leaves any paper trail behind.[32]

Notes

1 Fondation nationale des sciences politiques, archives Michel Debré, 2 D 11, letter
   from Constantin Melnik, Debré's security adviser, 29 November 1961.
2 Archives nationales (AN), 5 AG/FBDP 1–95. The Bureau de documentation et
   de presse missions, led by Michel Delaborde (1962–69) and Jean-François Bourie
   (1969–74), collected information about French and African presidents, but also
   checked what was written about Foccart.

3 Georges Figon, 'J'ai vu tuer Ben Barka', *L'Express*, 10 January 1966.

4 AN, 5 AG/FBDP 42–53, affaire Ben Barka (1965/66).

5 Even when they came to Paris unofficially, Foccart asked the Paris police to protect them. As a consequence, police reports represent the main source in the Foccart files to follow the everyday activities of African presidents in Paris and to identify the persons they meet. The crisis in the former Belgian Congo is significant: as he could not officially meet Moïse Tshombé in Africa, Félix Houphouët-Boigny (often accompanied by François Tombalbaye and Antoine Hazoume, SDECE agent) used to see him in his house in Marnes-la-Coquette.

6 AN, 5 AG/FBDP 56. Foccart's role at the Élysée (1969–73). *L'Humanité, Le Canard enchaîné, Minute, Aux écoutes, Pan!* and *Le Crapouillot* became his worst enemies. On 24 April 1968, *Minute* openly spread a rumour according to which Foccart was a Soviet mole, alias 'Colombine' or 'Topaz' (5 AG/FBDP 54, réseau 'Topaz'). This is the issue at the centre of Alfred Hitchcock's film *Topaz*, which was based on the 'Sapphire affair' in which Foccart was accused of being in touch with the Kremlin as De Gaulle was dealing with Moscow. The film was banned under this title in France.

7 AN, 5 AG/FPR 597 et 624, Letters from Colonel Robert Roussillat (1958–62).

8 AN, 5 AG/FPR 200, French intelligence service in Guinea (1959). Foccart received reports and notes directly from Service VIII whereas these papers should have been given to the director of the SDECE.

9 Fondation Charles De Gaulle, BR-RPF 669, correspondence with representatives in Côte d'Ivoire (1947–58). AN, 5 AG/FPR 174–5, Foccart's correspondence concerning Côte d'Ivoire (1958/59).

10 AN, 5 AG FPR 599, correspondence between Jacques Foccart and Maurice Robert (1958).

11 AN, 5 AG FPU 2020, Sénégal (May–August 1964). When dissensions appeared within the Lebanese community of Dakar, Mamoud Bourgi claimed publicly his friendship with Foccart.

12 Nick (1998: 757–809). Facsimile of commandant Vitasse report, emissary of General Massu in France between 18 May and 10 June 1958.

13 This section is based on interviews by the author with Foccart's collaborators: Paul Bouteiller (21 February and 30 June 2008), Pierre Decheix (23 November and 18 June 2008), Yves Jouhaud (13 December 2007), Martin Kirsch (3 January 2008), Maurice Ligot (24 October 2007), Alain Plantey (5 July 2004 and 26 January 2005), Fernand Wibaux (17 March 2005) and Pierre Voïta (4 January 2012).

14 AN, 5 AG/FPR 180–1, 184 bis, correspondence with Jacques Raphaël-Leygues (1963–74). AN, 5 AG/FPR 193–5, correspondence with Maurice Delauney (1965–72).

15 Fondation Charles De Gaulle, Roger Barberot's archives F-26/12–14 (embassy in Bangui, 1960–65) and 20–22 (private archives 1960s), correspondence of Roger Barberot.

16 AN, 5 AG/FPR 159, correspondence with Roger Barberot (1960–65); interview by the author with Jean Portafax (7 October 2010). The SCTIP is the French Cooperation police service and one of the two major French intelligence services active in post-colonial Africa.

17 AN, 5 AG/FPU 2001–2002, political situation in Gabon, 1964. Guy Ponsaillé, former colonial officer in Gabon who had become an oil tycoon at Elf, was sent as political adviser to Léon M'Ba. Bob Maloubier, former SDECE captain, also one of the French oil tycoons in Gabon, was called upon to establish a presidential intelligence service, the famous Presidential Guard (GP). Special Commissioner René Galy was appointed head of SCTIP (Cooperation police service) in Libreville. His mission was to reorganise the Gabonese intelligence service (Centre de documentation CEDOC), created by another French officer, Special Inspector Georges Conan, who was trained in Cameroon in the 1950s during the fighting against the UPC rebels, see Biteghe (1990).

18 AN, 5 AG/FPU 400, President Léon M'Ba. Letters from Maurice Delauney presenting different options for Léon M'Ba's succession; interview by the author with Maurice Delauney (4 April 2008).

19 Ecole militaire, centre de doctrine et d'emploi des forces, division recherche et retour d'expérience de l'armée de Terre, *Répertoire typologique des opérations*, t. 2, *Afrique*, 31–9, 51–76.

20 AN, 5 AG/FPR 162, French Embassy in the Central African Republic (1960–72). Letter from Ambassador Herly to Foccart, Bangui, 6 February 1968.

21 Service historique de la Défense, 10 T 640–1, Colonel Mehay's reports, French military adviser in Bangui, 1966.

22 This kinship is claimed by Bokassa, in reference to the personal links that tied European crowns to each other in early modern Europe.

23 Cf. Tshombé's press conference in Paris, on 12 October 1964, mostly inspired by Mauricheau and his team: 'Paris is an African and European capital, today more than ever. The new word that needs to replace Empire is more prosaic, it is the nuclear umbrella, protection by militaro-political accords … It is clear that Africa being under France, the losenge that is covered by France, it is nuclear protection that Africa needs to seek out (down as far as the Cape of Good Hope).' AN, 90 AJ 68, Congo-Léopoldville (1964/65).

24 Interview by the author with Philippe Lettéron, Mauricheau-Beaupré's deputy when he worked for Moïse Tshombé (14 December 2004 and 16 June 2005). AN, 90 AJ 51, 53, Philippe Lettéron's archives for Congo-Brazzaville (1963–80).

25 AN, 90 AJ 144 and 147, Tchad (1964–95).

26 AN, F 7, Direction centrale des Renseignement généraux 20070380, 5112 (art. 2), Jacques Foccart file. *Le Canard enchaîné*, 26 July 1995.

27 In 1969, during Alain Poher's interim presidency, Foccart had been dismissed. After his election, Georges Pompidou decided to keep this special office for Africa and called Foccart back to the Elysée. But President Pompidou reserved responsibility for the secret services at the Elysée for Pierre Juillet.

28 When Journiac died in a plane crash in 1980, Martin Kirsch took his place – he was also a former member of Foccart's office in the 1960s. Foccart disapproved of Giscard d'Estaing's behaviour with regard to African presidents, as exemplified by the case of Bokassa.

29 After 1988, Foccart no longer had the monopoly of African affairs in Chirac's entourage. A second organisation showed an interest in African issues – the Club 89, which

was led by Michel Aurillac and Maurice Robert. Robert Bourgi, son of Mahmoud Bourgi, took his first steps into the right-wing political camp through this organisation, where he became a kind of unofficial ambassador in Africa.

30 See Bat (2010). African presidents were visibly concerned by Foccart's health problems during Chirac's tour to Africa in July 1995.

31 Cf. Foccart and Gaillard (1997: 478): 'Chirac wanted a service that could follow and manage African affairs. At the same time, he wanted to receive the advice of an old gentleman who had experience but who no longer wanted to head a service and whose health no longer allowed him to do so.' Interview by the author with Fernand Wibaux (15 March 2005).

32 Foccart's files (FPU and FPR) are twice as large as President De Gaulle's files (5 AG 1). Foccart was the first of De Gaulle's collaborators to give his personal papers to the Archives nationales.

Part IV

Anglo-French relations

10

Whitehall, the French Community and the Year of Africa: negotiating post-independence diplomacy in West Africa

Mélanie Torrent

Although there was no equivalent to the French Year of Africa for Britain and its territories, the French experience in the period between September 1958 and November 1960 led British officials across Whitehall to reflect on their own strategies for colonial retreat. Macmillan had requested an 'audit' of empire in January 1957 and the independence of Ghana in March 1957 had bolstered constitutional conferences in British Africa (Hargreaves 1988: 181) while it also stimulated the nationalist movements in French West Africa. Macmillan's Winds of Change speech in February 1960 was primarily, as Geoffroy Chodron de Courcel, the French Ambassador in London, acknowledged in 1963, a 'political act'.[1] But overall, Britain's formal withdrawal was slower and more disparate and Britain found itself overtaken, virtually overnight, by the nature and pace of French decolonisation. An official from the West African Department of the Foreign Office commented over fifteen years later that independence in French West Africa had been 'quickly asserted'.[2] Even if one excludes the special case of Rhodesia/Zimbabwe, independence in British Africa occurred over more than a decade (1957–68). By the end of 1960, memories of Hola Camp in Kenya and the Nyasaland emergency in 1959 were still vivid; white settlers still constrained British strategies for imperial retreat in key parts of Southern, Central and Eastern Africa; and in West Africa itself, the future of the British Cameroons and The Gambia were yet to be settled.

Pioneered by William Roger Louis, the study of the 'official mind' remains crucial to the understanding of decolonisation, particularly when it leads historians to go beyond mere comparisons to investigate boundaries, linkages and transformations across (ex-)empires. This is the approach adopted by Martin Shipway and Martin Thomas in their most recent works, which provide a global, connected narrative of European decolonisation. Unsurprisingly, Franco-British relations in Africa have featured most prominently in studies of international institutions: Marc Michel and John Kent have demonstrated the delicate balance between rivalry and cooperation which Britain and France maintained in and over Africa in the 1950s, as they sought to maximise their power in UN and NATO politics; Véronique Dimier and Catherine Schenk have done so from the perspective of European Economic Community (EEC) integration and international economic relations. By comparison, exclusive spheres, the Commonwealth and the short-lived French Community, have attracted far less attention, even though officials on both sides of the Channel discussed them in detail. This chapter aims to contribute to the study of the nature, extent and impact of Franco-British relations in late colonial and post-colonial Africa – a vital object of current political and scholarly debates, as Tony Chafer's and Gordon Cumming's recent *From Rivalry to Partnership?* aptly demonstrates – by investigating Whitehall interpretations of the French Community.

Over the period, the Colonial Office, Commonwealth Relations Office and Foreign Office faced three interrelated tasks. First, they analysed the dynamics of French strategies to assess what, if anything, could be learnt. Secondly, they sought to maintain good relations with France, a NATO partner and European neighbour. Third, they devised connected but distinct relations with three major groups of African territories: the newly independent African states which now fell within the purview of the Foreign Office; their Commonwealth partners, particularly the new Asian and African Commonwealth countries, with which good relations had to be maintained; and finally, their own remaining African territories. Beyond Conakry, Yaoundé and Lomé, British resident ambassadors were installed in only two capitals of the Community's original states, Dakar and Abidjan. What influence did the early French Community and the Year of Africa have on British diplomacy in West Africa? British interpretations of African affairs at the beginning of the 1960s highlight the importance of two related questions: the impact of Franco-British relations on decolonisation strategies and the influence of the new Franco-African relations on Franco-British relations.

Franco-British relations in Africa in the 1950s: rivals and partners

In the post-war years, Labour's Foreign Secretary, Ernest Bevin, had identified Africa as a significant area to bolster Britain's global power and increase its influence in transatlantic and European dynamics. Africa was a source of raw materials to face the challenges of reconstruction; it offered strategic bases, particularly in the East, as Britain retreated from the Indian sub-continent but maintained key interests in the Middle East; and it even offered the possibility of exporting Labour's welfare project through the promotion of welfare and development – in reality a 'second colonial occupation' driven by British needs. Bevin's plans placed a strong Anglo-French axis at the centre of a wider alliance which would include the other European colonial powers and South Africa, Britain's Commonwealth partner. By the late 1940s, Britain's acute financial difficulties, its increasing distance from European plans for integration (Schenk 1996), political and economic differences in European colonial government (Dimier 2004: 273–8) and American restrictions on the use of Marshall funds overseas put an end to Bevin's 'Euro-Africa' (Kent 1989). But the Cold War, particularly after the Berlin blockade of 1948, the Chinese Revolution of 1949 and the Soviet Union's new aid offensive in the developing countries in 1955, meant that cooperation between colonial powers in Africa remained high on the Western agenda. For the Foreign Office, two key concerns prevailed: Western partners should consult as much as possible on colonial affairs; and the transfers of power should be managed in such a way as to prevent Communist expansion. As for the French (Keese 2007a), Cold War concerns dominated Britain's relations with and about Africa. This explains why the Foreign Office both welcomed talks with France (six-monthly high-level meetings were held until 1962, in Paris and London alternately) and chose to keep them out of the limelight, to avoid giving the impression that France and Britain were trying to 'remak[e] Africa'.[3] The costly Anglo-French debacle at Suez in 1956 had at least two consequences on Britain's policy in Africa. First, Britain's international reputation, particularly in the developing world, was a precious commodity that had to be salvaged: as Adam Watson at the Foreign Office African Department had predicted, the invasion ran counter to British interests on the continent. Second, while Suez had shown the limits of American support for British imperialist ventures, its aftermath also demonstrated Washington's cautious approach to African independence (Kent 2000): a key concern of American policy-makers was that in transferring powers, France and Britain should ensure that Africa remained in the Western orbit. For British officials across Whitehall, the birth of the French Community in 1958 was therefore an important development.

The French Community differed in virtually all aspects from the Commonwealth Whitehall was familiar with. The Commonwealth had grown steadily with no single constitution but through a series of agreed texts between Britain and its dominions; it functioned around regular Prime Ministers' Meetings, essentially managed by the Commonwealth Relations Office (CRO), but could take no binding decision for its members, all fully independent – and since the London Declaration of 1949, even the Crown was only its symbolic head. By contrast, the French Community, although it had evolved from the French Union of 1946, had come into existence with its own extremely detailed constitution, forming a complicated edifice around an executive council and a senate; Article 88 provided for further independence to be eventually granted but all international affairs lay firmly under French control.[4]

As one CRO official noted, British policy in Africa should seek 'to combat external threats to British-protected and Commonwealth territories in Africa, e.g. Communism, United Arab Republic (UAR) subversion and the Afro-Asian movement'.[5] Security concerns therefore loomed large in the assessments that the

Colonial Office, the CRO and the Foreign Office each made of the new French Community. Unsurprisingly, all three devoted attention to Guinea, which had voted '*non*' in the constitutional referendum of 29 September 1958 and from which all French personnel and assistance had subsequently been withdrawn.

Assessing the French Community: views from the Colonial Office and Commonwealth Relations Office

Only a few days after the French referendum, Colonial Secretary Alan Lennox-Boyd produced a paper entitled 'The Lessons of the Referendum in French Africa', in which he sought to answer three main questions. What effect would it have on British territories in West Africa? Could it be a model for Britain? And would it enhance European prestige in Africa? According to Lennox-Boyd, the referendum would have little effect on the tiny Gambia, whose independence seemed impossible, or on Nigeria, that as gigantic territory whose independence was being discussed at that very moment at the constitutional conference in London.[6] More worrying was Sierra Leone: kinship extended into Guinea across a long common border, and many Guineans worked in the diamond mines in Southeast Sierra Leone. Lennox-Boyd feared that events in Guinea might jeopardise Sierra Leone's otherwise smooth process towards independence. Talks of a possible union between Sierra Leone and Guinea, supported by the opposition to Sir Milton Margai's government, caused unease and Maurice Dorman, the British Governor, discussed the situation in Guinea when he visited the Ministry of Overseas France in November 1958.[7] But on the whole, the Governor saw little risk of widespread agitation: vigilance, rather than alarm, was in order.

The answer to Lennox-Boyd's second question was even clearer: the French referendum could not be a model. First, it had been 'part of a national stock-taking quite exceptional in its character and without a parallel'[8] in Britain. Secondly, British domestic opinion showed little sign of *cartiérisme*: 'conscience, prestige[,] international policy [and] purely commercial reasons' supported Britain's gradual decolonisation. Thirdly, Britain had always worked on a case-by-case basis. As a brief explained in starker terms in November 1959, British policy was 'neither theoretical [n]or haphazard': there were too many risks attached to independence 'by the stroke of a pen'.[9] The working party on small states advised the Colonial Office against a French-style constitution, giving 'overnight, as it were, a new status [to] a variety of territories',[10] and only really suitable, in any case, for areas which were 'not viable and too small to aspire to full independence'.[11] Policies should be allowed to change with circumstances, the Colonial Office believed. Guinea was a case in point: Britain's official policy was that 'independence and economic aid [were] mutually exclusive'[12] but in the Cold War context, forcing Guinea to choose, in effect, 'between subsidised dependence and unsubsidised independence'[13] amounted to virtual insanity.

Overall, however, Lennox-Boyd considered Guinea to be an exceptional case – which, if anything, proved that the referendum reflected the real wishes of the French Africans. Everywhere else, Lennox-Boyd saw 'striking and encouraging' support for continued relations between Europe and Africa, even if 'some of the larger or more prosperous territorial units in French Africa [may] after a time opt to leave the Community'.[14] The ultimate decision on the French Community was the result of a popular vote, despite the numerous limits which the colonial state and education placed on the process. For the Colonial Office therefore, the Community, like the Commonwealth, 'sustained the prestige of Europe throughout Africa'[15] and served as a rampart against Communism.

The attention of the Commonwealth Relations Office in the autumn of 1958 focused on Guinea and its projected union with Ghana, officially aired with the Accra Declaration of 23 November.[16] A comprehensive study of potential questions was undertaken[17] but the CRO thought the scheme unrealistic and only very loosely thought-out.[18] Much harder was the task of the Foreign Office, placed by De Gaulle's reaction to Guinea's vote in a virtually insoluble dilemma: maintaining good relations with France while preventing Guinea from falling into Communist hands, both policies being essential to Britain's Cold War objectives.

Foreign Office policy in Guinea

The Foreign Office had no doubt about France's Western credentials. France had used the Soviet argument to secure preferences for Africa in the Treaty of Rome of 1957 (Migani 2006: 251–2), monitored social movements, including trade unions, and sought to bring 'the African elites into Western universities'[19] to bolster European influence. For the Foreign Office, the French Community was 'a major contribution to African development in partnership with the West [and] a bold experiment which [made] for stability in Africa'.[20] French policy on Guinea, however, was a source of British concern. Whereas French officials disagreed over the nature and extent of Touré's 'Communism' (Keese 2007a: 596–9), the Foreign Office never really saw him as a Communist.[21] Even so, unless the West provided aid to Guinea, the British feared that he could end up in the Soviet camp; as Touré told the British in late 1959, '[i]f Satan himself had offered to buy Guinean goods and to help the Guinean people to survive, the offer would have been accepted'.[22] Early Foreign Office assessments received support from the Colonial Office. Britain had little to fear over Guinea's internal stability, Dorman suggested in November 1958. What mattered was its potential influence in the region and British policy should therefore be 'a) to restrain Guinea [and] b) to help Guinea'.[23] Improving Franco-Guinean relations therefore became a major Foreign Office objective.

The Foreign Office, supported in this by the US State Department, gave precedence to France on all Guinean matters. After 2 October 1958, Britain delayed its recognition of the new regime for the sake of French susceptibilities, as agreed between Foreign Secretary Selwyn Lloyd and Prime Minister Macmillan[24] and as reported to Louis Joxe at the Ministry of Foreign Affairs.[25] Even after the regime was recognised on 29 October, the Foreign Office made it very clear to both its representatives abroad and French officials that there was no 'desire to step into France's shoes'[26] or to 'seek to supplant [the French] in West Africa or indeed anywhere in Africa'.[27] The only goal was to keep Guinea in the Western camp. The British spoke about France in favourable terms to Diallo Telli, Touré's representative, even talking about De Gaulle's 'liberal'[28] policy in most colonial matters. Only when all hopes of seeing Paris support Guinea's membership in the UN finally failed did Britain give its own support: the Franco-Guinean dispute could not be allowed to damage Western – and therefore British – interests in the UN General Assembly.

A similar process occurred over the issue of diplomatic representation. The Foreign Office had three main reasons for seeking a direct presence in Guinea: blocking Communist activity, protecting the interests of Sierra Leone and supporting British firms (with investment in bauxite essentially).[29] However, at the request of French Minister of Foreign Affairs Couve de Murville,[30] Britain agreed to delay opening a diplomatic mission and considered accrediting its consul-general in Dakar to Guinea.[31] It also used the NATO meeting in November 1958 in Paris to emphasise that neither the Foreign Office nor the CRO supported plans for a Ghana-Guinea union – a scheme which Gladwyn Jebb in Paris, following conversations with Couve de Murville, had warned might lead to 'a real row involving a definite strain on Anglo-French relations'.[32] But the Foreign Office was also determined to press the argument that a clear Western presence in Guinea was necessary.[33] Anglo-American concerns over the Communist bloc's diplomatic relations with Guinea led Britain to open a diplomatic mission in January 1959. Selwyn Lloyd's meeting with De Gaulle in December 1958 probably convinced him further of Britain's delicate task.[34] The French president took Lloyd to task over Britain's support for Guinea's UN membership, which he saw – in line with British Togoland's and Ghana's independence – as a clear sign of British imperialist ambitions in the region. Wynn Normington Hugh-Jones was therefore sent as a chargé d'affaires only, and arrived in Conakry the day *after* his French counterpart, Francis Huré.[35]

But on the whole, Cold War concerns mattered more than the need to spare French susceptibilities – grounded, British diplomats thought, on hurt pride rather than sound realism. In late April 1959, Britain sought accreditation for its ambassador in Monrovia, G. H. Clarke[36] – and the British embassy in Washington even pressed for a resident ambassador, if Communist expansion was to be taken seriously.[37] The Foreign Office duly noted rising 'diplomatic activity, trade agreements, the gift of arms and military training advisers'[38] from the Soviet bloc – and Czechoslovakia particularly.[39] It was therefore urgent, the British told their American and French counterparts, to initiate a comprehensive policy of Western assistance to Guinea, including 'the appointment of Western Ambassadors, an increased Western share of Guinea's trade, measures to limit Communist arms shipments and advisers, supply of commodities which Guinea particularly needs such as rice, and the use of such other African influences on Guinea as we can enlist'.[40] What comes out of the British briefs is that the French should be persuaded to provide the bulk of the West's assistance to Guinea.[41] Britain's own assistance remained modest – with references by 1960 to English-language teaching and the gift of some police radio equipment (totalling about £1,000).[42]

Foreign Office concerns over Communism, Colonial Office interests in British West Africa – and, to a lesser extent, CRO affairs with Ghana – explain Britain's decision to receive Sekou Touré in London in November. Despite French worries over the visit, the British felt that the West should not be seen to be 'snubbing'[43] Guinea, particularly as Touré was then expected in Moscow. The visit was seen as an opportunity to address two objectives: 'to encourage any tendency in Guinea towards more friendly relations with the West [and] if possible to temper [Touré's] belligerence over issues affecting [British] territories'.[44] The Queen met with Touré and his wife; the Guinean President had conversations with British officials and with Macmillan himself on 10 and 12 November. Briefs were unambiguous: 'the Prime Minister should avoid being drawn into any discussion about French territories, particularly because of the sensitivity of the French about Guinea'.[45] In the event, Touré did criticise French policies over the meetings, but there is no evidence that British officials encouraged this[46] – and they were themselves relieved to see that their own colonial matters attracted little attention, possibly on account of Britain's early recognition of the regime.[47]

Chasse gardée? Constraints on British diplomacy in West Africa

Franco-Guinean relations were therefore a source of disquiet for British diplomats: if French officials showed 'indifference or even hostility'[48] when full independence was discussed, France's territories might look for other sources of support and the position of the West in Africa would be undermined. Officials in Whitehall therefore welcomed the transformation of the French Community in late 1959: Senghor's renewed appeal to France to 'convert the Community into a Commonwealth *à la française*' (Senghor 1962: 23), the request for full independence by the leaders of the Mali Federation to the Executive Council of the Community on 11–12 December 1959, and De Gaulle's speech in Dakar on 13 December 1959, paving the way for the series of independences of 1960.[49] Independence for the two French trusteeship territories, Cameroon on 1 January and Togo on 27 April, accelerated changes in the Community. In the space of twenty days in August 1960, ten new African states had emerged in West and Equatorial Africa. On the last day of the month, the Foreign Office noted: 'French policy has developed in a remarkably enlightened way during the past two years.'[50]

The changes of March 1960 also brought Jacques Foccart to the head of the Secretariat-General for Community Affairs, 'the eyes and ears of the [French] President' (Turpin 2009: 3), in charge of intergovernmental meetings and relations between De Gaulle and each of the African and Malagasy leaders. British officials in London and representatives in West Africa regularly noted that fears of British imperialism were an obsession among French officials, for whom the Commonwealth was still very much a British creature, if not a British pawn.[51] French suspicions were particularly frustrating for Britain as Africa was precisely one area where it suffered the most scathing attacks from its Commonwealth partners.[52] Again, Whitehall officials felt they faced an impossible task: ideally, information campaigns on the Commonwealth could dispel false assumptions and misinterpretations but in practice, such activity would only be seen as the sign that a British 'fifth column'[53] was operating in French spheres. The French ambassador in London sent reassuring reports to Paris in March 1960, repeating, in many ways, what British officials themselves were trying to convey during their meetings with Paris officials.[54] His recommendation was clear: the policies of Commonwealth states could not and should not be attributed to Britain; Franco-British rivalries should be left in the past.[55] But French officials in Africa remained highly suspicious of British motives. British ambassadors underlined the 'systematic inability [of the French] to see their influence declining';[56] reports from Yaoundé and Abidjan warned that although French dominance was well-established, French susceptibilities had not died down. With France appointing its first ambassador to Guinea in March 1961, Britain's decision to finally appoint its own resident ambassador in Conakry, Donald Logan, in July 1960 undoubtedly did little to help. Previously part of the British diplomatic staff in Washington, Logan reported that suspicions of Anglo-American plots were so strong that French involvement in the region was driven primarily by 'fear[s] of being supplanted by [the British] or the Americans'[57] at a time when Algeria was also slipping from France's grasp.

Despite French attitudes and contrary to French belief, the Foreign Office had no intention of replacing France in Africa. In June 1960, the British consul in Dakar was highly critical of the overwhelming French presence in Senegal but admitted that nothing should be done 'either publicly or confidentially with African Governments, which actively [sought] to damage or weaken French influence'.[58] The British ambassador in Conakry also reported in the summer of 1960 that any obstruction to France in the region was to be resisted as it would play 'straight into the hands of the Sino-Soviet bloc and inevitably reflect on France's Western allies in this continent'.[59] The Foreign Office unambiguously stated at the end of August 1960: 'the preservation of French influence in Africa

[was] a United Kingdom interest'; it was unwise to either 'discourage [or] seek to replace'[60] the French. French policy in Algeria and the nuclear tests carried out in the Saharan desert caused lasting damage to French relations with two of Britain's key Commonwealth partners, Ghana and Nigeria. But despite calls from a number of British representatives in Africa that London should distance itself from its European neighbour, Foreign Office advice was again clear: there was no need to support the French publicly; but there was equally no necessity to condemn them in public (Torrent 2012: 43). Balance, in this case, meant as little public involvement as possible.

British officials also considered that, in the short term at least, the wave of independences gave France a comparative advantage on the continent. In July 1960, the British ambassador in Paris observed that France's formal empire in sub-Saharan Africa would soon be gone: '[t]he length and difficulty of the negotiations for Malian independence showed'[61] the limits of French influence; but Britain still faced the more daunting task of transferring powers in East and Central Africa, where Kenya, the Rhodesias and Nyasaland posed acute problems (Murphy 1995).

The international relations which followed independence also hindered Franco-British cooperation. Strong bilateral relations emerged between a dominant France and each of its ex-African territories, except Guinea: individual cooperation agreements were signed in 1960, with military commitments, secret clauses and substantial Francophone African backing for France at the UN. As one British official in the West Africa Department would note in the late 1970s, the French Community had been 'fairly short-lived' but had generated strong 'defence commitments'.[62] The Colonial Office had seen Houphouët-Boigny as a fellow opponent of radical Pan-Africanism[63] and the Foreign Office now saw in his 'little NATO',[64] as British officials called the bilateral agreements between the Entente States (Côte d'Ivoire, Dahomey, Niger and Upper Volta) and France, a favourable sphere for maintaining French – and therefore Western – presence and influence beyond independence. Ex-French Africa, the Foreign Office knew, would constitute a key bloc in the UN[65] and the civil war which engulfed the ex-Belgian Congo in July 1960 confirmed this view: British and French positions at the UN may have differed but counting on most African states not to side with the East was crucial (James 1996).

British officials also interpreted the persistent close relations between French and African leaders in the light of past policies of assimilation, from the creation of the CFA Franc in 1945 and the Investment Fund for Economic and Social Development (FIDES), to creation of the French Union in 1946 (Chafer 2002b: 226). They identified distinctions in economic relations as the single most important stumbling block in cooperation across the ex-French and British empires. In May 1960, Ghana's suggestion that Guinea might be brought into the sterling bloc to check its deteriorating situation generated more worries than enthusiasm in London.[66] British diplomats were also aware of the limits that the EEC placed on their own relations with non-Commonwealth Africa. The Treaty of Rome in 1957 did open the way for a de-concentration of French power (Dimier 2005: 37–8) but the Foreign Office was keenly aware that France intended to use the EEC to build tighter links with its ex-empire and drive EEC-Africa relations.[67]

In the Cold War context, however, Britain also acknowledged that French economic aid, through the series of Franco-African cooperation agreements that privileged French capital, personnel and products, was crucial. This was particularly the case as British assistance to its empire and the Commonwealth remained very limited. The Colombo Plan of 1950 for Asia was extended to Africa in 1959–60, but unlike in the French sphere, there was no overall planning. Only in 1961 was the Department of Technical Cooperation established and even then, British assistance was partly the result of American pressure: British officials 'did not have any clear "development doctrine" or strategy' (Cumming 1995: 71). As Sir Roger Stevens admitted in May 1961, British assistance was indeed 'on a shoe-string basis and lacked urgency and drive'.[68] While both public and private French firms stood to gain from their privileged access to the African markets, British officials believed that French assistance came at the cost of 'genuine sacrifices for France'[69] and feared that France would eventually have to reduce financial commitments which no other Western power would want to take on. Some African states might seek 'to draw their aid from other sources'[70] but Britain had no intention of volunteering, at a time when France provided its ex-empire in Africa with as much aid as Britain gave the entire Commonwealth.[71] 'Eastern bloc penetration' was item 1 on the agenda of the meeting of British representatives in West and Central Africa in May 1961. The Commonwealth was a useful instrument for British policy as 'a representative group outside the Communist *bloc* yet capable of influencing it'. But it was also essential in British eyes that in the ex-French sphere, post-colonial relations blocked risks, albeit very low in most places, of Communist penetration. The nature and channels of Franco-African relations owed more to France's '*besoin de rayonnement*' (Chafer 2001: 173) but for Britain, results mattered more than motives, over which they had little influence and no direct control. Vague plans for common action in technical assistance[72] were made but never materialised, with the pattern of aid in each sphere weighing against joint action – even before De Gaulle vetoed Britain's application to join the EEC in January 1963.

Throughout the early stages of its relations with the ex-French empire, British officials were highly aware of French omnipresence. The Foreign Office highlighted that the French empire had been about the extension of France itself whereas the British empire had aimed to 'extend British rule' – allowing no notion of an 'Overseas Britain' which would match an 'Overseas France'.[73] The result, as British officials in London and West Africa noted, was that assimilation had led Francophone African leaders to see themselves as essentially 'Parisians' who happened to be black, whereas in Britain and its territories, leaders were 'English-speaking <u>Africans</u>',[74] with a clear sense of distinctiveness and none of the 'affection'[75] felt by their Francophone counterparts for the (ex-)metropole. This meant that within the foreign ministries of the newly independent African states, French officials remained extremely present and British representatives some-times had to deal with French nationals. The Canadian ambassador in Paris[76] and the British ambassador in Dakar[77] both noted that Paris had strengthened its hold over African states by fostering a very personal, private diplomacy between De Gaulle and individual heads of state, thereby encouraging African rivalries. These observations corresponded to France's real policies, which indeed aimed at maintaining French control in the affairs of African states (Dozon 2002; Médard 2002; Chafer 2002b: 235; Keese 2007a: 605).

Conclusions: The Year of Africa's legacy in British African policies

In the late colonial period, French developments were interpreted across Whitehall through three major prisms: the belief in Britain's global influence, the importance of securing Britain's prestige in the developing world and the need to check Communism in colonies and ex-colonies – its own and those of its Western partners. Lennox-Boyd's assessment in October 1958 remained valid: except in Guinea, the French had managed to effect a transition that both checked Communism and sustained Western prestige and interests in Africa. By the late 1970s, the Foreign Office considered that the Francophone West African States were still 'more economically and financially dependent on France, more reliant on French help for their security and more closely linked politically with France than ha[d] ever been the case between the Anglophone African countries and Britain.'[78] While the Foreign Office increasingly pressed for more African regional cooperation in West Africa, particularly after Britain joined the EEC in 1973, the French transition at the turn of the 1960s had secured what the British were hoping for: stability in partnership with the West.

As independences were celebrated in the course of 1960, the Foreign Office became the dominant voice in Whitehall. The French Community had ceased to exist; France was no longer a fellow colonial power in sub-Saharan Africa; by March 1961, the committee for relations with Community states had been replaced by the Council for African and Malagasy Affairs. Fairly sympathetic assessments of the experiment in 1959 were replaced by much starker comments on the part of British diplomats. The British representative in Dakar warned that the 'withering away of the Community was inevitable [,] hastened by French inability to adapt themselves psychologically to changed circumstances';[79] other British diplomats considered in 1961 that the French Community had been 'a vain attempt to "exorcise the demon of independence"'.[80] Events in the early 1960s confirmed that beyond common objectives, the nature and channels of decolonisation in the French and British spheres would be as different as their imperial rule had been. The second part of Lennox-Boyd's assessment rang very true: the French transition provided no model for the transfer of powers in Britain's remaining dependencies or for innovations in the Commonwealth.

As several historians have underlined, the ability of British policy-makers to accept the dilution of Anglo-African links within a multilateral Commonwealth stemmed from long-standing practices of indirect rule and the security of the Anglo-American partnership in the new world order (Smith 1978: 74). In contrast, the multilateral forums which emerged out of the French empire, the African and Malagasy Union (UAM) in early 1961, or the later African and Malagasy Organisation for Cooperation (OCAM), remained exclusively African and Francophone: unlike the Commonwealth therefore, they did not provide the opportunity to face the ex-colonial power collectively. Increasingly, the 'new' Commonwealth, now in a majority after the independence of Nigeria in October 1960, used meetings to criticise Britain's management of racial conflict and supported Black nationalist aspirations in the Central African Federation and South Africa – itself forced out of the organisation in March 1961. But the Commonwealth still met British objectives better than any other set of relations could: while allowing for non-alignment, it counted a vast majority of pro-Western countries; it came at a fairly low financial cost; it allowed for the full independence of all members, including Britain itself, whose officials pursued its privileged relations after 1961 with South Africa, its most important Africa partner; and, paradoxically, the very vocal criticism of Britain could be construed as a mark of international prestige, proving that ex-British colonies were no Western stooges.

Overall, French diplomacy remained far more engaged in and with West Africa than Britain, and rested on political, economic and administrative methods which the British chose not to have: there was no British equivalent of Foccart's Secretariat for African and Malagasy Affairs and France's highly presidentialised African diplomacy after 1961. By May 1962, the British ambassador in Paris, Sir Pierson Dixon, concluded that De Gaulle's character tended 'to perpetuate [French] self-reliance', making the French only 'prospective' partners for 'a common African policy'.[81] There was therefore consultation rather than cooperation on African policies between France and Britain at the turn of the 1960s and a clear sense, held throughout De Gaulle's mandates, that imperial boundaries had become diplomatic boundaries. At a time when Britain's interest and presence in its own Commonwealth sphere in Africa remained fairly low, engagement with the new Francophone states seemed to offer few attractions. In the Cold War, they were necessary Western allies rather than potential British partners. Politically, Foreign Office policy in the emerging ex-French states was dominated by the demands of Anglo-American and Anglo-French relations. Economically, the new countries needed high levels of assistance, which the

French were willing to provide, and their inclusion in the Franc zone made them unlikely trade partners. Only if Britain joined the EEC might these prospects change. In order to secure EEC membership, however, French approval was essential. The policy advocated by Sir Pierson Dixon was therefore to accommodate French susceptibilities in Africa, if Franco-British uneasy relations over Africa were ever to improve, and if European membership was to be gained in the short term. Diverging political traditions and economic competition in West Africa does not explain De Gaulle's veto in 1963 but certainly acted against Britain in French circles, as the Community was transformed into a French *pré carré* in West and Equatorial Africa.

The only exception to the rule was Guinea, where Britain, reluctantly, made choices it knew the French would resent. It certainly acted with the support of the United States, but British policy-makers did so primarily in Britain's own political and colonial interests. The organisation of France's bilateral and multilateral relations with the new African states meant that African affairs remained an extremely sensitive subject. France's *pré carré* was a constant factor in British African policies in the 1960s: as the French capital became the diplomatic 'clearing-house'[82] of Francophone Africa, Her Majesty's Ambassador in Paris became a vital source of insight into official French thinking on African affairs. As Martin Shipway argues, 'the British independence ceremony [was] a piece of myth-making' (Shipway 2008b: 749), with no equivalent in the French empire. But the Foreign Office was certainly under no illusion about British interests and the means to promote them: as the former colonial powers, France and Britain were the best placed to maintain Western influence in the region; and Paris, in the short term at least, was better able to maintain control over its ex-colonies. A strong French presence – if anything because of the lack of any better alternative – therefore remained a key British interest.

Notes

1 Centre des Archives Diplomatiques de Nantes (CADN), Londres (Ambassade), 378PO/1/1977, Ambassador to MAE, 24 January 1963. See also Ovendale (1995).
2 The National Archives, Kew (hereafter TNA), PRO, FCO/65/1832, *British Policy Towards Francophone Africa*, 19 May 1977.
3 TNA, PRO, FO371/137959, A. D. M. Ross, 24 February 1959.
4 TNA, PRO, CAB/129/98, 'Africa: The Next Ten Years', July 1959.
5 TNA, PRO, DO/35/9353, W. P. Oliver to Allen, 28 November 1958.
6 TNA, PRO, PREM/11/3340, *The Lessons of the Referendum in French Africa*, Alan Lennox-Boyd, 16 October 1958.
7 TNA, PRO, PREM/11/3340, Dorman to Lennox-Boyd, 14 November 1958.
8 TNA, PRO, PREM/11/3340, *The Lessons of the Referendum in French Africa*, Alan Lennox-Boyd, 16 October 1958.
9 TNA, PRO, PREM/11/2584, *Touré's visit to London*, Brief 4, November 1959.

10 TNA, PRO, CO/554/1614, Carter to Eastwood, 18 March 1959.
11 TNA, PRO, FO/371/137961, *Anglo-French Talks*, 8–9 June 1959.
12 TNA, PRO, PREM/11/3340, *The Lessons of the Referendum in French Africa*, Alan Lennox-Boyd, 16 October 1958.
13 Ibid.
14 Ibid.
15 TNA, PRO, FO/371/137960, *Macmillan-Debré Meeting*, 14 April 1959.
16 TNA, PRO, PREM/11/2894, Telegram Accra to CRO, 10 December 1958.
17 TNA, PRO, DO/35/9353.
18 TNA, PRO, FO/371/131425, *Draft record of Meeting*, FO, 26 November 1958.
19 TNA, PRO, FO/371/137960, Macmillan-Debré Meeting, 14 April 1959.
20 TNA, PRO, FO/371/137959, *Note on Anglo-French Talks on Africa, Prime Ministers' meeting*, 1959.
21 TNA, PRO, PREM/11/3340, Telegram, Conakry to FO, 14 May 1959.
22 TNA, PRO, PREM/11/2584, *Record of meeting, London, Macmillan-Touré*, 10 November 1959.
23 TNA, PRO, PREM/11/3340, Dorman to Lennox-Boyd, 14 November 1958.
24 TNA, PRO, PREM/11/3340, Selwyn Lloyd to Macmillan, 23 October 1958.
25 TNA, PRO, FO/371/131425, A. D. M. Ross, FO, to Sir George Young Bart, Paris, 3 December 1958.
26 TNA, PRO, PREM/11/3340, Telegram, FO to Dakar, 7 November 1958.
27 TNA, PRO, FO/371/131425, Ross to Bart, 3 December 1958.
28 TNA, PRO, PREM/11/3340, Telegram, Conakry to FO, 28 November 1958.
29 TNA, PRO, PREM/11/3340, Telegram, FO to Paris, 24 October 1958.
30 TNA, PRO, PREM/11/3340, Jebb to FO, 25 October 1958.
31 TNA, PRO, PREM/11/3340, Telegram, Conakry to FO, 28 November 1958.
32 TNA, PRO, PREM/11/2894, Jebb to FO, 25 November 1958.
33 TNA, PRO, PREM/11/2894, FO to UKDEL NATO, 25 November 1958.
34 TNA, PRO, PREM/11/3340, *Extract of Selwyn Lloyd-De Gaulle talks*, Matignon, 17 December 1958.
35 TNA, PRO, FO/371/138830, Hugh-Jones to Selwyn Lloyd, 9 February 1959.
36 TNA, PRO, FO/371/138836, *Tripartite talks: Guinea*, Note by J. H. A. Watson, 27 April 1959.
37 TNA, PRO, FO/371/138836, Hood, British Embassy (Washington) to A. D. M. Ross (FO), 23 April 1959.
38 TNA, PRO, FO/371/138836, Foreign Office to Washington Embassy, 29 April 1959.
39 TNA, PRO, FO/371/138877, P. L. Carter to J. H. A. Watson, 2 April 1959.
40 TNA, PRO, FO/371/138836, Guinea, J. H. A. Watson, *Brief for discussion with the Americans and the French*, 7 May 1959.
41 TNA, PRO, PREM/11/2584, Touré's visit to London, November 1959, Brief 1.
42 TNA, PRO, FO/371/138831, Note on behalf of Selwyn Lloyd to E. G. Andrews, Monrovia, 26 November 1959.
43 TNA, PRO, PREM/11/2584, *Touré's visit to London*, November 1959, Brief 4.

44 TNA, PRO, PREM/11/2584, FO to Lisbon, Algiers, Conakry, Dakar, Monrovia, Leopoldville, 6 November 1959.
45 TNA, PRO, PREM/11/2584, Touré's visit to London, November 1959, Brief 4.
46 TNA, PRO, FO/371/138831, Note on behalf of Selwyn Lloyd to E. G. Andrews, Monrovia, 26 November 1959; TNA, PRO, PREM 11/2584, *Record of meeting, London, Macmillan-Touré*, 10 November 1959.
47 TNA, PRO, FO/371/131425, *Draft record of Meeting*, FO, 26 November 1958.
48 TNA, PRO, FO/371/137959, A. D. M. Ross, 24 February 1959.
49 TNA, PRO, PREM/11/2888, Ambassador to FO, 2 March 1960.
50 TNA, PRO, FO371/46492, FO to Consulate (Dakar), 31 August 1960.
51 TNA, PRO, FO/371/137959, *Note on Anglo-French Talks on Africa, Prime Ministers' meeting*, 1959.
52 TNA, PRO, FO/371/137961, *Record of Anglo-French Talks*, 8–9 June 1959.
53 TNA, PRO, FO/371/138278, Embassy (Paris) to FO, 28 April 1959.
54 CADN, Londres (Ambassade), 378PO/1/1976, *Note sur la politique britannique en Afrique*, 14 mars 1960.
55 Ibid.
56 TNA, PRO, FO/371/154740, *Meeting of Representatives in West and Equatorial Africa*, London, 16–19 May 1961.
57 TNA, PRO, FO/371/146492, Embassy (Conakry) to FO, 28 July 1960.
58 TNA, PRO, FO/371/46492, Consulate General (Dakar) to FO, 13 June 1960.
59 TNA, PRO, FO/371/46492, Embassy (Conakry) to FO, 28 July 1960.
60 TNA, PRO, FO/371/46492, FO to Consulate (Dakar), 31 August 1960.
61 TNA, PRO, FO/371/46492, Embassy (Paris) to FO, 27 July 1960.
62 TNA, PRO, FCO/65/1832, *British Policy Towards Francophone Africa*, 19 May 1977.
63 TNA, PRO, PREM/11/3340, *The Lessons of the Referendum in French Africa*, Alan Lennox-Boyd, 16 October 1958.
64 TNA, PRO, FO/371/154739, *The ex-French States of West and Central Africa, notes for the London meeting*, 16–19 May 1961.
65 Ibid.
66 TNA, PRO, PREM/11/2894, Record of a conversation, Macmillan-Nkrumah, London, 2 May 1960.
67 TNA, PRO, FO/371/137960, *Brief on Anglo-French cooperation in Africa, 1959*; Telegram, 14 April 1959.
68 TNA, PRO, FO/371/154739, *Meeting of Representatives in West and Equatorial Africa*, 16 May 1961.
69 TNA, PRO, FO/371/137959, *Note on Anglo-French Talks on Africa, Prime Ministers' meeting*, 1959.
70 TNA, PRO, FO/371/154739, *The ex-French States of West and Central Africa*.
71 TNA, PRO, FO/371/154740, *Meeting of Representatives in West and Equatorial Africa*, 16 May 1961.
72 CADN, Londres (Ambassade), 378PO/1/1976, *Note sur la politique britannique en Afrique*, 14 mars 1960.
73 TNA, PRO, FCO/65/978, *Note on 'Differences between French and British attitudes*, October 1971.

74 TNA, PRO, FCO/65/978, Embassy (Dakar) to FO, 20 June 1963.
75 TNA, PRO, FO/371/146492, Embassy (Paris) to FO, 27 July 1960.
76 Library and Archives Canada, RG25, 12523, 20–FR-1–3–AFRICA, Embassy (Paris) to External Affairs, 1 October 1965.
77 TNA, PRO, *Meeting of Representatives in West and Equatorial Africa*, 16 May 1961.
78 TNA, PRO, FCO/65/1972, *British policy towards the Francophone countries of West Africa*, 14 April 1978.
79 TNA, PRO, *Meeting of Representatives in West and Equatorial Africa*, 16 May 1961.
80 Ibid.
81 TNA, PRO, FO/371/161371, Dixon to FO, 23 May 1962.
82 TNA, PRO, FCO/65/978, Embassy (Paris) to FO, *French policy in Black Africa*, May 1963.

11

A transnational decolonisation:
Britain, France and the Rhodesian problem,
1965–1969

Joanna Warson

In 2010, while Francophone Africa was commemorating fifty years of independence, Zimbabwe celebrated a smaller, though by no means less significant, anniversary. 18 April 2010 marked thirty years since the midnight ceremony, attended by Prince Charles and Bob Marley, when the red, green, black and gold flag of Zimbabwe rose for the first time (*The Times*, 1980, 18 April). It was therefore two decades after the independence of Francophone Africa that white minority-governed Rhodesia, 'the last outpost of the British Empire in Africa and the last colony in the continent', was transformed into majority-ruled Zimbabwe (*The Guardian*, 2010, 16 April).

The roots of the slow-paced decolonisation of Zimbabwe, known as Southern Rhodesia from 1901–65 and Rhodesia from 1965–79, lie deep in the history of white settlement in the region. A self-governing colony from 1923, Southern Rhodesia held a unique status within the British Empire, as a territory in which a white minority simultaneously maintained autonomy from the metropolitan colonial authorities and dominance over the country's African majority population. When the 'wind of change' began to blow through Africa in the 1960s, Southern Rhodesia's European government remained resolute in their determination to maintain 'the real bastion of Christian civilisation in Southern Africa' (Macleod, cited by Barber 1967: 181) in the face of rising anarchy and corruption in Black Africa and the spread of communism across the globe (Godwin and Hancock 1993: 3). On 11 November 1965 this intransigence led Ian Smith (Rhodesian Prime Minister, 1964–79) to make a Unilateral Declaration of Independence (UDI). Henceforth, as Coggins (2006), Meredith (1979) and others have explored, Southern Rhodesia was transformed into an illegal and unrecognised state, known simply as Rhodesia, which directly challenged British attempts to re-cast its role in the new post-colonial, Cold War-dominated world order.

This was also a time at which a new scramble for Africa was beginning.

As the former European colonial powers sought to revise their roles in post-independence Africa, a renewed inter-European competition was being played out on the African continent. This battle was particularly acute between Britain and France, geo-strategic rivals in Africa since the earliest European colonial ventures on the continent. In Rhodesia, where controversial evidence indicates France's 'tacit support' for Smith's illegal regime (Alden 1996: 15), this post-colonial, Anglo-French struggle can be clearly identified. Yet, despite this contentious evidence, French participation in this rebellious region of British Africa has been neglected by scholars. No historian has made an attempt to piece together the disparate elements of France's involvement in Rhodesia and present a systematic analysis of their significance to events on the ground in Rhodesia, as well as to the history of Anglo-French relations in the post-war world.

The aim of this chapter is to fill this void in the historiography and demonstrate that France had a complex and multifaceted Rhodesian policy. Drawing on a diverse range of French, British and Rhodesian primary source material, including Charles De Gaulle's Presidential archive and the papers of his closest advisers at the Secretariat of African and Malagasy Affairs, the Ian Smith collection and the archives of both the British Foreign Office and the French Ministry of Foreign Affairs, this discussion will first analyse the complexities of France's direct and indirect involvement in Rhodesia, and will then examine the motivations which lay behind France's participation in this region outside of its former colonial empire. Finally, building on the recent 'international turn' (Sluga 2011: 222) in the historical discipline, whereby historians have sought to analyse the 'webs of interaction' (McNeill and McNeill 2003: 3) between ideas, people and practices, across broad spatial and temporal boundaries, we will discuss the connections which existed between France's involvement in Rhodesia and its policies in Francophone Black Africa. By assessing not only the impact of French participation on the end of British rule in Africa, but also the ways in which France's own experiences of empire influenced its engagement in Rhodesia, this article will connect hitherto separated geographies, chronologies and archives, and provide a unique, transnational approach to decolonisation. Consequently, it will be possible to integrate France's Rhodesian policy into the abundant historiography on French policy in Francophone Africa, much of which fails to address the question of France's involvement outside of its traditional sphere of influence. This chapter will suggest therefore that the decolonisation of British Africa was closely intertwined with the end of French rule on the African continent.

A French Rhodesian policy?

At 11am on 11 November 1965, after months of failed negotiations, Ian Smith proclaimed Rhodesia's independence from Britain. This declaration signalled the beginning of what was to be a fourteen-year rebellion against British authority and 'a test of their global influence'.[1] France's official response to UDI reveals little out of the ordinary. The day after UDI, Maurice Couve de Murville (Minister of Foreign Affairs, 1958–68) condemned the action of the Rhodesian Front (RF), Rhodesia's white minority governing party, stating that France had no intention of recognising an independent Rhodesia. He also pledged to recall France's consul general from Salisbury and to stop purchasing Rhodesian tobacco.[2] In the months that followed, the French government confirmed its cooperation with Britain's sanctions programme by introducing an embargo on sugar purchases and petrol sales, suspending export credits to Rhodesia and by advising French industrialists to find new suppliers of chrome and asbestos.[3]

However, in reality, France's Rhodesian policy diverged significantly from this discourse of cooperation with the British. On 12 November 1965 France's representative in the UN abstained in a Security Council vote for the adoption of Resolution 216 which condemned the Rhodesian UDI, in marked contrast to the government's denunciation of the RF noted above. In order to justify this seemingly paradoxical stance, France gave the same explanation it had given for not participating in UN debates on Algeria during the Algerian War of Independence (1954–62): 'the conflict between the United Kingdom and South Rhodesia is not an international issue'.[4] France's position towards Rhodesia in the UN remained unchanged until May 1968 when in the wake of the Rhodesian Court of Appeal ruling in March 1968 the RF was permitted to carry out executions against murderers convicted and sentenced prior to UDI. Only then, France participated for the first time in a UN vote on Rhodesia, support-ing the extension of mandatory UN sanctions on all goods, including oil, under Security Council Resolution 253.[5]

The French barrier to Britain's sanctions policy was practical as well as theo-retical. In violation of British requests and UN legislation, French businessmen remained a common sight in Salisbury, as they built on commercial contacts established in years before UDI.[6] In the immediate aftermath of UDI, a powerful French financial group, identified only as TRANSACO, approached Ian Smith's government, with the approval of the French authorities, and indicated their interest in buying large quantities of Rhodesian tobacco and minerals. Charles Pollet, a TRANSACO representative, who was also in charge of the Rhodesian Information Office in Paris, travelled to Salisbury and returned with a 'glowing account'. This in turn led to increased enthusiasm among the French business community about the possibility of improved trading relations with Rhodesia. Much of the momentum for these economic contacts came therefore from France not Rhodesia and, had it not been for Rhodesian blunders such as their slow responses to French advances and ignoring of advice, notably by contacting the French tobacco monopoly directly rather than through the intermediary of TRANSACO, closer economic relations might have developed more quickly between France and Rhodesia.[7]

Despite these Rhodesian errors, France-Rhodesian deals were concluded in the post-UDI period. On 3 May 1966 the *Observer* gave details of the purchase of $10 million of Rhodesian tobacco by France, while on 7 June *Le Monde* reported the involvement of a French firm in an attempt by Pakistan to import 75,000 tons of Rhodesian steel.[8] French companies continued to be involved in the purchase of other sanctioned goods including sugar, asbestos and chrome, while the French state was repeatedly accused by the British government and press of being directly complicit in the 'most notorious example' of sanctions evasion: oil imports.[9] Furthermore, between January and March 1967 trade between Rhodesia and France in unembargoed commodities such as diamonds and precious stones increased by 106 per cent from 1966 levels.[10] As a result, in the first three months of 1967, France imported 200 per cent more Rhodesian merchandise than it had done in the same period in 1966.[11]

Moreover, despite France's vote in favour of UN Resolution 253 in May 1968, Franco-Rhodesian commerce persisted, through the direct actions of private French companies and the covert operations of the French state. French companies were frequently named by Britain in notes submitted to the UN Sanctions Committee, while French goods, particularly automobiles, continued to reach the country by indirect means, notably through Rhodesia's white-ruled neighbours, South Africa and Mozambique.[12] The scale of this indirect trading network is attested to in papers repatriated from the French Embassy in Pretoria which record how Renault and Peugeot retained a 50 per cent share of the Rhodesian automobile market in 1979, despite more than a decade of mandatory UN sanctions.[13] More anecdotally, in memoirs of her childhood in Rhodesia, Alexandra Fuller recalls being driven around the country in an 'avocado-green Peugeot' (2002: 104). This personal memory of French merchandise in everyday Rhodesian life provides additional evidence of the continued importation of French goods into the region after 1968. French officials, including those connected to Foccart's *cellule africaine*, also helped ensure that Rhodesian exports reached the world market, despite the international embargo. One 'great big hole' in the sanctions net imposed on Rhodesia was in the former French colony of Gabon, where, following the succession of Léon M'Ba in 1967 by the man who was to become one of France's best African friends, Omar Bongo, French officials were instrumental in the establishment of a sanctions-busting network whereby Rhodesian beef was exported via Libreville to numerous destinations across Africa and Europe.[14]

France's persistent commercial activity in Rhodesia contributed to the continued economic vitality of Rhodesia, with exports rising and shortages experienced only in luxury goods (Meredith 2006: 320). The affluent 'Rhodesian way of life' was sustained (Barber 1967: 182), with white wages ten times higher than black wages in 1970 (Godwin and Hancock 1993: 45). France, while not the only country involved in evading sanctions (companies from other Western democratic nations including West Germany, the USA and even Britain are among those accused of sanctions-busting), played an important role in maintaining this privileged lifestyle, the preservation of which permitted the Rhodesians to resist the introduction of majority rule, extending UDI and exacerbating Britain's troubles in the region.[15]

French private and public interests were also involved in providing Ian Smith's regime with arms and other military equipment. In the months directly preceding UDI, the French government approved the export of spare parts and projectiles to Rhodesia, while in September 1965 the Office Français d'Exportation de Matériels Aéronautiques requested permission to conclude a contract for the sale of nine Alouette III helicopters to the Rhodesian Royal Air Force.[16] It is possible to suggest therefore that France contributed directly to the strength of the Rhodesian military which, in turn, gave the country's white population the means and the confidence to declare UDI, safe in the knowledge that Britain would do little in response (Coggins 2006: 367). Away from the economic and military sectors, France also supported Rhodesia with intelligence. Ken Flower (Head of Rhodesia's Central Intelligence Agency), described in his memoirs how his opposite number at the Service de Documentation Extérieure et de Contre-Espionnage (SDECE) was 'always anxious to help', providing the RF with access to SDECE's 'best offices' to aid its efforts to break the diplomatic and economic isolation (1987: 74, 206). Central pillars of the Fifth Republic, notably those linked to the Presidential Palace, were therefore vital in the establishment and maintenance of UDI.

As well as providing a material lifeline, France's involvement in Rhodesia had psychological consequences in the region. French attitudes towards Rhodesia, notably the refusal to vote in the UN and the rumours and reality of military and financial deals, led many white Rhodesians to believe that France would offer diplomatic support to Ian Smith's regime.[17] These allegations were substantiated by the January 1966 announcement in the *Journal Officiel* that a Comité France-Rhodésie had been established to 'inform the French public of the background to the Rhodesian problem and other racial problems in Africa'. Led by right-wing writer and former Nazi collaborator, Marc Augier (also known by the pseudonym Saint-Loup), the society wrote a letter to Wilson in early 1966 criticising British policy in the region. In Rhodesia this letter was represented as proof that 'French Society Opposes Wilson'.[18] A parliamentary friendship group, the Comité parlementaire France-Rhodésie, led by Franck Cazenave, the Rassemblement Démocratique deputy for Gironde, provided further evidence to support the Rhodesian conviction that their cause had French backing. Cazenave's week-long visit to Rhodesia in late February and early March 1966, at the invitation of Ian Smith, was seen in Rhodesia as an 'unofficial good will mission'.[19] Smith also wrote at least five personal letters to Charles De Gaulle in which he openly expressed white Rhodesia's fraternal feelings towards France, as well as its hopes for further French support. A handwritten note indicating that the General himself confirmed receipt, as well as words of appreciation for De Gaulle's reply in the opening of a letter written by Smith in February 1966, demonstrate that De Gaulle himself was certainly aware of Rhodesian expectations and personally replied on at least one occasion.[20] It is possible to suggest, therefore, that Rhodesian anticipation of more formal French support was not merely a case of settler delusion. Thus, while the French government rejected all allegations that they would recognise Rhodesia, the fact that white Rhodesians identified France as a potential ally may have contributed to the RF's ability to maintain UDI, to the detriment of Britain and its global standing. Certainly, one should not overestimate the closeness of Franco-Rhodesian relations. France repeatedly denounced the RF and 'the existence in Southern Rhodesia of a racial minority government'.[21] However, it is clear from the extent of the French government's direct and indirect involvement in Rhodesia that France did have a Rhodesian policy which was crucial to developments in Rhodesia itself, as well as to Britain in the post-imperial world.

France's Rhodesian policy: pride or prejudice?

From 1923, Rhodesia occupied a unique and uncertain position within the British Empire, 'half-way between the status of colony and that of dominion of the Commonwealth'.[22] As the African continent moved towards independence in the 1960s, Rhodesia's paradoxical situation was heightened by its geographical location at the juncture between majority and minority governance, with independent African nation states on its northerly and westerly borders in contrast to the persistence of white rule in its southern neighbours of South Africa and Mozambique. Efforts to introduce a new kind of multiracial rule, distinct from the total segregation of apartheid and the perceived chaos of African government, further increased the complex circumstances in Rhodesia. Similarly ambiguous was France's Rhodesian policy in the period between 1965 and 1969. France's clandestine support for Ian Smith's illegal, white-minority government regime stood in opposition to France's reputation as a 'pioneer of decolonisation in Africa and champion of racial equality'.[23] It appears therefore that France's Rhodesian policy, like Rhodesia itself, was divided between the opposing demands from black Africans for independence and from settlers for the maintenance of white supremacy.

Despite being outside of France's colonial sphere, Rhodesia and its Anglophone neighbours formed part of France's African strategy throughout the post-war period. The first official French diplomatic representative arrived in Salisbury in 1947 and henceforth French economic and cultural interests in British Central Southern Africa grew exponentially.[24] In the immediate post-colonial period Rhodesia continued to form part of a wider French policy in which the African arena was used to guarantee France's 'claim to middle power status in the international system' (Bach 1986: 75). In Rhodesia, France found 'a new country', populated by amenable European settlers with an appetite for French luxury goods and rich with materials needed by French industry, such as potash.[25] Moreover, in the Cold War context, Rhodesia was a vital strategic asset due to its close proximity to the Indian Ocean.[26] Unsurprisingly therefore, once UDI was declared, France was reluctant to immediately sever its ties with the region, especially, as the Elysée acknowledged, as 'Rhodesia has some things in its favour'.[27] In a personal letter to De Gaulle, written in July 1968, Ian Smith further underscores the continued possibilities available to France in the region, asserting that 'French commercial interests have already established strong ties with South Africa and so are particularly well placed to fill part of the vacuum in Rhodesia'.[28] This explains France's unwillingness to cease completely its covert support for Ian Smith's regime, despite British, African and international criticism.

To France the opportunity in Rhodesia was even more appealing due to the fact that the power they would displace was their long-standing rival, Britain. The predominance of this anti-British sentiment in French decision-making towards Rhodesia can be seen in an announcement in an official bulletin in January 1966 which brought to 'the attention of French exporters ... the quarrel which presently exists between the Governments of Britain and Rhodesia'. The statement goes further, stating that 'the cessation of trade between these two countries [Britain and Rhodesia] ... represents a unique opportunity for French exporters'.[29] Such overt encouragement, framed by implicit references to Anglo-French rivalry, demonstrates the anti-British prejudice fuelling France's position towards Rhodesia, a sentiment which can also be detected in France's military involvement in the region. French companies played a significant part in the supply of arms and military equipment to Rhodesia's white minority government. This may have contributed to the strength of the Rhodesian military, a crucial factor in the British decision to adopt a policy primarily based upon economic sanctions, the effects of which the Ministry of Foreign Affairs acknowledged were 'negligible, at least minimal'.[30] Moreover, at least forty-one French-manufactured Alouette II and III helicopters, imported directly before 1965 or transferred via Rhodesia's *"grand frère" sud-africain'* after UDI, played a central role in white Rhodesia's protracted struggle with African nationalists which further elongated Britain's retreat from African empire.[31] It is possible to suggest therefore that France's active role in providing the RF with arms and military and aviation equipment was motivated, at least in part, by a deeply imbued Anglophobia. British government officials certainly thought this was the case, as can be seen by a note written some years later by a member of the Rhodesia Department at the Foreign and Commonwealth Office which described how the French, as 'substantial suppliers of arms to Rhodesia', contributed 'directly to prolonging a war which will, if it is fought to a finish, cause serious damage to British interests in Africa and elsewhere'.[32]

France's position towards Rhodesia in the UN further highlights the prevalence of Anglophobia in the minds of French policy-makers. The contradiction between France's condemnation of Rhodesia in intergovernmental correspondence and bilateral discussions with Britain, and its refusal to oppose the RF in a multinational arena, implies that France's position in the UN was not dictated exclusively by a belief in the principle of 'non-interference'. This incongruity did not go unnoticed by French policy-makers, including those at the Elysée. In particular, the decision to associate France with the petrol embargo against Rhodesia in December 1965 was criticised by the Secretariat of African and Malagasy Affairs, not only because of its conflict with France's claim in the UN that Rhodesia was 'an internal British affair', but also due to the potential negative consequences for 'the privileged position' of France in Southern Africa, in contrast to the status of Britain and the United States as 'enemies'.[33] This underscores the ways in which France's decision to abstain at the UN must be understood as a direct challenge to Britain's ability to end UDI, motivated by a deeply-rooted Anglophobia.

In May 1968, as a result of rising Third World pressure following the Rhodesian Court of Appeal ruling of March 1968, France voted in favour of UN mandatory sanctions against Rhodesia. At first glance, this shift in France's position towards Rhodesia in the United Nations appears to suggest that France's anti-British prejudice had been set aside.[34] Yet, France's U-turn in the UN was not mirrored in its policy on the ground. Franco-Rhodesian economic exchanges persisted in the period following France's vote in favour of Resolution 253, as can be seen by the role of the French authorities in establishing and maintaining commercial links between Rhodesia and Gabon which, in turn, permitted approximately 3,000 tons of Rhodesia beef per annum to be exported to Gabon in the early 1970s.[35] France's continued trade in the region is further underlined by an assertion made by Ian Smith in his aforementioned personal letter to De Gaulle in July 1968. In his letter, Smith expresses his hope that France's support for the UN mandatory sanctions against Rhodesia would 'not restrict the activities of French commercial interests to a degree that would make the continuation of trade with us through third countries impossible'. This statement implies that, notwithstanding the French government's official adherence to the British sanctions programme, French commercial agents continued to participate in Rhodesian trade on an unofficial and indirect basis.

In the months following the Appeal Court Ruling, France's Rhodesian Policy appears therefore to be more contradictory than ever, with France openly denouncing Rhodesia yet maintaining its covert support for the country's illegal regime. At the heart of this paradox was France's Anglophobia and what has been described as 'the Fashoda syndrome': the need to protect the French *pré-carré* from Anglophone encroachment (Chafer and Cumming 2010a: 1130). In the 1960s, new tensions in Anglo-French relations, ranging from clashes over the European Economic Community (EEC) to disagreements over transatlantic relations, Cold War alliances and the Concorde Project, intensified this enduring Anglo-French *mésentente* (Young 2006: 165–8). In 1967, when De Gaulle rejected Britain's application for membership of the EEC for the second time, these tensions increased exponentially. The outbreak of the Nigerian Civil War in the same year, in which France supported the Biafran separatists in their struggle against the British-backed Nigerian Federal Government, further exacerbated Anglo-French hostility (Warson 2009). Understood within this context, France's Rhodesian policy no longer seems so baffling. Moreover, in Rhodesia, this underlying Anglophobia collided with France's pursuit of *grandeur*. In Rhodesia, France found a new means of obtaining prestige: the elimination of its arch-rival from a region where France had traditionally been excluded. This sentiment is most notable in a 1965 brief found in the private archives of Jacques Foccart which describes how Britain had 'lost the initiative' in Rhodesia following 'a series of wrong calculations and a succession of failures'. This negative assessment is contrasted to the strength of France in Africa and the world, backed up by the ambitious claim that France had progressively replaced Britain in South Africa and was now poised to do the same in Rhodesia.[36] It was, therefore, a potent mix of prejudice against the British and a desire to re-assert French national pride which led France to adopt its complex and on occasion contradictory Rhodesian policy.

A transnational decolonisation? The impact of the independence of Francophone Africa on France's Rhodesian policy

The above discussion has revealed the presence of a complex and multifaceted French Rhodesian policy driven by an explosive mixture of French pride and anti-British prejudice. The fact that this policy was pursued in a region outside of France's traditional sphere of African influence sets it apart from French action in its former colonies in the immediate post-colonial period. Yet it is still possible to trace connections between France's policies towards Francophone Africa both during decolonisation and in the post-colonial period, and the policy France pursued in the British colony of Rhodesia. France's willingness to concede majority rule to its former colonies in Afrique Occidentale Française (AOF) and Afrique Equatoriale Française (AEF) was contingent upon its ability to retain influence in those regions after independence. In order to achieve this end France employed many different strategies, some of which can also be detected in its approach to Rhodesia, thus revealing the links between France's Francophone African policy and its Rhodesian policy.

In the immediate post-colonial period, France's African policy is widely acknowledged to have been fostered, not by the French Foreign Ministry, but directly by the Elysée palace, and in particular President Charles De Gaulle and his closest African adviser, Jacques Foccart (Chafer 2008: 39). France's Rhodesian policy was similarly a *'domaine réservé'* of the Elysée, as can be seen by the long-standing close contacts which existed between Jean Mauricheau-Beaupré and Philippe Lettéron from the Elysée's African cell and Sir Geoffrey Follows (former close adviser to Sir Roy Welensky who was the Smith government's 'entrée' into the Elysée) and P. K. Van der Byl.[37] This stands in stark contrast to the Ministry of Foreign Affairs reluctance to meet with Van der Byl or to endorse the visits of Frenchmen to Salisbury, as well as its apparent ignorance of large swathes of Franco-Rhodesian trade.[38] Moreover, as in Francophone Africa, the Elysée provided the main ideological impetus for France's Rhodesian policy. The main factor that determined French involvement in Rhodesia was the President, Charles De Gaulle, himself. The steadfast pursuit of prestige in the global arena and the desire to renew French national pride was based on De Gaulle's belief that 'without *grandeur*', 'France cannot be France' (De Gaulle 1954). Similarly influential was 'the famous "Anglo-Saxon" bloc of the General's historic imagination'.[39] This suspicion of Britain, as well as its American ally, permeated down through French government and into French society, infiltrating France's mindset towards Rhodesia. Elysée criticisms of France's association with the petrol embargo against Rhodesia in 1965 were, for example, justified by fears that sanctions against Rhodesia were little more than a pretext for Britain's closest ally, the United States, to intervene in the region.[40] Opposition to the British aircraft sent to Majunga, Madagascar in March 1966 to assist with the Royal Navy's Beira patrol to blockade oil shipments to Rhodesia was similarly conceived of as a British attempt to 'compromise the Francophones'.[41] The 'Fashoda syndrome', rooted in the personality of De Gaulle, was crucial, therefore, to the shape of France's Rhodesian policy.

The complex and overlapping *réseaux* which stemmed from the Elysée and formed the basis of France's post-colonial African policy often made it difficult to distinguish between the interests of individuals and the government (Chafer 2002a: 346; Médard 1997: 22–4). This intricate intertwining of private and state participation can also be seen in France's Rhodesian policy. Oral and written testimony reports that French officials provided Rhodesia with Gabonese business and political contacts, and oversaw the illegal Rhodesian trade through Libreville.[42] The French neo-colonial networks established in Gabon in the post-colonial period render this explanation plausible (Keese 2007a). Franco-Rhodesian personal contacts are equally opaque. The Ministry of Foreign Affairs distanced itself from any Rhodesian visitors to Paris, refusing to receive P. K. Van Der Byl throughout the late 1960s. Yet, P. K. met various current and former French government officials and diplomats, including Jean-François Poncet (Deputy Director for Africa, Ministry of Foreign Affairs, 1961–63),

Ernest-Antoine Seillière (Ministry of Foreign Affairs, 1964–7), Charles de Chambrun (Secretary of State for External Commerce, 1966–67) and Zinovy Peshkov (a Russian-born diplomat who represented France on diverse missions, including to South Africa, Japan and Taiwan).[43] It is unclear therefore how far the French state was directly involved and who was driving these economic and personal contacts. However, on the basis of the known links between Foccart's closest African advisers and high-ranking Rhodesian politicians, and the importance of one of France's best African 'friends', Gabon, in the Franco-Rhodesian connection, it is possible to speculate that France's Rhodesian policy, like its African policy as a whole, was the '*domain réservé*' of the Elysée.

As part of this broader strategy of maintaining French influence in Francophone black Africa following independence, economic links with former colonial territories were retained. Closely intertwined with the complex web of *réseaux*, these economic relations were characterised by clandestine dealings and informal contacts. These covert economic interactions were mirrored in France's commercial connections in Rhodesia, as can be seen in case of the French airline, Union des transports aériens (UTA). UTA, which first became active in Rhodesia in the early 1950s, maintained a strong presence in Rhodesia throughout the UDI period, with offices in Salisbury and Bulawayo.[44] Moreover, the French company was heavily embroiled in the trading network which tied Rhodesia to France and Gabon, organising tourist and trade visits to Salisbury and Libreville, and servicing the aircraft used to transport Rhodesian meat to this former French colony.[45] Strikingly, UTA, and in particular its Director of External Affairs, Daniel C. Richon, were closely associated with Foccart and his Africa Cell, providing regular updates and seeking Elysée approval for UTA activities in Rhodesia.[46] France's underhand, unofficial African dealings were not therefore confined to the Francophone regions of the continent, demonstrating the extent to which France's Rhodesian policy was informed by its experiences of decolonisation in Francophone Africa.

The practice of cultural *rayonnement*, whereby France sought to spread the French language and civilisation, was another means France used to maintain influence in Africa after independence. A similar strategy was adopted by France in Rhodesia. Efforts were made to foster the teaching of the French language in Rhodesian schools and universities, such as plans to introduce a television-based French-language teaching programme.[47] Moreover, in 1965 a 'Bureau d'Information Rhodésien' opened in Paris, with the aim to 'strengthen cultural and tourist relations between France and Rhodesia'.[48] While the bureau was not officially connected to the French government, the authorities did little to regulate its activities, and it was not until February 1977 that the office was ordered to close (Bach 1990: 189). This slow-paced official response appears to be an indication of the interest of the French in extending the policy of *rayonnement* to Rhodesia, a strategy usually reserved for regions already within the Francophone sphere. The example for France's Rhodesian policy was, therefore, France's policy in Francophone Africa. Moreover, Francophone Africa was itself often at the heart of France's covert dealings with Rhodesia, seen most obviously by the central position of Gabon in Rhodesia's sanctions-busting efforts. The existence of these transcontinental connections demonstrates how the decolonisation of French and British Africa was inextricably linked.

Conclusions

The idea of a French Rhodesian policy is not something that has hitherto existed in the historiography of Rhodesia's Unilateral Declaration of Independence. However, through the close analysis of all available diplomatic source material, this chapter has revealed that France was directly involved in Rhodesia on a political, military, economic and cultural basis in the period between 1965 and 1969. This French participation had a significant impact on the course of events in Rhodesia, contributing to the physical and psychological ability of Rhodesia's white settlers to maintain UDI and creating further obstacles to Britain's successful resolution of the crisis. As such, France's Rhodesian policy is vital to understanding the slow-paced decolonisation of Rhodesia.

Alongside this alternative angle on Anglo-Rhodesian relations, French involvement in Rhodesia also provides us with a new approach to France's African policy. The strategies employed by France in Rhodesia echoed in many respects those first tested in Francophone Africa, notably the covert economic dealings, emphasis on *rayonnement* and Elysée dominance. Francophone Africa also directly participated in the Franco-Rhodesian *réseaux*. Furthermore, in Rhodesia France faced many of the same opportunities for *grandeur* that it had previously identified in Francophone Africa. Despite attaining independence in 1960, France's former colonies remained vital to France's international status in the post-colonial period. Similarly, the Rhodesian problem gave France a chance to play an important role on the world stage, as can be seen by the recognition of the British government, white Rhodesians and black Africans alike that France was of pivotal importance in the resolution of the Rhodesian crisis.[49] Rhodesia also provided a springboard into British Africa and the opportunity to obtain prestige through the expansion of France's economic and cultural sphere into regions which had previously been out of reach. France's Rhodesian policy was therefore shaped by the independence of Francophone Africa in 1960, with transnational forces crossing the African continent from French-dominated West Africa to Anglophone southern Africa.

However, the complex and often contradictory nature of France's Rhodesian policy suggests that the experience of decolonisation in Francophone Africa was not the sole impetus behind France's decision to embroil itself in this region outside of its former colonial sphere. An alternative stimulus for France's Rhodesian policy can be located in the long-standing Anglo-French rivalry. Ever since Fashoda all French activity in Africa had been conducted with one eye on the British. In the context of Anglophone Africa, the impact of this 'Fashoda syndrome' was all the more explosive. France's knowledge of the difficulties of decolonisation in a settler colony should have meant that France was in an ideal position to aid Britain in its resolution of the Rhodesian problem. However, France's stubborn refusal to share the wisdom gained from these experiences underlines the crucial role played by France's resentment of Britain. To the French, Rhodesia served a dual purpose. In this landlocked African country, France could simultaneously restore national pride and act upon a deeply-rooted anti-British prejudice. It was this unique intermixing of pride and prejudice that fashioned France's attitudes and activities in Rhodesia.

Rhodesia was a region previously untouched by the stresses and strains of Anglo-French rivalry. Yet, as the 'wind of change' blew in Africa, Britain and France's divergent imperialisms became divergent post-colonial policies and the artificial national boundaries imposed on Africa by European colonialism ceased to be an obstacle to France and Britain's geo-strategic competition. This re-enactment of the Anglo-French colonial rivalry in the post-imperial epoch has left its mark on Britain and France's African policy and persists in creating an obstacle to Anglo-French cooperation on the African continent in the twenty-first century. As these two rivals remained on opposing sides in Africa, the decolonisation of different African regions became inseparably interlinked. France's own experience of decolonisation in Francophone Africa collided with a deeply rooted Anglophobia and shaped its participation in this region outside of its traditional sphere of influence. This in turn impacted upon Britain's ability to deal with the Rhodesian crisis and draw a line under its African imperial venture. The end of empire in Rhodesia did not therefore follow a single, linear path shaped solely by the coloniser and the colonised. Instead the transnational decolonisation of Rhodesia was a multifaceted process, fashioned by forces unbounded by national borders, continents and hemispheres.

Notes

1 Ministère des Affaires Etrangères (MAE) (2006), *Documents Diplomatiques Français (DDF) 1966*, vol. 2. Bruxelles: P. I. E.-Peter Lang, pp. 966–9. 385, Anonymous, *La crise rhodésienne*, 6 June 1966.

2 MAE. (2003). *DDF 1965*, vol. 2, p. 584. 259, Couve de Murville, Minister of Foreign Affairs, to de Courcel, French Ambassador, UK, 11 November 1965.

3 MAE. (2006). *DDF 1966*. Vol. 1, pp. 708–9. 275, Anonymous, *La France et l'Afrique du Sud devant la crise rhodésienne*, 28 April 1966.

4 Centre des Archives Diplomatiques de Nantes (CADN), Londres/1506/577, Diplomatie to New York, 12 November 1965.

5 MAE. (2009). *DDF 1968*, vol. 2, pp. 542–3. 261, Anonymous, *Politique Française à l'égard des résolutions de l'ONU concernant la Rhodésie*, 27 September 1968.

6 MAE, EU-Europe/Grande Bretagne/252/347, De Courcel to Couve de Murville, 23 March 1966.
7 Cory Library, Grahamstown (CL), Smith Collection (SC)/9/TS4/4, Van der Byl to Smith, 11 February 1966; CL, SC/9/TS4/7, Van der Byl, 1966; TNA, PRO, FCO36/589/7, Isolani, Rhodesia Department, 19 May 1969.
8 TNA, PRO, FO 371/188007/14, Luanda to FO, 5 May 1966; Anonymous, 'Le Pakistan aurait conclu deux importants contracts avec la Rhodésie', *Le Monde*, 7 June 1966.
9 TNA, PRO, FO 371/188007, Morgan, Labour Party Overseas Secretary, 1 November 1967, Bodleian Library, Oxford (BL), MS Wilson c. 896.
10 BL, MS Wilson c. 896, *Analysis of the Economic Sanctions Against Rhodesia*, 1967.
11 BL, MS Wilson c. 896, Morgan 1 November 1967.
12 TNA, PRO, FCO36/1907/17, Barlow, Rhodesia Department, to Colvin, British Embassy, Paris, 10 June 1976.
13 CADN, AD, Pretoria/91, Le Seac'h, French Vice Consul, Johannesburg, 27 November 1979.
14 TNA, PRO, FCO36/795/1, Dutton, Rhodesia Department, 25 February 1971; Van der Byl (1969, April). SC/12/TS3/67. Grahamstown:CL; Interview by Joanna Warson with Van der Syde, Rhodesian Civil Servant, 28 March 2011, Bournemouth: UK.
15 MAE, Direction Afrique-Levant (DAL), Rhodésie, 4, *Commerce avec la Rhodesie*, 26 July 1967.
16 CADN, Londres/1506/9513, Diplomatie to Londres, 28 May 1965; CADN, Londres/1506/12415, Diplomatie to Londres, 29 September 1965.
17 Franklin, 'Rhodesia at War', *The Guardian*, 3 March 1966.
18 Anonymous, 'French Society Opposes Wilson', *Rhodesian Herald*, 7 February 1966.
19 CADN, Londres/1506/369/70, Paris to London, 20 February 1966.
20 Archives Nationales (AN), Fonds Foccart, 5AG/FPR/302, Smith to De Gaulle, 24 December 1965; 11 February 1966; 17 February 1967; 14 August 1967; 2 July 1968.
21 CADN, Londres/1506/12506, Paris to New York, 11 October 1965.
22 MAE, DAL, Possessions Britanniques (PB)/16-105, Beauliex, French Consul Nairobi to Madagascar, 5 OCtober 1949.
23 CADN, Londres/1506/41850/81, Lusaka to Paris, 14 October 1965.
24 CADN, Salisbury, 1/9, Francières, French Vice Consul, Salisbury, to MAE, 4 November 1947.
25 MAE, DAL, PB/16/38, Warren, French Vice Consul, Salisbury, to Beaudoin, French Consul in Nairobi, 7 October 1950; MAE, DAL, PB/16/18, Francières to MAE, 24 November 1947; MAE, DAL, sud-est africain britannique (SEAB) 1966/13/245, *Exportation de potasse vers la Rhodesie*, 23 May 1966.
26 MAE, DAL, SEAB1966/13/245, Bellivier, Head of the French General Consulate, Salisbury, to MAE, 30 August 1966.
27 AN, 5AG/1/Ély/248, *Situation Diplomatique*, 12 November 1964.
28 AN, 5AG/1/Ély/215, Smith to De Gaulle, 2 July 1968.
29 CL SC/9/TS4/7. 001(R), 1966; TNA, PRO, FO371/188007/4, Paris to FO, 11 March 1966.

30 MAE, DAL, SEAB1966/13, *Sanctions contre la Rhodésie*, 2 September 1966.
31 CADN, Pretoria/90/647, Legendre, French Ambassador, South Africa, to MAE, 30 August 1973; CADN, Pretoria/90, *Bulletin de Documenation* (n° 376), 13 October 1977.
32 TNA, PRO, FCO 36/1907/17, Barlow to Colvin, 10 June 1976.
33 CADN, Londres/1506/148, Seydoux, French Representative, UN, to Diplomatie, 9 April 1966; AN, 5AG/FPR/302, Anonymous, nd.
34 MAE. (2009). DDF 1968, vol. 2, pp. 542–3, 261, Anonymous, *Politique Française à l'égard des résolutions de l'ONU concernant la Rhodésie*, 27 September 1968.
35 Van der Byl (1969, April). CL, SC/12/TS3/67. Interview with Van der Syde, 28 March 2011; AN, 5AG/FPU/915, Richon, Director of External Relations, UTA, to Gavois, Technical Advisor, MAE, 14 May 1973.
36 AN, 5AG/FPR/302, *Note sur les causes et les conséquences possibles d'une aggravation de la crise rhodésienne*, nd.
37 BL, Welensky Papers, 231/14.6, Secret Minute to PM, 7 May 1968; CL, SC/9/TS4/11, Van der Byl, 1966; CL, SC/15/TS3/8, Van der Byl to Smith, 8 March 1971.
38 MAE, DAL, Rhodesie, 4, MAE, *Demande d'audience du Ministre rhodésien d'Information*, 6 November 1968; MAE, DAL, SEAB1966/13, *Projet de voyage en Rhodésie de M. Cazenave*, 16 February 1966; TNA, PRO, FO 371/188007/14, Bridges to Palliser, 23 May 1966.
39 House of Lords Hansard, vol. 270, col. 135, Gladwyb, 11 December 1965.
40 AN, 5AG/FPR/302, Anonymous, nd.
41 House of Commons Hansard. Vol. 749, Col. 1822, Rees, Labour MP, 5 July 1967; AN, 5AG/FPR/302, *L'Angleterre et l'échéance rhodésienne, et l'affaire de Majunga*, nd.
42 CL, SC/12/TS3/67, Van der Byl, April 1969
43 MAE, DAL, SEAB1966/13, *Note pour M. Soutou*, 24 March 1966; MAE, DAL, Rhodésie, 4, *Demande d'audience du Ministre rhodésien d'Information*, 6 November1968; Van der Byl (1966). SC/9/TS4/11. Grahamstown: CL.
44 CADN, Pretoria/90/647, Legendre to MAE, 30 August 1973.
45 AN, 5AG/FPU/2132, Richon to Foccart, 1 November 1971; AN, 5AG/FPU/915, Guillaume to Doumenc, Regional Manager for Southern Africa, UTA, 18 March 1972; AN, 5AG/FPU/915, Ribo, French Ambassador, Gabon, to Foccart, 24 March 1972; TNA, PRO, FCO36/1907/6, Callaghan, UK Foreign Secretary), to NY, 22 March 1976.
46 AN, 5AG/FPU/2132, Richon to Foccart, 1 November 1971.
47 CADN, Salisbury/5/1295, MAE to Salisbury, 17 March 1969.
48 CADN, Salisbury/9/202, Bellivier to MAE, 21 May 1969.
49 TNA, PRO, FO371/187982, Cortazzi, West & Central African Department, to Peck, British Embassy, Dakar, 11 January 1966.

Part V

Nationalist trajectories, border issues and conflicted memories

12

The changing boundaries of resistance: the UPC and France in Cameroonian history and memory

Thomas Sharp

From its inception in 1948, the persistent demand of the *Union des Populations du Cameroun* (UPC) for French Cameroon's independence progressively distinguished it from the more moderate stance of the dominant nationalist parties in French sub-Saharan Africa (Joseph 1977: 337). Beginning in the early 1950s, the party increasingly predicated independence upon unification with the British Cameroons, a dual aim that appeared as a direct challenge to the metropole's continued presence in the region (Johnson 1970: 673; Gardinier 1963: 44). This threat was further underlined by the French administration's perception of the UPC as a communist movement. (LeVine 1964: 153; Keese 2008: 134–5; Deltombe, Domergue and Tatsitsa 2011: 158–81). France's attempts to suppress UPC activities finally resulted in riots throughout the south-west of the territory in May 1955, and the administration's proscription of the party in July. The majority of the leadership went into exile to sustain a diplomatic campaign for the party's aims, while from December 1956 UPC militants remaining within the territory began an armed guerrilla struggle, so that French Cameroon became the only territory in which major armed opposition against colonialism occurred in French sub-Saharan Africa (Johnson 1970: 671; Joseph 1974: 428). By the close of 1961, the two demands of the UPC had been ostensibly achieved, with the now-independent French territory and British Southern Cameroon being united on 1 October. The new Cameroonian government, however, under the presidency of Ahmadou Ahidjo, maintained close political, economic, technical and military ties to France (Joseph 1977: 343; Bayart 1978: 45–50).[1] As a consequence, the UPC's more radical leadership persisted in both seeking alternative extra-metropolitan connections abroad and directing the internal guerrilla insurgency for another decade, vowing to continue its resistance for 'true' independence against a 'neo-colonial' regime.

Studies of the close political and economic links that persisted between France and certain of its former territories in sub-Saharan Africa have often been limited by their neglect of concomitant political networks that were based upon a continued *rejection* of this privileged relationship.[2] A longer-term analysis that includes structures of opposition to *la présence française* reveals not only that continuities of resistance have existed alongside those of collusion, but also the complex ways in which these competing political modalities have interacted with each other over time – in history, politics and memory. By following the historical, political and commemorative trajectory of the UPC over the past fifty years, a more complete, yet ultimately more complex, picture of Cameroon's post-colonial relationship with France begins to emerge. First of all, and confirming arguments of scholars such as Bayart (1993) and Médard (2005), the Cameroonian government's responses to the UPC's initial uprising, as well as its later responses to the uprising's legacy, reveal that the close ties of cooperation that have existed between France and Cameroon over the past fifty years cannot be reduced to a static model of dependency dictated by Paris. Instead, the Cameroonian government has been able to use the UPC's subversive opposition as a means to actively negotiate and effectively exploit its relationship with France in order to strengthen its own political position.

Secondly, this interaction of UPC opposition and government cooperation, which refutes the dependency paradigm, cannot be reduced to a static antagonism between two distinct and fixed political groups. Structures of opposition and cooperation regarding the French presence in Cameroon were subject to shifting, overlapping and often uncertain memberships and transnational connections. As a result, analytical categories of 'collusion' and 'resistance' cannot be easily attached to any particular historical or political actor. The unstable and partial nature of these categories further emerges from the fact that their associated labels – such as 'neo-colonial', 'subversive', and 'anti-colonial' – have been variously re-assigned and re-appropriated by the Cameroonian actors themselves, according to political exigencies. The subjective process of re-assigning and re-appropriating these labels, both during the UPC uprising and in its subsequent commemorations, is evident among both state and non-state actors, who could be supportive, indifferent or hostile to France's close ties with Cameroon.

Cameroon's relationship to France has therefore been continuously open to shifting alliances and interacting networks of opposition and cooperation, representing a variety of political objectives that refutes conventional analytical categories of dependency, collaboration and resistance. The political and historical subjectivities that have been articulated around such a relationship have similarly been open to constant negotiation and appropriation by various actors in Cameroon. The overall result has been the creation of a complex and ever-evolving legacy, both of the French presence and of the groups that variously opposed or accepted it. To explain this multifaceted and dynamic relationship with France, this chapter examines two aspects of the UPC uprising during the 1960s, and two elements of its commemoration since the 1990s. These examples represent moments when networks of cooperation with, and opposition to, the French presence appeared at their most interconnected and indeterminate. At these junctures, categories of 'resistance' and 'collusion' became blurred, as the relationship to France was subject to intense negotiation, exploitation and interpretation by various political actors from Cameroon.

The UPC's resistance to the privileged relationship, 1960–1971

Following the UPC's prohibition and the start of its armed struggle within the French territory from 1956, the majority of the party's leadership sought refuge abroad, first in British Cameroon (which itself outlawed the party in 1957), then Khartoum, Cairo, Conakry and Accra, from where it issued numerous printed and verbal appeals to various international organisations, and from where it directed the guerrilla insurgency on Cameroonian territory.[3] After independence in 1960, the Cameroonian government's decision to maintain close links with Paris ensured the continuation of opposition activities by the UPC's more radical membership both at home and abroad, who collectively refused Ahidjo's offer of political amnesty.[4] Somewhat paradoxically, however, it was the perpetuation and scale of such opposition that significantly influenced Yaoundé's decision to strengthen and sustain its links to France throughout the 1960s, until the uprising's defeat in 1971. A recognition of the UPC's activities thus contributes to Chafer's (2002b: 2–3) critique of the view that the French presence in its former sub-Saharan territories was the natural extension of a congenial colonial encounter, or that it was an arrangement entirely dictated by the foreign policy concerns of Paris. A fuller understanding of the varied trajectories and complex interactions around which Franco-Cameroonian relations have formed must therefore begin not only with a de-centring of 1960 as a rupture, but a further de-centring of the former metropole as the decisive element in shaping these relations.

Although the Ahidjo regime did indeed sign a series of cooperation accords with France in 1960 (Atangana 1997: 104), the influence of the UPC's continued activities refutes a simplistic reduction of these agreements to a French desire to maintain a foothold in Africa. The decision by President Ahidjo to sign the accords, especially those concerning defence,[5] was also a domestic response to the destabilising effects the UPC posed in relation to a newly-independent state, particularly as it lacked the ability to suppress the uprising on a military level, as well as the capacity to undermine its popular support base through national development projects (Oyono 1990: 39).[6] That Cameroonian foreign policy could be determined by the domestic concerns of Yaoundé and the activities of the UPC, as much as by the interests of France, is evidenced by Cameroon's diplomatic relations beyond its Parisian channels. In September 1960, Ahidjo's stated opposition to the Casablanca group was not the result of a categorical desire to remain close to the Brazzaville group and help France maintain a foothold in Africa, but more specifically related to Nkrumah's support for the uprising (Oyono 1990: 69). Extending beyond Africa, although Cameroon's normalization of relations with the People's Republic of China in 1964 can be viewed as following the lead of De Gaulle's recognition in that same year, by once again de-centring Paris and focusing on the specific political context of Cameroon, one finds that Ahidjo's previous reluctance to recognise the PRC was equally founded upon the latter's support for the UPC.[7]

As a consequence, it is perhaps unsurprising that after the collapse of the UPC's major international support networks and the definitive defeat of its guerrilla forces by the 1970s, Ahidjo made signals that he wished to renegotiate the cooperation accords with France (Oyono 1990: 191). This is not to argue that the defeat of the UPC did not suit French aims nor that it signalled a significant rupture between Yaoundé and Paris.[8] It is instead to nuance an extant historical image, since an acknowledgement of the UPC's opposition to Franco-Cameroonian ties reveals that this relationship could be founded upon mutual interests rather than an imposed dependency, and that it could be enacted as a pragmatic domestic response to internal opposition.[9] Ahidjo was able to actively exploit both the UPC's opposition and the close relationship with Paris in order to secure his own hold on the state apparatus, perhaps most directly evidenced by his introduction of a prolonged State of Emergency that was enforced by French military and technical support.[10] As a result, the opposition of the UPC to the Franco-Cameroonian relationship was at the same time complicit in its affirmation.

Subversive students, 1962–1965

By widening the scope of analysis beyond the competing foreign support networks that directly pertained to the armed conflict, the international connections utilised by Yaoundé and the UPC are demonstrated to be neither entirely distinct nor constituted by homogeneous political memberships. In the realm of education, both the Cameroonian government and the UPC utilised the same international channels and institutions to train Cameroonian youth abroad for their competing political visions of an independent Cameroon. The consequent overlap of these networks generated internal tensions within each camp that began to reveal the indeterminate and shifting boundary that existed between notions of anti-colonial resistance and those of neo-colonial collusion regarding Cameroon's relationship with France.

A comparative study of the UPC's internal bulletins with reports written by government security services in the first half of the 1960s reveals not only that the UPC's exiled leadership was increasingly staffed by Cameroonians educated in Paris, but also that both the UPC and the Ahidjo government were simultaneously sending Cameroonian youth to be educated at the same universities in the

Eastern Bloc and China. The coexistence of UPC and government-sponsored youth within these 'communist' universities first of all created an acute atmosphere of apprehension among government security services within Cameroon during the first years of the 1960s.[11] From 1965, this resulted in the wrongful arrest of many Cameroonians returning from university courses in the East who were suspected of being 'subversives' working for the UPC, but who were subsequently released when it was discovered that they were on government-sponsored courses and thus posed no threat to the state.[12] In a similar development, the appearance in Accra of young UPC militants who had been educated in Paris aroused the suspicion among established elements of the exiled leadership that the new arrivals were 'saboteurs' employed by the French and Cameroonian governments.[13] These suspicions eventually led to the inward collapse of the exiled leadership in 1962, positing the 'old guard' of the original *Bureau du Comité Directeur* (BCD) against the newly-formed *Comité Révolutionnaire* (CR) of the Parisian students. The group's diplomatic struggle similarly turned in on itself, with accusations of 'neo-colonialism' and collaboration with France increasingly directed at opposing factions rather than the Ahidjo regime.[14]

Although education was at the heart of the nation-building project in the Third World (Westad 2006: 93), students could also be seen to enter political spaces as potential saboteurs due to their mobility and sensitivity to economic change, which in turn constituted their political membership as more flexible, and therefore their loyalty as more questionable (Durham 2000: 118). The potential for subversive students was especially acute in the case of Cameroon due to the ongoing insurgency, and in this particular instance uncertainty over the allegiance of Cameroonian youth educated abroad serves to demonstrate that the competing international networks formed by the UPC leadership and the Ahidjo government were not as distinct as their avowed animosity would suggest. A complex negotiation of political loyalties becomes evident, as notions of 'neo-colonialism' or 'subversion' were not fixed to any particular group, but could be reassigned according to specific political exigencies. In addition, scholarship applications written by Cameroonian youth, which were intercepted by government security forces, reveal that the vast majority of these students were motivated by personal desires for socio-economic advancement, and openly declared no political allegiance to either Yaoundé or the UPC.[15] As such, the avowed apolitical position of many scholarship students demonstrates that actors did not only ascribe political labels to further their own political agenda, but that these labels could also be actively refused to further individual socio-economic aims.

The overlapping of insurgent and government-sponsored education programmes abroad, moreover, caused the UPC leadership and Cameroonian security services to become suspicious of students who did not obtain scholarships through their approved channels. As a result, both insurgent and government authorities sought to control students' access to foreign educational resources in similar ways. Cameroonian security forces demonstrated a propensity to arrest those students returning to the country who had not obtained official permission from the government before leaving for education abroad, especially when this education had taken place at communist universities where UPC-sponsored students were known to be present.[16] In a similar fashion, the BCD labelled as 'colonial agents' those who provided or obtained scholarships without their approval – accusations that began with, and were primarily directed at, those Cameroonians who had sided with the Parisian-educated leadership of the *Comité Révolutionnaire*. On one occasion, the leadership of the BCD and CR had even attempted to persuade the Ghanaian authorities to imprison members of the opposing faction following a grenade attack on a meeting of the BCD in Accra.[17]

With the internal armed insurgency increasingly losing ground to a sustained assault by Franco-Cameroonian forces, and with Ahidjo applying increasing diplomatic pressure on the UPC's African sponsors through newly-created political institutions such as the OAU and OCAM (Terretta 2010: 192), the UPC's efforts to contest the state's metropolitan links were increasingly confined to strategies of rhetoric and representation through press releases and communiqués. Yet even these more limited efforts at opposition to Franco-Cameroonian relations were being progressively undermined by the internecine fighting between the BCD and the CR, so that the representation of the struggle soon became the struggle for representation. Each faction sought to control access to foreign financial and political support through published denunciations of former comrades as 'neo-colonial' stooges.[18] Just as the internal armed wing of the UPC began to fragment and pursue separate agendas in the name of the 'uprising',[19] so too did the exiled leadership begin to lose its cohesion as it competed for what external resources remained in the name of the UPC. The disintegration of the UPC leadership and the suspicions of government security services consequently serve to demonstrate how a complex political reality contributed to the shifting and re-assignable categories of political belonging, with which Cameroonians attempted to successfully negotiate the country's domestic and transnational political connections.

Changing alliances and the politics of history: the UPC and the Biya regime

Uncertain political alliances and overlapping international networks therefore significantly contributed to an indeterminate understanding of who and what constituted instances of collusion and resistance. Within more recent domestic debates about the Cameroonian state that centre upon its past and present relationship with France, the UPC accordingly occupies a somewhat ambiguous position. Since the introduction of multi-partyism in the early 1990s, the history of the uprising has been adopted by, and adapted for, a variety of competing political projects of both government and opposition. The various appropriations of this legacy once again indicate that the interconnected networks of opposition and association that have constituted Cameroon's relationship with France have never been static, and that accompanying categories of 'neo-colonialism' and 'anti-colonial resistance' cannot be permanently ascribed to particular groups. The impermanency of these labels means that they can, however, be re-appropriated and re-assigned for a variety of political projects – a process that is as true in the commemorative politics of the present as it was during the uprising itself.

By 1972, with both the internal armed insurgency and the activities of the UPC's exiled leadership no longer posing a threat, President Ahidjo was able to consolidate his hold on the Cameroonian state apparatus, which included official measures to render the UPC a taboo subject within the country (Jua and Nyamnjoh 2002). It would take an additional fifteen years and a new president before the UPC would be officially acknowledged in Cameroon's history of anti-colonialism, as demonstrated by a passage in President Paul Biya's 1987 political manifesto, *Communal Liberalism*:

> The independence of our country was hard won by many worthy children of the land, whose names unfortunately have remained taboo for the past quarter of a century … It is to these people that I am making this sincere and patriotic appeal for them to join us in the on-going struggle against neo-colonialism, with a view to acquiring freedom for Cameroonians. (159)

Biya's remarks appeared to indicate a rupture with Cameroon's past relationship with France and a new historical opening for the UPC. This was succeeded by a further political opening in 1991, when the ban on the party was lifted and it was allowed to participate in Cameroon's new multi-party democratic process. Under pressure from international donors' demands for 'good governance', as well as growing domestic discontent (Joseph 1997, Krieger 1994), Biya's apparent liberalisation of politics and history suggested that for the first time in decades, the socio-economic and political possibilities for Cameroonians would be disencumbered from the patrimonial networks of government and its past neo-colonial links with France. As a result, hundreds of former UPC militants returned from abroad, including surviving members of its exiled leadership (Asong and Chi 2001: 668).

The democratic process was quickly stalled by the president's political manoeuvring, however, and in spite of the West's previous demands for good governance and Biya's denunciations of 'neo-colonialism', Paris continued to be Cameroon's principal source of financial, technical and military support in what was still a de facto single-party state (Amin 2004: 162). In addition, the newly legalised UPC was unable to effectively exploit its own historical legacy of resistance to Cameroon's 'neo-colonial' past in order to contest the Biya regime's continued links to Paris, as the party leadership once again fell into dispute and split into rival factions. Of these factions, only the group led by Ndeh Ntumazah consistently sought to denounce the Cameroonian government's continued ties to France and to seek political alternatives abroad.[20] Ntumazah's limited material and financial resources, however, as well as his preoccupation with overcoming the internal divisions within the UPC, once more restricted such opposition to a limited dissemination of pamphlets and publications produced abroad.[21]

Conversely, it was President Biya who was able to most effectively exploit the legacy of the UPC's resistance, allowing him to disguise the incongruence of his own declared policy towards French 'neo-colonialism' and consolidate his hold on power. It was furthermore the divisions of the re-legalised UPC that largely enabled such a strategy, and even assisted in maintaining Cameroon's privileged relationship with France. This was achieved by Biya's shrewd combination of a public *rapprochement* with the UPC and his maintenance of a highly restricted democratic process.[22] Biya's admission of deceased UPC leaders into the 'pantheon of national heroes' in 1991 and his offer of cooperation towards the party – which took place in the context of very limited opportunities for political participation – soon compelled the leaders of the two remaining UPC factions, Augustin Fréderic Kodock and Henri Hogbe Nlend, to abandon their oppositional activities and pursue official posts within the government, a government that still maintained questionable ties to Paris.[23] As a result, Biya's political appropriation of the UPC legacy and the subsequent acceptance of government positions by Kodock and Henri Hogbe Nlend – as former members of the opposition – allowed the Biya regime to demonstrate the credentials of democratic 'good governance' to the international community, which would enable continued access to French financial aid. Due to Biya's political manoeuvring and the UPC's weakness, therefore, both the party and its legacy failed to represent a stable and coherent opposition to the Cameroonian state's ties to France and in this instance can even be said to have reinforced such ties. The political boundary between resistance and collusion that centres upon the Franco-Cameroonian relationship, a boundary which the UPC was supposed to represent, consequently remained indistinct and uncertain in political reality.

The UPC as neo-colonial collaborator: the 'anglophone problem'

In present-day Anglophone West Cameroon, which constituted the former British Southern Cameroons, there is a widespread perception that unification with the French territory in 1961 has led to a growing marginalisation of the Anglophone minority in the nation-state project.[24] The project is portrayed as having been controlled by an assimilated Francophone political elite that seeks to dispossess Anglophones not only of their political and economic power, but also of their cultural heritage and identity (Konings and Nyamnjoh, 2003: 2; Eyoh 1998: 263). A historical narrative has subsequently emerged to justify a two-state solution to the problem of marginalisation, through a return to the pre-unification boundaries. The claim has been exhorted by several Anglophone political organisations created during the 1990s, the most prolific of these arguably being the Southern Cameroons National Council (SCNC).[25] The claims of groups like the SCNC appear to echo the historical demands of the UPC in the 1960s, as they are largely based upon accusations of political dispossession against the Cameroonian state that have been engendered by the government's 'neo-colonial' ties to France.

The history of UPC activities in the British Southern Cameroons has been relatively little studied, in large part due to the lack of insurrectionary violence that actually occurred there (Takougang 1996: 8). By widening the analysis to include the Anglophone perspective, the history of Cameroon's relationship with France – and how the UPC relates to such a history – is once again shown to be more complex than a simple antagonism between two distinct and static camps of 'neo'- and 'anti'-colonialists. Although Anglophone nationalists, like the UPC during the 1960s, claim that 'true' independence must be predicated upon freedom from French influence and 'neo-colonial' practices, the party continues to occupy an ambiguous historical position in the Anglophone nationalist narrative. In this narrative, the UPC uprising does not provide a precedent of resistance to neo-colonialism which Anglophone nationalists can lay claim to for political legitimacy, as it has done for the post-liberalisation UPC and for the Biya government. Rather, neo-colonialism in the Anglophone narrative is constituted not only by the more tangible political and economic agreements between Yaoundé and Paris, but by a more generalised 'Francophone' culture of violent assimilation and centralisation that continued after independence. This culture had taken root among Francophone Cameroonians during the colonial period as a result of the strong metropolitan presence, and was subsequently unleashed upon the Anglophone territory via unification in 1961. As a consequence, the UPC are not portrayed as a force that resisted neo-colonial forces in the former British territory, but as one that both represented and enabled it, due to the party's Francophone roots, its violent campaign for unification, and its shared belief with the Ahidjo regime that 'only a unitary government can guarantee the security and unity of a reunified Cameroon' (Ngoh 1990: 199).

The idea of a Francophone 'Other' in the Anglophone nationalist narrative represents the boundaries of historical identity that must correspond to the territorial boundaries demanded by its secessionist claims. This re-drawing of boundaries is further required to be justified on moral grounds, so that a homogenous Anglophone culture of peace and democracy is posited against a threatening Francophone culture of violence and autocracy. The SCNC thus portray their pre-unification history as one of collective progress towards freedom interrupted by the 'neo-colonial' Francophone project of violent assimilationism. In contrast to the liberalism and democracy inherited from the British, the SCNC posit the 'moral bankruptcy' of Francophones, denouncing 'the Francophone corrupt culture' of rigid bureaucracy and violence that was 'copied' from the metropole and imposed on the Southern Cameroons after unification ('About Us' 2009).[26] A history of the Southern Cameroons written by a well-known Anglophone nationalist academic and activist (Anyangwe 2008: 12–13) similarly represents this 'neo-colonial' culture of Francophone Cameroonians as being wilfully derivative of French practice. Ahidjo's decision to sign the Co-operation Accords with France is consequently described as an 'aping' of French colonial practice, labelling him as a '*centralisateur et Jacobin*' and a 'black *Gaulliste*' who would soon put an end to the 'vibrant democracy' of British Southern Cameroon after unification.[27] The violent nature of this inherited Francophone culture is evidenced by Ahidjo's suppression of UPC opposition with the aid of French troops, which the author even goes so far as to label 'genocidal' (Anyangwe 2008: 13).

The contradictions that accompany Anglophone nationalism's re-drawing of identity and history maintain the UPC in an indeterminate position regarding Cameroon's relationship with France, as the party simultaneously appears as both a victim and perpetrator of this Francophone culture of aggressive assimilationism. As opponents to the Yaoundé-Paris alliance who bore the brunt of its violent, indeed even 'genocidal', suppression of dissent, the UPC is located outside and against this neo-colonial culture. In order to maintain the homogeneous and exclusive identity of the Anglophone victim, however, the opposition and victimisation of the UPC in relation to French neo-colonialism must be transmuted into complicity. In the Anglophone narrative, the UPC's Francophone origins, and the armed struggle by which it pursued unification, subsequently relocates the party in the neo-colonial Francophone culture of violent Jacobinism. The ambiguities that such historical representations produce become most visible in the Anglophone portrayal of UPC-affiliated refugees in Southern Cameroon from 1955. Although these Francophone refugees are acknowledged to be fleeing the dictatorship and oppression of the Franco-Cameroonian alliance (Alemanji 2008: 3), the fact that their presence also allowed the UPC's unification campaign to take hold in Southern Cameroon (Takougang 1998: 10), causes their presence to be portrayed as that of a 'Trojan Horse' that 'hi-jacked' the territory's peaceful progress towards independence (Alemanji 2008: 3).[28] Unification therefore becomes 'a conspiracy by ungrateful asylees' who 'abused the hospitality of their host country by plotting to subvert its political life and to steal the country' (Anyangwe 2008: 25).

Anglophone nationalists' association of the UPC and the Ahidjo regime within this Francophone culture is not, however, an invention of the present. In 1960, during the plebiscite campaign to determine the form of Southern Cameroons' independence, the Cameroon People's National Congress (CPNC)

– who supported British Cameroon's integration into Nigeria – asked in one of its pamphlets: 'Who amongst you would like to live in French Cameroons, a country red with the blood of thousands of innocent victims killed by terrorists and the Ahidjo regime?' (Ngoh 2001: 151). As is the case in more recent Anglophone narratives, the CPNC located this Francophone culture of violence in opposition to British political culture: 'In the Southern Cameroons and Nigeria, political differences are settled by arguments and by the ballot box. In French Cameroons political differences are settled by guns and poison' (ibid.: 151). The shifting and indeterminate boundaries of political identification are once again evident, as the CPNC's portrayal of the UPC as violent 'terrorists' echoes the portrayal of the UPC by the Ahidjo government (Hubenelle, 'Le Cameroun à trois mois de sa réunification', 1961), a government that the CPNC was conversely trying to distance itself from.

The reality of unification in Southern Cameroon was more complex, of course. In the UN plebiscite that was to determine the unification question, it was Southern Cameroonians themselves who voted to join the French territory – they were not forced to do so by the UPC. The plebiscite, however, did not give the option of independence for Southern Cameroon in and of itself, only by joining either the newly-independent state of Nigeria or that of *La République du Cameroun* (Awasom 2000: 110). The attitude of Anglophone nationalist historians – that the plebiscite represented a 'catch 22' for Southern Cameroonians – is evident in their frequent quotation of the Fon of Bafut's remark at the Mamfe Plebiscite Conference in August 1959: 'To me the French Cameroons is "Fire" and Nigeria "Water". Sir, I support secession without unification.' (Personal Correspondences, Bamenda 2012; cited from Welch 1966: 207) The explanations for why Southern Cameroonians chose unification are as multiple as the possible reasons (Ngoh 2001; Awasom 2000; Takougang 1996), but it appears that the UPC has served as a useful historical scapegoat for the fact that it put the unification option on the table in the first place, and supported it ardently (Anyangwe 2008: 32). As a result, the party was seen as the vehicle that enabled French colonial – and Francophone neo-colonial – practices to take hold in Southern Cameroon.

Conclusion

Throughout the past fifty years, the enduring presence of France in Cameroon is not in doubt, and neither is its ability to shape the country's political landscape. If, however, *la présence française* is a central subject around which understandings of 'collusion', 'resistance' and 'dependency' have been articulated in the context of French Africa, then the difficulty of ascribing these categories in Cameroon demonstrates two important points. First of all, analyses of the continued ties between France and its former African colonies have been too focused on the actions of Paris, which has resulted in an over-simplification of the complex and various ways in which Africans themselves have engaged with this relationship. Secondly, the consequent complexity of the Cameroonian example shows the difficulty of presenting a generalised picture of post-colonial Francophone Africa, whether at ten, thirty or fifty years old. This complexity is not only evident in the concrete economic and political manifestations of the Franco-Cameroonian relationship, but also in how it has been subjectively interpreted and commemorated by Africans themselves. For the academic, therefore, the historical significance and legacy of this relationship is never fixed or complete, but continuously constructed according to the scope and focus of the analytical gaze.

Importantly, however, what may appear as an indeterminate and incomplete picture in academic analysis, has, for certain Cameroonians, been demonstrated as providing a constant source of political opportunity over the past fifty years. The ability to exploit various political modalities, and to detach labels from one particular group and re-assign it to another was, and still is, an important strategy in order to negotiate a complex political and historical landscape, a landscape where the past and continued presence of France is still perceived to matter in terms of access to political and socio-economic opportunities. The contested and ambiguous legacy of the Franco-Cameroonian relationship, and the inter-dependent networks of opposition and cooperation that have formed around it, represent attempts by a variety of actors in Cameroon to utilise a wide range of resources – political, economic, symbolic and commemorative – in order to take advantage of *la présence française*, whether in apparent opposition or collusion. Even if the concrete economic and political links of the French presence in Cameroon will eventually fade, the history of this presence may continue to provide a vital resource for Cameroonians attempting to navigate the country's political landscape, as it has done already.

Notes

1 Numerous examples of the UPC's attacks on President Ahidjo's 'neo-colonial' regime can be found in issues of the party newspaper, *La Voix du Kamerun*, which continued to be published from Cairo, Accra and Conakry after the leadership's exile. Multiple copies can be found in the Archives Départementales de la Seine-Saint-Denis (ADSSD), Fonds du PCF, archives de la section de politique extérieure (261 J 7).

2 In the (often limited) Anglophone literature, this trend first became evident in the 1980s with works such as John Chipman's *French Power in Africa* (Chipman 1989). In both French and English works, the idea that Franco-African relations were essentially constituted by elite networks of cooperation or clientelism has again resurfaced, evidenced by the attention given by both academics and journalists to François-Xavier Verschave's slogan of '*Françafrique*' (Verschave, 1998).

3 Numerous examples can be found in ADSSD, 261 J 7. In addition Meredith Terretta (2010) offers a comprehensive and insightful analysis of the UPC's representation

in foreign governments and Third World organisations (such as the Afro-Asian Solidarity Organisation) during this period, *c.*1957–65.

4 Ahidjo had been Prime Minister of the French territory since February 1958, and was Paris' favoured candidate for the presidency.

5 The defence agreement allowed the use of 'direct' and 'indirect' military aid by French troops, who were moreover to remain under the command of the French, rather than Cameroonian, government (Ahidjo, Lettre du Premier Ministre Camerounais, February 1960).

6 In an interview with *Le Monde* (Hubenelle, 'Le Cameroun à Trois Mois de sa Réunification', 12 July 1961), Ahidjo expressed his repeated opinion that social as well as political developments were needed to combat UPC 'terrorism'.

7 At a press conference in Yaoundé, February 1964, Ahidjo is reported to have said: 'Si nous ne reconnaissons pas la Chine communiste, ... ce n'est pas parce qu'elle est communiste, c'est parce que nous avons constaté qu'elle s'ingérait dans nos affaires en aidant la subversion. Si nous avions la preuve que la Chine Populaire ne s'ingérait plus dans nos affaires intérieures nous ne verrions aucun inconvénient à la reconnaître, à voter pour son admission à l'ONU.' Quoted in ADSSD, 261 J7, Declaration by the UPC's Comité Révolutionnaire (n° 05/64/CP/SE/CR), 1964: 2.

8 Kofele-Kale (1981: 216) states that Ahidjo's 1973 decision to opt out of the French-controlled OCAM 'was touted in the official press as evidence of Cameroon's determination to neutralize French control over its sovereignty'. He then adds, however, that 'Had the withdrawal from OCAM been followed by a withdrawal from the franc zone ... then government claims about pursuing an independent foreign policy not constrained by French interests would have been more plausible.'

9 Torrent (2012) presents a thorough analysis of how the domestic issue of the UPC uprising influenced Ahidjo's more 'pragmatic' foreign policy concerns throughout the 1960s and 1970s.

10 'Proclamation d'Etat d'urgence' (1960).

11 'Activities of Cameroonians who have studied in Communist countries', 1962.

12 'Activities of Cameroonians who have studied in Communist countries', 1965.

13 In the view of Deltombe, Domergue and Tatsitsa (2011: 525–35), it was the lack of time spent by these students in Cameroon compared to their time in Paris that was fundamental to the initial hostility of the BCD.

14 This rather nebulous dispute is played out over numerous (unclassified) bulletins in the Archives départementales de la Seine-Saint-Denis, with perhaps the most accessible (albeit heavily biased) presentations of the debate being a pamphlet published by the BCD entitled 'La Vérité sur le "Comité Révolutionnaire"' (261 J 7, December 1963) and a document by the CR entitled 'Après les événements d'Accra' (261 J 7, April 1963). It is similarly articulated in a document written by Ndeh Ntumazah of the BCD entitled 'Mercenaries Rule Kamerun', reprinted in Asong and Chi (2001: 115–16).

15 A document sent by the District Chief of Federal Security in Buea to the Director of Federal Security in Yaoundé on 27 November 1965 – as just one example among several – contains numerous intercepted applications written by Cameroonians to 'subversive' countries such as Ghana and the USSR. None of these applications

demonstrates any political leanings whatsoever; they only indicate a desire to make use of further education facilities that were unavailable in Cameroon. 'Activities of Cameroonians who have studied in Communist countries', 1962.

16 'Activities of Cameroonians who have studied in Communist countries', 1965.

17 ADSSD, 261 J7, 'La Vérité sur le "Comité Révolutionnaire"': 12–21.

18 ADSSD, 261 J7.

19 The increasing lack of the UPC's military cohesion becomes evident in French military reports ('Synthèse Historique sur les événements du Cameroun, 1960–62', 1962).

20 Documents given to the author by Pius Fruh Wallah in Bamenda, Cameroon in 2011 showed that there was regular correspondence between the Ntumazah faction and the British Labour Party on this.

21 The most prolific of these was the *Cameroon Monitor*, published from London and edited by Frank Russell and Diana Davies from the late 1980s and throughout the 1990s.

22 Such actions reflect Bayart's (2000: 255) assertion that the actions of African political leaders under the scrutiny of the 'international community' 'take place in at least two dimensions: those of the visible and the invisible, the world of the day and the domain of the night'.

23 Hogbe Nlend was given the post of Minister of Scientific and Technical Research by Biya after the 1997 presidential elections. Kodock was appointed to the government as Minister of State for Planning and Regional Development from 1992 to 1994 and then as Minister of State for Agriculture from 1994 to 1997. He was again Minister of State for Agriculture from 2002 to 2004 and Minister of State for Planning from 2004 to 2007.

24 Both French Cameroun and British Cameroon became UN trust territories in 1946, and in February 1961, a year after French Cameroun had gained independence (becoming *La République du Cameroun*), residents of British Cameroon were issued with a UN plebiscite which gave them two options for their own independence: they could join an independent Nigeria or the independent Republic of Cameroon. British Northern Cameroon chose integration with Nigeria and became part of that state in June 1961, while Southern Cameroon chose to 'unite' with *La République du Cameroun*, to become *La République Fédérale du Cameroun* in October 1961. In 1972, however, Ahidjo abolished Cameroon's federal status and enacted a highly centralised 'unitary state'.

25 The Anglophone political movement is in no way homogeneous, however, and is largely split between the North West and South West provinces. Konings and Nyamnjoh (2003: 18) have observed that the South West political elite prefer a ten-state federal option to the SCNC's 'two-state' solution, as they believe that the latter would allow the North West elites to dominate the entire political apparatus of South Cameroon.

26 The SCNC website ('About Us', 2009) states, for example, how 'Anglo-Saxon culture flourished as democratic political institutions took firm roots in national life' and that the withdrawal of the British after reunification was 'at the displeasure of many inhabitants who had grown to cherish the British ways of life'.

27 Anyangwe (2008: 2) similarly posits an idealised British political culture, creating a territory that was 'based on the Westminster model and a thriving and vibrant democracy from 1954 to 1961'.

28 After the UPC was banned in the Southern Cameroons by the British Administration in 1957, its work was continued by the One Kamerun Party, formed by Ndeh Ntumazah in July of that year.

13

A fragmented and forgotten decolonisation: the end of European empires in the Sahara and their legacy

*Berny Sèbe**

You are already dead. How can one dare to speak to you of independence, you who are not even present in the places where the decisions about independence are taken?

Mohamed Ali Ag Ataher Insar, former chief of the Kel Antassar Tuaregs, Mali (1990: 96).

There was never such thing as a 'Year of the Sahara' in Africa: although most of the Saharo-Sahelian zone was granted nominal independence in 1960, the process of decolonisation of the Sahara proved to be much more protracted and complex than elsewhere in Africa. This fate was perhaps unavoidable for a territory that lay between the Algerian conflict on the one hand, and the peaceful decolonisation of French West Africa (AOF) on the other. Because the post-colonial history of the Sahara has tended to be absorbed more or less artificially within the national narratives to which it came to belong (with or without the consent of its populations), the decolonisation processes at work in the Sahara, and their consequences, have remained neglected territory for a long time.

By looking at the fragmented and forgotten decolonisation of the Sahara as a whole, and by considering some of its long-term side effects from a Saharo-centric perspective, this chapter intends to redress this historiographical imbalance and to offer an alternative interpretation of the end of Empire in the Sahara, from the perspective of its human and geographical realities rather than through the polities which have absorbed it, willingly or unwillingly. It questions the role and impact of post-colonial African states on ethnic groups which straddle several countries born as a result of the end of empire, a situation not uncommon in many regions of the continent. Against this background it tests out an interpretative model of decolonisation which posits decolonisation, not as an emancipatory process a priori, but as a factor of political fragmentation that was the product of Western-inspired supposed nation-states suddenly imposed on populations, whose specificity had often been better preserved under colonial rule and who became marginalised as a result of the decolonisation process. It posits that the legacy of this process has been one of post-colonial instability. Lastly, this chapter offers an insight into an ultimately unsuccessful attempt to unify politically and economically large spaces in Africa, and as such complements existing knowledge of other initiatives or projects in the region, such as the Mali Federation or attempts to retain the unity of French West Africa at independence.

Home to four major ethnic groups (Arabs, Tuaregs, Moors and Tubus) and displaying a clear desertic identity in the 3.5 million sq. miles straddling the Tropic of Cancer and running from the Atlantic Ocean to the Red Sea, the Sahara was entirely absorbed by European imperial powers in the late nineteenth and early twentieth centuries (Dufourcq 2009). New, artificial boundaries between British, Italian, Spanish and French zones of control were drawn, while the French, who had obtained the lion's share, further divided it within their own empire (between Algeria, French West Africa, French Equatorial Africa and the two protectorates of Morocco and Tunisia, where they often fixed previously unclear boundaries). When anti-colonial movements started to challenge imperial rule north of the Atlas Mountains and south of the Sahel, Saharan populations remained generally so quiet that the French tried to merge all their Saharan territories into a Common Organisation of Saharan Regions (OCRS, 1957–62), an initiative which sought to give reality to a project that had been mooted several times before: the idea of a French Sahara (Capot-Rey 1953; Bélime 1955; Chenntouf 1986; Sèbe 2010). However, this obvious attempt to retain power over the newly-discovered mineral and oil resources of the region (and access to nuclear testing facilities) failed to erase decades of administrative compartmentalisation. Each sub-division of the Sahara subsequently obtained independence with the non-Saharan territories it used to be attached to: in the south, Mauritania, Mali, Niger and Chad, in the north, Algeria. In the meantime, Libya had become self-governing in 1951, and Anglo-Egyptian Sudan had followed suit in 1956. Later, after an attempt to 'departmentalise' the Western Sahara, the Spaniards left it in 1975, only for Morocco (until now) and Mauritania (until 1979) to annex it. Whereas official government narratives of decolonisation in North Africa have tended to emphasise the concept of the liberation of an oppressed but homogeneous population from the colonial yoke, such an approach seems economical with the truth in the case of the Sahara. In many cases, decolonisation seems to have denied Saharan populations a geopolitical existence rather than, as is more often the case in other regions, granting it one.

This process of colonial division has led to a long-term reconfiguration of the territorial, ethnic and sociocultural borders of the Sahara, going against the geographical unity of the region which had been so potent before the advent of European colonialism. The belated French initiative to bring about a hasty and ephemeral reunification through the creation of the OCRS was unable to prevent a definitive post-colonial fragmentation that has hindered nomadic lifestyles and turned Saharan populations into minorities in all the countries in which they live (Fèvre 1983: 275–301; Dayak 1992, 1996; Bourgeot 1995). Although this was not necessarily a problem in itself, it has proved to be a major factor of dissatisfaction among Saharan populations in many countries in the area – especially Mali, Niger and Chad.

The colonial fragmentation of the Sahara

The European conquest of the Sahara, which unfolded as part of the late nineteenth century 'Scramble for Africa', did not mean the dismantling of a completely homogeneous ensemble; rather, it amounted to the reorganisation by external agents, and along much more rigid lines, of a space where competing communities and ethnicities had constantly negotiated their coexistence, trying to make the most of a vast and borderless territory. The very definition of the limits of the Sahara is not unproblematic, as it is mostly defined in opposition to its margins, and does not possess the ethnological unity, or the correspondingly clear-cut divisions, which colonial observers hastily described: for instance, the classic ethnic divisions perceived in colonial times (generally, between Arabs, Tuaregs and Tubus) tended to mask other divisions within each entity, such as the opposition between nomadic and sedentary populations. In other cases, these latter categories could lead to an over-simplification of local social structures. The Sahara was also traditionally perceived as a territory of 'white' populations (whiteness being defined in a broad sense, phenotypically and socially) as opposed to 'black Africans' south of it. This perception tended to overshadow the fact that, in all likelihood, 'black' sedentary populations in the oases generally outnumbered the 'white' nomads who, however, had traditionally retained power until the independence of the various nations which ended up covering the vast space of the Sahara (Bourgeot 2000).

The colonial period added a new dimension to the century-old distinctions prevalent among Saharan populations, based on skin colour, religion and way of life: that of state and administrative boundaries decided in faraway places and imposed in a top-down approach (insofar as the colonial administration had the means of enforcing them), reflecting various political traditions with no local roots. The continuum of arid territory to which the Arabs refer as *Sahra* (literally: dry, barren land) ended up divided between four European colonial powers: France, Britain, Italy and Spain.

While Saharan exploration had long been dominated by German and British explorers in the nineteenth century, French colonial claims on the Sahara forestalled their rivals (Porch 1984). However, the fact that separate French military corps (the '*Coloniaux*' from the south and the '*Algériens*' from the north) conquered the Sahara from their respective bases created internal boundaries which remained almost unnoticeable as long as the French controlled these various areas, but they planted the seeds of future divisions which will be discussed later in this chapter (Ageron 1978; Kanya-Forstner 1969, 1972; Frémeaux 2010).

Beyond the 'French Sahara', Great Britain, Italy and Spain administered significant shares of the margins, fixing boundaries which have survived decolonisation and still divide the Sahara. These colonial divisions, imposed gradually over half a century, disrupted traditional trade routes, while pre-colonial political ensembles and the logics of territorial relations were shaken. Because colonial penetration had generally proceeded from a coast, the new order seemed to be doubly alien: not only were the colonisers Christians, but the centres of decision were situated beyond the Sahara itself, with orders coming from as far away as Dakar, Algiers, Tripoli or Cairo – or even Paris, London, Rome or Madrid. With this generally came unwelcome administrative frameworks and tax requirements. Local populations resented this new order and tried to escape whenever possible by crossing boundaries which had no palpable reality (Berridge 2011), or rose up against the colonising power when the prospect of victory was in sight. The most serious rebellion took place during the First World War, when Kaocen ag Kedda, a leader who combined a modern understanding of warfare and a subtle political acumen, led the Tuareg revolt of 1915–17. The memory of this collective uprising set a precedent to which later advocates of the unity of the Sahara systematically referred. Its ultimate failure can perhaps be seen as symptomatic of the impossibility of attaining this goal (Decraene and Zuccarelli 1994: 100–7).

Imperial control over Saharan populations was consolidated during the interwar years, with the Tuaregs enjoying favourable treatment in the French sphere as a result of their willingness to collaborate with the colonisers, and also probably due to a national collective feeling of passion towards them which I have called elsewhere 'Saharomania' (Sèbe 2011). The Second World War demonstrated the strategic importance of the Sahara as a space to be crossed and occupied and led to the departure of the Italians from Libya, with the French replacing them in the Fezzan and the British elsewhere.

In the 1950s, French authorities tried to use the question of access to resources as an opportunity to unify their Saharan possessions. Coal had been found in Algeria as early as 1917 and, during the war, copper had been discovered in Mauritania and Niger, and tin in Niger. By the early 1950s the French government encouraged mining exploration, ultimately leading to the discovery of significant oil reserves in Edjeleh (Algeria) in 1956 (Boissonnade 1982). These new economic prospects, combined with the outbreak of the Algerian War two years earlier and the independence of the two protectorates of Morocco and Tunisia in 1956, led the French to devise plans to unify their Saharan territories and prepare for them a political future distinct from that of the neighbouring regions, all of which seemed to aspire to a form of independence that threatened the metropole's interests (Boilley 1993; Bourgeot 2000). The only colonial attempt to unify the Sahara along geopolitical lines therefore stemmed from self-interest, yet it had the potential to re-shape the future of the region at the very moment when decolonisation processes were being set in motion throughout most of the French Empire.

An impossible unification?

Significantly, the project of unification of the Sahara under French rule was formally presented to the French National Assembly by an African political leader: it was through law No. 57–27 of 10 January 1957 that Félix Houphouët-Boigny, future Ivoirian president and leader of the Rassemblement Démocratique Africain (RDA) at the time, proposed to establish the OCRS, with the stated purpose to finance the development (*mise en valeur*) of the region and the socio-economic promotion of local populations with a share of the new oil revenue (Boilley 1993; Sèbe 2010). Comprising the Saharan territories of Algeria, Mauritania, the French Soudan (modern Mali), Niger and Chad, it created a de facto 'French Sahara' that was justified on developmental grounds, a rationale that was customary for Britain and France after 1945 to defend the persistence of their colonial systems (Cooper 2002: 62–5). The remit of the OCRS appeared generous in principle and American observers praised its achievements (Sèbe 2010), yet it bore the features of a last and desperate attempt to cling to oil-rich territories[1] which also presented the added advantage of offering easily accessible nuclear testing sites. Moreover, the principle of autonomy enshrined in the June 1956 framework law (*loi-cadre*) was at odds with the fact that the OCRS was administered directly from Paris, with the duty of OCRS general delegate performed by a Minister of the Sahara based in the French capital, following the creation of the Ministry of the Sahara in June 1957 (Bourgeot 2000).

Although the economic, political and geostrategic interests which the OCRS was able to serve were difficult to conceal and had met with outright rejection from the outset in Algerian nationalist circles, the initiative had been made easier by the generally cooperative attitude of Saharan populations who, by the 1950s, had become accustomed to French administration and even enjoyed certain material benefits that came with it (Vallet 1990). Remarkably, the Tuaregs of the Southern territories of Algeria did not rise against the French authorities during the Algerian war (Frémeaux 2002), notably because the conditions imposed by the *pax gallica* since the battle of Tit (1902) benefited them in general (unlike their former vassals, the sedentary peasants – the *harratin* – who increasingly sided with the Algerian liberation front).

General De Gaulle believed that the stable political situation that prevailed in the Sahara, and the shared desire of nomadic populations to escape the post-colonial domination of Arab or Black African administrators, would allow France to safeguard its own geostrategic, energy-related interests, centred around the three pillars of oil, natural gas and nuclear testing sites (Chenu 1994: 221–33). The OCRS survived the mutation of the French Union into the French Community, and even the independence of Mali, Niger and Chad (which joined the organisation as independent states), but the greatest threat to its survival was the outcome of the Algerian war, inasmuch as the key financial resources for the organisation came from Algerian oil.

Several West African countries involved in the OCRS (especially the poorest ones like Niger) turned a blind eye to the breach of sovereignty the organisation brought about. As observed in 1960 by the American Consul General in Dakar, it offered them the opportunity to benefit from oil revenue from a territory lying beyond their borders:

> The two other states of the former federation of French West Africa [beyond Niger] which could benefit from OCRS assistance are Mauritania and Soudan [present-day Mali]. It will be recalled that prior to OCRS' change of status last year, there was in Black Africa a definite suspicion as to the real political aims of the French government in the creation of the original OCRS. This led to a policy of aloofness on the part of the states bordering the desert areas of Algeria.

> However, OCRS came later to be considered as hardly more than another convenient source of technical and economic aid. Niger, which really had never shown active resistance against OCRS, was the first, and so far the only, state in the former Federation of F.W.A., to sign the appropriate agreements.

> [...] The President of the Mauritanian Assembly, Sidi El Moktar, had stated in a radio broadcast on March 15, 1959, that his country was in favour of joining the OCRS, now that the latter had become a strictly economic organisation.'[2]

In contrast, Modibo Keïta's Mali, which expressed its 'solidarity towards the Algerian people and its honourable representative the Provisional Government of the Algerian Republic'[3] and later used the argument of French sympathies towards the Tuaregs to explain the 1963/64 uprising in the north of the country, took a much more critical stance with regard to the OCRS.

Yet, the major obstacle to de Gaulle's plans remained a potentially independent Algeria, the government of which would seek to stop this transfer of resources. Negotiations with the Provisional Government of the Algerian Republic stalled on several occasions on the question of the Sahara, as FLN negotiators were adamant that the Territoires du Sud had to be included in the negotiations alongside the coastal Algerian departments, and that there could be no peace agreement without the Sahara (Malek 1995). The August 1957 departmentalisation of the Algerian Sahara had reinforced FLN suspicions of the ultimate goals of the French in the region and seemed to justify their insistence on considering all Algerian departments together. The French finally gave in and the OCRS disappeared with the independence of Algeria. The only attempt to give Saharan populations a coherent geopolitical entity had been too late to be successful.

Post-colonial fragmentation and conflict in Saharan territories

Decolonisation posed a new challenge to the geographically homogeneous but sociologically diverse and commercially and culturally interconnected regions of the Sahara. Instead of being loosely divided between four European powers, as it had been in the previous decades, by 1975 no fewer than eleven countries controlled some part of Saharan territory. Nomadic life suddenly became threatened by the strict enforcement of boundaries which used to be only nominal (Dayak 1992: 52 and 61–3).

A few attempts to remedy this situation were made, but they were too blatantly nationalist and aggressive to be successful. Moroccan attempts to annex Mauritania before it was granted independence were stopped by the new Mauritanian government's unwillingness to submit to Rabat, by the geographical obstacle of the Spanish Sahara, and by the French military operation 'Ecouvillon' (1958–9) (see Chapter 6 by Camille Evrard in this volume). Although it appears today as a clear case of expansionism, some scholars, such as Odette du Puigaudeau, backed Moroccan claims over Mauritania in the late 1950s on the grounds that it would spare Hassaniyya-speaking nomads the hassle of crossing borders that threatened their nomadic way of life (Du Puigaudeau 1962). Rabat also claimed vast swathes of the west of Algeria shortly after independence (Farsoun and Paul 1976). Partly in response to such attempts, the Organisation of African Unity adopted in 1963 the principle of inviolability of borders inherited from the colonial period (Touval 1967). Moreover, the Spanish withdrawal from the Rio de Oro and Saguia al Hamra provinces in 1976 and the ensuing conflict between Morocco, Mauritania and the Polisario Front exposed the complex problems raised by any attempt at redrawing the political map of the region (Hodges 1987). As the great Pan-African and Pan-Arab designs withered away, Saharan regions seemed to remain condemned to an even greater degree of fragmentation than during the colonial period.

The post-1969 Libyan regime was the only regional power that demonstrated any willingness to address the problem of the artificial divisions imposed on Saharan populations. Muammar Qaddafi's background as a nomad and his revolutionary geopolitical designs led him to advocate the idea of the 'United States of the Sahara' (Georgy 1998). Libyan hegemonic ambitions in the region made the Guide of the Revolution present himself alternately or simultaneously as an Arab, African or Saharan leader, trying to play on these three geographical dimensions (Hottinger 1981; Otayek 1986; Grégoire 2004; Bennafla 2004). Libyan territorial claims over Chad (including the ephemeral attempt to merge

Chad and Libya in 1981), and continued Libyan logistical support for rebels from a variety of countries of the Saharo-Sahelian region, were often justified on the grounds of Saharan solidarity and the need to foster the installation of regimes friendly to the Libyans in order to prepare for greater political convergence and the opening up of Saharan borders (Otayek 1984). In spite of repeated failures in the 1980s (Lacoste 1986), Kadhafi still called in 1997 for a Grouping of Saharan states bringing together Chad, Burkina Faso, Mali, Niger and Libya, therefore giving a second birth to his project of a 'United States of the Sahara'. It was followed in 1998 by the launch of a 'Community of Sahelo-Saharan States', with a view to creating a space of free circulation for goods and people, similar in principle to the European Union. The project was given a new lease of life in 2006 in the form of the project of the 'Great Sahara' (Cherfaoui 2006). Although it was meant to include twenty-eight states, it failed to deliver the zone of free circulation that it had promised (Perrin 2009), and Qaddafi's death in 2011, sealing the end of his regime, has halted all talk of such an initiative. In any case, the presence of underground resources (uranium in Niger, iron in Mauritania, oil and natural gas in Algeria and Libya) makes any unification of the Sahara more difficult to undertake, as each country seeks to retain control over the revenue their resources generate.

In stark contrast with the pre-colonial situation which presented an extremely porous, almost borderless open space, the post-colonial fragmentation of the Sahara had an impact on its inhabitants at several levels. It led to confrontations between states and within states, and partitioned major ethnic groups.

At the state level, unsolved colonial disputes often led to long-lasting confrontations. This was particularly the case of the dispute between Chad and Libya over the Aouzou strip, which resulted from an unratified Franco-Italian agreement of 1935 and led to an 'African Thirty Years' War' until the International Court of Justice arbitrated in favour of Chad in 1994 (Lanne 1982; Wright 1989; Burr and Collins 1999). The unofficial 'Sands war' between Morocco and Algeria in 1963 also had colonial roots, given that the French had been unwilling to define once and for all a border between their flagship colony and one of their protectorates (Heggoy 1970). Finally, the hasty departure of the Spanish from the Western Sahara led to the longest-lasting conflict the Sahara has witnessed since the independence of the region, with Moroccan and Mauritanian expansionist plans frustrating the establishment of the Sahrawi Arab Democratic Republic advocated by the Polisario Front (Barbier 1982; Hodges 1987; Caratini 1989; Saint Maurice 2000; Mohsen Finan 1997; Zunes and Mundy 2010).

Post-colonial fragmentations within countries with Saharan territory have also been numerous and resulted mainly from colonial boundary-making which, as we have seen above, tended to entrust chunks of the Sahara to the jurisdiction of neighbouring regions and therefore placed the future of the region in the hands of decision-makers who were external to it. Policies which had an impact on

Saharan populations were discussed either in Arabic-speaking Maghrebi administrations for the northern half of the Sahara, or in French-speaking African
capitals for the southern half of the desert. This situation led to constant tensions
between the administrative centres of power and their Saharan territories, sometimes turning into full-fledged conflict, as happened in the case of the Tuareg
and Tubu populations in Mali, Niger and Chad on several occasions – in the
case of Mali, almost immediately after independence.

The space dominated by the Tuaregs, which became divided between five
post-colonial states after independence (Algeria, Libya, Mali, Niger, Burkina-
Faso), had been traditionally organised around four major federative poles.
Independence disrupted the cohesion of this ensemble: two poles ended up
in Arab-dominated Algeria and, to a far lesser extent, Libya (Kel Ahaggar and
Kel Ajjer) and one in each of the Black-African-dominated newly independent Saharo-Sahelian countries (Kel Tademekkat in Mali and Kel Aïr in Niger)
(Claudot-Hawad 1990: 12). The notion of a Sahara français, first voiced by
the likes of Robert Capot-Rey or Emile Bélime and then materialised through
the OCRS, had been viewed favourably by Tuareg leaders, who perceived the
opportunity to achieve a reunion of confederations enjoying considerable territorial freedom (Ag Ataher Insar 1990: 97). Although the concept of a 'Tuareg
nation' was not as deeply entrenched as has often been claimed in an attempt to
justify Tuareg rebellions (Bisson 2003), nomadic populations were by definition
favourable to any initiative preserving their ability to follow freely the opportunities offered by pasture for their herds. This is one of the reasons why the period
preceding decolonisation is seen retrospectively as a moment of greater freedom
than the present by the Tuaregs themselves (interview, Moussa Ag Assarid,
2012).

By a twist of fate, decolonisation threatened the modus vivendi that the
Tuaregs had found with colonial administrations (Clauzel 1992; interview,
Moussa Ag Assarid, 2012). The Tuaregs also realised that, having resisted for
long the prospect of a European type of schooling for their children, they would
be put at a disadvantage in the new post-colonial entities, to the benefit of other
ethnic groups (some of whom had been their hereditary enemies or vassals). The
transfer of power of the early 1960s meant a loss of authority of the Tuaregs to
the benefit of their former slaves in Niger and Mali, while in Algeria the new
post-colonial authorities tried to neutralise gradually the authority of Tuareg
amenokals (customary leaders). Revealingly, when an Algerian journalist asked in
1962 the Hoggar *amenokal* Bey ag Akhamouk what he thought about the independence of Algeria, this was his response: 'Before, it was the French who were
in command of us, now it is the Arabs' (Gast 2004: 87). More recently, Moussa
ag Assarid, a spokesperson for the National Liberation Front of the Azawad
(MNLA), goes as far as to say that the post-colonial period has been just another
form of colonisation for ethnic minorities (interview, Moussa Ag Assarid, 2012).

Indeed, the first Tuareg rebellion took place in Northern Mali as early as 1963, in the Adrar des Iforas, against Modibo Keïta's socialist regime. The area was subsequently placed under military control (Boilley 1999: 271–350). It was in Northern Mali that a variety of social, economic and political factors came to a head, leading a Tuareg movement to seek an independent homeland – a request which had been put forward to the French authorities by more than three hundred chiefs of villages and confederations as early as 1957, but which was not successful (interview, Moussa Ag Assarid, 2012). The French ambassador to Mali between 1964 and 1968, Pierre Pelen, offered an insightful summary of the various reasons that led to this uprising:

> The Tuaregs are ... nomadic populations and independent by nature and, as they can be found, geographically speaking, straddling three frontiers, they can easily escape any administrative control. However, the French authorities had established with these tribes a kind of *modus vivendi*, which had led to relative peace in the region.
>
> With the independence of Mali, the problem was again posed, as the Malian government decided to enforce at any price the existing national regulations, and to levy tariffs and táxes from these nomadic populations, without taking into account the particular conditions of the 'Tuareg economy'. If this had been a simple reluctance of the Tuareg [*sic*] to fulfil their obligations vis-à-vis the state, the whole question would have been less grave; however, it became poisoned by a racial conflict. The white Tuaregs have, effectively, always been hesitant to accept the authority of the Blacks, whom they distrust and whom they regard as an inferior race, from which they once took slaves to carry out non-aristocratic tasks. The Malian officials, who are all of the Black race, have attempted not only to control the resources deriving from taxation for their own benefit, but also to strengthen their authority over these nomads. The results of this policy were no surprise as the Malian Tuaregs fled to Algeria and Niger to avoid this persecution, until the Malian government signed agreements with the governments in Algiers, and then in Niamey, that allowed the Malian armed forces – with the collaboration of the frontier posts of friendly states – to pursue rebels who sought refuge on their territory.[4]

The exodus brought about by the repression of the Malian army against both the rebels and civilian populations sympathetic to them, the disruption to trade generated by the creation of the Malian franc, as well as a clear drive towards sedentarisation, further disrupted customary practices and embittered inter-ethnic relations. The memory of the opportunities, which seemed to open up as a result of this armed uprising, has since fuelled Tuareg secessionist dreams in the Sahel up to the present day. Thus, the MNLA proclaimed unilaterally in early 2012 the independence of the Azawad. (This name stands for a loosely defined region including northern Mali, where MNLA leaders believed that they could establish a majority rule government defending Tuareg interests.) (*Africa Confidential*, 2012, 22 June). These secessionist aspirations tend to indicate that, in some cases, the artificial association between Saharan and non-Saharan territories and cultures may have reached its breaking point.

The situation described results in part from a large-scale disruption in inter-ethnic and caste relationships, which has seen the Tuaregs losing the privileges and prestige that had been traditionally bestowed upon them as the economics of the region dramatically shifted. As the exploitation of the rich underground resources only marginally called upon local manpower, unemployment forced young workers to migrate away from the traditional Tuareg areas to find work: northern Nigeria or Côte d'Ivoire for those from the South, and Libya for those of the North. Those who stayed at home faced bleak prospects and felt all the more helpless as they had to face the combined assaults of unsympathetic govern-ments and severe droughts. By the mid-1970s, the Tuaregs of the Ahaggar had lost most of their social standing and class superiority, their slaves and even some of their land (Vallet 1990: 88). Efforts to co-opt the Tuareg through political decentralisation failed after a relatively short period (Seely 2001), while recurring economic problems, the complete failure of policies of sedentarisation, due to the fact that former nomads were not offered alternative means of earning their lives, and inter-regional collaboration, which closed possible escape routes, all contributed to making the Tuaregs feel that they were being cornered by hostile forces, often leading to violent rebellions.[5]

It was against this backdrop that a passive form of collective resistance of the younger generations developed, encapsulated in the concept of *teshumara* (possibly from the French *chômeur*, though this etymology is often challenged). Starting from a contestation of traditional Tuareg values (combined with a situa-tion of socio-economic failure), it gradually evolved towards a full-fledged armed resistance in the 1990s, thanks in large part to Libyan encouragement (Hawad 1990). When an uprising took place in Tchin-Tabaraden (Niger) in May 1990, it reflected the frustration of essentially nomadic populations who had been denied the right to decide their post-colonial future and felt marginalised in all the countries that covered their traditional living space. Understandably, all states which had the potential to become embroiled with the problem reacted swiftly to nip the revolt in the bud. However, regional coordination against the rebellion failed to stop the vicious circle of state repression and further upris-ing, and the rebellion subsequently spread to Mali, lasting until 1995 and then periodically resuming until the present day (Dayak 1992; Salifou 1992; Grégoire 2000). Perceived French sympathies towards nomadic Saharan populations (and especially the Tuaregs) have repeatedly led to the former colonial power being accused in Bamako and Niamey of interference in national conflicts,[6] whereas in reality uncontrolled socio-economic and cultural disruptions, stemming from inadequate political systems, were the main source of discontent (Boilley 2005).

In recent years, the combined effects of the almost complete disappearance of tourism in the region as a result of Islamist terrorism and banditry, as well as the increased awareness of the commercial value of underground resources (especially oil and uranium), have fuelled continuing dissatisfaction with the central governments, leading to regular outbursts of violence, or at least a state of almost permanent instability, in Northern Niger and Mali. Thus, the case of the Tuareg populations, who represent around 1.5 million people (Pandolfi 1998: 29) who are divided between five countries (in each of which they represent a minority), is emblematic of the frustrations (and associated political challenges) caused by a fragmented post-colonial destiny.[7]

Conclusion

Stemming from the belief that interpretations of decolonisation have all too often been fashioned around the geopolitical realities shaped at independence, regardless of their limited adequacy to reflect local allegiances and dynamics, this chapter has attempted to offer an alternative interpretation of decolonisation processes in Africa, revolving around the post-colonial fate of the various ethnic entities which populated the Sahara at the end of the empires. Interpreting the consequences of the 'Year of Africa' through the lens of fragmentation rather than that of emancipation offers a salutary revision of the impact on minority (especially nomadic) communities of decolonisation.

Though this chapter focuses on the case study of the Saharan region, it raises questions that could be usefully extended to other regions of Africa where decolonisation did not prove to be a factor of stability or emancipation of minorities. In addition, it invites us to reflect upon the possible benefits of initiatives tending to develop larger regional entities, which would have overcome the legacy of colonial borders (Mamdani 2009). As the secession of northern Mali makes the headlines at the time of writing, it is more pressing than ever to reflect upon the causes of the continued dissatisfaction of most Saharan populations with their central governments.

However, any appraisal of the impact of decolonisation on the Sahara and its inhabitants should avoid constructing an idealised retrospective pre-colonial homogeneity, as this vast region has always been a very complex socio-political space. Yet, it is beyond doubt that the colonial period added another long-lasting layer of divisions, leading to a durable post-colonial fragmentation of its various groups and making it often more difficult for local populations to negotiate their survival and adapt to changing environmental conditions after independence. Artificial divisions allocated Saharan territories to various political entities governed from *outside* the Sahara – geographically and culturally – leading, ironically, to accusations of the imposition of colonial-style overrule fifty years on from decolonisation.

Because few Saharans had been trained enough to play leading political roles in their own countries, they remained absent from the corridors of power and the majority of post-colonial policies have appeared unsympathetic to dislocated, disorganised and sometimes forcibly sedentarised Saharan populations. Although long-established traditions of trans-Saharan trade have remained significant in spite of the enforcement of previously theoretical borders (Scheele 2010; Ahmida 2011), and migration across the Sahara has become substantial over the last few decades (Marfaing and Wippel 2004), the disruption caused to the social and economic dynamics of Saharan societies by the post-colonial fragmentation of their once vast territory is indisputable.

The failure of the OCRS project meant that the fate of the Sahara was to remain fragmented as a result of the decolonisation process. Deprived of any significant political weight in any of the post-colonial countries to which they belonged, facing the abrupt end of the 'gentlemen's agreement' which allowed nomadic populations to coexist in peace with colonial authorities (interview, Ag-Assarid, 2012), Saharan populations only marginally benefited from the considerable mineral resources that their territories concealed.

Paradoxically, the French project of unification of the Sahara was given a new lease of life (but from a different political standpoint) when Muammar Qaddafi attempted to implement his idea of a 'United States of the Sahara'. Ultimately, his project failed, not only because his neighbours feared the overwhelming weight of a Libyan-led ensemble, but also because Western interests (and French in particular) preferred to retain their power of influence over a large number of weaker and often rival entities. It is only due to the extreme mobility across the Sahara of Al-Qaeda in the Islamic Maghreb (AQIM) that Western preferences shifted recently: regional cooperation is now openly encouraged, as reflected in the American Pan-Sahel Initiative and Western support to the Tamanrasset-based regional command for joint counter-terrorism operations (Keenan 2007; 2009: 158–75). Thus, an extremely mobile terrorist group has finally recreated a sense of borderless space which so many generations had craved for. This conception of the Sahara as a vast open space, combined with the potential for cross-border illegal activities, may well account, in part at least, for the relative appeal of AQIM among some Saharan populations (such as in Northern Mali), in spite of its strict interpretation of Islam, which is at odds with local traditions.

For Saharan populations the legacy of decolonisation is thus a mixed one, as they frequently feel that they have been denied the right to self-determination which had justified so many struggles for independence. As such, they appear as clear losers of the 'balkanisation' process that took place in the 1960s. Speaking for the Tuaregs, Amuzzar ag Eshim perspicaciously encapsulated the problem: 'the French destroyed the tissue of our nation and when they departed, they not only did not weave it again, but they left it to the claws of others, who destroyed it further and plucked it so much that it does not have the slightest possibility to be restored' (cited by Claudot-Hawad 2002: 81).

The fragmentation of the Sahara, and the frustrations that it has brought about, are still a major factor of instability and under-development in the region today. Writing in 1965 about Northern Mali, French Ambassador Pierre Pelen somewhat prophetically concluded his report by observing that 'This sector is calm for the moment, but it does not seem that the problems confronting the region have been resolved'.[8] Fifty years on, the issues which led to the 1963/64 rebellion are more acute than ever and demands for self-determination have never been louder. In a striking irony, the fragmentation of the Sahara has led to the formulation of demands which, if successful, would lead to a further partition of the region, given that a unification of all Saharan regions has become a clearly unattainable goal. The legacy of the geopolitical partition of the Sahara is far-reaching, and this explains many of the problems that have engulfed the Saharo-Sahelian region over the last half-century.

*Note from the author: A first draft of this chapter was presented at the Independence and Decolonisation seminar organised by the Institute for Historical Studies at the University of Texas at Austin. The ideas expressed here were further developed on the occasion of the Year of Africa conference in Portsmouth. The author wishes to thank the audience of both events as well as the commentators of his papers, Benjamin C. Brower and Tony Chafer and Alex Keese, for their useful comments on the chapter. Heartfelt thanks also go to Steffen Prauses and Theo Schley for their assistance in Paris. As usual, all errors remain the responsibility of the author.

Notes

1 US State Department (1957). NARA Archives, College Park, MD, RG 59, General Records of the Department of State, Lot files (Africa), 1944–63, box 1, country files, entry 3109, folder A6 (Algerian Petroleum), K. S. Cate, 'Report from Europe', 10 December 1957.

2 US State Department (1960). NARA Archives, College Park, MD, RG 59, General Records of the Department of State, Central Decimal Files, 1960–63, box 2571, 851T.00/2–960, American Consul-General to State Department, despatch 'OCRS Economic and Technical Assistance to Niger', 9 February 1960.

3 Archives of the French Ministry of Foreign Affairs (MAE), Direction des Affaires africaines et malgaches, sous-série Mali 1959–1969, 1, Chargé d'Affaires de France for the French Embassy in Bamako to Secrétaire d'Etat aux Affaires Etrangères, *Dépêche hebdomadaire*, 29 August 1961.

4 MAE, Direction des Affaires africaines et malgaches, sous-série Mali 1959–1969, 17, Pierre Pelen, French Ambassador in Bamako to Courve de Murville, Minister of Foreign Affairs (n° 36), 24 February 1965.

5 MAE, Direction des Affaires africaines et malgaches, sous-série Mali 1959–1969, 17, Fernand Wibaux, French Ambassador in Bamako, to Couve de Murville (n° 2141), 28 September 1963.

6 MAE, Direction des Affaires africaines et malgaches, sous-série Mali 1959–1969, 17, Telegram from Guidi, French Foreign Ministry, Direction des Affaires africaines et malgaches, to French Embassy in Bamako (n° 107/108), 5 March 1964.
7 The parallel case of the Tubu populations of Chad leads to a similar conclusion (Wauthier, 1995: 214; Bennafla, 2003).
8 MAE, Direction des Affaires africaines et malgaches, sous-série Mali 1959–1969, 17, Pierre Pelen, French Ambassador in Bamako to Couve de Murville (n° 36), 24 February 1965.

14

Through the prism of the *cinquantenaire*: Côte d'Ivoire between *refondation* and Houphouët's legacy

*Kathrin Heitz**

Under the leadership of its first president Félix Houphouët-Boigny, Côte d'Ivoire, the economic heavyweight of the ex-AOF, became a central pillar of what has been termed *Françafrique* (Verschave 1998). Houphouët-Boigny had served as a minister in several French cabinets in the second half of the 1950s and his close ties with France continued after independence in 1960. He agreed to a permanent French military base, right next to the international airport in Abidjan. The French expatriate community in Côte d'Ivoire, the biggest in Sub-Saharan Africa, increased five times after independence, from roughly 10,000 at independence to around 50,000 in the mid-1980s (Smith 2011). Informal net-works in politics and business were maintained, so that dependencies persisted. Hence, what 'really' changed at independence, as some argue, was the judicial status of the (former) colony (Cooper 1999: 582), reducing national sovereignty to quasi-independence (Jackson 1990: 16–20). The actual implication of this landmark in Ivoirian history has remained a controversial subject ever since and became centre-stage in the jubilee year.

Laurent Gbagbo, Houphouët's historical opponent – trained as a historian with a PhD from France – held the presidency in 2010, the year of the 50th anniversary of independence, and his government was in charge to organise the official celebrations.[1] As is to be expected, Gbagbo intended to make a clean break with the past, advertised with the catchphrase 'second independence'.

However, it was not the occasion of the jubilee that brought the issue of the Franco-Ivoirian relationship back into the focus of Ivoirian politics. At least, since the interposition of France at the outbreak of the armed rebellion in 2002, issues of national sovereignty were repeatedly debated in public discourse. Politics had been gravitating around Ivoirian identity and sovereignty with both its inward and outward dimensions since the death of *Le vieux*, the founding-father Houphouët-Boigny, in 1993.

Hence, the *cinquantenaire* – the French term for the 50th jubilee of independence – came at a moment of deep national crisis. At its 50th anniversary, Côte d'Ivoire was divided into two competing political camps,[2] manifest in the administrative partition of the country into a rebel-held North and government-controlled South. The armed rebellion that had started in September 2002 was at an advanced stage of a peace process in 2010. Nevertheless, by 7 August 2010, the day of the *cinquantenaire*, the northern half was still in the hands of the rebel movement *Les Forces Nouvelles*, even though the state administration had partially returned to the North. The southern half, including both the capital city (Yamoussoukro) and the economic hub (Abidjan), had remained under the government of President Laurent Gbagbo, in office since 2000. Apart from the *cinquantenaire*, Ivorians were in anticipation of yet another important event, namely the first post-conflict presidential elections.[3] In the long run, those gave hope for the reunification of the country; as a competition, however, they were inclined to sustain differences between the camps, for the time of the jubilee year.

Although large parts of national day celebrations can be said to have a rather fixed form, Côte d'Ivoire's political landscape set the stage for multiple *mises en scène* of the nation and its history. This chapter is based on the analysis of my observation of a commemoration in the rebel-held part, and information about the small, non-public ceremony that the government had organised as the official celebration.

The scenarios can roughly be grouped into two different types of ceremony. Those at district level largely followed the script of previous independence celebrations as initiated under the founding-father Houphouët-Boigny. As has been the case in many newly independent states, these celebrations used elements of the universal decorum that are locally appropriated and reinterpreted every year.[4] I will refer to this type as the conventional celebration and juxtapose it to the government's official jubilee that aimed to break with this style. In a figurative sense, one may read this break as a break with the 'houphouëtist' mode of politics that strove to preserve *la Françafrique*. I will argue that the aim to signal a rupture with the 'houphouëtist' system failed, nevertheless, as it was not just a break with Houphouët's post-colony and France; but a break with the 'universal decorum' of national day celebrations.[5]

The chapter proceeds by juxtaposing and comparing the two types of jubilee in reference to universal elements of national day celebrations and collective memories of Ivoirian independence celebrations. Such a contextualisation is necessary, as present-day celebrations are based on previous ones, either by drawing on their imagery or by using them as a counter-image.[6] It is the imageries of previous ceremonies that still serve as a reference and shape expectations today. Whereas political positions are mirrored in the commemoration ceremonies, performances also have a projective dimension (Boehm 2007). Hence, the contribution ends by relating the imagery of the official *cinquantenaire* with the political events of the first post-conflict elections.

The data of the commemoration ceremony in the rebel-held North are based on observations during the events in Côte d'Ivoire's mountainous West (Man and Podiagouiné), supported by video recordings and photographs, as well as informal talks with participants. Information about the official celebration in the South is based on a review of newspaper articles, published sources from two *cinquantenaire* conferences and secondary sources, particularly N'Guessan's recent studies (2011: 55–72).[7] As the chapter aims at discussing political dynamics through the prism of the *cinquantenaire*, I will first provide the background to the conflicting setting in which the jubilee took place.

Domestic struggle or neo-colonial conspiracy?

Much has been written lately by scholars of various disciplines as to how the country renowned for its political stability and economic success in the 1960s and 1970s could be plunged into such a severe military-political crisis (examples are Akindès 2004; McGovern 2011; Bouquet 2011). Analysts generally link the causes for the violent crisis to the power vacuum after the over thirty years of rule of the first President, Félix Houphouët-Boigny (Banégas and Fratani 2007). The integration achieved under the 'Houphouët-Boigny system' (Akindès, 2004), which depended on the redistribution of state revenues to opponents, virtually collapsed in the harsher economic environment of the late 1980s.

When the charismatic 'father of the nation' died in office in 1993, a fierce competition among possible successors for the Presidency erupted that eventually split the country into different political camps. The divisions ran increasingly along the lines of the country's ethno-regional groups. The same centrifugal forces that split the former unity/central party (the PDCI) in 1994, divided the students' union (FESCI) in 1998 and eventually the army in 2002 (Konaté 2003). Intellectual circles, too, have not remained unaffected. Particularly the university campuses and some of their eminent figures were at the forefront of the development of an ideology based on autochthony. President Henri Konkan Bédié, the successor of Houphouët, had a group of scholars who developed the ethno-nationalistic ideology of '*Ivoirité*', Ivoirian citizenship (Arnault and Blommaert 2009). This ethno-nationalistic rhetoric was used as an ideological tool to exclude the northern part of the population and its candidate (Dozon 2000). The consequence was that although elections were held in 1995 and 2000, they brought candidates with little legitimacy to power, as other contenders with good prospects had been excluded from the vote in advance. Eventually, in 2002, a failed *coup d'état* turned into a full-fledged rebellion which cut the country into two halves.

Two versions dominate the public discourse as to why there is a crisis and what politics the country should adopt in its relationship to France (Yéré 2007). One explanation emphasises that the Ivoirian crisis is an inner-Ivoirian struggle for state control; whereas the second portrays the conflict as classic neo-colonial interference, in which France tries to install a puppet regime.

The first explanation stressing the domestic struggle posits that 'northerners' – that is ethno-linguistic groups who originate from the North, many of which have migrated to the South – have become marginalised by the state and treated like second-class citizens after Houphouët's death. The ultranationalist ideology *Ivoirité* served as an instrument to change the conditions for the criteria of the eligibility of the president with the effect that the promising candidate of the marginalised northern population, Alassane Ouattara, was banned from running for the presidency in 1995 and 2000. This is how in 2000, Laurent Gbagbo came to power under circumstances that he himself famously called 'calamitous'. Two years later, mid-rank officers of the national armed forces tried to oust him from power. They failed in the South, but managed to capture the northern half of the country, where the population shared their grievances. According to this first version, northern youngsters took up arms to fight against their exclusion and for elections that include their candidate, which ultimately should give them access to the state's power and wealth.

On the other side of the conflict, in the pro-Gbagbo camp whose partisans live mostly in the South, these allegations of exclusion are denied and it is argued that there is hardly any state in which foreigners can become president. By saying so they allude to and insist on Alassane Ouattara's family links to Burkina Faso. However, the main focus of their discourse emphasises the 'neo-colonial' relationship between France and Côte d'Ivoire. They suspect that France is behind the insurgents and their candidate. According to this view, France sees its economic interest threatened by Gbagbo's Socialist and anti-neo-colonial attitude and his attempts to diversify business relationships. From this perspective, Gbagbo was defined as a threat to French hegemonic interests, and had to be removed (Kessé 2005; Yéré 2007; Charbonneau 2008a). Those who privilege this view found their fears confirmed at several occasions: for instance, when France all too soon recognised the rebels, or 'terrorists' in some of their parlance, as partners at the peace negotiation table in 2003; or when the French president, Jacques Chirac, ordered the destruction of the Ivoirian Air Force in November 2004, after Gbagbo broke the cease-fire and bombarded French positions, leaving nine French peace-keepers dead. Moreover, to add another instance, the French military shot into a crowd of Ivoirian protesters during tensions.[8] In this view, decolonisation had not been a true change of relationships between France and Côte d'Ivoire; but a transfer of power to a moderate elite under the leadership of Houphouët-Boigny.

Certainly, both tales contain elements of 'truths', but this is not at issue here. For my argument it is important to note that they stress different aspects while downplaying others. The two opposing political camps came up with different scenarios for the jubilee celebration that mirror these political positions: one more conventional and the other based on the idea to create a counter-image. Although the *raison d'être* of a commemoration ceremony is a past event, they have a clear link to the present. Different aspects are picked out from the past and displayed according to needs in the present and the immediate future. Such an understanding of commemorative events highlights their projective dimension and message to the audience assembled. In the following part, I will discuss previous independence celebrations that created a particular imagery of Ivoirian celebrations. In the following and final part of this chapter, I will refer to the projective dimension of the *cinquantenaire* and link my analysis to the first post-conflict presidential elections at the end of the jubilee year.

Independence celebrations in Côte d'Ivoire

During the first decades of Houphouët-Boigny's rule, Côte d'Ivoire's economy flourished and independence ceremonies were celebrated with glamour and *grandeur*. To develop the different regions, the celebration rotated through the major towns of the country. For instance, district towns received a tarmac road, a sports stadium or a residence for the president (N'Guessan 2011; Förster 2012).

The independence celebrations of these early times of independence created an imagery that deeply shaped Ivoirian imaginations of such celebrations. In Man, such a celebration was held in 1969 (*Abidjan Matin*, 7 August). Even from remote towns inhabitants mobilised and participated (B. Lai, personal communication, 7 August 2010). A part of the elder generation in the region of Man wax lyrical about these past celebrations and produce almost paradise-like descriptions of abundance. In a large part of the population, Houphouët-Boigny acquired the status of a demigod. As another elderly man put it: 'Houphouët is not a man, Houphouët is God' (P. Tia, personal communication, 15 June 2011). This generation uses harsh words when asked about the present celebrations: 'they are nil today; it is just the name that stays ... There are no good celebrations any longer, everybody stays home' (A. Seu, personal communication, 15 June 2011). In former times the population had stayed until nightfall, as another informant remembers nostalgically (M. Fofana, personal communication, 14 June 2011).

These early grand celebrations are remembered as Houphouët-Boigny's independence celebrations. Given the economic decline, however, celebrations at that scale were no longer possible (T. Förster, personal communication, 30 July 2012). Nevertheless, the reiteration of the yearly independence celebration merged into an imagery of what I call the conventional or standard Ivoirian independence celebration. This celebration follows a recurring procedure with the participation of similar representatives and social groups. A dozen interviews with elderly locals revealed which elements are seen as constitutive of the independence celebration.[9] The main ceremony is expected to be held at a central public place in town. Guests from afar and participants from the entire region, and also from remote villages, are expected to be present. For the region of Man, these are chiefs, the members of the committee, women's dance groups and mask-bearers. At the heart of descriptions was always the parade, particularly the military parade but also the march of the socio-professional groups (F. Dohi, personal communication, 2 August 2010). Further important elements mentioned were official speeches and the reception and distribution of food afterwards. A few informants also mentioned competitions organised at the occasion of the national day (V. Bleu, personal communication, 2 August 2010; L. S. Sably, personal communication, 4 August 2010).

This shared imagination of elements and imageries that are constitutive of a successful independence celebration orients itself at an international decorum including the display of national symbols, parades, speeches and receptions (Fauré 1978; Lentz 2010). As often, folkloristic elements add local flavour to national performances (Tirefort 1999). Furthermore, new elements from the global *mediascape* may also be appropriated and included (Förster 2012). In the next part I will describe the *cinquantenaire* modelled according to this conventional style in the northern part of Côte d'Ivoire.

The *cinquantenaire* in the rebel-held parts (Man)

Even if the ceremonies of the *cinquantenaire* in the rebel-controlled North oriented themselves at the universal decorum appropriated during the postcolony, they demonstrated a considerable degree of variations (for Korhogo, see Förster, 2012). The variations at district level can be explained with the decentralised structure of the rebel administration and the local political leaderships of the respective communities. The biggest military parade of the rebels took place in Bouaké, the headquarters of the rebel movement and second largest city of Côte d'Ivoire. In the following, I will describe the celebration in Man.

The city of Man is the district capital of the Region of Tonkpi with about 150,000 inhabitants. Before the violent political crisis, this region used to be a major tourist resort famous for its mountains and mask performances (Reed 2003). In 2010, the city was a mere shadow of its former self. By the time of the *cinquantenaire*, administrative powers had been effectively transferred to the state administration, although the (ex) rebels remained in charge of crucial elements such as the local armed forces and the tax system (Heitz 2009). What this meant for the commemoration in Man was that the ceremony was organised under the administrative leadership of the prefect, whereas the military parade was commanded by the local rebel leader.

To mark the anniversary, a group of local sports teachers took the up-coming celebrations as an opportunity to organise a football tournament for the boys' clubs in Man.[10] They obtained the support of the rebel commander of Man for their initiative. The final for the *coupe du cinquantenaire* was supposed to be played in the stadium of Man on the eve of the jubilee. This, however, was occupied by a political rally promoting the re-election of president Gbagbo.[11]

Early in the morning of 7 August, marquees were pitched up along the road at the Place de la Paix, the central square of Man, where parades had commonly been held. For the dignitaries, sofas were put up. Dressed in local gowns, a large delegation of chiefs from the neighbourhoods took their seats in the shade of one of the tents. At the other end, the Manding women's association dressed in white honoured the celebration with their presence, as well as representatives of religious communities.

The groups mentioned so far constitute official representatives of their respective social groups that are always called to participate at such occasions. The roadsides filled up with mostly young persons until it was crammed. The photographers had taken up their positions waiting for the arrival of the dignitaries in their limousines. A clown entertained the spectators in his funny dress in national colours with bells.

Throughout the ceremony, whenever there was a break for the animator, the historic 'Indépendence ChaCha' from Congo was played (Dorsch 2010: 133). This was one of the most direct references to the historical times of 1960 throughout the ceremony.

At this point, the zone commander, the rebel chief of Man, arrived with some of his *garde rapprochée* (security staff). The troops stood to attention and the zone commander inspected and saluted them, accompanied by the commander in charge of the parade. Most of the civil and military staff of the rebels was present. The next person arriving was the prefect of the region of Man, Amani Michel, accompanied by prefects from neighbouring prefectures and sub-prefectures. The mayor of Man, Dr Albert Flindé, and his deputies followed; as well as Sriki Blon Blaise, representing the region, alongside other representatives from the camp of the president in the South. The prefect (state) and the commander (insurgent) inspected the troops together and saluted in front of the flag and fanfare. According to protocol, the commander walked behind the prefect.

The cohabitation of rebels and state officials – former belligerents and political opponents – had reached a temporary, stable form. Blon Blaise made a donation of petrol to the rebels for their provision of security.

The prefect went to the wooden rostrum covered in the national flag to deliver his speech. It was summarised in the press as follows: '… Côte d'Ivoire celebrates today its fifty years of independence and this gives us the opportunity to use the rear-mirror to prepare the future. During forty years, our country has been at the forefront of development in the sub-region. This was brought to an end by the war. Côte d'Ivoire still has its potential and the mountainous areas as well …'.[12] This prefect clearly referred to the flourishing years under Houphouët-Boigny, but downplayed the fact that Côte d'Ivoire's economic decline goes back to the 'houphouëtist' period. By claiming that Côte d'Ivoire could regain its former status without mentioning that the relationship with France had to be altered, he revealed in subtle ways his political affiliation, the anti-Gbagbo Rassemblement des Houphouëtistes pour la Démocratie et la Paix (RHDP). In the rest of his speech he listed the progress made in the different domains of education, infrastructure and health services by reading out detailed numbers that nobody seemed to be able to follow.

At the celebration in Man, the programme of the official jubilee at the national level was not at all mentioned. In Podiagouiné in the south of Man, the sub-prefect reported on the national history conferences of the official national committee. These conferences were seen as biased in favour of Gbagbo (N'Gguessan 2011: 59–60). The prefects and sub-prefects made their personal choices of what to mention of the official celebration and of what to leave out completely – choices which obviously reflected their political attitude.

Although Amani Michel had demanded that the celebrations should be an opportunity to learn from the past, no one seemed to be prepared to actually take a critical look at past events during these times of crisis. Little was commemorated of what had happened in 1960, apart from the fact that it happened. Neither the prefect nor the sub-prefect spoke about decolonisation or the time leading up to 1960. The commemoration was not so much about independence from France nor about the first fifty years. Rather than a backward glance, minds were hopefully directed towards the future. Most of the time, participants talked about the *cinquantenaire* as a moment when the country would move on and get back to the glorious times of the Ivoirian economic 'miracle' after independence.

In Man, there was a short comic cameo in which Houphouët-Boigny was mimicked as an old, trembling man holding a speech. Noteworthy, in this sketch, was the fact that Houphouët was not linked to the glorious years of the Ivoirian miracle, but to the more recent times.

The next element was the military parade. First, standard-bearers passed presenting a shining trimmed national flag. Then, three platoons in red berets armed with Kalashnikovs followed marching in step to the drums and trumpets of the fanfare. Afterwards, military vehicles were presented. The procession was continued by the *dozow*, the hunters of the local hunter association. During the violent conflict in 2002, they had fought on the side of the rebels. They were accompanied by traditional music, stopped and formed a semicircle in front of the dignitaries and showed some of their quick dance steps.

The procession continued with social and cultural groups: ethno-regional associations (e.g. the Senufo of Korhogo), professional associations (wax tissue sellers, bakers, shoe-cleaners), NGOs for the development of the region, sports associations (football and karate), brevets du *cinquantenaire* wearing T-shirts with its symbol. Most groups stopped for a short time in front of the dignitaries, made a small performance and received a small tip.

A *Dan* mask, popularly called 'the long mask', due to its stilts made its appearance. The mask has been promoted as a symbol of the region (Reed 2003). Its display in public ceremonies linked to the state has become customary since colonial times (Steiner 2007). It danced to the beats of a drum, so that the audience cheered out loud.

Next came the karate club. Particularly the small boys and girls impressed the audience with their short performance. The sociocultural parade was brought to an end by motorbikes, coaches and trucks of the merchant association. The audience was now invited for a reception at the residence of the prefect. Distinguished guests were invited inside, others had to sit in tents outside.

According to these observations, the independence celebrations seemed to be held in the public realm, with state officials and representatives of the population. The *cinquantenaire* was less celebrated within the families, compared to the *fête du mouton* (Eid al-adha), for example, which is celebrated in the mosque, at home with a meal, new clothing and visitors. These observations show that local reasons to celebrate, unrelated to the anniversary, contributed to the *grandeur* of the festivities in the smaller towns around Man. Podiagouiné had received the status of a sub-prefecture two years ago and for the second time it used a bigger celebration to invite 'powerful authorities' in order to promote the community.

The pitfalls of the 'second independence'

President Laurent Gbagbo, a historian, was in charge of organising the official celebration of Côte d'Ivoire's jubilee of independence. In line with the *refondation*, Gbagbo's political programme, the fiftieth anniversary of independence was to be(come) Côte d'Ivoire's 'second independence' or rather true independence from France (Smith 2011; N'Guessan 2013). A constitutive element of the ideology of the *refondation* is its anti-neocolonialist critique that advocates a new relationship with France. To underline this aspect, Gbagbo was the only Francophone head of state to reject France's invitation to send Ivoirian troops to parade on the French national day, 14 July, to mark the fiftieth anniversary of the 'Year of Africa'.

The Historian-President Laurent Gbagbo set up a national commission to prepare the jubilee, the Commission nationale préparatoire du cinquantenaire de la Côte d'Ivoire (CNPCICI). He appointed another historian, Pierre Kipré, as its president. The major concern of the government's programme was to revise the conventional historiography and imagery and to give voice to marginalised aspects of history beyond the figure of Houphouët-Boigny (N'Guessan, 2013).[13]

The conventional independence celebration was associated with independence festivals of Houphouët-Boigny's regime, which had always adopted a decisively pro-French tone. The approach chosen to 'disconnect the fiftieth-anniversary commemorative event from the name and person of Houphouët-Boigny …

the *Übervater* of Ivoirian independence' was actualised by breaking with the 'Houphouët-style remembering' (N'Guessan 2013: 287). The extravagant military and social parades were postponed. Just a small military parade was held on the forecourt of the presidential palace in private.[14] The message was to avoid the usual 'dancing and singing' (N'Guessan 2011: 65) and to start working for a better future, with real independence. Hence, Côte d'Ivoire's incumbent regime celebrated with a small, non-public act inside the Palace walls reserved for an illustrious few.

The central programme that Kipré and the CNPCICI organised – instead of a grand popular feast – constituted of a series of intellectual conferences, held previous to 7 August. The conferences took place in different non-university towns, all of them in the government-controlled South. Following these international colloquiums with participants from Africa, Europe and Asia, the national commission for the organisation of the jubilee published some of the contributions in a series (Kipré and Aké 2011a, 2011b). In the foreword of the first volume, Kipré writes that contrary to other fiftieth anniversary celebrations, Ivoirian society wished to reflect collectively on five essential issues in West Africa, to take stock and make recommendations for future action. The conference dealt with regional conflicts and national independences, economic conditions, agriculture and food security, environmental issues and conservation and the significance of independence (Kipré 2011b: 7). Although innovative, a lecture series in French was not very accessible for the majority of the population.

The book on regional conflicts and independence in West Africa addressed the autocratic face of Houphouët-Boigny's regime (Kipré and Aké, 2011b). A contribution about Ernest Boka who was the first president of the Ivoirian Supreme Court serves as example. An outspoken critic of the 'neo-colonialist politics' of Houphouët-Boigny and France, he resigned in 1963 to protest against the arbitrary arrests of individuals linked to the attempted coup of 1963 (allegedly due to a (communist) conspiracy against the presidency) and died in custody under dubious circumstances (Brou Cho 2011: 33–46). Another contribution looks beyond the domination of the single-party system that covered social divisions and crises, and stresses that to the current day the unions remain politicised (Yapi 2011: 153–64). Kipré and Aké show self-confidently that France is not the only partner of Côte d'Ivoire and they trace the history of Sino-Ivoirian relations (Kipré and Aké 2011b; Seka and Kouakou, 2011).

The contributions of the conferences were to convey the message that the idea of a golden past contrasted with a negative image of the present is erroneous (Kipré 2011: 8). In a video-interview placed on the publishing house's website, Kipré particularly emphasised the significance of the series for Africa in general and West Africa in particular (interview with Pierre Kipré, 2011). In line with the *refondateurs*' main explanation of the crisis, Kipré attributes to the project an international mission of intellectual revolution, rather than a domestic one.

The opposition refused to participate in the conferences with the argument that the CNPCICI was pro-Gbagbo, which was not a completely unfounded accusation, as the post-electoral period revealed.[15] Indeed, this bias seems characteristic of many events organised or supported by the CNPCICI. There hardly seemed to have been common grounds on and events in which both political camps were able to unite as Ivoirians.

What remained free from politicisation was the *pagne du cinquantenaire*, the special fabric with the logo of the event, although it was promoted by Simone Gbagbo, the first Lady and politician in her own right. The *pagne*[16] was produced in several variations, most of them in the national colours, in green and orange on a white background. Its price was between 5,000 and 12,500 CFA francs (1€ equals 655 CFA francs), depending on the quality. According to my observation, nobody wore the fabric except for elite members linked to the national level. However, in this milieu, individuals from both political camps used the *pagne*. Social class, not political belonging, seemed decisive.

The contrast with the conventional commemoration certainly worked at the national level for some circles. However, the dissemination of the re-writing of Côte d'Ivoire's historiography was limited due to the intellectual format of the conferences. In some way, the rupture with the conventional style was perceived as if there had not been any ceremony at all, given the extremely high expectations for a spectacular *cinquantenaire*. A businessman in his late forties commented with disappointment that hardly any projects – such as construction of new infrastructure, public buildings, roads, etc. – had been undertaken (P. Tokpa, personal communication, 27 July 2010). As Bidi commented in an opposition newspaper on the government's commemoration, it was a 'lost opportunity' for a big celebration.[17]

The celebrations in Man and other districts were modelled along the lines of a conventional ceremony and resisted in a certain way the rupture that the government's jubilee had sought. Hence, one could argue that the imagery of the independence ceremony *à la Houphouët-Boigny* 'has been in part kept going performatively' in prefectures and sub-prefectures throughout the country (Connerton 1989: 43).

The celebrations at the district levels, particularly in the North, were based on the 'Ivoirianised' framework of the universal decorum. They were not a mere repetition of so-called Houphouët-style celebrations, for the celebrations did not actively remember the glory of Houphouët-Boigny's times. Quite to the contrary, in Man Houphouët-Boigny was ridiculed as an old man who still clung to power, whereas in Korhogo the founding father was not mentioned at all (Förster 2012). In these respects, the local arenas showed that the conventional Ivoirian celebration had emancipated itself from the *Übervater* Houphouët-Boigny and quite self-consciously staged the nation in the local environment by making use of and creatively appropriating a universally applied form of public performance.

Conclusion: the retreat into the palace

Throughout the programme of the official *cinquantenaire*, the rhetoric of the 'second independence' has nurtured the theory of French manipulation of Ivoirian politics. It was towards the end of the jubilee year that the old master narrative of a French conspiracy developed its full potential and became a 'self-fulfilling prophecy' (Piccolino 2012: 15).

In late 2010, presidential elections were held in which the nation was to choose in a run-off between Laurent Gbagbo, the candidate of the *refondateurs*, and the candidate of the coalition RHDP, Alassane Ouattara, from the North. Due to mistrust between the candidates (International Crisis Group [ICG] 2011: 7), a modus operandi was put in place that requested the UN to follow closely the work of the national election commission and subsequently to certify the vote, which was a novelty in international election supervision (ICG 2011: 7). According to the Ivoirian Election Commission and the UN, the outgoing president Laurent Gbagbo lost the vote. The Constitutional Council, the highest Ivoirian court 'with the authority to validate the vote', and whose president was close to Laurent Gbagbo, produced a different outcome (Bassett 2011: 473). The votes of several pro-Ouattara strongholds were cancelled and Gbagbo declared to be the winner of the run-off. Surrounded by their respective supporters, Gbagbo and Ouattara were sworn in as presidents of Côte d'Ivoire. The international community including major African political bodies such as the African Union (AU) and the Economic Community of West African States (ECOWAS) supported Ouattara as the democratically elected president.

For Gbagbo's supporters, however, the picture looked quite different. The fact that the verdict of the highest Ivoirian court was nullified by the international community constituted in their eyes a violation of Ivoirian sovereignty. To them, the situation was an iteration of *Françafrique* and Gbagbo another victim on the long list of French interference to preserve its own hegemonic interests. In this conspiracy narrative, France pulled the strings behind the UN to install its puppet to preserve the anachronistic system of *la Françafrique* (Piccolino 2012). Two publications criticised the international military intervention harshly in the rhetoric of the anti-neocolonialism. For instance, 'Une guerre coloniale' (a colonial war) (Casanova: 2011), 'Démocratie néocoloniale de la France' (Baniafouna 2011); 'Le coup d'Etat de trop de la France en Afrique' (yet another French *coup d'état* in Africa) (Gnangui 2011); 'La bataille de la seconde independence' (the battle for the second independence) (Charvin 2011); or, in the words of the president of the official commission for the *cinquantenaire*: citizens should defend their independent state, 'even against other citizens who are linked to exterior powers who are in favour of the post-colonial state' (Kipré 2011: 9).

A large part of the population as well as quite a few international observers bought into this well-established pattern of explanation, as it had so often been true for the Cold War years. As Smith (2011) eloquently puts it: 'The long history of Françafrique – its obscurity of informal networks and alliances in business and in high politics that were underlined by the presence of the French military battalion – created a credible basis for a different version of "facts".' The rallying cry of a 'second independence' had somehow prepared Gbagbo's followers throughout the jubilee year for such a confrontation. The only consistent course of action following the rhetoric of the *refondateurs* was to mount resistance – with words and weapons – to what was perceived as international interference spearheaded by France.

However, the rhetoric of the second independence refused to acknowledge that the end of the Cold War and the democratic wave signalled the end of an era (Young 2004: 24). The old explanatory model of French hegemonic interests is no longer able to account for the dynamics after the end of the post-colony. In the age of human rights and global democratic governance, further issues are at stake. Not every project between France and Côte d'Ivoire is of a neo-colonial character. Côte d'Ivoire has long diversified its international relations, as the contributions to the conferences of the *cinquantenaire* have themselves emphasised (Seka and Kouakou 2011). Furthermore, France has lost the privileged position it once had in Ivoirian business. Apart from cocoa, the oil sector has become key to the Ivoirian economy. France, however, does not dominate either of these two sectors (Smith 2011).

The conventional Ivoirian independence celebration was portrayed by the pro-Gbagbo movement as an anachronistic remnant of the 'houphouëtist' post-colony. In the symbolic language and imagery of the *cinquantenaire*, the rupture with the conventional Ivoirian celebration translated into the political language of the *refondateurs* as a rupture with the 'houphouëtist' system and France. This interpretation, however, neglects the universal character of the conventional Ivoirian celebration whose model it has appropriated. Laurent Gbagbo celebrated the *cinquantenaire* of Côte d'Ivoire in a secluded way, almost in private, shielded from the public, when politics and the nation are exactly about the public, the national social space and the common future.

In retrospect, the projective dimension of the *cinquantenaire* stands out more clearly. In this light, the retreat of the ceremony into the presidential palace foreshadowed Gbagbo's attempt to cling to power and his withdrawal into the bunker. It was not just from the French that Gbagbo eventually dissociated himself, but from the international community of states.

* Note from the author: I would like to express my gratitude to the editors of this volume and Till Förster for their comments on earlier versions of this chapter. I am most indebted to Konstanze N'Guessan who generously shared her thoughts and unpublished work on the Ivoirian jubilee with me.

Notes

1 Laurent Gbagbo has published a small book on the socio-economic aspects on the eve of independence (Gbagbo 1982).

2 The two political camps are far from being compact; but we can distinguish a pro-government or pro-Gbagbo and an anti-Gbagbo camp. Both camps were organised in cross-party alliances: *La Majorité Présidentielle* (LMP) and *Le Rassemblement des Houphouëtistes pour la Démocratie et la Paix* (RHDP). As McGovern has pointed out, the Ivoirian conflict was often a figuration of three, one of them bridging the two opposite sides in conflict (McGovern 2011: 36–41).

3 The country was not engaged in an election campaign on 7 August 2010; it was only at the eve of the *cinquantenaire* that president Gbagbo announced to hold elections before the end of the year.

4 On the concept of appropriation see Hahn (2008).

5 Houphouët-Boigny shaped Côte d'Ivoire during forty years, before and after independence. According to Akindès (2004), Ivoirian politics under Houphouët was based on a politico-economic arrangement, the 'houphouëtist' system or the 'houphouëtist' compromise. This arrangement included the already mentioned relationship to French business and politics, as well as his achievement of national cohesion which was largely based on the redistribution of state revenues to opponents.

6 An imagery constitutes of an assemblage of images and imaginations, saturated with shared meanings that are particularly image-based.

7 Konstanze N'Guessan investigates the official celebration of the Ivoirian state as her PhD project. Her field reports were published online in the framework of a comparative project of official commemoration ceremonies in Francophone Africa headed by Carola Lentz (Lentz 2011).

8 For a more detailed analysis see Charbonneau (2007: 166–9).

9 Further information on the small corpus of a dozen interviews with elderly persons aged between 63 and over 80 about their memories of 1960 and the independence celebrations in the 1960s and 1970s is given elsewhere (Heitz 2013).

10 Lately at least, football games are often locally organised to mark big events, including national day celebrations.

11 Bamba (2010, August 9), 'Philippe Attey aux populations de Man – "Gbagbo ou rien"'.

12 Souleymane (2010, August 9), 'Cinquantenaire à Man, Blon Blaise offre dix millions: La population en colère'.

13 For an excellent comparative analysis of the counter-narrative presented by the official commission on the occasion of the *cinquantenaire* in contrast to histories of independence reiterated under Houphouët-Boigny, see N'Guessan (2013).

14 Bidi (2010, August 9), '50 ans de la Côte d'Ivoire: Grand cinquantenaire, petit défilé'.

15 Aké N'Gbo, who was the president of the Cnpcici's scientific commission, served as prime minister in Gbagbo's illegal government. Pierre Kipré, the president of the Cnpcici, supported Gbagbo wholeheartedly as his ambassador in France.

16 Cloth produced by UNIWAX: cinquantenaire-*pagne*.

17 Bidi (2010, August 9) '50 ans de la Côte d'Ivoire: Grand cinquantenaire, petit défilé'.

15

Chad's political violence at 50: bullets, ballots and bases

David Styan

Chad is arguably the least cohesive and most bloodstained state to emerge from the decolonisation of French Equatorial Africa in 1960. This chapter takes the Chadian state's 50th anniversary as a prism to examine selected aspects of the political violence which has marked the lives of Chadians throughout the half century.

The chapter is divided into four sections: first it chronicles the events and debates surrounding the delayed 50th anniversary in Chad itself, contrasting the ceremony and diplomatic fanfare of January 2011 with the critical domestic debate surrounding the anniversary. It also examines the unique place that the country occupies in French Gaullist iconography, Chad being the birthplace of the Free French forces in 1940, the 70th anniversary of which overlapped with that of the *cinquantenaire*.

The second section examines the nature of Chadian authoritarianism. Two traits are noted as having characterised successive presidential regimes in Chad; first a systematic rejection of political compromise, political differences invariably being resolved via bullets and coercion; secondly a generalised acceptance of impunity for past crimes.

Thirdly, the text asks to what degree French forces have served to protect and legitimise successive Chadian regimes, and whether the continued presence of foreign armed forces has facilitated or constrained domestic political violence. At independence Chad signed a standard bilateral defence accord with Paris, under which French troops have made several substantive military interventions (notably in 1969, 1983 and 1986) to defend those in power in N'Djamena against both domestic rebellions and Libyan incursions. Since 1986 Chad has hosted around 1,200 troops of France's Operation Epervier, based principally in N'Djamena and the eastern town of Abéché.[1] In 2008/10 the French were joined temporarily by EU then UN military forces, the multilateral presence justified in part by a need to contain violence across Chad's eastern border in

Sudan's Darfur province.[2] France's 2008 Defence White Paper and cost-cutting heralded the closure of bases elsewhere in Africa. Yet French troops remain in Chad, with a revised bilateral military accord under negotiation in 2012.[3]

Finally the text briefly considers the increasing role that elections and the ballot box have played in the evolution of politics and the strengthening of President Idris Déby. Electoral legitimisation has been important in several ways. The 50th anniversary of the Chadian state marked the consolidation of his own two decades in power, and was adroitly used to boost his international legitimacy in the run-up to Chad's, repeatedly postponed, legislative elections. Held a month after the anniversary celebrations, these reflected the high degree of presidential patronage over *both* the ruling party and the fissiparous opposition groupings. Idris Déby himself was then effortlessly re-elected for a fourth presidential term in April 2011. Formal electoral procedures have been crucial to the legitimisation of French and European officials' interactions with Déby and his governments, as underscored by the centrality of the August 2007 Political Accord between opposition and presidential camps (International Crisis Group 2010).

It is hardly surprising that neither 'success' nor 'stability' was being celebrated by the bulk of Chad's population on the 50th anniversary. Successive governments have been chronically unstable, their rule invariably violent. Those in power in N'Djamena (which retained its colonial name, Fort Lamy, until 1971) have faced threats from armed rebellion in one or more regions of the country continuously since 1966. Formally, there has only been one text-book coup, the military overthrow of President Tombalbaye in April 1975. Yet his death was the culmination of army dissent over the decade-long war in the north. The subsequent failures of the military junta to either consolidate or share power triggered further fragmentation of the armed forces. This brought civil war to the capital itself, and interventions by both French and Libyan troops. It established a template for subsequent challenges to Chadian government, whereby incumbents would be replaced only by rebel raids on the capital. Such raids were successful in 1982 and 1990 (Burr and Collins 1999: 102–12, Haggar 2007). Attacks were repeated in 2006, when rebels were stopped in the suburbs of the capital; and in February 2008 the presidential palace was surrounded before the rebels were vanquished, largely by helicopters flown by foreign pilots. There is no credible estimate of the number of Chadians killed during successive rounds of civil war, nor of the cumulative loss of life due to recurrent famine and the state's chronic inability to provide either basic healthcare or adequate famine relief. However, Hissene Habré's rule (1982–90) alone resulted in the deaths of 40,000 Chadians through imprisonment, torture and extra-judicial killings (Abakar 2006; Human Right Watch 2012). In addition to extreme political violence, on almost all indicators of human development Chad (usually accompanied by its Francophone neighbours Niger and Central African Republic) regularly features in the bottom ten countries. Conversely, it is habitually near the top of indices of global corruption.

Chad's 50th-anniversary celebrations

André Malraux formally granted Chad its independence at midnight on 10–11 August 1960. Fifty years later most former Francophone colonies held their anniversary ceremonies on independence day itself. However, in Chad the event was celebrated with a five-month delay; President Idris Déby hosting 14 African heads of state and thousands of guests in central N'Djamena on 11 January 2011. Those attending included all of his fellow Francophone African heads of state, French defence minister Alain Juppé, and – in what would prove to be the final foreign trip of his career – Libya's leader Muammar Qaddafi.

Guests and locals gathered before a fifty-metre triumphal arch draped in the colours of the Chadian flag, the centrepiece of a vast newly built square flanked by a victory statue depicting heroic male and female fighters. They were surrounded by a somewhat surreal collection of globes, balls and lamps strewn across a vast, barely finished, concrete esplanade where – until just a few months earlier – Chad's main military garrison had stood since colonial times.

The context and reasons for the delays to the anniversary celebrations say more about Chadian public life than the pomp and symbolism of the ceremony itself. Several factors played a role in the postponement. First, patronage and corruption: N'Djamena's mayor had been charged with organising the celebrations, but had been imprisoned along with several colleagues early in 2010. His arrest, on corruption charges linked to public contracts, was the latest in a series of arrests in the personal entourage of President Idris Déby and his ruling party, the Mouvement Patriotique du Salut (MPS). While the fraudulent contracts did not relate to preparations for the anniversary, they triggered one of the regular waves of arrests which have been a key element in the President's strategy of political control, keeping his allies in check via the switchback of patronage and allegations of embezzlement. Many of those arrested in 2009/10, including both the mayor himself and the head of the ruling party, were subsequently discreetly released, in part because their support was required in the run-up to the 2011 presidential and legislative elections (*La Voix*, 2010, August 26).

Secondly, the delay allowed some of the numerous public works programmes in N'Djamena itself to be completed. While the extensive damage wrought by the fighting and looting of February 2008 had been largely patched up by early 2010, far greater destruction was wrought by the government's grandiose plans to reconstruct the city. After 2008 the government began a haphazard demolition programme in residential areas. These *déguerpissements* initially began as a form of collective punishment against quarters which had risen up against the government during the rebels' brief occupation of much of the city in February

2008. Over time they metamorphosed into broader plans to rebuild the capital via a series of ambitious infrastructure projects, funded by the windfall oil revenues of 2006–08. In July 2010 the centrepiece of reconstruction, a vast Place Cinquantenaire, replacing the army camp which since the 1940s had faced the city's central square, cathedral and presidential palace, was officially inaugurated.[4] By this time, a ministerial decree had already been passed on 1 July formally postponing the anniversary celebration by five months to 11 January 2011. However, few people in N'Djamena were aware that the celebrations had been postponed. Thus on Independence Day itself there was considerable confusion; while workers were told in a radio broadcast that the 11th was a bank holiday, this was contradicted by the presidency. On the day itself, the local press noted '[To] general surprise … the military parade, programmed and announced by the national radio, did not take place'.[5]

Famine and floods also help explain the postponement of Chad's *cinquantenaire*. In mid-2010 Chad and its Sahelian neighbours were wracked by famine; with two million Chadians, mostly in the central Sahelian belt, facing malnutrition; while in the regions around Lake Chad and bordering Niger, a quarter of the population faced starvation. Deaths during this, the last month of the *soudure* period of penury between harvests, were estimated in the tens of thousands. Livestock deaths were far higher in both Chad and Niger, sapping livelihoods further for the coming years. Flash floods in late July 2010 also devastated parts of both N'Djamena and Faya Largeau in the north, adding to the misery caused by demolitions.[6]

Finally, and perhaps most importantly in terms of the Chadian state, by postponing the event by five months Déby effectively turned the *cinquantenaire* into a celebration of his own power. By holding the anniversary celebration in January 2011, he ensured media coverage of that commemoration occurring between the 20th anniversary of his seizure of power (on 1 December 1990), and the presidential elections of April 2011.[7] Five days after the anniversary celebrations, the ruling party held a congress which endorsed Déby's candidature. The MPS then duly gained a majority in the legislative elections of February, with Déby being re-elected for a fourth presidential term in April by 88 per cent of the votes cast. Both polls were boycotted by most opposition groups.

France and Chad: double anniversaries

The *mise en scène* of hastily constructed parade-ground, triumphal arch and statuesque baubles viewed by the dignitaries in N'Djamena were built literally on the foundations of Gaullist France's enduring historical ties with Chad. The new Place Cinquantenaire was built over the demolished military garrison which had served first French then Chadian troops throughout the twentieth century. One cannot understand the persistence of France's military ties to the independent

Chadian state without reference to the rather specific place that this north-east slice of Afrique Equatoriale Française (AEF) occupies in the history of Gaullist France.

André Malraux, who represented De Gaulle at the independence ceremonies of four AEF states in succession during his tour of August 1960, noted the centrality of Chad to the Free French in his independence speech in what at that point was still a small garrison town on the river Chari:

> For you, for us, for the world, this city constitutes a meeting point of history and liberty.

> This is yet a more emotional night for us as your destiny and that of Free France have fulfilled themselves side by side. From this city started the adventure that led General Leclerc to Strasbourg; here, Governor Eboué combined the noblest loyalty to France with the most lucid confidence in the African qualities, and established the principles, the results of which we are celebrating together. May a Rue du General Leclerc and a Rue Félix Eboué meet in your city, at a Place d'Indépendance!

Under AEF's governor Felix Eboué, Chad was the first colony in the Empire to declare for De Gaulle, General Catroux subsequently rallying to De Gaulle in Fort Lamy.[8] Thus in 1940/41 Chad was the military kernel from which evolved De Gaulle's embryonic Free French military forces, the launch-pad for the first combat operations against the Italians at Koufra, the oasis in south-east Libya. The battle of Koufra prompted Leclerc's famous pledge to 'fight to Strasbourg', subsequently indelibly embedded in the military iconography of the Free French.[9] The military garrison Camp des Martyrs, demolished to make way for the Place Cinquantenaire by Senegalese and South Korean contractors for the anniversary, bore the name 'Camp de Koufra' until the 1990s. Indeed the Régiment de Marche du Tchad, within which were subsumed the Régiment de Tirailleurs Sénégalais du Tchad, remains to this day a mechanised unit in the French army. These ties and anniversaries continue to be maintained and renewed. In October 2010 a 200-strong French delegation led by the Fondation Charles De Gaulle visited N'Djamena to mark the 70th anniversary. It included grandchildren of both De Gaulle and Maréchal Leclerc.

Just as plans for celebrations of the 50th anniversary did not go entirely according to script, the original 1960 ceremony was not without hiccups. The balcony from which independence was to be declared was accessible only by climbing awkwardly through a window. Midway through Malraux's speech there was also a power failure, meaning that he and Tombalbaye read their statements by torchlight, providing what has proved to be the enduring image of the evening in the broader iconography of 1960.[10] Yet while Chad thus occupies a unique symbolic place in the 50th-anniversary historiography, in terms of the political analysis of the states that emerged from Afrique Occidentale Française (AOF) and AEF it is an outlier, its politics having been far more violent than other Francophone central and west African states, as examined in this chapter.

While for most Chadians day-to-day survival was a more pressing concern than the *cinquantenaire*, the anniversary did prompt limited public debate among Chad's small, beleaguered intellectual milieu. The independent bi-weekly *N'Djamena bi-Hebdo* carried several articles reflecting on the anniversary. Outspoken historian Gali Ngothé Gatta and former Minister Hourmadji M. Doumagor published highly critical assessments of independence, while blogs based abroad also hosted debates on the anniversary.

Gatta, a veteran Chadian politician and academic, lamented:

> From our fifty years of independence, we have spent thirty to forty in petty battles, killing and destroying each other, and we have never thought of stopping this tragic cycle ... Yes, we underwent a 'forty-years war' that does not promote any vision for society, except to satisfy the appetites of some nomad groups that are unable to live with the others, and to which state power gives a legitimacy to pillage this State and other sections of Chadian society ... From where does this bloodstained idea come to us that through corruption, pillage and vandalism a people gets rich and its leaders become respectable and dignified men?[11]

Doumagor, a technocrat with extensive ministerial and economic experience, underscored the 'aggressive opulence of a governing nomenklatura, which has taken over the resources of the country' while highlighting Chad's economic calamities, notably the failures of the cotton sector and nomadism. Like Gatta, he blamed the failures of the state on the unhealed divisions of the civil war: '... in Chad, the Frolinat rebellion undermined the foundations of the nation, created insurmountable tribal barriers and exacerbated the fixation of identities today'.[12]

Five decades of political violence

As noted in the introduction to this chapter, two aspects of political violence overshadow the unstable political landscape of the Chadian state since independence in 1960 and are reflected in the literature chronicling its evolution.[13] The first is the manner in which actual or threatened violence determined both the change of successive regimes and the manner in which they wielded political power when in office. Power-sharing, attempts at political compromise or reconciliation between contenders for power have been almost entirely absent from Chad's political lexicon since independence.[14] This trait appears, somewhat paradoxically, linked to a second aspect of power: the way that successive rulers have encouraged a climate of impunity for those involved in past violence. Calls for formal reconciliation, due legal process or reparations are systematically eschewed once loyalty and subservience to the new power have been established.

This pattern has become a structural reality within Chadian politics, rather than simply reflecting specific conjunctures, or the lack of functioning legal systems.

Intense rivalry among Chad's minuscule (and initially almost entirely southern) elite immediately before and after independence in 1960 was a portend of what was to follow. A rapid turnover of unstable post-*Loi-cadre* governments (see Shipway, Chapter 1 in this volume) between 1958 and 1960 saw François Tombalbaye outmanoeuvre Gabriel Lisette to emerge as premier. Within five months of independence, Tombalbaye had banned parties other than the ruling Parti Progressiste Tchadien (PPT, formally a regional branch of the Rassemblement Démocratique Africain, RDA) and dissolved the National Assembly, whose *députés* vainly attempted to resist the move. Civilian politics rapidly adopted a heavily personalised and authoritarian character, the premier repeatedly arresting perceived rivals during 1962/63. Brutal and arbitrary rule by Tombalbaye appointees in the regions triggered reaction in the form of uprisings, with that of Mangalmé, east of Mongo, in late 1965 acting as a catalyst for wider revolt, particularly among northerners (Lanne 1998, Haggar 2007).

These early developments set the stage for factors which have since become generic to each successive stage of what has been – indeed continues to be – a near-perpetual violent struggle to seize and maintain state power in Chad, often involving foreign powers (notably Libyan, Sudanese or French). Six successive phases of violence can be schematically summarised as follows: first, Tombalbaye's initial authoritarian misrule, noted above, triggered riots in 1963 and 1965; a second phase of violence opened with the formation of the largely northern rebel force, the Front de Libération Nationale du Tchad – Frolinat – in 1966. It waged guerrilla warfare from the late 1960s onwards, defining the template of Chadian politics. To counter this, in 1969 French forces in Chad were boosted to 3,000, the largest such intervention force since the ending of the Algerian war (Yacoub 2006: 55).

While Frolinat forces, partially backed by Libya, were initially contained, a third phase of violence began in April 1975 with the military coup of General Félix Malloum overthrowing Tombalbaye. Fighting in the north continued until an accord was reached between Malloum's military administration and Hissein Habré's faction of Frolinat in 1978. The fourth phase, de facto civil war between 1979 and 1982 in which both Libyan and French forces play key roles, included two rounds of extensive fighting in the capital itself between rival factions of Frolinat, which were temporarily halted only after complex international involvement. Habré's tortuous eight-year reign was dominated regionally by the re-incursion and then defeat of Libyan forces, prompting renewed French military interventions (Operations Manta in 1983 and Epervier from 1986). Domestically his rule involved particularly brutal methods of internal repression.

A brief, relatively pluralist interregnum followed the overthrow in 1990 of Habré by one of his commanders, Idris Déby, backed by French forces. Déby's two decades of subsequent rule can be seen as a sixth phase of Chadian politics. He tightened his grip on power via repression and control of the electoral process from 1993 onwards. The financial stakes of state power increased significantly from 2003 with the advent of oil exports. The cycle of violence resumed in 2005; triggered by Déby instigating constitutional reforms to allow him to remain in power and prompting several close aides and family members to defect, triggering civil war via rebellions based partly in Sudan. Rebel forces attacked N'Djamena in both April 2006 and, far more seriously, in February 2008 when, after two days of clashes, only French, Libyan and mercenary support saved Déby.

As this overview indicates, notwithstanding innumerable accords, peace deals and repeated constitutional changes, political compromise and accommodation has been almost entirely absent from Chad's political history. This is not simply a case of a lack of accommodation *between* either different political forces within the capital or within linguistic or ethnic groups in the regions. Rather, violence has invariably systematically pre-empted compromise *within* groups. This reflects what May and Charlton, in an analysis of what they termed Chadian 'warlordism', referred to as '[T]he propensity of its factions to resort to force as a first, rather than a last resort ...' (1989: 17).

The term 'warlordism' gained widespread currency in the 1990s. It was used to analyse ostensibly new actors and modes of political violence, most notably in civil wars in Zaire/DRC, and the interrelated conflicts in Liberia and Sierra Leone, the term often being deployed loosely within broader conceptions of these as 'failed states' (Reno 1998). A systematic comparative analysis is beyond the scope of this chapter, but two observations can be drawn from Chad's political trajectory. First, in the Liberian and Sierra Leonean cases, the emergence of militias and 'warlords' was synonymous with civil wars that marked decisive ruptures in post-independence politics of those countries, ultimately prompting state-collapse. Wars were eventually ended, in part via armed external intervention, and variants of pluralist politics (featuring new actors) were subsequently reconstructed as part of 'state-building'. In Liberia, militia leaders were prosecuted. In Chad's case, rather than constituting a rupture, what Charlton and May refer to as 'warlordism' has been the *dominant*, indeed defining feature of post-independence politics and the maintenance of the state. It has also been supported by external powers. The second observation, central to the concerns of this book, is that this pattern of politics has been unique within Francophone Africa. The trajectories of Niger and Mali, the Sahelian states sharing the same French colonial heritage, have been markedly different to that of Chad.

Chadian politics is studded with examples of this: the composition and evolution of Frolinat itself illustrates the trend (Buijtenhuis 1984a, b); divisions between different factions and leaders impaired the Front's effectiveness, and rivalry between Hissene Habré and Goukouni Oueddei, and their respective

Forces armées du nord (FAN) and Forces armées populaires (FAP) fighters, was at the heart of both the successive stages of civil war and the ineffectiveness of the Transitional Government of National Unity (GUNT), from 1979 onwards. The nature of such violent relations within and among Frolinat forces is analysed in depth by both Doornbos (1982) and Buijtenhuis (1984a, b).

Further schisms in 1989 triggered Habré's disastrous falling-out with his close aides Idris Déby (then his presidential adviser and former Chief of Staff) and Hassan Djamous, head of the Forces armées nationales tchadiennes (FANT), the latter widely regarded as architect of the defeat of the Libyans in 1987. Both men fled, along with arms and allies, into Sudan on 1 April 1989, from where they launched the raid which overthrew Habré. Djamous was captured in fighting and is presumed to have been personally tortured to death by Habré himself.[15]

A near-identical pattern of internal schism was reproduced in 2005 when some of Idris Déby's closest aides, including veteran military leader Mahamat Nouri, and close Zaghawa relatives within Déby's entourage fled to Sudan following the President's decision to alter the constitution to enable him to stand for re-election for a third time. Despite the ensuing rebellion, he was duly elected successfully in April 2006. Nouri and Timane Erdimi subsequently headed two of the disparate rebel forces which, via a series of loose rebel alliances, repeatedly attempted to overthrow Déby by force in 2006–09. Despite initial substantial backing from Sudan, the rebels themselves were beset by internal rivalries. Indeed, communication failures between rebel factions during their siege of Déby's palace in N'Djamena on 1–2 Februrary 2008 in part explain why their otherwise successful *razzia* ultimately failed.

Fissiparous politics are not restricted to military factions and rebel groups; a similar pattern of failure to cooperate can be seen within civilian political forces. This was evident both within groups allied to the ruling MPS and among opposition groups. The civilian Coordination of Political Parties for the Defence of the Constitution (CPDC), led by spokesman Ibni Omar Mahamat Saleh, was created to challenge the constitutional change proposed in 2005 to allow Déby to seek a third presidential mandate. However, after initial success, the CPDC was plagued with internal dissent and weaknesses; divisions were exacerbated after Ibni Omar was abducted and killed by men linked to Déby during the fighting of February 2008 (Marchal 2009, Amnesty International 2008).

This fragmentation of civilian forces is evidently not unique in Francophone Africa. Equally, it is a structural part of the manner in which Idris Déby masterfully controls both his allies and opponents via patronage. Patronage ties largely dominate Chad's small political stage, power and wealth being inextricably linked in a system where access to the state and its resources has reinforced a winner-takes-all approach to politics. This was the case from the outset, notably vis-à-vis Chad's economic mainstay, the cotton industry, with its price stabilisation and state marketing organisation. After 2003 the stakes rose considerably with the onset of oil production. In 2007–09 oil receipts were over US$1bn a year, small by Gabonese or Angolan standards, but colossal given the size and nature of Chad's minuscule ruling elite. As noted, the defection of key members of Déby's entourage, including the oil minister, in 2005 was triggered by struggles over access to oil rents. Similarly, Déby's extensive arms purchases and recourse to foreign mercenaries, including the helicopter pilots (reputedly Ukrainian, Mexican and Algerian) who saved his skin in February 2008 – in the process wreaking destruction in N'Djamena – were all purchased with windfall oil revenues.[16]

Impunity and individuals

The second characteristic of note is the manner in which a culture of near total impunity for past deeds has taken root among the relatively small number of individuals involved in Chadian politics. While Tombalbaye himself was killed in the 1975 coup, most of the other actors in the last four decades were reintegrated into political life. General Wadal Abdulkader Kamougué, who coordinated the 1975 coup, initially resisted Habré, but then became a minister under both Habré and Déby. Felix Malloum, who replaced Tombalbaye before himself being ousted from power in 1979, went into exile before returning to Chad in 2002. Even the arch opponent of Habré and Déby, Goukounni Oueddei, finally returned from exile to N'Djamena in 2010, even participating in the 50th anniversary celebrations.

Hissene Habré's case remains both the most flagrant and by far the most convoluted case of de facto impunity among Chadian politicians. After ousting Habré in 1990, Idris Déby authorised the 1992 Commission of Enquiry into abuses under Habré, agreed during the period of National Conference debates. While the Enquiry was completed, and its findings fully published (Abakar 2006), there has still been no trial of Habré, despite extensive lobbying and the initiation of legal procedures in several jurisdictions. Habré remains in exile in Senegal, despite repeated abortive attempts both to have him tried there, under either African Union or Senegalese auspices, or extradited to Belgium, where legal procedures have been opened by former victims. Déby is clearly ambivalent about this, not least because of his own participation in Habré's violence, despite frequently stating that he would like to see Habré tried internationally. With over 40,000 extra-judicial deaths during his eight years of rule, Habré's case is the most mediatised and protracted judicial saga in Africa.[17]

An additional example of impunity is the fact that many leaders and fighters involved in rebellions against Déby since 2005 have repeatedly been brought into his administration once they have rallied to him. Mahamat Nour, whose forces threatened N'Djamena in April 2006, subsequently became defence minister; some militia leaders who participated in the February 2008 assaults on the capital also later joined the government, with their armed followers receiving positions in the army. A final example is provided by the fact that the Commission of Enquiry formed, in part following French pressure, to investigate the extra-judicial killing of CPDC opposition leader Ibni Omar during those same assaults in February 2008, did identify those responsible for his abduction. However, there were no subsequent arrests or trials, reinforcing the widespread impression of arbitrary rule and impunity.[18]

France's military presence in Chad

This third section briefly sketches France's protracted military presence in Chad, asking what role military ties have played in the maintenance and regulation of internal political violence. France trained and equipped Chad's minuscule army from the outset and French troops have been stationed in Chad for most of the five decades since independence. However, their relationship with those in power in N'Djamena has rarely been straightforward. The notion of a 'neocolonial' puppet-master is of little analytical use, not least because French interests are multifaceted, have changed over time, and have more often than not been beset with internal uncertainties as to what policy to adopt when faced with successive Chadian leaders, phases of civil war and regional threats.

For comparative purposes, it should be noted that Chad's military arrangements with the departing colonial power were slightly different to those of other states which emerged from AOF and AEF (see Joly, Chapter 5 and Evrard, Chapter 6 in this volume). On 16 August 1960 the Tombalbaye government did sign a defence accord with France, similar to those with other former African colonies. However, French forces remained formally in control of Chad's three northern provinces – Borkou, Ennedi and Tibesti – until 1964, when the initial agreement was replaced with a 'technical assistance' accord. This in turn was amended on 6 March 1976 under Malloum's military government.

As noted already, in the 1960s French forces intervened several times against northern rebels in defence of N'Djamena, and French officials retained key civilian and military posts throughout the state well after that. For the past 35 years governments in power in N'Djamena have sporadically offered rhetorical criticism of the continued presence of French troops, yet in practice all have relied on their firepower. The assistance agreement remains in force, and it was under its provisions that French forces provided the logistical support which saved Idris Déby in February 2008, defending the airport, thus protecting Déby's helicopters and facilitating supplies of ammunition from Libya.

Schematically, French military interventions in Chad can be grouped into three categories: military actions in *support* of the power in place; strategic decisions *not* to intervene when the incumbent is threatened by rebels, thus facilitating their overthrow (Tombalbaye in 1975; GUNT in 1982, then Habré in 1990) and thirdly actions to defend the *territorial integrity* of Chad. This last category includes actions against Libya's seizure of the Aouzou strip (Operations Manta 1983, thence Epervier 1986). However, the distinction between domestic and foreign intervention has rarely been clear-cut: Libya also supported Frolinat, then Goukounni Oueddei against Habré; Sudan has repeatedly offered support to rebels, most particularly those among Zaghawa communities who straddle the border with Darfur. The latter have included both Déby's move against Habré in 1990 and the rebellions of 2005–09 against Déby himself.

France's military presence in Chad has never been purely bilateral. Broader geostrategic interests have frequently played a key role: these included Chadian troops being a springboard for interventions elsewhere, notably in the Central African Republic and both Congos, as well as the Cold War confrontation with Libya over their territorial claims to the Aouzou Strip. Since the end of the Cold War several trends have been evident; first there have been moves to 'multilateralise' France's military presence in Chad (Chafer 2005). This informed French support for the European force in 2008/09, thence its planned replacement by a UN force (Styan 2012). Both proved short-lived; neither led to a reduction of French forces or expenditure in Chad. A geostrategic 'division of labour' still casts France in a 'gendarme' role in the Sahel, currently both in relation to Islamist groups and an unstable post-Qaddafi Libya. The importance of this regional context is explicitly flagged in the 2008 Defence White Paper, which notes the rise of Sahelian terrorism and trafficking as justifications for the maintenance of bases in Africa (France 2008: 154). France's military presence also continues to have a logistical dimension; the north of Chad remaining an ideal desert training-ground for French plans, pilots and missiles.

Thus foreign military presence in Chad, and the actions or omissions of foreign forces vis-à-vis Chad's own political life, continue to be linked to external factors; since 2003–05 external involvement in Chadian politics has been inextricably intertwined with Western perceptions and policies towards Darfur; since 2003–05 around 250,000 Darfurian refugees have sought refuge in Eastern Chad. Given Déby's own roots (both as a Zaghawa and in terms of the Sudanese logistical and political support which brought him to power in 1990), he has expended considerable military and political capital on both containing the threat from those members of his entourage who fled to Sudan in 2005 and managing international resources directed towards Darfur. This culminated in the latest phase of seesaw relations with Sudan, a rapprochement with Sudan's President al-Bashir in January 2010, brokered in part by Qatar and Qaddafi's Libya.

Conclusion: the ballot box, constitutional rule and external legitimacy

Within the context of the decades of violence examined here, the phrase 'the consolidation of peace' has a hollow, quaint ring to it. Yet in relative terms it is an accurate summary of Idris Déby's effectiveness, first in quashing then co-opting his opponents. As such he has both reinforced and refined his domination and manipulation of military power, rendering it synonymous with control of the state and its revenues, a template which has evolved through successive phases of violence – outlined earlier in the text – which have punctuated Chad's five decades of independence.

Clearly the fact of military rule alone does not distinguish Chad's political history from that of other states that were carved out of AOF and AEF fifty years ago. Yet the chapter has suggested that the nature of violence and impunity prevalent in Chad has its specificity in relation to the form and duration of military rule elsewhere in the region. This is partly due to the manner in which violence has undermined the emergence of alternative sources of power – be they economic, political or social – from emerging and playing a role in the evolution of the state and its institutions.

A brief comparison with neighbouring Niger helps to illustrate this. Niger too has seen successive coups and military rulers since 1960; since 1991 alone there have been three successive constitutions. A coup in 1999 prompted the promulgation of the current, fifth republic, which has been far from stable since. Yet throughout successive political crises, including that of 2009/10, Nigerian politics has been shaped by *competing* political elites, operating in a political space ordered via tacit rules and successive compromises between competing elements within both the military and civilian party elites. The military is thus one actor among many, in part playing a regulatory role. In Chad under Habré or Déby, this would be inconceivable, military commanders owing personal loyalty to the presidency, and being organised partially along militia lines. Similarly, within the Nigerian political space, broader social forces, including students and civil society associations, are able to act autonomously of the state, articulating ideas via a relatively free and pluralist media.

Thus President Mamadou Tandja's attempts, which began in 2009, to unconstitutionally extend his rule for a fourth term eventually led to his overthrow in a classic 'corrective' military coup in February 2010. Soldiers removed the President after he had dissolved the National Assembly and Constitutional Court in an attempt to illegally prolong his rule. The military received the backing of the civilian political elite, and then facilitated the subsequent elections and resumption of civilian rule. Part of this resumption initially involved holding Tandja and those closely associated with him to account for their actions. On the surface, there appeared therefore to be little question of impunity as has repeatedly been the case in Chad, although Tandja was subsequently released in mid-2011, pending further investigations.

Chad's culture of impunity for past crimes has been consolidated under Déby in several ways: for example, patronage and pardons have been granted to militia leaders who have rallied to his side and he has adopted a contradictory stance towards those Chadians and international bodies seeking to try his former ally Hissene Habré for atrocities committed in the 1980s. Déby's relationship with President Omar al-Bashir of Sudan has also blended both impunity and realpolitik; four years of proxy wars and scorched-earth policies, wreaking violence and misery upon both Darfur and eastern Chad, being abruptly replaced by alliance and bilateral military cooperation in 2009.

French forces have served to protect and legitimise successive Chadian regimes. As such, the presence of foreign troops has not constrained domestic political violence, instead providing legitimacy for those in power in N'Djamena. Again, this is not unique to Chad, but such military ties have remained in place despite changes effected elsewhere, notably Senegal and Côte d'Ivoire, where French forces have distanced themselves from the defence of incumbents, and withdrawn troops. As such, the presence of Epervier in Chad appears increasingly anomalous. As noted earlier, in *de jure* terms, the genesis of France's military presence was both strategically and financially apart from the network of French forces based elsewhere on the continent, having been funded as a stand-alone 'external operation' ('OpEx') ever since the mid-1980s campaigns against Libya. In practice, over the decades, it had become a permanent element of French military projection in the Sahel and central Africa, something Idris Déby has repeatedly played to his advantage. As noted, the *cinquantenaire* coincided with French bases elsewhere being either closed completely, as in Dakar, or scaled back, as in Djibouti. French financial and strategic objectives in Africa are clearly in flux. Yet neither the 'rupture' in Franco-African relations pledged by President Sarkozy in 2007, nor the election of his socialist successor François Hollande in 2012, appear to have prompted a fundamental reappraisal of ties between Paris and Ndjamena. The protracted renegotiation of bilateral defence accords with Chad, promised in the Defence White Paper of 2008, continued throughout 2011/12.

However, while the total withdrawal of French forces from Chad are not yet envisaged, broader security equations in the Sahel, coupled with budgetary pressures in Paris, will be determinant in shaping the role played by France in the coming decades of Chadian independence. Regionally, the 2011 overthrow of Qaddafi, in which France played a leading role, has had extensive economic and political repercussions for the Sahelian states. During the military campaign, both President Déby and his counterpart in Niger warned Paris of the destabilising impact of the Libyan war on the Sahel. Inter-communal strife in southern Libya has repercussions for northern Chad. In Niger the return of 250,000 migrant workers and loss of remittances has undermined the economy. In Mali, the influx of former fighters and their arms contributed to the successes of first Tuareg then Islamist insurgencies in paralysing the state. These upheavals complicate the longer-term outlook for Franco-Chadian ties. While France is less willing to intervene to support African allies, broader insecurity in the Sahel weighs in favour of Paris maintaining operational military bases in Chad. For his part, President Déby will continue to push for increased financial recompense for hosting such troops. In turn he will use both the international legitimacy and revenues gained from their presence to burnish his profile as a pillar of stability in the Sahel. A critical alliance with successive governments in Paris has served him well for two decades. As such, the somewhat ad hoc, but predominantly military character of the 50th-anniversary celebrations was apposite.

Notes

1 France also maintains a smaller outpost in the northern town of Faya Largeau. For historical background on Epervier, see Burr and Collins (1999); on France's contemporary military role, see ICG (2006: 16–19).
2 On the 2008/09 EU force in Chad, see Tubiana (2008: 53–65); Styan (2012); Helly (2009).
3 The 2008 White Paper reforms include the renegotiation of defence accords with all former French colonies in Africa. By early 2012 the Chadian accord had not been concluded. Canada's state radio reported on France's military presence during the *cinquantenaire* in a broadcast entitled 'Neo-colonialism in Chad' (CBC, 2010).
4 APA, 'N'Djamena gets facelift before independence golden jubilee', 29 July 2010: www.apanews.net/spip.php?article129183. Accessed 16 August 2010.
5 CEFOD, press review: www.cefod.org/spip.php?article2479. Accessed 16 August 2010.
6 UN Integrated Regional Information Networks, 'CHAD: Flood victims contend with thugs, cholera and hippos', 17 November 2010: http://reliefweb.int/node/375087, accessed February 2012.
7 *N'Djamena Bi-Hebdo*, Nos 1336 (13–16 January 2011) and 1337 (17–24 January 2011).
8 A fact today commemorated by a rather forlorn fountain in the 12ème arrondissement of Paris.
9 For the Ministry of Defence's official history, see: www.cheminsdememoire.gouv.fr/page/affichecitoyennete.php?idLang=en&idCitoyen=29. Accessed February 2012.
10 Radio France Internationale used the 'torch' as the link to Tombalbaye's speech in their 'Découvrez les objects symboles des indépendances africaines' on their website throughout 2010. RFI (2010).
11 This and other quotations translated from French by the author. Gatta (2010).
12 Gatta's *Une indépendance en fumée* (NBH 1276), Doumgor's *Cinquante ans d'échecs des Etats* (NBH 1285), for Makaila, http://makaila.over-blog.com/
13 The standard sources include: Lanne (1998); May (1989). Buijtenhuis's publications (1984a, 1984b) provide a detailed dissection of FROLINAT. See also Mahamat Saleh Yacoub (2005). The latter provides an invaluable overview of the formation and disintegration of Chad's diverse armed forces, drawing particularly on extensive interviews with key players.
14 The one period where power-sharing was attempted, 1978–82, triggered civil war: see *Politique Africaine* (1984). The August 2007 Political Accord has proved ineffectual;

see Tubiana (2008), Roland Marchal (2009) as well as International Crisis Group (2006, 2010).

15 Mahamat Hassan Abakar, who chaired the enquiry into Habré, has published several works on Habré and political violence of the 1980s. Abakar (2006: 101) narrates how the publication of a photo of Djamous's mutilated body, by *N'Djamena Hebdo*, became a key symbol of the 1992 Commission of Enquiry's report into atrocities under Habré, which Abakar chaired. N'Djamena's international airport is now named after Djamous.

16 CCFD-Terre Solidaire (2012) provides an overview of Chad's arms purchases. ICG (2009) details the impact of oil on violence.

17 US-based advocacy group Human Rights Watch continues to play an active role in attempts to bring Habré to trial. See www.hrw.org/en/habre-case

18 Mahamat Saleh Haroun, Chad's leading film director, argues that impunity permeates politics and society in a more complex manner, a fact reflected in several of his films, most explicitly *Daraat* (2006) and *L'homme qui crie*, the film which won the Jury prize in Venice in 2010.

Bibliography

Abakar, M. H. (2006). *Chronique d'une enquête criminelle nationale: le cas du régime de Hissein Habré, 1982–1990*. Paris: L'Harmattan.

Adda, J. and Smouts, M.-C. (1989). *La France face au Sud: le miroir brisé*. Paris: Karthala.

Adebajo, A. (ed.) (2009). *From global apartheid to global village: Africa and the United Nations*. Scottsville: University of KwaZulu-Natal Press.

AFP (Agence France Presse) (2010, February 9). Kouchner veut une alliance des Européens et des Américains face à la Chine en Afrique. *Jeune Afrique*.

Ag Ataher Insar, A. M. (1990). La scolarisation moderne comme stratégie de résistance. In H. Claudot-Hawad (ed.) (1990). *Touaregs, exil et résistance* [special issue]. *Revue du Monde musulman et de la Méditerranée*, 57(3), 91–7.

Ageron, C.-R. (1978). *France coloniale ou parti colonial?* Paris: PUF.

Ageron, C.-R. (1992). Les Etats africains de la Communauté et la guerre d'Algérie. In C.-R. Ageron and M. Michel (eds), *L'Afrique noire française: l'heure des indépendances* (pp. 229–54). Paris: CNRS editions.

Ageron, C.-R. (1997). La guerre psychologique de l'Armée de Libération Nationale dans algérienne. In C.-R. Ageron (ed.), *La guerre d'Algérie et les Algériens, 1954–1962* (pp. 201–29). Paris: Colin.

Ageron, C.-R. and Michel, M. (eds) (1992). *L'Afrique noire française: l'heure des indépendances*. Paris: CNRS Editions.

Ahluwalia, D. P. S. (2010). *Out of Africa: post-structuralism's colonial roots*. Oxford: Abingdon; New York: Routledge.

Ahmida, A. A. (ed.) (2011). *Bridges across the Sahara: social, economic and cultural impact of the trans-Sahara trade during the 19th and 20th Centuries*. Newcastle: Cambridge Scholars Press.

Akindès, F. (2004). *The roots of the military-political crises in Côte d'Ivoire. Research Report*: Vol. 128. Uppsala: Nordiska Afrikainstitutet.

Akpo-Vaché, C. (1996). Souviens-toi Thiaroye! La mutinerie des tirailleurs sénégalais du 1 décembre 1944. *Guerres mondiales et conflits contemporains*, 1(181), 21–6.

Alden, C. (1996). From policy autonomy to policy integration: the evolution of France's role in Africa. In C. Alden and J.-P. Daloz (eds), *Paris, Pretoria and the African continent: the international relations of states and societies in transition* (pp. 11–25). Basingstoke: Macmillan; New York: St. Martin's Press.

Alemanji, M. (2008). *A miscarriage of justice at the United Nations: the missing link in the case of South Cameroons independence.* Unpublished article.

Amin, J. A. (2004). Paul Biya's foreign policy: the promise and performance. In J. M. Mbaku and J. Takougang (eds), *The Leadership Challenge in Africa: Cameroon Under Paul Biya* (pp. 153–87). Trenton, NJ: Africa World Press.

Amnesty International (2008, December). *Double misfortune: deepening human rights crisis in Chad.* London: Amnesty.

Anonymous. (1969, August 7). Indépendance Man 1969. La fête à la montagne. *Abidjan Matin.*

Anyangwe, C. (2008). *Imperialistic politics in Cameroon: resistance and the inception of restoration of the statehood of Southern Cameroons.* Bamenda, Cameroon: Langaa RPCIG.

Ardant, P. (1965). Le Néo-colonialisme. Thème, mythe et réalité. *Revue française de science politique,* 15(5), 837–55.

Arendt, H. (1968). *The origins of totalitarianism* (new edn). San Diego; New York: A Harvest Book.

Arnaut, K. and Blommaert, J. (2009). Chtonic science: Georges Niangoran-Bouah and the anthropology of belonging in Côte d'Ivoire. *American Ethnologist,* 36(3), 574–90.

Ashton, C. (2011, February 15). *Statement by the EU High Representative Catherine Ashton on the legislative elections in Chad* (European Union). www.consilium.europa. eu/uedocs/cms_Data/docs/pressdata/EN/foraff/119306.pdf (Accessed January 2012).

Asong, L. T. and Chi, S. N. (2001). *Ndeh Ntumazah: a controversial autobiography.* Bamenda, Cameroon: Patron Publishing House.

Assemblée Nationale (2008). *No. 1332: Rapport d'information sur la politique de la France en Afrique.* Paris: Commission des Affaires Etrangères.

Assidon, E. (1978, February). De l'opération Ecouvillon à l'intervention en Mauritanie. *Le Monde Diplomatique,* 33.

Atangana, M. R. (1997). French Capitalism and Nationalism in Cameroon. *African Studies Review,* 40(1), 83–111.

Audigier, F. (2003). *Histoire du S. A. C.: la part d'ombre du gaullisme.* Paris: Stock.

Awasom, N. F. (2000). The reunification question in Cameroon history: was the bride an enthusiastic or a reluctant one? *Africa Today,* 47(2), 91–119.

Bach, D. (1986). France's involvement in sub-Saharan Africa: a necessary condition to middle power status in the international system. In A. Sesay (ed.), *Africa and Europe: from partition to interdependence or dependence?* (pp. 75–85). London: Croom Helm.

Bach, D. (1990). *La France et l'Afrique du Sud: histoire, mythes et enjeux contemporains.* Paris: Karthala; Nairobi: Credu.

Bagayoko-Penone, N. (2003). *Afrique: les stratégies française et américaine.* Paris: L'Harmattan.

Balandier, G. (1951). La Situation coloniale: approche théorique. *Cahiers internationaux de sociologie,* 11, 44–79.

Bamba, S. (2010, August 9). Philippe Attey aux populations de Man – 'Gbagbo ou rien'. *Notre Heure.* www.abidjan/net (Accessed 9 August 2010).

Bancel, N. (1999). *Entre acculturation et révolution. Les mouvements de jeunesse et les sports dans l'évolution politique et institutionnelle en AOF (1945–1960).* Unpublished doctoral thesis, University of Paris I, Paris.

Banégas, R. and Marshall-Fratani, R. (2007). Côte d'Ivoire: negotiating identity and citizenship. In M. Boas and K. C. Dunn (eds), *African guerrillas. Raging against the machine* (pp. 81–110). Boulder, CO: Lynne Riener Publishers.

Baniafouna, C. (2011). *La Démocratie néocoloniale de la France: 5 cartes électorales pour un président de la communauté internationale en Côte d'Ivoire.* Paris: L'Harmattan.

Barber, J. P. (1967). *Rhodesia: the road to rebellion.* London, New York: Oxford University Press.

Barbier, M. (1982). *Le Conflit du Sahara occidental.* Paris: L'Harmattan.

Bassett, T. J. (2011). Winning coalition, sore loser: Cote d'Ivoire's 2010 presidential elections. *African Affairs*, 110(440), 469–79.

Basso, J. (1992). Les Accords de coopération entre la France et les Etats africains franco-phones: leurs relations et leurs conséquences au regard des indépendances africaines (1960–1970). In C.-R. Ageron and M. Michel (eds), *L'Afrique noire française: l'heure des indépendances* (pp. 255–83). Paris: CNRS Editions.

Bat, J.-P. (2006). Les «archives Foccart» aux Archives Nationales. *Afrique et Histoire*, 5, 189–201.

Bat, J.-P. (2010). De la fin de Foccart à la mort de Bongo: l'impossible liquidation de la cellule Afrique de l'Elysée (1988–2009). *Cahiers d'histoire immédiate*, 37/38.

Bat, J.-P. (2011). Le rôle de la France après les indépendances. Jacques Foccart et la *Pax Gallica*. *Afrique contemporaine*, 235, 43–52.

Bat, J.-P. (2012). *La Politique de la France en Afrique: le syndrome Foccart, 1959–2010.* Paris: Gallimard.

Bat, J-P. and Geneste, P. (2010). Jean Mauricheau-Beaupré: de Fontaine à Mathurin, JMB au service du Général. *Relations Internationales*, 142, 87–100.

Bauer, K. (2007). *Kleidung und Kleidungspraktiken im Norden der Côte d'Ivoire: Geschichte und Dynamiken des Wandels vom Ende des 19 Jahrhunderts.* Berlin: Lit.

Bayart, J.-F. (1978). The political system. In R. Joseph (ed.), *Gaullist Africa: Cameroon under Ahmadu Ahidjo* (pp. 45–81). Enugu, Nigeria: Fourth Dimension Publishers.

Bayart, J.-F. (1993). *The state in Africa: the politics of the belly.* London: Longman.

Bayart, J.-F. (2000). Africa in the world: a history of extraversion. *African Affairs*, 99(395), 217–69.

Bélime, E. (1955). *Gardons l'Afrique.* Paris: Nouvelles Editions Latines.

Bennafla, K. (2003). La Réactivation des échanges transsahariens: l'exemple tchado-libyen. In G. Marfaing and S. Wippel (eds), *Les relations transsahariennes à l'époque contemporaine* (pp. 89–112). Paris: Karthala; Zentrum Moderner Orient.

Bennafla, K. (2004). De la guerre à la coopération: les dangereuses liaisons tchado-libyennes. In O. Pliez (ed.), *La Nouvelle Libye* (pp. 111–38). Paris: Karthala.

Benoist, J.-R. de (1979). *La Balkanisation de l'Afrique occidentale française.* Dakar: Les Nouvelles Editions Africaines.

Benoist, J.-R. de (1982). *L'Afrique occidentale française de 1944 à 1960.* Dakar: Les Nouvelles Editions Africaines.

Benot, Y. (1994). *Massacres coloniaux 1944–1950: la IVe République et la mise au pas des colonies françaises.* Paris: La Découverte.

Berridge, W. J. (2011). 'What the men are crying out for is leadership': the Khartoum police strike of 1951 and the battle for administrative control. *Journal of Imperial and Commonwealth History*, 39(1), 121–42.

Beslay, F. (1984). *Les Regueibat, de la paix française au Front Polisario*. Paris: L'Harmattan.

Bidi, I. (2010, August 9). 50 ans de la Côte d'Ivoire: Grand cinquantenaire, petit défilé. *Nord-Sud*. //www.abidjan.net (Accessed 9 August 2010).

Bierschenk, T. and Spies, E. (2010). Introduction: Continuities, dislocations and transformations: 50 years of independence in Africa. *Africa Spectrum*, 45(3), 3–10.

Bisson, J. (2003). *Mythes et réalité d'un désert convoité: Le Sahara*. Paris: L'Harmattan.

Biteghe, M. N. (1990). *Echec aux militaires au Gabon*. Paris: Chaka.

Biya, P. (1987). *Communal liberalism*. London: Macmillan.

Black, D. and Williams, P. (eds). (2010). *The international politics of mass atrocities: the case of Darfur*. New York: Routledge.

Blanchard, P. and Bancel, N. (2005). *La Fracture coloniale. La société française au prisme de l'héritage colonial*. Paris: La Découverte.

Bodin, M. (2000). *Les Africains dans la guerre d'Indochine, 1947–1954*. Paris: L'Harmattan.

Boehm, G. (2007). *Wie Bilder Sinn erzeugen: Die Macht des Zeigens*. Berlin: Berlin University Press.

Boilley, P. (1993). L'Organisation commune des régions sahariennes (OCRS): une tentative avortée. In P. Boilley, E. Bernus, J. Clauzel and J.L. Triaud (eds), *Nomades et commandants: administration et sociétés nomades dans l'ancienne AOF* (pp. 214–39). Paris: Karthala.

Boilley, P. (1999). *Les Touaregs Kel Adagh: dépendances et révoltes: du Soudan français au Mali contemporain*. Paris: Karthala.

Boilley, P. (2005). Un complot français au Sahara? Politiques françaises et représentations maliennes. In GEMDEV (ed.), *Mali-France: regards sur une histoire partagée* (pp. 163–82). Paris: Karthala.

Boissonnade, E. (1982). *Conrad Kilian, explorateur souverain*. Paris: France-Empire.

Bossuat, G. (2003). French development aid and cooperation under De Gaulle. *Contemporary European History*, 12(4), 431–56.

Bouquet, C. (2011). *Côte d'Ivoire. Le désespoir de Kourouma*. Paris: Armand Colin.

Bourgeot, A. (1995). *Les Sociétés touarègues: nomadisme, identité, résistances*. Paris: Karthala.

Bourgeot, A. (2000). Sahara: espace géostratégique et enjeux politiques. *Autrepart*, 16, 21–48.

Bourgi, A. (1979). *La Politique française de coopération en Afrique: le cas du Sénégal*. Paris: Librairie générale de droit et de jurisprudence.

Bourgi, R. (1980). *Le général de Gaulle et l'Afrique Noire (1940–1969)*. Paris: Librairie générale de droit et de jurisprudence.

Bourmaud, D. (2000). French political culture and African policy: from consensus to dissensus. *Monograph No. 50, Franco-South African dialogue: sustainable security in Africa*. www.iss.co.za/Pubs/Monographs/No50/Chap 5/htm (Accessed 6 June 2010).

Brou Cho, J. (2011). L'affaire Boka Ernest et le régime d'Houphouët-Boigny en Côte d'Ivoire (avril 1964). In P. Kipré and N. G.-M. Aké (eds), *Conflits régionaux et indépendances nationales en Afrique de l'Ouest. Actes du colloque d'Abengourou, 26–28 février 2010* (pp. 31–45). Paris: L'Harmattan.

Brunschwig, H. (1983). *Noirs et Blancs dans l'Afrique noire française, ou, comment le colonisé devient colonisateur (1870–1914)*. Paris: Flammarion.

Buijtenhuijs, R. (1984a, December). Le Frolinat à l'épreuve du pouvoir: l'échec d'une révolution africaine. *Politique africaine*. Paris: Karthala.

Buijtenhuis, R. (1984b). *Le Frolinat et les guerres civiles du Tchad (1977–1984): la révolution introuvable*. Paris: Karthala.

Burr, J. M. and Collins, R. O. (1999). *Africa's Thirty Years War: Chad, Libya and the Sudan, 1963–1993*. Boulder, CO: Westview Press.

Cadenat, P. (1983). *La France et le tiers-monde: vingt ans de coopération bilatérale. Notes et études documentaires, n° 4701–4702*. Paris: La documentation française.

Campbell, D. (1998). *Writing security: United States foreign policy and the politics of identity* (rev edn). Minneapolis: University of Minnesota Press.

Campmas, P. (1978). *L'Union soudanaise R .D .A*. Abidjan: Editions Communication Intercontinentale.

Capot-Rey, R. (1953). *Le Sahara français*. Paris: Presses Universitaires de France.

Caratini, S. (1989). *Les Rgaybāt (1610–1934)* (Vol. 1). Paris: L'Harmattan.

Caratini, S. (2001). Les Sahraouis: un peuple sans territoire. In L. Cambrézy and V. Lassailly-Jacob (eds), *Populations réfugiées: de l'exil au retour* (pp. 183–210). Paris: Institut de recherche pour le développement.

Caratini, S. (2003). *La République des sables: anthropologie d'une révolution*. Paris: L'Harmattan.

Casanova, R. (2011). *Putsch en Côte d'Ivoire: Une guerre coloniale de Nicolas Sarkozy*. Paris: L'Harmattan.

CCFD-Terre Solidaire (2012). *Le Développement piégé: les transferts d'armes et le développement au Tchad*. Paris: CCFD.

Cerny, P. (1983). *The politics of grandeur: ideological aspects of de Gaulle's foreign policy*. London: Pinter.

Chafer, T. (2001). French African policy in historical perspective. *Journal of Contemporary African Studies*, 19(2), 165–81.

Chafer, T. (2002a). Franco-African relations: no longer exceptional? *African Affairs*, 101(404), 343–63.

Chafer, T. (2002b). *The end of empire in French West Africa: France's successful decolonization?* Oxford and New York: Berg.

Chafer, T. (2005). Chirac and 'la Françafrique': no longer a family affair. *Modern and Contemporary France*, 13(1), 7–23.

Chafer, T. (2008). From Confidence to Confusion: Franco-African Relations in the Era of Globalisation. In M. S. Maclean and J. Szarka (eds), *France on the World Stage: Nation State Strategies in the Global Era* (pp. 37–56). Basingstoke: Palgrave Macmillan.

Chafer, T. and Cumming, G. (2010). Beyond Fashoda: Anglo-French security cooperation in Africa since Saint-Malo. *International Affairs*, 86(5), 1129–47.

Chafer, T. and Cumming, G. (2010). Cinquante ans de politique africaine de la France. *Afrique contemporaine*, 235, 53–62.

Chafer, T. and Cumming, G. (eds) (2011) *From rivalry to partnership? New approaches to the challenges of Africa*. London: Ashgate.

Chaffard, G. (1965). *Les Carnets secrets de la décolonisation*. Vol. 1. Paris: Calmann-Lévy.

Chaffard, G. (1967). *Les Carnets secrets de la décolonisation*. Vol. 2. Paris: Calmann-Lévy.

Chaigneau, P. (1984). *La Politique militaire de la France en Afrique*. Paris: CHEAM.

Chaker, S. (ed.) (1987). Berbères: une identité en construction [special issue]. *Revue du Monde musulman et de la Méditerranée*, 44(2).

Charbonneau, B. (2008a). *France and the new imperialism: security policy in Sub-Saharan Africa*. Aldershot: Ashgate.

Charbonneau, B. (2008b). Dreams of empire: France, Europe, and the new interventionism in Africa. *Modern and Contemporary France*, 16(3), 279–95.

Charbonneau, B. (2009). What is so special about the European Union? EU-UN Cooperation in crisis management in Africa. *International Peacekeeping*, 16(4), 546–61.

Charbonneau, B. (2010). France. In D. Black and P. Williams (eds), *The international politics of mass atrocities: the case of Darfur* (pp. 213–31). New York: Routledge.

Charbonneau, B. (2012a). 'War and Peace in Côte d'Ivoire: Violence, Agency, and the Local/International Line', *International Peacekeeping* 19(4): 508–24.

Charbonneau, B. (2012b). 'Les Effets du prisme de l'Atlantique sur les relations de sécurité Nord-Sud: Le cas de l'Afrique francophone', in Dorval Brunelle (ed.), *Repenser l'Atlantique* (pp. 395–418). Brussels: Bruylant.

Charles, B. (1992). Le role de la violence dans la mise en place des pouvoirs en Guinée. In C.-R. Ageron and M. Michel (eds), *L'Afrique noire française: l'heure des indépendances* (pp. 361–73). Paris: CNRS Editions.

Charvin, R. (2011). *Côte d'Ivoire 2011: La bataille de la seconde indépendance*. Paris: L'Harmattan.

Chenntouf, T. (1986). L'assemblée algérienne et l'application des réformes prévues par le statut du 20 septembre 1947. In C.-R. Ageron (ed.), *Les Chemins de la décolonisation de l'empire français, 1936–1956* (pp. 367–75). Paris: CNRS Editions.

Chenu, R. (1994). *Paul Delouvrier, ou, la passion d'agir: entretiens avec Roselyne Chenu*. Paris: Le Seuil.

Cherfaoui, Z. (2006, April 12). Le nouveau 'fantasme' de Kadhafi sur le Sahara. *El Watan*.

Chikh, S. (1984). L'enjeu saharien dans la guerre d'Algérie. In P. Baduel (ed.), *Enjeux sahariens* (pp. 95–7). Paris: CNRS Editions.

Chipman, J. (1989). *French power in Africa*. Oxford: Basil Blackwell.

Cissoko, S. M. (2005). *Un Combat pour l'unité de l'Afrique de l'Ouest:la Fédération du Mali (1959–1960)*. Dakar: Les Nouvelles Editions Africaines du Sénégal.

Claudot-Hawad, H. (ed.) (1990). *Touaregs, exil et résistance* [special issue]. *Revue du Monde musulman et de la Méditerranée*, 57(3).

Claudot-Hawad, H. (2002). *Touaregs: apprivoiser le désert*. Paris: Gallimard.

Clauzel, J. (1989). *Administrateur de la France d'outre-mer*. Marseille: Jeanne Laffitte.

Clauzel, J. (ed.) (2003). *La France d'outre-mer (1930–1960): témoignages d'administrateurs et de magistrats* (2nd edn). Paris: Karthala.

Clayton, A. (1988). *France, Soldiers and Africa*. London: Brassey's Defence.

Clayton, A. (1994a). *Histoire de l'armée française en Afrique (1830–1962)*. Paris: A. Michel.

Clayton, A. (1994b). *The wars of French decolonization*. London: Longman.

Coggins, R. (2006). Wilson and Rhodesia: UDI and British policy towards Africa. *Contemporary British History*, 20(3), 363–81.

Cohen, W. (1971). *Rulers of empire: the French colonial service in Africa*. Stanford, CA: Hoover Institution Press.

Cole, J. (2001). *Forget colonialism?: Sacrifice and the art of memory in Madagascar*. Berkeley, CA: University of California Press.

Colombani, O. (1991). *Mémoires coloniales: La fin de l'Empire français d'Afrique vue par les administrateurs coloniaux*. Paris: La Découverte.

Conklin, A. L. (1997). *A mission to civilize: the republican idea of empire in France and West Africa, 1895–1930*. Stanford, CA: Stanford University Press.

Connelly, M. (2001). Rethinking the Cold War and decolonization: the grand strategy of the Algerian war for independence. *International Journal of Middle East Studies*, 33(2), 221–45.

Connelly, M. (2003). *A diplomatic revolution: Algeria's fight for independence and the origins of the post-Cold War era*. New York, Oxford: Oxford University Press.

Connerton, P. (1989). *How societies remember*. Cambridge: Cambridge University Press.

Constantin, F. and Coulon, C. (1979), Les relations extérieures de la Mauritanie. In Centre de recherches et d'études sur les sociétés méditerranéennes and Centre d'étude d'Afrique noire (eds), *Introduction à la Mauritanie*. Paris: Editions du Centre National de la Recherche Scientifique.

Cooper, F. (1994). Conflict and connection: rethinking colonial African history. *American Historical Review*, 99(5), 1516–45.

Cooper, F. (1996). *Decolonization and African society: the labor question in French and British Africa*. Cambridge: Cambridge University Press.

Cooper, F. (1999). Decolonisation in Africa: an interpretation. In K. A. Appiah and H. L. Gates, *Africana: the encyclopaedia of the African and African American experience*. (pp. 571–83). New York: Basic Civitas Books.

Cooper, F. (2002). *Africa since 1940: the past of the present*. Cambridge: Cambridge University Press.

Cooper, F. (2005). *Colonialism in question: theory, knowledge, history*. Berkeley, CA: University of California Press.

Coquery-Vidrovitch, C. (1988). The transfer of economic power in French-speaking West Africa. In P. Gifford and W. R. Louis (eds), *Decolonization and African independence: the transfers of power, 1960–1980* (pp. 105–35). New Haven, CT: Yale University Press.

Coquio, C. (ed.). (2006). *Des Crimes contre l'humanité en République française (1990–2002)*. Paris: L'Harmattan.

Corbett, E. M. (1972). *The French presence in Black Africa* (1st edn). Washington, Black Orpheus Press.

Costantini, D. (2008). *Mission civilisatrice: le rôle de l'histoire coloniale dans la construction de l'identité politique française* (trans. J. Ferdinand). Paris: La Découverte.

Crowder, M. (1987). Whose dream was it anyway? Twenty-five years of African independence. *African Affairs*, 86(342), 7–24.

Cumming, G. (1995) *Aid to Africa: French and British policies from the Cold War to the new Millenium*. Aldershot: Ashgate.

Cumming, G. (2005). Transposing the 'Republican' model? A critical appraisal of France's historic mission in Africa'. *Journal of Contemporary African Studies*, 23(2), 233–52.

Cunliffe, P. (2012). 'Still the spectre at the feast: comparisons between peacekeeping and imperialism in peacekeeping studies today', *International Peacekeeping* 19(4), 426–42.

Cuttier, M. (2007). *Portrait du colonialisme triomphant: Louis Archinard (1850–1932)*. Paris: Lavauzelle.

Dabezies, P. (1978). L'armée et le pouvoir dans le Tiers-Monde. *Annuaire du Tiers-Monde*, IV, 255–65.

Darby, P. (2004). Pursuing the political: a postcolonial rethinking of relations international. *Millennium*, 33(1), 1–32.

Darwin, J. (2005). A fourth British Empire? In M. Lynn (ed.), *The British Empire in the 1950s: retreat or revival?* (pp. 16–31). Basingstoke: Palgrave Macmillan.

Dayak, M. (1992). *Touareg: la tragédie*. Paris: Robert Laffont.

Dayak, M. (1996). *Je suis né avec du sable dans les yeux*. Paris: Robert Laffont.

De Gaulle, C. (1954). *Memoires de guerre: l'appel, 1940–1942*. Paris: Plon.

De Gaulle, C. (1964). *Major addresses, statements and press conferences of General Charles de Gaulle, May 19, 1958–January 31, 1964*. New York: French Embassy Press and Information Division.

De Gaulle, C. (1970). *Discours et messages*. Paris: Plon.

De Gaulle, C. (1986). *Lettres, notes et carnets, janvier 1961–décembre 1963*. Paris: Plon.

Debré, M. (1988). *Trois républiques pour une France: mémoires. III: Gouverner, 1958–1962*. Paris: A. Michel.

Decraene, P. and Zuccarelli, F. (1994). *Grands Sahariens à la conquête du désert des déserts*. Paris: Denoël.

Deltombe, T., Domergue, M. and Tatsitsa, J. (2011). *Kamerun! Une guerre cachée aux origines de la Françafrique, 1948–1971*. Paris: La Découverte.

Denard, B. (1998). *Corsaire de la République*. Paris: Robert Laffon.

Dewitte, P. (2004). L'immigration: l'émergence en métropole d'une élite africaine. In P. Blanchard and S. Lemaire (eds), *Culture impériale, 1931–1961: les colonies au coeur de la République* (pp. 199–212). Paris: Autrement.

Diagne, A. (1991). *Le Sénégal et la guerre d'Indochine: récit de vie des vétérans*. Unpublished masters dissertation, Université Cheick Anta Diop, Dakar.

Diagouraga, M. (2005). *Modibo Keita: un destin*. Paris: L'Harmattan.

Diallo, A. (2008a). Sékou Touré et l'indépendance guinéenne: déconstruction d'un mythe et retour sur l'histoire. *Outre-Mers*, 96(358–359), 267–88.

Diallo, A. (2008b). *Sékou Touré 1957–1961: Mythe et réalités d'un héros*. Paris: L'Harmattan.

Diawara, M. (1998). *In Search of Africa*. Cambridge, MA and London: Harvard University Press.

Dijkstra, H. (2010). The military operation of the EU in Chad and the Central African Republic: good policy, bad politics. *International Peacekeeping*, 17(3), 395–407.

Dimier, V. (2004). *Le Gouvernement des colonies: regards croisés franco-britanniques*. Bruxelles: Editions de l'Université de Bruxelles.

Dimier, V. (2005). Construire l'Association: entre l'Europe communautaire et l'Afrique indépendante. *Matériaux pour l'Histoire de Notre Temps*, 77.

Doornbos, P. (1982). La Révolution dérapée: la violence dans l'Est du Tchad (1978–81). *Politique africaine*, 7, 5–13.

Dorsch, H. (2010). Indépendance Cha Cha: African pop music since the independence era. *Africa Spectrum*, 45(3), 131–46.

Doty, R. (1996). *Imperial encounters: the politics of representation in North-South relations*. Minneapolis: University of Minnesota Press.

Dozon, J.-P. (2000). La Côte d'Ivoire entre démocratie, nationalisme et ethnonationalisme. *Politique Africaine*, 78, 445–62.

Dozon, J.-P. (2002). L'état français contemporain et son double, l'état franco-africain. *Cahiers du Centre de Recherches Historiques*, 30. http://ccrh.revues.org/index432.html (Accessed 30 January 2010).

Dozon, J.-P. (2003). *Frères et sujets: la France et l'Afrique en perspective*. Paris: Flammarion.

Duffield, M. (2007). *Development, security and unending war*. Cambridge: Polity.

Dufourcq, J. (2009). Les tensions de l'océan sahélien. *Cahier du Centre d'Etudes et de Recherches de l'Ecole Militaire*, 13, 7–9.

Dulphy, A. (2005). La guerre d'Algérie dans les relations franco-espagnoles, *Cahiers de la Méditerranée*, 71.

Dulucq, S. and Zytnicki, C. (2005). Penser le passé colonial français: entre perspectives historiographiques et résurgence des mémoires. *Vingtième siècle. Revue d'histoire*, 86(2), 59–69.

Dulucq, S., Coquery-Vidrovitch, C., Frémigacci, J., Sibeud, E. and Triaud, J.-L. (2006). L'écriture de l'histoire de la colonisation en France depuis 1960. *Afrique et histoire*, 2(6), 235–76.

Durand, P.-M. (2007). *L'Afrique et les relations franco-américaines des années soixante: aux origines de l'obsession américaine*. Paris: L'Harmattan.

Durham, D. (2000). Youth and social imagination in Africa: introduction to parts 1 and 2. *Anthropological Quarterly*, 73(3), 113–20.

Echenberg, M. (1991). *Colonial conscripts: the tirailleurs Sénégalais in French West Africa, 1857–1960*. Portsmouth, NH: Heinemann.

Echenberg, M. (2009). *Les Tirailleurs sénégalais en Afrique occidentale française (1857–1960)*. Paris: Karthala.

Ecole nationale de la France d'outre-mer (1998). *L'Administrateur colonial, cet inconnu: étude historique et sociologique d'une promotion de l'Ecole nationale de la France d'outre-mer*. Paris: L'Harmattan.

El Mellouki Riffi, B. (1989). *La Politique française de coopération avec les Etats du Maghreb (1955–1987)*. Paris: Publisud.

Evans, M. (2011). *Algeria: France's undeclared war*. Oxford: Oxford University Press.

Evrard, C. (2008). *La Transmission du pouvoir militaire en Mauritanie, 1956–1966*. Unpublished masters dissertation, Université Paris 1, Paris.

Eyoh, D. (1998). Conflicting narratives of Anglophone protest and the politics of identity in Cameroon. *Journal of Contemporary African Studies*, 16(2), 249–276.

Faes, G. and Smith, S. (2000). *Bokassa Ier: un empereur français*. Paris: Calmann-Lévy.

Fané Z. (2008). *La Politique étrangère du Mali, 1960–2008. Permanences, ajustements et perspectives. Action extérieure d'un Etat sahélien enclavé*. Unpublished doctoral thesis, University Paris X, Nanterre, Paris.

Farsoun, K. and Paul, J. (1976). War in the Sahara: 1963. *Middle East Research and Information Project (MERIP) Reports*, 45, 13–16.

Fauré, Y.-A. (1978). Célébrations officielles et pouvoirs africains: symbolique et construction de l'Etat. *Canadian Journal of African Studies*, 12(3), 383–404.

Fauré, Y.-A. and Médard, J.-F. (eds) (1982). *Etat et bourgeoisie en Côte d'Ivoire: études*. Paris: Karthala.

Ferrage, P. M. (1918). *Petit Manuel français-Bambara*. Paris: Imprimerie Militaire Fournier.

Fèvre, F. (1983). *Les Seigneurs du désert: histoire du Sahara*. Paris: Presses de la Renaissance.

Flory, M. (1976). Sanction de l'évaluation et rigidité du système de coopération. In J. Touscoz (ed.), *L'Evaluation de la coopération Nord-Sud: l'exemple de la coopération entre pays francophones*. Montreal: Presses de l'Université du Québec.

Flower, K. E. N. (1987). *Serving secretly: an intelligence chief on record; Rhodesia into Zimbabwe, 1964 to 1981*. London: John Murray.

Foccart, J. (1964). Préface. In M. Ligot. *Les Accords de coopération entre la France et les états africains et malgache d'expression française*. Paris: Documentation française.

Foccart, J. (1997 et seq.). *Journal de l'Elysée*. Paris: Fayard/Jeune Afrique.

Foccart, J., and Gaillard, P. (1995). *Foccart parle: entretiens avec Philippe Gaillard*. (Vol. 1). Paris: Fayard/Jeune Afrique.

Foccart, J., and Gaillard, P. (1997). *Foccart parle: entretiens avec Philippe Gaillard*. (Vol. 2). Paris: Fayard/Jeune Afrique.

Fogarty, R. (2008). *Race and war in France: colonial subjects in the French Army, 1914–1918*. Baltimore, MD: Johns Hopkins University Press.

Foltz, W. J. (1965). *From French West Africa to the Mali Federation*. New Haven, CT and London: Yale University Press.

Forget, M. (1992). Mauritanie 1977: Lamantin. Une intervention extérieure à dominante air. *Revue historique des armées*, 186, 88–89.

Förster, T. (2012). Imagining the nation: independence ceremonies under rebel domination in Northern Côte d'Ivoire. *African Arts*, 45(3), 42–55.

Francart, L. (2002). *Maîtriser la violence: une option stratégique* (2nd edn). Paris: Economica.

France. (2008). *Défense et sécurité nationale: le livre blanc*. Paris: Odile Jacob/La Documentation française. www.ladocumentationfrancaise.fr/rapports-publics/08400 0341/index.shtml (Accessed 1 August 2013).

France-Sénat. (2006). *No. 450: Rapport d'information sur la gestion des crises en Afrique subsaharienne*. Paris: Commission des Affaires Étrangères.

Frémeaux, J. (1997). La guerre d'Algérie et le Sahara. In C.-R. Ageron (ed.), *La guerre d'Algérie et les Algériens, 1954–1962* (pp. 93–110). Paris: Colin.

Frémeaux, J. (2002). The Sahara and the Algerian War. In M. Evans (ed.), *The Algerian War and the French army, 1954–1962* (pp. 76–87). Basingstoke: Palgrave Macmillan.

Frémeaux, J. (2006). *Intervention et humanisme: le style des armées françaises en Afrique au XIXe siècle.* Paris: Economica.

Frémeaux, J. (2010). *Le Sahara et la France.* Paris: Soteca.

Fuller, A. (2002). *Don't let's go to the dogs tonight: an African childhood.* Basingstoke: Picador.

Gaillard, P. (1995), *Foccart parle. Entretiens avec Philippe Gaillard* (Vol. 1). Paris: Fayard/ Jeune Afrique.

Gallisot, R. (1984). Les nouveaux Etats: essai de typologie, in C. Coquery-Vidrovitch (ed.), *Décolonisations et Nouvelles Dépendances: Modèles et contre-modèles idéologiques et culturels dans le Tiers-Monde* (pp. 51–63). Villeneuve-d'Ascq: Presses de l'Université de Lille.

Gardinier, D. E. (1963). *Cameroon: United Nations challenge to French policy.* London: Oxford University Press.

Gast, M. (2004). *Tikatoûtin: un instituteur chez les Touaregs, itinéraire d'un apprenti ethnologue.* Seyssinet: La Boussole.

Gatta, G.N. (1985). *Tchad: guerre civile et désagrégation de l'Etat.* Paris: Présence Africaine.

Gatta, G. N. (2010, October). Notre indépendance: 50 ans partis en fumée. *Ndjamena bi-Hebdo,* 1317, 18–20.

Gauthereau, R. (1986). *Journal d'un colonialiste.* Paris: Editions du Seuil.

Gautron, J.-C. (1980). La Communauté et le processus de décolonisation sous la Ve République. In Institut d'études politiques de Bordeaux (ed.), *La Politique africaine du Général de Gaulle (1958–1969)* (pp. 17–30). Paris: A. Pedone.

Gbagbo, L. (1982). *La Côte-d'Ivoire: économie et société à la veille de l'indépendance (1940–1960).* Paris: L'Harmattan.

Georgy, G. (1998). *Le Berger des Syrtes.* Paris: Flammarion.

Géré, F. (2010). Contre-insurrection et action psychologique: tradition et modernité. *Focus stratégique,* 25.

Gifford, P. and Louis, W. R. (eds). *Decolonization and African independence: the transfers of power, 1960–1980.* New Haven, CT: Yale University Press.

Ginio, R. (2006). African colonial soldiers between memory and forgetfulness: the case of post-colonial Senegal. *Outremers: Revue d'Histoire,* 94(350–1), 141–55.

Ginio, R. (2010). French officers, African officers and the violent image of African colonial soldiers. *Historical Reflections,* 36(2), 59–75.

Glaser, A. and Smith, S. (2005). *Comment la France a perdu l'Afrique.* Paris: Calmann-Lévy.

Gnangui, A. (2011). *Côte-d'Ivoire, 11 avril 2011: Le coup d'Etat de trop de la France en Afrique.* Paris: L'Harmattan.

Godwin, P. and Hancock, I. (1993). *'Rhodesians never die': the impact of war and political change on White Rhodesia c. 1970–1980.* Oxford and New York: Oxford University Press.

Golan, T. (1981). A certain mystery: how can France do everything that it does in Africa – and get away with it? *African Affairs,* 80(318), 3–11.

Gordon, P. H. (1993). *A certain idea of France: French security policy and the Gaullist legacy.* Princeton, NJ: Princeton University Press.

Goscha, C. (2011). *Vietnam: Un Etat né de la guerre, 1945–1954*. Paris: Armand Colin.

Gounin, Y. (2009). *La France en Afrique. Le Combat des anciens et des modernes*. Bruxelles: De Boeck.

Granvaud, R. (2009). *Que fait l'armée française en Afrique?* Marseille: Agone.

Grégoire, E. (2000). *Touaregs du Niger: le destin d'un mythe*. Paris: Karthala.

Grégoire, E. (2004). Les relations politiques et économiques mouvementées du Niger et de la Libye. In O. Pliez (ed.), *La nouvelle Libye* (pp. 97–109). Paris: Karthala.

Grosser, A. (1984). *Affaires extérieures: la politique de la France, 1944–1984*. Paris: Flammarion.

Grossetti, M. (1986). Enseignants en coopération. Aperçus sur un type particulier de trajectoires sociales. *Revue française de sociologie*, 27(1), 133–48.

Grovogui, S. (2001). Come to Africa: A Hermeneutics of Race in International Theory. *Alternatives: global, local, political*, 26(4), 425–48.

Guéna, Y. (1962). *Historique de la Communauté*. Paris: Fayard.

Guillemin, J. (1982). Les campagnes militaires françaises de la décolonisation en Afrique sub-saharienne. *Le Mois en Afrique*, 198–9, 124–41.

Guinea. (1982). Evolution des rapports franco-guinéens. *Révolution Démocratique Africaine No. 193* (2nd edn). Conakry: Imprimerie Nationale Patrice Lumumba.

Guirma, F. (1991). *Comment perdre le pouvoir? Le cas de Maurice Yaméogo*. Paris: Chaka.

Gutelius, D. (2006). War on terror and social networks in Mali. *ISIM Review*, 17, 38–9.

Haggar, B. I. (2007). *Histoire politique du Tchad sous le régime du Président François Tombalbaye 1960–75: déjà le Tchad était mal parti!* Paris: L'Harmattan.

Hahn, H. P. (2008). Diffusionism, appropriation, and globalization: some remarks on current debates in anthropology. *Anthropos*, 103(1), 191–202.

Hargreaves, J. (1988). *Decolonization in Africa* (2nd edn 1996). London: Longman.

Hawad. (1990). La *teshumara*, antidote de l'état. *Revue du Monde musulman et de la Méditerranée*, 57(3), 123–38.

Heggoy, A. A. (1970). Colonial origins of the Algerian-Moroccan border conflict of October 1963. *African Studies Review*, 13(1), 17–22.

Heitz, K. (2009). Power-sharing in the local arena: Man – a rebel-held town in Western Côte d'Ivoire. *Africa Spectrum*, 44(3), 109–31.

Heitz, K. (2013). Recollections from the times of independence. Talks with elderly people in western Côte d'Ivoire. In O. Goerg, J.-L. Martineau, and D. Nativel (eds), *Vivre les indépendances en Afrique. L'événement et ses mémoires 1960–2010*. Rennes: Presses Universitaires de Rennes.

Helly, D. (2009). Eufor Tchad/RCA. In G. Grevi, D. Helly and D. Keohane (eds), *European security and defence policy: the first ten years (1999–2009)* (pp. 339–51). Paris: Institute for Security Studies, European Union.

Hesseling, G. (1985). *Histoire politique du Sénégal: institutions, droit, et société*. Paris: Karthala.

Hettier de Boislambert, C. (1978). *Les fers de l'espoir*. Paris: Plon.

Hodges, T. (1984). *Western Sahara: The roots of a desert war*. Chicago, IL: Lawrence Hill Books (published in French 1987).

Hogard, J. (1957, January). L'Armée française devant la guerre révolutionnaire. *Revue de Défense nationale*, 143, 77–89.

Hottinger, A. (1981). L'Expansionnisme libyen: Machrek, Maghreb et Afrique noire. *Politique étrangère*, 46(1), 137–49.

Hubenelle, D. (1961, 12 July). Le Cameroon à trois mois de sa réunification. *Le Monde*.

Human Rights Watch (2012). *The case against Hissène Habré: legal documents*. www.hrw. org/en/habre-case (Accessed 12 December 2011).

Ignatieff, M. (2003). *Empire Lite*. London: Vintage.

International Crisis Group (2006, June). Tchad: vers le retour de la guerre? *Rapport Afrique No. 111*. Brussels and Nairobi: ICG.

International Crisis Group. (3 March 2011). *Côte d'Ivoire: faut-il se résoudre à la guerre? Rapport Afrique de Crisis Group* (Report No. 171). www.crisisgroup.org/-/media/ Files/africa/west-africa/cote-divoire/171%20Cote%dIvoire%20–%faut-il%20se%20 resoudre%20a%201a%20guerre (Accessed 1 August 2013).

International Crisis Group. (2009, August). Tchad: sortir du piège pétrolier. *Briefing Afrique* No. 65. Brussels and Nairobi: ICG.

International Crisis Group. (2010, August). *Tchad: au déla de l'apaisement. Rapport Afrique No. 162*. Brussels and Nairobi: ICG.

Interview de Pierre Kipré (2011). www/editions-harmattan.fr/index.asp?navig=catalogue andobj=livreandno=35275 (L'Harmattan website, Accessed 1 December 2012).

Jackson, R. (1990). *Quasi-states: sovereignty, international relations and the Third World*. Cambridge: Cambridge University Press.

Jacquemot, P. (2011). Cinquante ans de coopération française avec l'Afrique subsaharienne: une mise en perspective. *Afrique contemporaine*, 238, 43–57.

James, A. (1996). *Britain and the Congo crisis, 1960–1963*. London: Macmillan.

Jeanneney, J.-M. (1963). *La Politique de coopération avec les pays en voie de développement*. Paris: Commission d'étude de coopération avec les pays en voie de développement.

Johnson, W. R. (1970). The Union des Populations du Cameroon in rebellion: the integrative backlash of insurgency. In R. I. Rotberg and A. A. Mazrui (eds), *Protest and power in Black Africa* (pp. 671–92). Oxford: Oxford University Press.

Joly, V. (2000, March). La fin de la présence militaire française au Mali. *Revue Historique des Armées*, 218, 39–55.

Joly, V. (2006). *Le Soudan français de 1939 à 1945: une colonie dans la guerre*. Paris: Karthala.

Joly, V. (2009). *Guerres d'Afrique: 130 ans de guerres coloniales: l'expérience française*. Rennes: Presses Universitaires de Rennes.

Jones, B. G. (ed.). (2006). *Decolonizing international relations*. Lanham, MD: Rowman & Littlefield.

Joseph, R. (1974). Ruben um Nyobé and the 'Kamerun' rebellion. *African Affairs*, 73(293), 428–44.

Joseph, R. (1976). The Gaullist legacy: patterns of French neo-colonialism. *Review of African Political Economy*, 6, 4–13.

Joseph, R. (1977). *Radical nationalism in Cameroun: social origins of the UPC rebellion*. Oxford: Oxford University Press.

Joseph, R. (1997). Democratization in Africa after 1989: comparative and theoretical perspectives. *Comparative Politics*, 45(2), 49–71.

Jua, N. B. and Nyamnjoh, F. B. (2002). Scholarship production in Cameroon: interrogating a recession. *African Studies Review*, 45(2), 49–71.

Juppé, A. and Schweitzer, L. (eds) (2008). *La France et l'Europe dans le monde: livre blanc sur la politique étrangère et européenne de la France, 2008–2020*. Paris: Documentation française.

Kaba, L. (1989). *Le 'Non' de Guinée à de Gaulle*. Paris: Chaka.

Kaké, I. B. (1987). *Sékou Touré: le héros et le tyran*. Paris: Jeune Afrique.

Kanya-Forstner, A. S. (1969). *The conquest of the Western Sudan: a study in French military imperialism*. Cambridge: Cambridge University Press.

Kanya-Forstner, A. S. (1972). French expansion in Africa: the mythical theory. In R. Owen and B. Sutcliffe (eds), *Studies in the Theory of Imperialism* (pp. 277–94). London: Longman.

Keenan, J. (2005). Waging war on terror: the implications of America's 'New Imperialism' for Saharan peoples (pp. 619–47). In J. Keenan (ed.), The Sahara: Past, Present and Future [special issue]. *Journal of North African Studies*, 10(3–4).

Keenan, J. (2009). *The dark Sahara*. London and New York: Pluto Press.

Keese, A. (2003). 'Quelques satisfactions d'amour propre': African elite integration, the Loi-Cadre and involuntary decolonisation of French tropical Africa. *Itinerario*, 27(1), 33–57.

Keese, A. (2007a). First lessons in neo-colonialism: the personalisation of relations between African politicians and French officials in sub-Saharan Africa, 1956–66. *Journal of Imperial and Commonwealth History*, 35(4), 593–613.

Keese, A. (2007b). *Living with ambiguity: integrating an African elite in French and Portuguese Africa, 1930–61*. Stuttgart: Franz Steiner.

Keese, A. (2008). A culture of panic: 'Communist' scapegoats and decolonization in French West Africa and French Polynesia, 1945–1957. *French Colonial History*, 9, 131–45.

Keese, A. (2011). Rigged elections? Democracy and manipulation in the late colonial state in French West Africa and Togo, 1944–1958'. In M. Thomas (ed.), *The French Colonial Mind. Volume 1: Mental maps of empire and colonial encounters* (pp. 324–45). Lincoln, NE and London: University of Nebraska Press.

Keiger, J. F. V. (2001). *France and the world since 1870*. London: Arnold.

Keita, M. (1965). *Discours et interventions*. Bamako (self-published).

Kent, J. (1989). Bevin's imperialism and the idea of Euro-Africa 1945–49. In M. Dockrill and J. Young (eds), *British foreign policy, 1945–56* (pp. 47–76). Basingstoke: Macmillan.

Kent, J. (1992). *Internationalization of colonialism: Britain, France and black Africa, 1939–56*. Oxford: Oxford University Press.

Kent, J. (2000). The United States and the decolonization of Black Africa, 1945–63. In D. Ryan and V. Pungong (eds), *The United States and decolonization: power and freedom* (pp. 168–87). London: Palgrave Macmillan.

Kessé, A. B. (2005). *La Côte d'Ivoire en guerre: le sens de l'imposture française*. Paris: L'Harmattan.

Kessler, M.-C. (1999). *La politique étrangère de la France: acteurs et processus*. Paris: Presses de Sciences Po.

Kipré, P. (2011). Avant-propos. In P. Kipré and N. G.-M. Aké (eds), *Conflits régionaux et indépendances nationales en Afrique de l'Ouest. Actes du colloque d'Abengourou, 26–28 février 2010* (pp. 7–10). Paris: L'Harmattan.

Kipré, P., and Aké, N. G.-M. (eds) (2011a). *Conflits régionaux et indépendances nationales en Afrique de l'Ouest: Actes du colloque d'Abengourou, 26–28 février 2010.* Paris: L'Harmattan.

Kipré, P., and Aké, N. G.-M. (eds). (2011b). *Les Conditions économiques de l'indépendance à l'ère de la mondialisation: Mythes et réalités en Afrique de l'Ouest. Actes du colloque de San Pedro, 10–14 mars 2010.* Paris: L'Harmattan.

Kofele-Kale, N. (1981). Cameroon and its foreign relations. *African Affairs*, 80(319), 197–217.

Kolodziej, E. A. (1974). *French international policy under De Gaulle and Pompidou: the politics of grandeur.* Ithaca, NY and London: Cornell University Press.

Konaté, Y. (2003). Les enfants de la balle. De la fesci aux mouvements des patriotes. *Politique Africaine*, 89, 49–70.

Konings, P. and Nyamnjoh, F. B. (1994). The Anglophone problem in Cameroon. *Journal of Modern African Studies*, 32(4), 207–29.

Konings, P. and Nyamnjoh, F. B. (2003). *Negotiating an Anglophone identity: a study of the politics of recognition and representation in Cameroon.* Leiden and Boston: Brill.

Kouassi, Y. (1994). Contribution humaine de l'Afrique noire à l'effort de guerre en Indochine (1947–1954), *Revue Historique des Armées*, 194, 6–16.

Kouchner, B. (2006, December 27). Au Darfour, des massacres et du pétrole. *Le Monde*.

Krieger, M. (1994). Cameroon's democratic crossroads, 1990–1994. *Journal of Modern African Studies*, 32(4), 605–28.

Kroslak, D. (2007). *The role of France in the Rwandan Genocide.* London: Hurst.

Kurtz, D. (1970). Political integration in Africa: the Mali Federation. *Journal of Modern African Studies*, 8(3), 405–24.

La Voix (2010, August 26). *Affaire Zen Bada: Déby sonne-t-il la fin de la partie?* http://tchad online.com/affaire-zen-bada-deby-sonne-t-il-la-fin-de-la-partie (Accessed 1 December 2011).

Labrousse, A. (1971). *La France et l'aide à l'éducation dans 14 états africains et Malgache: analyse critique de la politique suivie par la France entre 1959 et 1970 pour accorder son aide a l'éducation dans 14 états africains et Malgache d'expression française.* Paris: UNESCO; International Institute for Educational Planning.

Lacoste, Y. (1986). Quelques réflexions sur les problèmes géopolitiques du Sahara. *Revue de l'Occident Musulman et de la Méditerranée*, 41(41–2), 283–90.

Lacroix, A. (1965). Problème de défense en Afrique Noire francophone et coopération militaire française. *Mémoire du CHEAM*, 3995.

Lanne, B. (1982). *Tchad-Libye: la querelle des frontières.* Paris: Karthala.

Lanne, B. (1998). *Histoire politique du Tchad de 1945 à 1958: administration, partis, élections.* Paris: Karthala.

L'Année politique 1960 (1961). Paris: Grand Siècle.

Laurent, S. (2008, March 20). Bockel victime de ses positions sur la Françafrique? *Le Figaro*.

Laurent, S. (ed.) (2011). *Les espions français parlent. Archives et témoignages inédits des services secrets français*. Paris: Nouveau monde.

Lentz, C. (2010). *Ghana@50: celebrating the nation – debating the nation* (Working paper 120). Mainz, Germany: Department of Anthropology and African Studies, Johannes Gutenberg University of Mainz. www.ifeas.uni-mainz.de/workingpapers/AP83.pdf (Accessed 27 May 2011).

Lentz, C. (ed.) (2011). *Afrika@50. Vor-Ort-Berichte von den Unabhängigkeitsjubiläen in Kamerun, Madagaskar, DR Kongo, Benin, Côte d'Ivoire, Gabun, Mali, Nigeria und Burkina Faso* (Working paper 126). Mainz, Germany: Department of Anthropology and African Studies, Johannes Gutenberg University of Mainz. www.ifeas.unimainz. de/workingpapers/AP126.pdf (Accessed 21 December 2011).

Léon, A. (1991). Colonisation, enseignement et éducation. Paris: L'Harmattan.

LeVine, V. T. (1964). *The Cameroons: from mandate to independence*. Los Angeles: University of California Press.

Lewin, A. (1990). *Diallo Telli: Le Tragique destin d'un grand Africain*. Paris: Jeune Afrique Livres.

Lewin, A. (2009). *Ahmed Sékou Touré (1922–1984), Président de la Guinée de 1958 à 1984* (Vol. 1. 1922–1956). Paris: L'Harmattan.

Leymarie, P. (2010, July 19). Saint-Cyr, nous voilà! *Le Monde diplomatique: Défense en ligne*. http://blog.mondediplo.net/2010–07–19–Saint-Cyr-nous-voila (Accessed 19 July 2010).

Liauzu, C. and Manceron, G. (2006). *La colonisation, la loi et l'histoire*. Paris: Syllepse.

Lindqvist, S. (1996). *Exterminate all the brutes*. New York: The New Press.

Louis, W. R. (2007). *Ends of British Imperialism, The Scramble for Empire, Suez and Decolonization*. London: I.B. Tauris.

Luckham, R. (1982, March). Le Militarisme français en Afrique. *Politique africaine*, 5, 95–110.

Luckham, R. (1982, June). Le Militarisme français en Afrique. *Politique africaine*, 6, 45–71.

Luckman, R. (1982). French militarism in Africa. *Review of African Political Economy*, 24, 55–84.

Lunel, P. (1991). *Bob Denard, le roi de fortune*. Paris: Édition n° 1.

Lunn, J. (1999). Les Races guerrières: racial preconceptions in the French military about West African soldiers during the First World War. *Journal of Contemporary History*, 34(4), 517–36.

Lynn, M. (ed.) (2005). *The British Empire in the 1950s: retreat or revival?* Basingstoke: Palgrave Macmillan.

MacDonald, M. S. (2009). The challenge of Guinean independence, 1958–1971. Unpublished doctoral thesis, University of Toronto, Toronto.

Malek, R. (1995). *L'Algérie à Evian: histoire des négociations secrètes, 1956–62*. Paris: Le Seuil.

Malraux, A. (1960, August 10). Discours de Fort-Lamy. www.malraux.org/index.php/motsclefs/1014–independanceafrique.html (Accessed 20 September 2010).

Mamdani, M. (2009). *Saviors and survivors: Darfur, politics, and the war on terror*. New York: Pantheon Books.

Mann, G. (2006). *Native sons: West African veterans in the twentieth century.* Durham, NC: Duke University Press.

Marchal, R. (2009, June 4). Understanding French policy toward Chad/Sudan? A difficult task (1). http://africanarguments.org/2009/06/04/understanding-french-policy-toward-chadsudan-a-difficult-task-1/ (Accessed June 2009).

Marfaing, L. and Wippel, S. (eds) (2004). *Les Relations transsahariennes à l'époque contemporaine, un espace en constante mutation.* Paris: Karthala.

Marten, K. (2004). *Enforcing the peace: learning from the Imperial Peace.* New York: Columbia University Press.

Martin, G. (1985). The historical, economic and political bases of France's African policy. *Journal of Modern African Studies,* 23(2), 189–208.

Martin, G. (1995). Continuity and change in Franco-African relations. *Journal of Modern African Studies,* 33(1), 1–20.

May, R. and Charlton, R. (1989). Warlords and militarism in Chad. *Review of African Political Economy,* 16(45–6), 12–26.

McGovern, M. (2011). *Making war in Côte d'Ivoire.* London: Hurst.

McNamara, F. T. (1989). *France in Black Africa.* Washington, DC: National Defense University Press.

McNeill, J. R and McNeill, W. H. (2003). *The Human Web: A Bird's-Eye View of the World.* New York: W. W. Norton and Company, Inc.

Médard, J.-F. (1997). France-Africa: within the family. In D. Della Porta and Y. Mény (eds), *Democracy and corruption in Europe.* London: Pinter.

Médard, J-F. (2002). «La Politique est au bout du réseau».Questions sur la méthode Foccart. *Cahiers du Centre de Recherches Historiques,* 30. http://ccrh.revues.org/index612.html (Accessed 30 January 2010).

Médard, J.-F. (2005). France and sub-Saharan Africa: a privileged relationship. In U. Engel and G. R. Olsen (eds), *Africa and the north: between globalization and marginalization.* Oxford and New York: Routledge.

Meimon, J. (2005). *'Et pourtant elle tourne'. L'institutionnalisation contrariée de la coopération française au développement (1958 à 1998).* Unpublished doctoral thesis, Université Lille 2, Lille.

Meimon, J. (2007, September). L'invention de l'aide au développement: discours, instruments et pratiques d'une dynamique hégémonique. Questions de recherche No. 21. Paris: CERI.

Mérand, F. and Rakotonirina, H. M. (2009, June). La Force européenne au Tchad et en Centrafrique: le baptême du feu. *Politique africaine,* 114, 105–25.

Meredith, M. (1979). *The past is another country: Rhodesia 1890–1979.* London: André Deutsch.

Meredith, M. (2006). *The state of Africa: a history of fifty years of independence.* London: Free Press.

Mesli, S. (2009). La Grève de mai-juin 1968 à l'Université de Dakar. In P. Dramé and J. Lamarre (eds), *Societies in crisis: a global perspective* (pp. 101–19). Laval: Presses de l'Université Laval.

Messmer, P. (1992). *Après tant de Batailles.* Paris: Albin Michel.

Messmer, P. (1998). *Les Blancs s'en vont: récits de décolonisation.* Paris: Albin Michel.

Michel, M. (1982). *L'Appel à l'Afrique. Contributions et réactions à l'effort de guerre en AOF, 1914–1919*. Paris: Publications de la Sorbonne.

Michel, M. (2002) Au travers des archives Foccart: les relations franco-africaines de 1958 à 1962. *Cahiers du Centre de Recherches Historiques*, 30. http://ccrh.revues.org/index592.html (Accessed 30 January 2010).

Michel, M. (2003). *Les Africains et la Grande Guerre: l'appel à l'Afrique (1914–1918)*. Paris: Karthala.

Migani, G. (2006). L'Association des TOM au marché commun: histoire d'un accord européen entre cultures économiques différentes et idéaux politiques communs, 1955–1957. In M.-T. Bitsch and G. Bossuat (eds), *L'Europe unie et l'Afrique: de l'idée d'Eurafrique à la Convention de Lomé I* (pp. 233–52). Bruxelles: Groupe de Liaison des Historiens auprès des Communautés.

Migani, G. (2008). *La France et l'Afrique sub-saharienne, 1957–1963: histoire d'une décolonisation entre idéaux eurafricains et politique de puissance*. Bruxelles and Oxford: P. I. E. Peter Lang.

Ministère des Affaires Etrangères. Commission de publication des documents diplomatiques, f. a. (2002 et seq.). *Documents diplomatiques français 1964–1968*. Brussels: P.I.E. Peter Lang.

Mitterrand, F. (1953). *Aux frontières de l'Union française*. Paris: Julliard.

Mitterrand, F. (1957). *Présence française et abandon*. Paris: Plon.

Mohsen-Finan, K. (1998). *Sahara occidental: les enjeux d'un conflit régional*. Paris: CNRS Editions.

Morgenthau, R. S. (1964). *Political parties in French-speaking West Africa*. Oxford: Oxford University Press.

Mortimer, E. (1969). *France and the Africans, 1940–60: a political history*. London: Faber.

Mortimer, R. (1972). From Federalism to Francophonia: Senghor's African policy. *African Studies Review*, 15(2), 283–306.

Muller, J. (1958, May). La Subversion menace-t-elle l'Afrique noire? *Revue de Défense Nationale*, 158.

Murphy, P. (1995), *Party Politics and Decolonization: the Conservative Party and British Colonial Policy in Tropical Africa, 1951–1964*. Oxford: Clarendon.

Ndoye, M. (1995). La Fédération du Mali à l'épreuve de l'indépendance: chronique d'un échec. *Africa (Roma)*, 50(2), 151–75.

Neuberger, B. (1976). The African concept of Balkanisation. *Journal of Modern African Studies*, 14(3), 523–9.

Ngoh, V. J. (1990). *Constitutional developments in Southern Cameroons, 1946–1961: from trusteeship to independence*. Yaoundé: CEPER.

Ngoh, V. J. (2001). *Southern Cameroons, 1921–1961. A constitutional history*. Aldershot: Ashgate.

Ngom, M. and Diouf, M. (2010, April 3). Mali: Mamadou Diouf, professeur d'histoire à l'UCAD – Pourquoi le Président Houphouët-Boigny n'a jamais voulu de la Fédération du Mali. *Wal Fadjri: l'aurore*.

N'Guessan, K. (2011). Côte d'Ivoire. In C. Lentz (ed.), *Afrika@50. Vor-Ort-Berichte von den Unabhängigkeitsjubiläen in Kamerun, Madagaskar, DR Kongo, Benin, Côte d'Ivoire, Gabun, Mali, Nigeria und Burkina Faso* (Working paper 126) (pp. 58–72). Mainz,

Germany: Department of Anthropology and African Studies, Johannes Gutenberg University of Mainz. www.ifeas.unimainz.de/workingpapers/AP126.pdf (Accessed 1 December 2012).

N'Guessan, K. (2013). Independence is not given, it is taken. Nationalist History/ies on the occasion of the 50th anniversary of Ivorian independence. *Nations and Nationalism*, 19(2), 276–95.

Nick, C. (1998). *Résurrection, naissance de la Ve République, un coup d'Etat démocratique*. Paris: Fayard.

Nora, P. (ed.). (1986). *La Nation: le territoire, l'état, le patrimoine*. Paris: Gallimard.

Olsen, G. R. (2009). The EU and military conflict management in Africa: for the good of Africa or Europe? *International Peacekeeping*, 16(2), 245–60.

Onana, C. (2003). *La France et ses tirailleurs: enquête sur les combattants de la République 1939–2003*. Paris: Duboiris.

Orford, A. (2003). *Reading humanitarian intervention: human rights and the use of force in international law*. Cambridge: Cambridge University Press.

Orwin, E. M. (2008). Of couscous and control: the bureau of Muslim soldier affairs and the crisis of French colonialism. *The Historian*, 70(2), 263–84.

Otayek, R. (1984). La Libye face à la France au Tchad: qui perd gagne? *Politique africaine*, 16, 66–85.

Otayek, R. (1986). *La Politique africaine de la Libye*. Paris: Karthala.

Ould Saleck, M. (1979). L'Armée mauritanienne est pour la paix. *Revue africaine de stratégie*, 2(2), 4–9.

Ovendale, R. (1995). Macmillan and the wind of change in Africa, 1957–1960. *Historical Journal*, 38(2), 455–77.

Oyono, D. (1990). *Avec ou sans France? La politique africaine de la France depuis 1960*. Paris: L'Harmattan.

Pahlavi, P. (2007–8). Political warfare is a double-edged sword: the rise and fall of the French counter-insurgency in Algeria. *Canadian Military Journal*, 8(4), 53–63.

Pandolfi, P. (1998). *Les Touaregs de l'Ahaggar*. Paris: Karthala.

Pascallon, P. (ed.). (2004). *La Politique de sécurité de la France en Afrique*. Paris: L'Harmattan.

Passeron, A. (1962). *De Gaulle parle: des institutions, de l'Algérie, de l'armée, des affaires étrangères, de la Communauté, de l'économie et des questions sociales*. Paris: Plon.

Péan, P. (1983). *Affaires africaines*. Paris: Fayard.

Péan, P. (1990). *L'homme de l'ombre. Eléments d'enquête autour de Jacques Foccart, l'homme le plus puissant et le plus mystérieux de la Ve République*. Paris: Fayard.

Périès, G. and Servenay, D. (2007). *Une guerre noire: enquête sur les origines du génocide rwandais (1959–1994)*. Paris: La Découverte.

Perrin, D. (2009). *La Gestion des frontières en Libye*. Florence: Robert Schuman Centre for Advanced Studies, European University Institute. http://hdl.handle.net/1814/12257 (Accessed 19 March 2010).

Piccolino, G. (2012). David against Goliath in Côte d'Ivoire? Laurent Gbagbo's war against global governance. *African Affairs*, 111(442), 1–23.

Politique Africaine (1984, December). Le Tchad [special issue]. *Politique africaine*, 16.

Porch, D. (1984). *The Conquest of the Sahara*. New York: Knopf.

Pourtier, R. (2010). L'éducation, enjeu majeur de l'Afrique post-indépendances. Cinquante ans d'enseignement en Afrique? Un bilan en demi-teinte. *Afrique contemporaine*, 235, 101–14.

Puigaudeau, O. du (1962). *Le Passé maghrébin de la Mauritanie*. Rabat: Ministère d'Etat chargé des affaires islamiques.

Quermonne, J.-L. (1957). L'Organisation commune des régions sahariennes selon la loi du 10 janvier 1957. *Bulletin juridique et politique de l'Union française*, 11(2), 273–93.

Rabemananjara, J. (1958). *Guinée: Prélude à l'indépendance*. Paris: Présence Africaine.

Radio-Canada. (2010, August 17). *Neo-Colonialism in Chad?* [radio broadcast]. www.cbc.ca/thecurrent/africa (Accessed December 2011).

Randrianja, S. and Ellis, S. (2009). *Madagascar: A Short History*. London: Hurst.

Reed, D. B. (2003). *Dan Ge performance: masks and music in contemporary Côte d'Ivoire*. Bloomington, IN: Indiana University Press.

Reno, W. (1998). *Warlord politics and African states*, Boulder, CO: Lynne Rienner.

RFI. (2010). *Découvrez les objets symbols des indépendences africaines*. www.rfi.fr/afrique/20100818–decouvrez-objets-symboles-independances-africaines (Accessed August 2009).

Richmond, O. (2011). *A post-liberal peace*. New York: Routledge.

Roche, C. (2001). *Le Sénégal à la conquête de son indépendance, 1939–1960: chronique de la vie politique et syndicale, de l'Empire français à l'indépendance*. Paris: Karthala.

Rothchild, D. (1966). The limits of federalism: an examination of political institutional transfer in Africa. *Journal of Modern African Studies*, 4(3), 275–93.

Rothermund, D. (2006). *The Routledge companion to decolonization*. London and New York: Routledge.

Rouvez, C. (1994). *Disconsolate empires: French, British, and Belgian military involvement in post-colonial Sub-Saharan Africa*. Lanham, MD and London: University Press of America.

Said, E. W. (1993). *Culture and imperialism*. New York: Vintage.

Saint Maurice, T. de (2000). *Sahara occidental 1991–1999: l'enjeu du référendum d'autodétermination*. Paris: L'Harmattan.

Salifou, A. (1992). *La Question touarègue au Niger*. Paris: Karthala.

Sanmarco, L. and Mbajum, M. (2007). *Entretiens sur les non-dits de la décolonisation: confidences d'un administrateur des colonies*. Paris: Editions de l'officine.

Şaul, M. and Royer, P. (2001) *West African challenge to empire: culture and history in the Volta-Bani anti-colonial war*. Athens, OH: Ohio University Press.

Scheck, R. (2010). French colonial soldiers in German prisoners of war camps (1940–1945). *French History*, 24(3), 420–46.

Scheele, J. (2010). Traders, saints and irrigation: reflections on Saharan connectivity. *Journal of African History*, 51, 281–300.

Schenk, C. (1996). Decolonization and European Economic Integration: the Free Trade Area Negotiations, 1956–58, *Journal of Imperial and Commonwealth History*, 24(3), 444–63.

Schmidt, E. (2005). *Mobilizing the masses: gender, ethnicity and class in the nationalist movement in Guinea, 1939–1958*. Portsmouth, NH: Heinemann.

Schmidt, E. (2007). *Cold War and decolonization in Guinea, 1946–1958.* Athens, OH: Ohio University Press.

Schwab, P. (2004). *Designing West Africa.* New York: Palgrave.

Sèbe, B. (2010). In the shadow of the Algerian war: the United States and the Common Organisation of Saharan Regions (OCRS), 1957–62. *Journal of Imperial and Commonwealth History,* 38(2), 303–22.

Sèbe, B. (2011). Exalting imperial grandeur: the French Empire and its metropolitan public. In J. M. MacKenzie (ed.), *European empires and the people: popular responses to imperialism in France, Britain, the Netherlands, Belgium, Germany and Italy* (pp. 19–56). Manchester: Manchester University Press.

Seck, I. (1993). *La Stratégie culturelle de la France en Afrique.* Paris: L'Harmattan.

Seely, J. C. (2001). A political analysis of decentralisation: coopting the Tuareg threat in Mali. *Journal of Modern African Studies,* 39(3), 499–524.

Seibert, B. H. (2007, November). *African adventure? Assessing the European Union's military intervention in Chad and the Central African Republic* (Working paper). Cambridge, MA: MIT Security Studies Program.

Seibert, B. H. (2008, March). EUFOR Tchad/RCA: a cautionary note. *European Security Review,* 37, 1–4.

Seka, P. R., and Kouakou, C. K. (2011). Regard sur les relations économiques entre la Chine et la Côte d'Ivoire. In N. G.-M. Aké and P. Kipré (eds), *Les Conditions économiques de l'indépendance à l'ère de la mondialisation. Mythes et réalités en Afrique de l'Ouest. Actes du colloque de San Pedro, 10–14 mars 2010* (pp. 115–47). Paris: L'Harmattan.

Senghor, L. S. (1962). *African Socialism.* London: Pall Mall Press.

Shapiro, M. J. (1997). *Violent cartographies: mapping cultures of war.* Minneapolis: University of Minnesota Press.

Shapiro, M. J. (2004). *Methods and nations: cultural governance and the indigenous subject.* New York: Routledge.

Shipway, M. (2008a) 'Transfer of destinies', or Business as usual? Republican invented tradition and the problem of 'independence' at the end of the French Empire. *The Round Table: The Commonwealth Journal of International Affairs,* 97(398), 747–59.

Shipway, M. (2008b). *Decolonization and its impact: A comparative approach to the end of the colonial empires.* Malden, MA and Oxford: Blackwell.

Shipway, M. (2011). Thinking like an empire: Governor Henri Laurentie and postwar plans for the late colonial French 'Empire-State'. In M. Thomas (ed.), *The French Colonial Mind. Volume 1: Mental maps of empire and colonial encounters* (pp. 219–50). Lincoln, NE and London: University of Nebraska Press.

Siriex, P.-H. (1957). *Une nouvelle Afrique: AOF 1957.* Paris: Plon.

Slater, D. (2004). *Geopolitics and the post-colonial: rethinking North-South relations.* New York: Wiley-Blackwell.

Sluga, G. (2011). Editorial for transnational cluster. *Journal of Global History,* 6(2), 219–22.

Smith, S. (2010). *Voyage en postcolonie: Le nouveau monde franco-africain.* Paris: Grasset.

Smith, S. (2011, May 19). The Story of Laurent Gbagbo. *London Review of Books.* www.

lrb.co.uk/v33/n10/stephen-w-smith/the-story-of-laurent-gbagbo (Accessed 19 May 2011).

Smith, T. (1978). A comparative study of French and British Decolonization. *Comparative Studies in Society and History*, 20(1), 70–102.

Smouts, M.-C. (1979). *La France à l'ONU: premiers rôles et second rang*. Paris: Presses de la Fondation nationale des sciences politiques.

Sot, M. (2002). *Etudiants africains en France, 1951–2001*. Paris: Karthala.

Souleymane, B. (2010, August 9). Cinquantenaire à Man. Blon Blaise offre dix millions: la population en colère. *Notre Heure*. www.abidjan.net (Accessed 9 August 2010).

Southern Cameroon National Council (2009). *About Us*. www.scncforsoutherncameroo ns.net/index.php?option=comcontentandview=articleandid=46andItemid=27 (Accessed 8 January 2012).

Steiner, C. B. (2010). The invisible face: masks, ethnicity, and the state in Côte d'Ivoire. In R. R. Grinker and C. B. Steiner (eds), *Perspectives on Africa. A reader in culture, history, and representation*, 2nd edn (pp. 514–20). Oxford: Wiley-Blackwell.

Stoler, A. L. and Cooper, F. (1997). Between metropole and colony: rethinking a research agenda. In F. Cooper and A. L. Stoler (eds), *Tensions of empire: colonial cultures in a bourgeois world* (pp. 1–37). Berkeley: University of California Press.

Styan, D. (2012). EU power and armed humanitarianism in Africa: evaluating European Security and Defense Policy in Chad. *Cambridge Review of International Affairs*, 25(4), 651–68.

Suret-Canale, J. (1970). *La République de Guinée*, Paris: Editions Sociales.

Suret-Canale, J. (1982). From colonization to independence in French Tropical Africa: the economic background, in P. Gifford and Wm. R. Louis (eds), *The transfer of power in Africa: decolonization 1940–1960* (pp. 445–81). New Haven, CT and London: Yale University Press.

Suret-Canale, J. (1998). Les Banques d'affaires et l'Outre-Mer dans les années 1950. In Ministère de l'Economie, des Finances et de l'Industrie (ed.), *La France et l'outre-mer: un siècle de relations monétaires et financières* (pp. 486–95). Paris: Comité pour l'histoire économique et financière de la France.

Takougang, J. (1996). The Union des Populations du Cameroun and its Southern Cameroons connection. *Revue Française d'Histoire d'Outre-Mer*, 83(310), 7–24.

Tangri, R. (1976). Conflict and violence in contemporary Sierra Leone chiefdoms. *Journal of Modern African Studies*, 14(2), 311–21.

Terretta, M. (2007). A miscarriage of revolution: Cameroonian women and nationalism. *Stichproben: Wiener Zeitschrift für kritische Afrikastudien*, 12, 61–90.

Terretta, M. (2010). Cameroonian nationalists go global: from forest *maquis* to a pan-African Accra. *Journal of African History*, 51(2), 189–212.

Thomas, M. (ed.) (2011). *The French colonial mind. Volume 1: Mental maps of empire and colonial encounters*. Lincoln, NE and London: University of Nebraska Press.

Thomas, M., Moore, B., and Butler, L. J. (2008). *Crises of empire: decolonization and Europe's imperial states, 1918–1975*. London: Hodder Education.

Tirefort, A. (1999). Aux antipodes du Tam-tam, la fête coloniale en Côte d'Ivoire pendant l'entre-deux-guerres. In O. Goerg (ed.), *Fêtes urbaines en Afrique. Espaces, identités et pouvoirs* (pp. 167–79). Paris: Karthala.

Titley, B. (2002). *Dark age: The political odyssey of Emperor Bokassa.* Montreal: McGill Queens Press.

Tocqueville, A. (1991). *Oeuvres,* Vol. 1, ed. J. André. Paris: Gallimard.

Tønnesson, S. (2009). *Vietnam 1946: how the war began.* Berkeley, CA: University of California Press.

Torrent, M. (2012). *Diplomacy and nation-building in Africa: Franco-British relations and Cameroon at the end of empire.* London: I. B. Tauris.

Touré, A. S. (1958a, August 25). Speech. In Guinea. (1982). Evolution des rapports franco-guinéens. *Révolution Démocratique Africaine No. 193* (2nd edn) (pp. 17–25). Conakry: Imprimerie Nationale Patrice Lumumba.

Touré, A. S. (1958b, October 26). Speech at Cinema 'Vox', Conakry. In J. Rabemananjara (1958). *Guinée: Prélude à l'indépendance* (pp. 163–75). Paris: Présence Africaine.

Touscoz, J. (1976). *L'évaluation de la coopération Nord-Sud: l'exemple de la coopération entre pays francophones.* Montréal: Presses de l'Université du Québec.

Touval, S. (1967). The Organization of African Unity and African borders. *International Organization,* 21(1), 102–27.

Tshimanga, C., Gondola, D. and Bloom, P. (eds) (2009). *Frenchness and the African diaspora: identity and uprising in Contemporary France.* Bloomington, IN: Indiana University Press.

Tubiana, J. (2008, April). *The Chad-Sudan proxy war and the 'Darfurization' of Chad* (Sudan Human Security Baseline Assessment Working Paper 12). Geneva: Small Arms Survey.

Turpin, F. (2002). Jacques Foccart et le RPF en Afrique noire sous la IVᵉ République. *Les Cahiers du Centre de Recherches Historiques,* 30. http://ccrh.revues.org/index572.html (Accessed 1 October 2012).

Turpin, F. (2009, August) Jacques Foccart et le secrétariat général pour les affaires africaines et malgaches. *Histoire@Politique, Politique, culture, société,* 8. www.histoire-politique.fr/index.php?numero=08andrub=dossieranditem=83 (Accessed 30 January 2010).

Turpin, F. (2010). *De Gaulle, Pompidou et l'Afrique (1958–1974): décoloniser et coopérer.* Paris: Indes savantes.

UN Security Council (2010). *Report of the Secretary-General on the United Nations Mission in the Central African Republic and Chad.* New York: United Nations.

Vaïsse, M. (1998). *La grandeur: politique étrangère du général de Gaulle, 1958–1969.* Paris: Fayard.

Vallet, M. (1990). Les Touaregs du Hoggar entre decolonisation et indépendances (1954–1974). In H. Claudot-Hawad (ed.). *Touaregs, exil et résistance* [special issue]. *Revue du Monde musulman et de la Méditerranée,* 57(3), 77–90.

Varnoteaux P. (1998). Le centre interarmées d'essais d'engins spéciaux. Origine et enjeux d'un champ de tir opérationnel. In M. Vaïsse (ed.), *La IVe République face aux problèmes d'armement* (pp. 535–42). Vincennes: ADDIM.

Verrier, A. (1986). *The road to Zimbabwe, 1890–1980.* London: Cape.

Verschave, F.-X. (1998) *La Françafrique: le plus long scandale de la République.* Paris: Stock.

Verschave, F.-X. (2000). *Noir silence: qui arrêtera le Françafrique?* Paris: Edition des Arènes.

Villatoux, M.-C. (2007). *Guerre et action psychologiques en Algérie.* Paris: Service Historique de la Défense.

Villatoux, P. and Villatoux, M.-C. (2005). *La République et son armée face au «péril subversif»: guerre et action psychologique en France.* Paris: Indes savantes.

Visier, C. (2003). *L'Etat et la coopération: la fin d'un monopole.* Paris: L'Harmattan.

Walker, R. B. J. (2010). *After the globe, before the world.* New York: Routledge.

Warson, J. (2009). *Britain, France and the Nigerian Civil War, 1967–1970.* Unpublished undergraduate dissertation, London School of Economics and Political Science, London.

Wauthier, C. (1995). *Quatre présidents et l'Afrique: De Gaulle, Pompidou, Giscard d'Estaing, Mitterrand: quarante ans de politique africaine.* Paris: Seuil.

Weiskel, T. C. (1988). Independence and the longue durée: the Ivory Coast 'Miracle' reconsidered. In P. Gifford and W. R. Louis (eds), *Decolonization and African independence: the transfers of power, 1960–1980* (pp. 347–80). New Haven, CT: Yale University Press.

Welch, C. (1966). *Dream of unity: pan-Africanism and political unification in West Africa.* Ithaca, NY: Cornell University Press.

Westad, O. A. (2006). *The global Cold War: Third World interventions and the making of our times.* Cambridge: Cambridge University Press.

White, L. (2000). *Speaking with vampires: rumor and history in colonial Africa.* Berkeley, CA: University of California Press.

Wilder, G. (2005). *The French imperial nation-state: negritude and colonial humanism between the two World Wars.* Chicago: University of Chicago Press.

Wolfgram, M. A. (2011). *'Getting history right': East and West German collective memories of the Holocaust and war.* Lewisburg, PA: Bucknell University Press.

Wood, R. S. (1973). *France in the World Community.* Leyden: Sijthoff.

Wright, J. (1989). *Libya, Chad and the Central Sahara.* London: Hurst.

Yacoub, A. (2006). *Les Relations franco-tchadiennes dans les années soixante.* Paris: Publibook.

Yacoub, M. S. (2005), *Tchad: des rebelles aux seigneurs de guerre: la désagrégation de l'armée nationale.* Ndjamena: Al-Mouna.

Yapi, A. (2011). La Crise interne à l'UGTCI de 1968: ébranlement de l'unité syndicale et instinct de survie du régime PDCI-RDA. In P. Kipré and N. G.-M. Aké (eds), *Conflits régionaux et indépendances nationales en Afrique de l'Ouest. Actes du colloque d'Abengourou, 26–28 février 2010* (pp. 153–62). Paris: L'Harmattan.

Yéré, H.M. (2007). Reconfiguring nationhood in Côte d'Ivoire? In C. Obi (ed.), *Perspectives on Côte d'Ivoire: between political breakdown and post-conflict peace. Discussion Paper Nordiska Afrikainstitutet, 39, 50–65.*

Young, C. (1994). *The African colonial state in comparative perspective.* New Haven, CT and London: Yale University Press.

Young, C. (2004). The end of the post-colonial state in Africa? Reflections on changing African political dynamics. *African Affairs,* 103(410), 23–49.

Young, J. W. (2006). Franco-British relations during the Wilson Years. In A. Capet (ed.), *Britain, France and the Entente Cordiale since 1904* (pp. 162–83). Basingstoke: Palgrave Macmillan.

Zimmerman, S. (2011). *Living beyond boundaries: West African servicemen in French colonial conflicts, 1908–1962*. Unpublished doctoral thesis, University of California, Berkeley.

Žižek, S. (2008). *Violence: six sideways reflections*. New York: Picador.

Zunes, S. and Mundy, J. (2010). *Western Sahara: war, nationalism and conflict irresolution*. Syracuse, NY: Syracuse University Press.

Index

AAMC 81
Abidjan 97, 128–30, 137, 139, 142–3, 145, 156, 162, 219–20, 222, 230
Accra 39, 193, 200 (n.1)
ACCT 123
Addis Ababa 121, 131
ADS 147
ADSSD 200 (n.1)
AEF 3, 8, 22, 24–5, 120, 140, 179, 205, 233, 237, 243, 245
Africa cell 146–8, 174
African and Malagasy Organisation for Cooperation 166
African and Malagasy Union 166
African Labour Code 22
African Union 230
Afrique Equatoriale Française, see AEF
Afrique Occidentale Française, see AOF
Ag Assarid, Moussa 212
Ahidjo, Ahmadou 189, 191–5, 197–9, 200 (n.1), 201 (n.4–7, n.9), 202 (n.24)
aid policy 4, 121, 123–5
AL (Armée de Libération) 92–4, 102 (n.3)
Algeria 4, 6, 16, 19, 22, 33, 40, 47, 61–2, 69, 71, 74 (n.7), 76–9, 82–8, 90, 93–4, 100, 102 (n.5), 107, 110–11, 122, 128, 146, 162, 205, 207–13, 242
Algerian War of Independence 63–4, 66–7, 76–7, 80–3, 85, 87, 90, 93–4, 99, 107, 204, 207–9, 239
Algiers 79, 110, 140, 207, 213
ALN (Armée de Libération Nationale) 87
Al-Ousseini, Songhay Alhaman 82
Amayas, Marly Ag 82
Anglo-French relations 172, 179

Anglo-French rivalry 177, 183
Anglophone Africa 165, 196–9, 202 (n.25–6), 203 (n.27)
Anyangwe, Carlson 198, 203 (n.27)
AOF 3, 10, 21, 23–4, 30–3, 37–8, 41, 51, 55, 61–73, 76–7, 79, 82–3, 87, 92–3, 120, 140, 179, 204–5, 209, 219, 237, 243, 245
Aouzou Strip 211, 244
Apithy, Sourou-Migan 25, 46–7
AQIM 216
Arab 32, 76, 100, 205–6, 209–10, 212
arms 175
army (colonial) 91, 93, 97, 99–101
army (national) 91–2, 94, 96–102
Army of Liberation (Moroccan), see AL
Asia 62
Assembly of the French Union 20
Aw, Mamadou 85

Ba, Amadaou 82
Ba, Tamsir 53
BAG 32, 37
Balafrej, Ahmed 93
Balandier, Georges 110
balkanisation 5, 55, 216
Bamako 45, 54, 72, 75, 77, 80, 83, 85–7, 214
Bangui 127, 142
Bao Daï 23
Barka, Mehdi Ben 136
Barry III, see Ibrahima, Barry
Bayrou, Maurice 37
BCD 193–4, 196, 201 (n.13–14)
Beaufre, General André 76

Bélime, Emile 212
Benin 125
  see also Dahomey
Berber 102 (n.3, n.5)
Bérété, Framoi 36
Beslay, François 97
Bevin, Ernest 156
Bey ag Akhamouk 82, 212
BIRD 96
Biya, Paul 195–7
blood debt 6
Bockel, Jean-Marie 115
Bokassa, Jean-Bédel 144, 150 (n.22, n.28)
Bonfils, Charles 37–8
Bongo, Albert-Bernard (or Omar) 115, 143, 174
Bonifay, Paul 70
Boucheseiche, Georges 136
Bourges, Yvon 8
Bourguiba, Habib 123
Bourgund, General Gabriel 93
Brazzaville Conference (1944) 17–19, 21, 23, 27
Britain 10, 15, 26, 28 (n.3), 31, 38–41, 79, 87, 155, 160–5, 171–80, 202 (n.20, n.26), 203 (n.27–8), 205–8
British empire 15, 26, 38–9, 155–6, 158–9, 164, 171, 175–6, 178–9, 189, 191, 196–9, 202 (n.24)
Brouin, Georges 9
Bruhat, Jean-Louis 8
Burkina Faso 125, 211–12, 222
  see also Upper Volta

Cairo, *see* Egypt
Cameroon 3, 7, 11, 22–3, 28 (n.10), 85, 113, 123, 125, 128, 139, 150 (n.17), 155, 161, 189–200, 201 (n.5, n.8, n.13, n.15), 202 (n.15, n.20, n.24–5)
capitalism 16, 32
Capot-Rey, Robert 212
CAR 107, 113, 115, 125, 128, 144–5, 234, 244
  see also Bangui
Carney, G. E. A. 38
Casablanca 107
Casamance 53
CCFD 248 (n.16)
CEDOC 150 (n.17)
CEFEO 76
cellule africaine, see Africa cell
Central African Republic, *see* CAR

Chaban-Delmas, Jacques 93
Chad 5, 11, 22, 74 (n.13), 107, 113, 115, 122, 125, 127–8, 144, 147, 205–6, 208–12, 233–47, 248 (n.16, n.18)
Chambard, Roger 93
Chauvet, Paul 25–6
CIEES 77
cinquantenaire 219–21, 223–4, 226–7, 229–31, 232 (n.3, n.13), 233, 236, 238, 247 (n.3)
civilising mission 4
CNPCICI 227–9
Cold War 19, 77, 87, 107–8, 113–15, 118, 157–9, 166, 177, 179, 231, 244
Colonial Office (UK) 156, 158–9, 161, 163
colonial violence 10, 107–8, 111–12, 114, 117–18
commemoration 11
Commonwealth 80, 156–7, 159, 161–4, 166, 176
Communauté, see Community
communism 7–8, 32, 44, 47, 50–1, 54, 65, 76, 79–80, 87, 111, 113–14, 157, 159–60, 164–5, 189, 202 (n.15)
Community, French 2, 7, 25, 27, 30–1, 51, 78–81, 84–5, 88, 90–1, 95, 142, 156–9, 161, 163, 165
Condé, Sory 33
CONFEMEN 123, 131
Congo 16, 125, 145–6, 149 (n.5), 225, 240, 244
Congo (Brazzaville) 8, 46, 128, 139, 143, 145, 191, 244
Congo (Léopoldville/Kinshasa) 5, 145–6, 149 (n.5), 150 (n.23–4), 163, 225, 240, 244
Cooper, Frederick 16–18
coopération 4, 10, 90, 100–2, 104 (n.25), 120–33, 142
Cornut-Gentille, Bernard 32, 34, 37
Côte d'Ivoire 3–4, 8–9, 11, 19–20, 23–4, 37, 107–8, 113, 115–17, 122, 125, 129, 131, 139, 146–7, 163, 208, 214, 219–31, 232 (n.2, n.5), 246
Coulibaly, Ouezzin 36
Council of State 26
Council of the Republic 20
coup d'état 7, 46, 54, 221
Courcel, Geoffrey Chodron de 155
Couve de Murville, Maurice 160
CPDC 241, 243
CPNC 198–9

CPS 140
CR 193–4, 201 (n.14)
Crimea 110
CRO 156–60
Cusin, Gaston 93
Czechoslovakia 86, 161

Daddah, Moktar Ould 95–6, 100
Dahomey 8, 25, 46–7, 68, 79, 122, 163
    see also Benin
Dakar 23, 34, 38–9, 45–51, 53, 56 (n.14),
    69–70, 77–9, 81–2, 84–7, 91, 93–4,
    97, 128–30, 137, 149 (n.11), 156,
    160–1, 165, 207, 209, 246
De Gaulle, Charles 2–3, 6–8, 16, 18–19,
    27, 30–1, 34, 41–2, 47, 49, 67, 78, 80,
    85, 87, 94, 113, 120, 123, 135–43,
    145–8, 149 (n.6), 151 (n.32), 159–62,
    164–7, 172, 176–7, 179–80, 192,
    208–9, 236–7
Debré, Michel 80–1, 83, 96, 102, 140
Déby, Idris 5, 234–6, 239–47
decolonisation 1, 3–5, 10, 16–17, 23, 44–8,
    51, 53–4, 55 (n.4), 61–3, 73, 92,
    107–10, 112–15, 135, 143, 155–6,
    166, 171–2, 179, 182–3, 204–5, 210,
    212, 215
Decraene, Philippe 86
defence agreements 95–8
Defferre, Gaston 9, 15–16, 18, 21–6, 28
    (n.4), 33, 93
Delavignette, Robert 21
democracy 16, 20, 32, 37, 109, 175, 194–5,
    198, 202 (n.26), 203 (n.27)
Denise, Auguste 9
Deriaud, Paul-Charles 8
Dia, Mamadou 9, 49–53, 84, 137, 140
Diallo, Yacine 35, 36
Diané, Lansana 33–4, 65
Diawadou, Barry 35–6
Dien Bien Phu 33, 66, 69, 72
Diffre, Thadée 9
Diori, Hamani 123
Dixon, Sir Pierson 167
Djibouti 113, 115, 246
DOM-TOM 138, 140
Dorman, Maurice 39
Doustin, Daniel 8
DSG 32

Eboué, Félix 237
ECOWAS 230

education 1, 7–8, 10, 34, 62, 67–71, 73,
    76–7, 121–33, 192–3, 212, 226
Egypt 15, 77, 200 (n.1), 207
El Moudjahid 77
Elysée 178, 180–2
EMA 115
EMGDN 83
Empire 1, 3, 9–10, 15, 17, 27, 38, 61,
    63–6, 68, 73, 88, 110–14, 120–1, 142,
    150 (n.23), 155, 163–4, 172, 177,
    183, 204, 208, 215, 237
ENFOM 21
Europe 3, 10, 15, 40, 44–5, 63, 77, 79, 111,
    115–17, 122, 138, 150 (n.22, n.23),
    155–9, 163, 171–2, 177, 205–6, 210,
    212, 228, 234, 244
European Economic Community (EEC)
    156, 164–5, 167, 179
European Union (EU) 117–18, 211, 233,
    247 (n.2)

FAC 123–4, 127–30
FAN 241
Fanon, Frantz 111
FANT 241
FAP 241
Far East 76
Fashoda syndrome 183
Fassi, Alla el 92
Faure, Edgar 21
Fellagha 83
FESAC 128
FESCI 221
FIDES 163
Fifth Republic 3, 5, 16, 27, 30, 136, 142
First World War 6, 63, 207
Flanders 16
FLN 16, 40, 66–7, 76, 80, 83, 85–6, 209
Foccart, Jacques 2, 4–8, 10, 44, 48–9,
    52, 55 (n.1), 85, 87, 94, 102, 112,
    135–48, 149 (n.5, n.6, n.8), 150
    (n.27–9), 151 (n.30, n.32), 162, 166,
    174, 179–80
Follows, Geoffrey 180
forced labour, abolition of 20, 23
Foreign Legion 65
Foreign and Commonwealth Office 177
Foreign Office 155–7, 160–4
Fournier-Bidoz, Robert 8, 139
Fourth Republic 16–17, 19–21, 32, 66,
    138, 140
Fouta Djallon 32

FPR 148
FPU 148
Françafrique 1, 5, 7, 115, 120, 136, 148,
    200 (n.2), 219–20, 230–1
Franco, Francisco 93
Franco Rhodesian relations 173–83
Francophonie 4
Free French Forces 64, 72, 74 (n.13), 138,
    233, 237
French Community, *see* Community, French
French Equatorial Africa, *see* AEF
French Union 3, 17–21, 24, 38, 77–8, 82,
    88, 111, 138, 157, 163, 209
French West Africa, *see* AOF
FROLINAT 144, 238–41, 244, 247 (n.13)
Fulbe 35–6

Gabon 4, 37, 55 (n.2), 113, 115, 125, 128,
    143, 150 (n.17), 174, 181–2, 242
Gaillard, Félix 93
Gallieni, Joseph 110
Gambia 155
Garbay, General Pierre 69–70, 72, 74 (n.13)
Garcia, André 127
Gardet, General 79, 83
gendarme de l'Afrique 114–15
Geneva 76
Germany 63–4, 75, 206
Ghana 28 (n.3), 79, 159–60, 163, 201
    (n.15)
Ghana, independence of (1957) 15, 18
GP 150 (n.17)
GPRA 85–6
Gold Coast, *see* Ghana
grandeur 179, 182, 223, 227
Grunitzky, Nicolas 26
Guèye, Lamine 57 (n.21), 84
Guinea (Conakry) 5, 8–10, 20, 27, 30–43,
    47, 64, 76, 78–9, 86, 137, 149 (n.8),
    156, 158–63, 165, 200 (n.1)
GUNT 241, 243

Habré, Hissene 239–46, 248 (n.15, n.17)
Haiphong 107
harki 66
Hassan II 136
Hawaii 109
Hettier de Boislambert, Claude 45, 48–51,
    53–4, 85
Hogard, Commander Jacques 77
Hogbe Nlend, Henri 196, 202 (n.23)
Houphouët-Boigny, Félix 4, 8–9, 19–21,

    23–5, 36, 38–40, 113, 136–40, 142,
    145–6, 149 (n.5), 163, 208, 219–23,
    226–9, 232 (n.13)

Ibrahima, Barry 32, 36
ICG 230, 247 (n.1)
Ifora 82–3
Illi, Attaher Ag 82
immigration 6, 110
imperialism 1, 32, 92, 108–11, 157, 162,
    205
impunity 242, 245
independence 1–3, 6, 8–11, 15–16, 18,
    21, 28 (n.10), 30–5, 38, 40–2, 61,
    64, 73, 76, 80, 82, 84, 87, 91–2,
    100, 102, 113, 120–1, 148, 160–1,
    165, 167, 171–3, 176, 179, 182, 189,
    198–9, 202 (n.24), 208–10, 212, 215,
    219–20, 223, 225, 227–8, 232 (n.13),
    237, 239, 245
insurgency 7, 16, 19, 28 (n.10), 189, 193
Indochina 4, 6, 8, 17, 19, 23–4, 33, 61,
    63–7, 71–3, 74 (n.13), 76, 81, 90,
    107, 110, 113
Interahamwe militia 5
Israel 15, 87

Janot, Raymond 51, 142
Jebb, Gladwyn 160

Kaba, Lansiné 34
Keïta, Madeira 41, 83
Keïta, Modibo 10, 45–53, 56 (n.14), 57
    (n.21), 75, 78, 80–7, 209, 213
Keïta, Paul Lalifa 78
Kel Ahaggar 212
Kel Aïr 212
Kel Ajjer 212
Kel Tademekkat 212
Kenya 155, 163
Kirby, Dennis 39–40
Kodock, Augustin Frédéric 196
Korea 113
Kouchner, Bernard 118
Koufra 237
Kourouma, Koly 36
Kunta, Bunama 82
Kuwait 100

la Coloniale 110
Laos 65
Laurentie, Henri 23

Lavenon, Paul 8
Law of 23 February 2005 4
Law of 23 June 1956, *see Loi-cadre*
Léglise, Gérard 35–6
Lennox–Boyd, Alan 158–9, 165–6
Lettéron, Philippe 180
Liberia 240
Libya 100, 116, 144, 205, 207, 211–12,
    214, 216, 233–4, 239, 243–4, 246
Lloyd, Selwyn 160
Loi-cadre 9, 15–8, 20–4, 26–7, 28 (n.4),
    33–4, 38, 41, 44, 46, 91, 208, 239
London 38, 155, 157, 161, 207
Lopez, Antoine 136
Lorillot, General Henri 76
Luang Prabang 65
Lyautey, Louis-Hubert-Gonzalve 110

Macmillan, Harold 160–1
Madagascar 15, 19, 22–3, 28 (n.10), 61, 72,
    74 (n.13), 107, 110, 122, 125, 127–8,
    130, 140, 180
Magal 49
Maghreb 77, 127, 129, 212
Mali 10, 31, 42, 45–55, 75, 77, 80–8,
    122, 125, 161, 205–6, 209, 211–13,
    215–16, 240, 246
    see also Soudan
Malloum, Felix 239, 242–3
Malraux, André 87, 235, 237
Man (Côte d'Ivoire) 11, 221, 223–6, 229
Mangin, General Charles 63
manipulation 2–3, 5, 47–9, 53–5, 230,
    245
Mauricheau-Beaupré, Jean 145–6, 180
Mauritania 7, 10, 79, 90–102, 103 (n.19),
    112, 122, 125, 205, 207–11
Mayotte (La Réunion) 115
Mazarin, Cardinal 136
M'Ba, Léon 4, 143, 150 (n.17), 174
Messmer, Pierre 3, 24, 34, 79
Miferma, *see* SNIM
militarism 107, 110, 113–15
military operation 90–6, 99–100, 102
military pensions 6, 64
Ministry of Overseas France 21–2
Ministry of the Sahara 208
Mitterrand, François 16, 20, 28 (n.4), 138
MNLA 212–13
Mobutu, Joseph-Désiré 5
Moisan, Roland 136
Mollet, Guy 15–16, 19, 21–2, 77

Monde, Le 18, 86, 174
Monnerville, Gaston 19
Moor 205
Morocco 77, 87, 91–4, 97, 99–100, 102,
    104 (n.24), 107, 126, 128, 136, 191,
    205, 207, 210
Morocco, independence of (1956) 15, 91
Moscow 50, 78
Mouragues, Albert-Louis 93
Mourier, Paul 97–8
Moutet, Marius 22
Mozambique 176
MPS 235, 241
Muller, Colonel Jean 78
Muridiyya 49
Muslim 49, 122

Naegelen, Marcel-Edmond 19
Nasser, Gamel Abdul 15
National Assembly 18–22, 24–5, 35, 208,
    239, 245
nationalism 15, 31, 38–40, 44, 76–7, 198,
    210, 221
NATO 113, 116–17, 156, 160, 163
Nazi 66, 175
N'Diaye, Valdiodio 50–1, 53, 57 (n.21)
N'Djamena 127, 144, 233–6, 240–3, 246,
    248 (n.15)
neo–colonialism 1, 8, 9, 16, 18, 27, 101,
    108–9, 114, 136, 144, 180, 189–90,
    192–8, 222, 227
networks 2, 9, 121, 180–2, 191–2, 200
    (n.2), 231
New York 41
Nguyen Ai Quoc (Ho Chi Minh) 111
Niang, Ousmane 65
Niger 46, 77, 79, 82–3, 122, 125, 163,
    205–9, 211–12, 214–15, 234, 236,
    240, 245–6
Nigeria 39, 146, 158, 163, 166, 199, 202
    (n.24), 213–14, 245
Nkrumah, Kwame 15, 18
Ntumazah, Ndeh 196, 201 (n.14), 203
    (n.28)
Nyobé, Ruben Um 28 (n.10)

OCAM 142, 166, 201 (n.8)
OCRS 82, 205–6, 208–10, 212, 216
oil 1, 78, 136, 150 (n.17), 173–4, 205, 209,
    211, 215, 231, 236, 240, 242, 248
    (n.16)
Oldham, Alan Trevor 39–40

Operation Cornue 96, 99
Operation Ecouvillon 91–2, 94–6, 102, 210
Operation Epervier 233, 239, 246, 247
    (n.1)
Operation Lamantin 92, 100
Operation Manta 239
Operation Ouragan 94–5
Operation Tiede 94
Oueddei, Goukouni 240, 242, 244
Ouefkir, Colonel Mohamed 136
Ould Cheikh, Mohammed Mahmoud 82,
    97
Oulliminden 82
Ounif, Béni 87
Ouremba, Keïta 35

Pan-Africanism 39, 163, 210
Pan-Arabism 210
Pan-Sahel Initiative 216
Paris 8–9, 20–4, 26, 33, 36–8, 41, 47,
    49–50, 64, 77, 80, 83–6, 93–4, 101,
    129, 136, 142, 144–5, 147, 149
    (n.5), 150 (n.23), 160, 162–7, 180–1,
    191–3, 195–6, 198, 200, 201 (n.4,
    n.13), 207–8, 233, 246–7
Parisot, Jean-Paul 33, 36
PCF 19–20, 32–3
    see also Communism
PDCI 20, 221
PDG 20, 30–8, 40–2
peace operations 108, 117–19
Pearson, David 38–9
Péchoux, Laurent 8
Pierre, François 48, 52–3
Pignon, Léon 21, 23–6, 57 (n. 23)
Pineau, Christian 22
PLR 144
Poher, Alain 136
Polisario Front 91, 99–100, 210–11
Polynesia 8
post–colonial 1–2, 6–7, 10–11, 16, 31, 73,
    135, 156, 171, 176, 179–80, 204–6,
    209, 211–12, 214–16, 230
PPT 239
PRA 78
PRC 192
propaganda 10, 19, 32, 35, 39, 61–3,
    66–71, 73, 76, 80, 83
Pruvost, Hubert 36–7

Qaddafi, Muammar 210, 211, 216, 235,
    244, 246

rayonnement 181–2
RDA 20, 31–7, 39–40, 76–7, 139, 208, 239
Referendum of 28 September 1958 6, 30,
    32, 45, 47, 50, 140, 158
réseaux, see networks
RF 173, 175–6, 178
RFI 247 (n.10)
RHDP 226, 230
Rhodesia (Southern) 10, 155, 163, 171–83
Rio de Oro (Spanish Sahara) 94, 210
Robert, Maurice 138–9, 144, 151 (n.29)
RPF 138–9, 141, 148
RPR 146–7
Rwanda 1, 5, 115

SAARF 137
Sahara 11, 66, 77–8, 80, 82–3, 85, 90, 92,
    102 (n.4), 163, 204–12, 214–17
Saharomania (in France) 207
Sahrawi Arab Democratic Republic 211
Saleck, Mustafa Ould 100
Saller, Raphaël 36
sanctions 173–4, 177–8, 182
Sands war 211
Sangha 8
Sanmarco, Louis 5
Sano, Mamba 36
Sassou-Nguesso, Denis 115
SCNC 197, 202 (n.25, n.26)
Scramble for Africa 171, 206
SCTIP 143, 149 (n.16), 150 (n.17)
SDECE 79–80, 82, 86, 94, 135, 137–9,
    143–4, 146, 149 (n.5, n.8), 150
    (n.17), 175
Second World War 6, 9, 17, 61–4, 66, 68,
    72, 74 (n.10), 75–6, 90, 92, 107,
    111–12, 129, 207
Secretary for African and Malagasy Affairs 2,
    5, 44, 48, 54, 94
security 45, 49, 54, 107, 110, 113–18, 157,
    228, 246
Seguiet el Hamra (Spanish Sahara) 94, 99,
    210
Senegal 9–10, 38, 42, 45–54, 56 (n.14), 57
    (n.20–1), 63–4, 68– 9, 72, 74 (n.13),
    79–80, 84–6, 93, 113, 115, 125, 127,
    129, 131, 237, 242, 246
Senghor, Léopold Sédar 9, 21, 24–5, 27,
    49–51, 84, 123, 129, 140, 161
Sétif 107
Sidibé, Captain Mamadou 81
Sierra Leone 31, 39–40, 158, 240

Smith, Ian 171–2, 175–7, 180
SMR 79
SNIM 104 (n.25)
socialism 15, 19, 21–2, 93, 146, 213
Soudan, French 10, 31, 41–2, 45–7, 49–54,
  55 (n.5), 57 (n.20), 75–86, 208–9
  see also Mali
Souma, Amara 36
Soumaré, Abdoulaye 52–3, 77
Soustelle, Jacques 83
South Africa 176–7, 179
Spain 92–4, 99, 102 (n.5), 211
Spanish Sahara 94–5, 99–100, 102 (n.5),
  104 (n.24), 210
  see also Western Sahara
student organisations 63, 77
Sudan 205, 233, 239–41, 244
Sudan, independence of (1956) 15
Suez 15, 153, 157

Tanoh, Amon 129
Tauzière, Victoria 7
Taya, Maaouiya Ould 100
teachers 121–3, 126, 129, 131, 133 (n.1)
Teitgen, Pierre–Henri 21–2
Telli, Diallo 160
Territoires du Sud (Algeria) 209
teshumara 214
Tessalit 77
Thiaroye 75
tirailleurs sénégalais 61, 63–4
Tirant, René 8
Togo 21, 26, 46, 76, 79, 83, 87, 92–3, 122,
  125, 160
Tombalbaye, François 144, 234, 239,
  242–3, 247 (n.10)
Touati 83
Touré, Ahmed Sékou 8–9, 20, 30, 33–41,
  47, 50, 53, 78–9, 137, 159–61
trade unions 63, 79
Tric, Robert 122
Tsirinana, Philibert 28 (n.10)
Tuareg 82, 205–9, 212–16, 246
Tubu 205–6, 212
Tunis 77
Tunisia 72, 74 (n.13), 80, 93, 126, 205, 207

UAM 166
UDD 47
UDI 171, 173, 175–6, 178, 182
UDS-PFA 49
UDSR 20, 138

Union of Soviet Socialist Republics
  (USSR) 86–7, 113, 122, 149 (n.6), 157,
  159, 161–2, 201 (n.15)
United Kingdom, *see* Britain
United Nations (UN) 30, 41, 85, 108,
  112–3, 117–18, 121, 156, 160, 163,
  173–4, 178, 199, 202 (n.24), 230,
  233, 244
United Nations Trusteeship
  Territories 21, 26, 28 (n.3)
United States (US) 1, 41, 87, 109, 113, 146,
  159, 161–2, 175, 178, 216, 242, 248
  (n.17)
United States of the Sahara 210–11, 216
universities 123–4, 126, 128–31
UPC 11, 139, 189–99, 200 (n.1, n.3), 201
  (n.6, n.9), 202 (n.19), 203 (n.28)
Upper Volta 7–8, 46, 56 (n.14), 72, 122,
  163
  see also Burkina Faso
UPS 51, 53
uranium 211, 215
US-RDA 77–8, 80–2, 85–6
UTA 181

Verschave, François-Xavier 1–2, 5, 114, 120,
  136, 200 (n.2), 219
Vichy 66
Viet Minh 19, 65–7, 76
Vietnam 66
Vietnam (Haiphong) 107
violence 10–11, 35–9, 62, 64–6, 74 (n.13),
  86, 107–8, 110–15, 117–19, 198,
  214–15, 233–4, 238–45, 248 (n.15,
  n.16)
VPP 57 (n.23)
VSN 124

Western Sahara 91, 99–100, 205, 211
  see also Spanish Sahara
Wibaux, Fernand 16, 54, 85–7, 147–8
Wilson, Harold 175
Western Sahara 91, 99–100, 110, 211

Yaméogo, Maurice 56 (n.14)
Year of Africa 15, 155–6, 215, 227
Young, Crawford 20
Youssef, Sakiet Sidi 93

Zaire, *see* Congo (Léopoldville/Kinshasa)
Zimbabwe 171
  see also Rhodesia